American Buildings and Their Architects

AMERICAN BUILDINGS AND THEIR ARCHITECTS

American Buildings and Their Architects

VOLUME 1

THE COLONIAL
AND NEOCLASSICAL STYLES

William H. Pierson, Jr.

OXFORD UNIVERSITY PRESS
New York   Oxford

Oxford University Press

Oxford   New York   Toronto
Delhi   Bombay   Calcutta   Madras   Karachi
Petaling Jaya   Singapore   Hong Kong   Tokyo
Nairobi   Dar es Salaam   Cape Town
Melbourne   Auckland

and associated companies in
Beirut   Berlin   Ibadan   Nicosia

First published in 1970 by Doubleday & Company, Inc., Garden City, New York
First issued in paperback in 1976 by Anchor Books, Garden City, New York
This paperback edition published in 1986 by Oxford University Press, Inc.,
200 Madison Avenue, New York, New York 10016,
by arrrangement with the author

Oxford is a registered trademark of Oxford University Press

Library of Congress Cataloging-in-Publication Data
Pierson, William Harvey, 1911–
American buildings and their architects.
Vols. –5 by William H. Jordy.
Reprint. Originally published: Garden City, N.Y. :
Doubleday, c1970–c1978.
Includes bibliographical references and indexes.
Contents: v. 1. The colonial and neoclassical
styles—v. 2. Technology and the picturesque—
[etc.]—v. 5. The impact of European modernism in
the mid-twentieth century.
1. Architecture—United States. 2. Architects—
United States. I. Jordy, William H. II. Title.
NA705.P5   1970   .720'.973   86-16348
ISBN 0-19-504216-6 (pbk.: vol. 1)

6 8 10 9 7 5
Printed in the United States of America
on acid-free paper

TO MY WIFE

Contents

List of Illustrations

Except where otherwise indicated the
photographs used for the illustrations
were made by the author.

Acknowledgments

This book has its origins in many rewarding years of association with my colleague in the adventure, Professor William Jordy of Brown University. Although we agreed at the beginning that we would write separate volumes, rather than collaborate in all four, we have nevertheless maintained a lively discourse with one another and both the shape and direction of this volume is in no small measure a result of that exchange. My thanks to Professor Jordy for sharing this experience with me.

Another formative influence has come from a course on American Art which I teach at Williams College. Twenty years of dialogue with students have drawn me ever more deeply into American architecture and much of the substance of this volume is a direct result of that involvement. My next expression of gratitude, therefore, must be to those young men who have provided the provocation in which ideas have been born. I am also grateful to the President and Trustees of Williams College, first for their generosity in providing financial support through the 1900 Fund, but most especially for the friendly spirit with which they have granted me leave so that I could carry out my research and writing. My colleagues in the Williams College Art Department, Professor S. Lane Faison, Jr. and Professor Whitney S. Stoddard, have also cheerfully assumed the added burdens occasioned by my absence, and for this I am deeply grateful.

Equally important in the successful conduct of my work were the four years spent as Executive Secretary to the Carnegie Study of the Arts of the United States. This responsibility provided the opportunity for extensive travel in this country and together with additional travel on my own made it possible for me to visit every major building which I have discussed. It also brought me into direct and productive contact with leading architectural historians in the American field. I would like to thank both Carnegie Corporation of New York and the University of Georgia for this rewarding experience.

Numerous individuals have also been influential in giving shape to the book. Through the inspired teaching of the late Karl Lehmann of New York University my eyes were opened to the wonders of architecture as an art of space; and the late Carroll L. V. Meeks, who directed my doctoral thesis at Yale, was the first to arouse my enthusiasm for nineteenth-century America. With respect to English architecture, my understanding was enormously enriched by a brief but stimulating association with Sir John Summerson. Several revealing discussions with him made embarrassingly clear the extreme provincialism of my views on the relationship between English and American architecture, and his lucid and beautiful writings have been an inspiration to me in my own efforts. Assistance of a special kind was also rendered by Mrs. H. Richard Archer and Mrs. Alex Shaw. Mrs. Archer served as a research and editorial assistant, while Mrs. Shaw assumed all responsibilities for the preparation of the manucript. In addition, I received invaluable help with respect to matters of content and style from Professor Don Gifford of the Williams College English Department. The freehand drawings used for all plans and schematics were made by my associate in the Williams College Art Department, Professor H. Lee Hirsche. For all this I would like to express my deepest appreciation.

The monumental task of acquiring high quality photographs for the illustrations was greatly facilitated by the superb collection of color negatives made for the Carnegie Study of the Arts of the United States by Sandak Inc. of New York. Special thanks, therefore, go to Victor and Harold Sandak, who have generously made this material available and who have provided the splendid photographs from which approximately one third of my illustrations have been reproduced. I am also grateful to the following photographers, amateur and professional, who have permitted me to use their photographs: Wayne Andrews, Louis Frohman, Ernest LeClaire, Samuel A. Roberson, and Whitney S. Stoddard.

A number of other photographs have been obtained from various government, public, and private sources. Specifically, I would like to thank the following for their willingness to let me use their material: Avery Architectural Library, Columbia University; The Edwin J. Beinecke Library, Yale University; Boston Athenaeum; Chapin Library, Williams College; Country Life, Ltd.; The Historical Society of Pennsylvania; Houghton Library, Harvard University; The Library of Congress; Maryland Historical Society; Massachusetts Historical Society; The Metropolitan Museum of Art; The National Buildings Record (England); New York Graphic Society, Ltd.; New-York Historical Society; The New York Public Library; Pennsylvania Academy of the Fine Arts; Public Buildings Service, General Services Administration; Society for the Preservation of New England Antiquities; University of Virginia; Valentine Museum, Richmond, Va.; Virginia State Library, and the Warner House Association, Portsmouth, N.H.

In order to make many of my photographs it has been necessary to invade the privacy of both individuals and institutions, sometimes at great inconvenience to those concerned. Yet one of the most rewarding aspects of the entire undertaking has been the hospitality with which we have been received, and I would like to extend my thanks to the following for their kindness in opening their doors: Christ Church (Old North), Boston, Mass.; Christ Church, Philadelphia, Pa.; Colonial Williamsburg, Inc.; The Commonwealth of Massachusetts; The Diocese of Baltimore; Essex Institute, Salem, Mass.; First Baptist Meetinghouse, Providence, R.I.; Mr. and Mrs. Bruce Crane Fisher of Westover, Charles City County, Va.; Hammond-Harwood House Association, Annapolis, Md.; Historic Charleston Foundation, Charleston, S.C.; Historic St. Luke's Restoration, Smithfield, Va.; King's Chapel, Boston, Mass.; Mrs. Karl Lehmann, Haydenville, Mass.; Marblehead Historical Society, Marblehead, Mass.; Monumental Church, Richmond, Va.; Old Colony House, Newport, R.I.; Old

Ship Meetinghouse, Hingham, Mass.; Royall House Association, Medford, Mass.; St. Francis of Assisi Church, Ranchos de Taos, N.M.; San Jose Mission, Old Laguna Pueblo, N.M.; San Jose Mission, San Antonio, Tex.; San Xavier del Bac, Tucson, Ariz.; The South Carolina Historical Society, Charleston, S.C.; Thomas Jefferson Memorial Foundation, Charlottesville, Va.; Thoroughgood House Foundation, Norfolk, Va.; Topsfield Historical Society, Topsfield, Mass.; Touro Synagogue, Newport, R.I.; Department of the Treasury, United States Government; Mr. and Mrs. Walker Pegram Warren of Bacon's Castle, Surry County, Va.; Wentworth-Gardner and Tobias Lear Houses Association, Portsmouth, N.H., and Wesleyan University, Middletown, Conn.

The task of locating and collecting the visual and documentary material has been greatly eased by the friendly cooperation of all those to whom I have turned for help, and I am particularly thankful to the following for the special efforts they have made in my behalf; Miss E. Boyd, Curator, Spanish Colonial Department, Museum of New Mexico; Abbott Lowell Cummings, Assistant Director, Society for the Preservation of New England Antiquities; Charles M. Dale, Wentworth-Gardner and Tobias Lear Houses Association; David Green, Church Hanborough, Oxford, England; Professor Henry-Russell Hitchcock, Smith College; Professor George Kubler, Yale University; Donald J. Lehman, General Services Administration; Bertram K. Little, Director, Society for the Preservation of New England Antiquities; Miss Helen G. McCormack, then Director, Gibbes Art Gallery, Charleston, S.C.; Professor Paul F. Norton, Chairman, Department of Art, University of Massachusetts; Mrs. Granville T. Prior, The South Carolina Historical Society; Miss Helen Cynthia Rose, Supervisor of Art Education, Richmond Public Schools; Dr. Alexander St. Ivanyi, Minister, The First Church of Christ, Lancaster, Massachusetts; Miss Dorothy Stroud, Sir John Soane's Museum; and Karel Yasko, Special Assistant to the Commissioner for Design, General Services Administration.

Then there were those who were willing to read my manuscript, either in part or in its entirety, so that I could see it through eyes other than my own. Their thoughtful responses have been a major factor in determining several matters of organization and style. Those whom I would like to thank are: James A. Bear, Jr., Curator, Thomas Jefferson Memorial Foundation, Monticello; Frederick D. Nichols, Chairman, School of Architecture, University of Virginia; Richard W. Hale, Acting Chairman, Massachusetts Historical Commission; Miss Anne Wardwell, Massachusetts State Historical Commission; and most especially my family, who have not only read and torn apart what I have written, but have had the patience to bear with the writing.

WILLIAM H. PIERSON, JR.

Williamstown, Massachusetts, 1968

PART I

Colonial America

CHAPTER I

The Background to the
Architecture of Colonial America

*Throughout this stream of human life, and thought, and ac-
tivity . . . men have ever felt the need to build; and from
the need arose the power to build. So as they thought they
built; for, strange as it may seem, they could build in no
other way. As they built, they made, used, and left behind
them records of their thinking . . . . Whatever the character
of the thinking, just so was the character of the building.*
LOUIS SULLIVAN

This is a book about architecture.

But why write a book about architecture? If you ask a mountaineer why
he climbs a mountain he will tell you, because it is there. Its fascination,
he will say, lies in its mystery, in the marvel of its physical structure, in
its ever-changing spatial vistas. It will vary with the light, with the weather,
and with the vantage point, but it will always be there, to quicken the
imagination and uplift the human spirit. Precisely the same is true of
architecture. It too is structurally coherent, it too is an experience in
space, time, and movement; and like the mountain, it challenges and
moves the mind and quickens the heart. But also like the mountain, it
fully reveals itself only to those who have the curiosity and the will to ex-
plore. This book has been written to provide a stimulus for such exploration.

If a work of architecture is like a mountain it is also very different:
a mountain as part of the natural world rejects man, permitting him to
intrude only to the extent of his physical endurance; a work of architecture as a product of the human intelligence embraces man, taking him
within itself to meet both his physical and emotional needs. Man participates in architecture. Of all the arts, it is the most intrinsically humanistic,
for more than any other it has a direct and continuing tie with the daily
functions of life. A painting or a piece of sculpture can exist independently
of outside concerns, with no other purpose than being itself; a building
cannot. It is meant to be occupied by people. This close and potentially
productive union with life itself gives to architecture a special organic
quality, and provides a variety of expressive possibilities unmatched by
any of the other arts.

A work of architecture is first of all an instrument of living. In its
most primitive form a building is an enclosure to shelter man from his

physical environment. Walls and a roof enclosing a simple space, these are all that are required to provide sanctuary from the rain, the wind, the cold. But civilized man has never been content with shelter alone. Very early in history he began to make distinctions between various forms of human activity. Working, playing, sleeping, worshiping, all were recognized as different provinces of life, each requiring a specific kind of space with special paraphernalia. To accommodate these increasing demands man caused the simple walls of the primitive shelter to give way to diverse and complex walls, decisively separating some spaces, coherently joining others. More than that, these same walls were no longer merely functional, dividing space for practical purposes. They also became alive as the means for aesthetic enrichment. In shape and surface they became objects of beauty, proportioned and adjusted for pleasing effect, sometimes in a manner totally unrelated to function. When this was made to happen, building acquired a new order of meaning and the simple shelter became architecture. In this sense, architecture can be compared to language. Words can be used for practical purposes such as describing objects, but when they are composed by a poet these same words not only describe, they also interpret. Above all, through euphony and structured rhythm, they incite sensations which are purely aesthetic which touch the emotions rather than the mind, and which have little or nothing to do with literal meaning. Like words, a work of architecture fulfills some useful end, but also like words it is capable of evoking aesthetic responses, of reaching those loftier regions of mind and heart which distinguish man from the animal.

But a work of architecture is not only a useful and beautiful object, it is also the product of a technique. It must be built. Like every work of art it is a combination of various materials brought together by human hands and human skills into a cohesive structural whole. Unlike painting and sculpture, architecture encloses space, and the technical means to achieve this are, of necessity, more precisely defined, more demanding and more complex. Consequently, the relationship between the *form,* or visual appearance, of a building and its structural components is direct. A building erected with vertical posts and horizontal beams will be basically rectilinear in shape, if arches and vaults are used some of the shapes will be curved; if the material of the outer walls is stone the texture will be rough, if it is steel and glass the surfaces will be smooth. For both technical and aesthetic reasons, therefore, the architect is forced to work within certain clearly defined limits. This imposes a discipline which is productive as well as restrictive. The push and pull which results from the competing demands of form on the one hand and structure on the other is one of the most fascinating aspects of architecture and unites in a state of dynamic equilibrium the seemingly hostile worlds of the poetic and the practical, the abstract and the real.

Style

Our approach to American architecture will be through two fundamental areas of expression, the design and ordering of space for both practical and aesthetic purposes, and the relationship of structure and materials to form. Together they constitute the ingredients of *style*. Because the concept of *style* is basic to architectural criticism, it is essential that we give some consideration to its meaning.

By style is meant the specific identifying characteristics of a building both as it appears to the eye and as it is known to exist in design and structure. Perhaps this idea can best be understood through an analogy. Each man, in spite of his uniqueness, is endowed with certain physical traits which relate him at once to a number of other human beings. Different races of man, for example, can be distinguished by the color of the skin. We recognize this as a major racial classification. By observing and relating other identifying features, however, such as the color of the hair and eyes, the shape, size and proportion of the body, and the manner of speech and movement, subgroups can be determined; and through this method, for one purpose or another, mankind can be divided into an infinite variety of types, or "styles."

Architecture may be analyzed and classified in the same way. Every building has certain conspicuous characteristics which relate it at once to other buildings with similar characteristics. All Gothic churches, for example, have pointed arches. Indeed, this structural and visual device has come to be recognized as a major manifestation of the Gothic style. But within this broad and obvious classification infinitely more subtle distinctions can be made. More discriminating observation discerns that the shape and proportions of the pointed arches of Gothic buildings in France are totally different from those in England. By collating these differences it is possible to determine French and English variants of the Gothic style. In the same manner, architecture of one period can be separated from that of another, the works of different architects distinguished one from another, and the evolution of style, either within a single period of history or within the life work of a single architect, can be readily defined. This is accomplished entirely through stylistic analysis, and the four aspects of form in architecture which provide the principal indices for such analysis are organization of space, proportion, scale, and ornament. We shall consider each of these separately.

Space

The substance of architecture is space, malleable, expressive, controlled; it is space enclosed by structure. In every building the practical requirements determine at once certain fundamental aspects of its space organization. It is obvious that the shape, size, and disposition of the main spatial components, both inside and out, must be appropriate to the purpose for which they are intended. But the fulfillment of function involves far more than the alleviation of some physical need. For space, in any form, is a visual experience to which men may respond in a variety of ways. These responses may be symbolic, they may be aesthetic, or they may be purely technical, but in any case they are conditioned by fundamental attitudes toward life itself; they grow from a common understanding of

FIGURE 1. *Parthenon, Athens, Greece, 447–438* B.C.

space as a physical environment, destined to serve emotional and intellectual as well as practical needs. Thus it is, that for each period in history space has taken on a special meaning, and each civilization has shaped its architecture to conform to and to express that meaning.

To the ancient Greeks, for example, the highest human achievement was the perfect mind in the perfect body. Reason and wholeness, these were the ideals toward which they aspired, ideals which found their purest expression in the science of geometry. "By beauty," wrote Plato, "I mean straight lines and curves and the surfaces or solids produced out of these . . . for . . . these are not beautiful relatively, like other things, but always and naturally and absolutely. . . ."[1] The space organization of the Parthenon is a consummate expression of this idea (Fig. 1). Its shape is a precise, clearly defined rectangle horizontally placed; its short ends are emphasized by the triangles of the pediments, which are formed by the angle planes of the roof. Each spatial component, such as one of the columns, is a self-contained geometric entity; at the same time it is an inseparable part of the whole. So emphatically is the equilibrium dependent upon reciprocal correspondence that it would be impossible to remove any single part without destroying the whole. The building is serene, poised and complete, and wholly dominated by a refined systematic geometry.

FIGURE 2. *Cathedral of Notre Dame, Amiens, France, thirteenth century.*

In contrast to the logical simplicity of the Greek temple the spatial organization of a Gothic cathedral such as Amiens (Fig. 2) is complex; and this very complexity is in itself a singular manifestation of the medieval mind. Where the ancient Greeks saw man as the measure of all things, the men of the Middle Ages saw him as insignificant before an omnipotent God. In the Greek temple the unity of independent parts gives to the building an articulate wholeness like that of the human body; in the Gothic cathedral, the individual part is engulfed by an intricate proliferation of ever-changing forms which suggest, in their diversity, the entire cosmos of nature. The principal spatial components of the cathedral are two narrow vertical masses of unequal length which intersect at right angles to form a cross. The over-all shape of the building, therefore, becomes a tangible symbol of the Christian faith. Beyond this, however, the major cross-shaped mass is cut into and dissolved by a forest of structural and decorative elements, presenting a variety of shapes, all thin, all vertically oriented and all tapering toward the top. Within the building (Fig. 3), the space is long and narrow, and points emphatically toward the high altar, which occupies a central position near the choir end of this dramatic spatial volume. The sense of direction thus begun is accelerated by the rhythmic pattern of the arcades which mark off, in a

FIGURE 3. *Cathedral of Notre Dame, Amiens, France, thirteenth century.*

sequence of rapid accents, the full length of the nave. At the same time that it extends toward the altar this narrow space also moves vertically. The thin lines of the colonnettes, which ascend unbroken from the piers to the splaying ribs above, compel the eye, with equal insistence, toward the dizzy and shadowed heights of the vaults. Thus a dynamic spatial tension between the horizontal and the vertical is established, a tension which unifies, at the same time that it sets apart, the earthly realm of the altar, where man through the sacraments comes into union with God, and the heavenly realm above toward which his soul aspires. These dramatically poised spatial effects defy the planes and solids of geometry, and excite the emotions rather than the mind; and in contrast to the reflective serenity of the Parthenon, they proclaim, in their visual animation, the impassioned faith of the Middle Ages. Thus the Parthenon and Amiens, each in its own way, presents both itself and its times through the character and organization of its spatial elements.

Proportion

Directly related to the shape and disposition of space is *proportion*. Since proportion is a dimensional matter, it can be considered as one aspect of shape. But proportion is more precise than shape, for where shape involves the generalities of outline, proportion is a specific matter of length in relation to width. If we say that the main mass of the Parthenon is a rectangle we are describing its shape. But if we say it is a rectangle nine units long by four units wide we are refining our description with the specific data of proportions. A positive relationship is thus established which then becomes an important clue to style; for just as all buildings in any given style show a consistent character of shape and orientation of space, so too they are conceived according to a consistent system of proportions. Like the building itself, the columns of the Parthenon are heavily proportioned, that is, their width is substantial in relation to their height. In contrast, the colonnettes of Amiens are extremely thin in proportion, counting for little more than lines as they rise to the full height of the vaults. Moreover, these qualities of thickness on the one hand and attenuation on the other are carried into every part of the respective buildings, so that the heavy proportions of the Parthenon give it weight and substance, whereas at Amiens the effect of the thin, drawn-out proportions is to make the building seem light and soaring. Even if there were no other means of stylistic determination these drastic proportional differences would be sufficient to establish the two buildings as representative of wholly distinct styles.

A more subtle distinction can be made between the Doric and Ionic orders as used by the Greeks of the fifth century B.C. Here we are dealing in each case with identical structural components, columns supporting an entablature, yet the two orders are very different; and one of the principal differences is a difference in proportions. The Doric column is squat and heavy, the Ionic (Fig. 4) is tall and slender; within the Greek system these proportions were always the same, thus a major distinction between the two is always immediately apparent.

Scale

Scale, like proportion, is a spatial concern. But where proportion may be defined as relative dimensions, scale is relative measure. Proportion is a relationship between length and width and is contained *within the object itself;* whereas scale is a relationship in size between the object and some constant unit of measure *outside the object.* In architecture that unit of measure is man. To understand this, consider what the result would be if the Parthenon were enlarged, *exactly as it is,* to twice its present size. Since all lengths in relation to widths would be the same, its proportions would remain unchanged, but its scale, in relation to man, would be doubled. A photograph made both before and after the change would not show the difference unless in each case an object or person were placed beside the building to establish a unit of reference. If, on the other

FIGURE 4. Temple of Athena Nike, Athens, Greece, fifth century B.C.

hand, the height of all the elements of the Parthenon were doubled but the widths were kept the same, the proportions would be drastically altered. The scale, however, would be unaffected. This is so because one dimension of every component of the building would remain unaltered in size and would thus serve as a unit of measure common to both instances against which the dramatic increase in height would be immediately apparent. In this case, photographs taken before and after the change would clearly indicate the new height, whether a scale figure were placed beside the building or not.

As a reflection of fundamental attitudes toward space, it is revealing that the Greeks, because of their preoccupation with geometric relationships, sought an ideal system of proportions. As we have just observed, this system, once established, was rigidly adhered to whether the building was large or small. The designers of the Gothic cathedrals, however, had no such rational objective. To them, the visual appeal of the church was to the emotions, not to the mind; and proportions were susceptible to infinite attenuation, commensurate with their drive toward awesome heights; and it was through carefully controlled scale, which established a constant relationship with man, that móving effects were sustained and intensified.

Ornament

Of all the indices to style *ornament* is perhaps the most obvious and therefore the most immediately useful. The buildings of any given style are characterized by a certain kind and degree of ornament. Furthermore, the specific ornamental devices themselves are generally developed in a manner consistent in shape, proportion, and scale with the other aspects of the style. In general, ornament may be of two types, *integral* and *applied*. The shallow concave channels, or flutes, on the columns of the Parthenon are integral. They are carved in the round shafts themselves and are intended not only to elaborate the surfaces, but also to accent the appearance of thrust as the columns reach vertically to support the entablature above. In the same building, however, the figural sculpture in the frieze is applied as pure visual enrichment, having no structural function. Similarly, the colonnettes and ribs are part of the structural system of Amiens and are therefore integral, whereas the figural sculpture in the tympanum over the main door is applied. One must also consider degree and character of ornament. Along with proportional differences, they constitute a major distinction between the Greek Doric and Ionic orders (compare Figs. 1 and 4). The Doric capital, for example, is a simple block ornamented only by its integral reverse-curve profile. The Ionic, in contrast, is composed of paired volutes carried on moldings which themselves are elaborately carved with applied ornament designed to complement their profiles. But whether ornament is integral or applied, its character provides an effective clue to style, and because ornament is one of the first things that one sees as one views a building it serves as an informative preface to the stylistic program as a whole.

Form and Structure

The distinction just made between integral and applied ornament brings us to one of the most intriguing aspects of architecture, the relationship between structure and form. Although we have already touched upon this problem briefly, it is so intimate a part of the evolution of American architecture that it is essential to consider it further. Throughout the history of architecture two fundamental and opposing attitudes toward this relationship have been in a constant shifting struggle for pre-eminence. One opinion holds that the form of a building should be a direct result *structural* of the materials and structural methods used. The other asserts that form should come first, with the architect free to design the building in any *visual* way he wishes. Materials and structural methods should then be made to conform to that design. The first point of view we will call the *structural,* the second, since it begins with the appearance of the building, we will recognize as the *visual.*

The Parthenon provides a supreme example of the structural point of view. The magnificent rhythm of its colonnade is one of the building's noblest assets. But when it was designed the columns were not placed in long rows primarily to create a rhythmic sequence, but to provide support for the superstructure of the building. The columns are the vertical posts upon which the horizontal lintel stones rest, and the rhythmic pattern which they create, although sensitively exploited by the Greeks, is nevertheless secondary to this basic function. The visual effect, therefore, is a direct product of the structural technique.

That the Greeks were consciously aware of this relationship is clearly revealed by the manner in which the columns are treated. The most efficient support that the designers could have employed would have been a simple rectangular post, having the same dimensions from top to bottom. This they did not use. Instead, they made the columns round, tapered them slightly toward the top, and shaped them so that their sides, instead of being straight lines, are long almost imperceptible curves of a parabolic type. By this subtle shaping, a structural element which might have appeared as nothing more than a totally inanimate pier, is made to come alive visually as a dynamic supporting member which, like the human arm, seems able to spring and stretch, even to push back against the weight imposed upon it from above. This visual expression of a directed physical activity is further enhanced by the carved fluting. The sharp vertical lines, formed where the flutes meet, emphasize the upward thrust; the delicate concave curves enliven the marble surface and make it seem capable of flexible expansion as it yields to the weight which it carries; and at the top, as though it were absorbing the downward pressure of the superstructure, the cushion of the capital swells out in a sweeping reverse curve. None of these visual devices in any way adds to the physical strength of the column, but together they transform an inert shaft of stone into a lively and gracious instrument of support, one which not only fulfills its mechanical function but visually proclaims with the utmost clarity how it does so.

The Romans took over from the Greeks the entire concept of the orders, but they used them in a very different way. This can best be illustrated by comparing the Parthenon (Fig. 1) with an early Roman temple, the Maison Carrée in Nîmes, southern France (Fig. 5). We recognize in this later building the basic Greek temple, a horizontal rectangular block with its long axis emphasized by the triangles of the pediments. But there is one significant difference. In the Parthenon the columns run all the way around the building, in the Maison Carrée they are freestanding only in the front. Here they form a porch behind which the walls of the main body of the temple have been brought out to the same plane as the side columns. If these walls had been left unadorned a clear distinction would have been made between the bearing walls and the columns as structural elements. But the Romans chose to do otherwise. A series of half columns was attached to the wall and continued around the building as an engaged colonnade. Used in this way the half columns perform no structural function whatsoever, for it is the walls and not themselves that are

FIGURE 5. *Maison Carrée,*
Nîmes, France, first century B.C.

supporting the building. The sole purpose of the engaged columns, therefore, is to continue the visual rhythm of the front colonnade. Consequently,
a device which had been developed by the Greeks basically as a means
of support was employed by the Romans as applied ornament to create
a particular visual effect. The Roman attitude toward the column, therefore, was *visual* rather than structural. Unlike the Greeks, whose building methods were limited to the post-and-lintel system, the Romans developed complex vaulting techniques which enabled them to enclose vast
and sensational interior spaces. But over the surfaces of these daring

vaults they found it necessary, in order to gratify an insatiable taste for the visually extravagant, to impose a rich veneer of elaborate applied ornament, much of which was derived from the structural devices of the ancient Greeks.

The question raised by this contrast in approach is not a qualitative one. We are not concerned in this instance with concepts such as good and bad. It does not necessarily follow that because the Greeks showed a greater concern for the expression of structure than the Romans did that they were therefore better architects. In fact, it could be argued that the Romans, through their command of space, were the greater of the two. To assume that structural purity is a condition of great architecture would be to relegate to a position of minor importance some of man's most imaginative architectural achievements, including many in America. This would be neither reasonable nor productive. The question that confronts us here is rather one of historical distinction. The important thing is that the Greeks and the Romans, motivated by wholly different objectives, conceived their architecture in correspondingly different terms; and unless we understand these terms we have no basis from which to interpret or judge their buildings. Stylistic analysis, therefore, is an analysis of kind and relationships, not of quality. To say that a building is Greek rather than Roman pinpoints it in time and location, and identifies it with a way of life. In this manner, the building is drawn into an historical orbit and the way is then clear for interpretation and evaluation. If space is the vocabulary of architecture and structure its grammar, then style is its syntax, and we cannot read the book of architecture until we have mastered the language in which it is written.

The Formation and Permeation of Style

Throughout Western history the evolution of style in architecture has been continuous and directly responsive to the changing conditions of man. The roots of style have penetrated deeply into the venerable realms of tradition and custom and have stretched from epoch to epoch and from place to place; nourishment has come from the manifold streams of life itself. But always the process of development has been the same. In its formative stage, each style at first merely hints at its ultimate character. Then through experiment and change, through expansion and refinement, it evolves a mature architectural idiom, unique, coherent and expressive. From this high point, it then spreads outward and downward through the entire fabric of the civilization which brought it into being. This process, which we will call the formation and permeation of style, may be likened to the eruption of a volcano, as its molten fires, which come from deep within the earth, rise irresistibly toward the summit, finally to surge over the crater edge and flood downward, cooling as they descend and leaving something of their substance and structure wherever they go. Finally, the fires go out, forms become rigid, and change becomes possible only through a new eruption.

The formative stage, which is the dynamic and aggressive phase in the evolution of style, always takes place at a high creative level. The many practical, technical, and aesthetic ingredients which ultimately join to form the character of a style are not brought together by the caprices of nature; they are channeled and molded by the human intelligence. This, of course, is true of every creative act in every realm of endeavor. But in architecture this creative intelligence involves a unique relationship. Foremost is the architect. It is to him that all the generative forces flow, and it is through his practical skills and poetic imagination that these same forces are commingled and freshened, ultimately flowering in a unique and coherent creation unlike anything that has ever been achieved before. But unlike the painter, the musician, and the poet, the architect cannot work alone. Behind him stands the patron, either an individual or a group, who represents society, who creates the challenge, who sets in motion those forces to which the architect addresses himself. Although it is the architect who performs the creative act, it is the patron who provides both the need and the means, for the patron is as essential to the productive process as blood is to the brain. No great work of architecture has ever been produced outside of an active patronage.

The relationship between the architect and the patron, and their respective roles in the creative process, are among the most fascinating aspects of the study of architecture. For each epoch in history the term "architect," if used at all, has had a very special meaning. During the Middle Ages, the period which forms the prelude to American architecture, the "architect" was in fact the master mason, qualified as such under the powerful medieval guild system, and actively involved in the actual building process itself. It was without question he who solved the complex problems of vaulting which made the Gothic style possible, and it was he who supervised the vast army of workmen and associated artisans who carried out the work. Conceptually, however, the great cathedrals, in which the Gothic style was formed, were as much the product of the collective mind of the Church itself as they were of the master masons. The soaring verticality, the glorious splendor of the stained glass, the shape and arrangement of spaces, all were motivated by the impassioned religious aspirations of the Church. To realize them the master mason functioned not as a professional architect but as a productive artisan whose primary responsibility was to solve the technical problems. The Gothic style, therefore, at least in its moment of full flower, was a style of the community rather than of particular individuals.

With the coming of the Renaissance and its attendant humanism, this situation changed dramatically. Stimulated by advances in science and technology, and brought closer to his fellow man by such far-reaching means of communication as celestial navigation and the printed book, man left the seclusion of the church and the monastery and reached out to embrace the world. Moreover, with the rise of individualism the professional architect emerged as the most creative force in the development of new architectural ideas. In the Middle Ages, with few exceptions, most of the master masons remained anonymous. From the Renaissance onward, however, we not only know the names of all the great architects, but also know much about their lives, and we can identify their works with relative ease. In many instances these men were forceful personalities and had some of the most inquiring minds of their time; under their aggressive leadership the formation of style took on a more personal, revolutionary, and frequently volcanic character.

Not all buildings in the history of architecture have been the work of such creative figures. Indeed, the vast majority have not been, and much of the architecture which we will be considering will be identified with the lower levels of creative activity. In many instances, especially in the colonial period, we will find the work to be anonymous. Yet the influence of the great men reaches far and deep, even when we are forced by historical circumstances to deal with seemingly insignificant buildings, we cannot analyze or evaluate them without making constant reference to those vital sources of creativity to which they owe their very existence. No style, regardless of the depth to which it may penetrate a culture, is without the shadow of the great personalities and the irresistible forces which brought it into being.

Architectural Prelude to Colonial America

During the first century and a half of its existence, America was a colonial society with links to different and diverse homelands; and in the study of the architecture of a colonial society the whole question of the formation and permeation of style assumes particular importance. This is so because colonies in general have drawn their cultural nourishment from the mother country; thus their architecture, like other aspects of their culture, has been largely imitative of that of the homeland, and permeation frequently has occurred through complex and sometimes devious channels. Proper evaluation of any colonial architecture thus requires that it be viewed not as an original style in its own right, but as an integral segment of the architectural development of the country from which it came.

During the early years of the settlement of America four great European nations established thriving colonies on the new continent, first the Spanish, then the English, the French, and the Dutch. By far the most important were the English. Not only did the English make the most determined effort, but unlike the mission-oriented Spanish settlements, the English colonies were Protestant and middle class and had a firm mercantile and agrarian economic base. These factors, combined with a radical political idealism, not only led to the Revolution and independence but ultimately formed the basis of the new nation. Our major attention, therefore, will be directed toward the English colonies, and our first concern will be the English architectural background, from which the early colonials took their inspiration.

By the early seventeenth century in England, at the very time when the colonization of America began, the formation and permeation of style, especially as it related to patronage, had begun to assume a peculiarly national character. There continued, of course, the established affluent and frequently enlightened patronage of the aristocracy, the state, and the church. It was these groups which provided both the practical and artistic opportunities for the leading architects and made it possible for them to think in the largest possible terms as free creative agents. From this combination of support and talent came the great architectural monuments of the period, monuments which set the character of the English styles.

A major factor in the changing patterns of English culture during the seventeenth century was the emergence of a powerful middle class. Primarily associated with the expanding mercantile activities of the nation, this segment of English society offered a new type of patronage to the architect; and its demands were of a special kind. Fiercely competitive and socially ambitious, but culturally insecure, they sought to emulate the aristocracy in every way they could—in dress, social behavior, and the trappings with which the upper class surrounded themselves. Their resources were more limited than those of the aristocracy and their building efforts therefore were more modest, but because of their desire to attain all the outward symbols of success and importance their standards of quality were high. The result was a wholly new level of architecture, one which was not only widespread and uniquely English, but one which also brought to a lower social stratum than ever before many of the finest aspects of the best and most advanced contemporary architecture.

Because it was imitative by choice, the work produced by this new order of men lacked originality; imitation and creativity have never been synonymous. Rarely, therefore, can the name of an outstanding architect be associated with English domestic work at this level. On the other hand, it provided an opportunity for ambitious skilled carpenters and masons to function as architects as well as builders, thus broadening the base of the whole profession.[2] Most especially, it injected a new competitive spirit into the crafts, and changed the character of the building trade. This general tendency was given additional impetus by the increasing availability of architectural and building handbooks, since they made possible a wide dissemination of uniform structural and decorative information. The ubiquitous middle-class style which resulted we shall call *low style,* primarily because it was directly derived from the *high style* of the aristocracy which it sought to emulate. The low style was conservative and almost totally devoid of that vitality and inventiveness which characterized the work of the great architects, but the level of craftsmanship was frequently high, and precisely because it was imitative it brought the refined taste of high patronage to a larger segment of English society.

In seventeenth-century England the permeation of style did not stop with the middle class. Life in the villages and on the farms was as much involved in the changing social and economic order as was life in the cities and on the landed estates. The architecture which grew up around this life showed a definite affinity with that of the higher styles. Yet it was also very different. Built by farmers, artisans, and yeomen, who were removed from the sophistications and pretensions of the urban areas, the buildings of rural England were the work of the common people. They represent, therefore, the *folk style* of the regions in which they are found.

This folk style differed from the low style in several important respects. First, because it was produced by plain and less literate men, it was simple. Sometimes it was even crude. But structural methods were straightforward, and on the whole the style had a natural vigor which was generally lacking in the more pretentious buildings of the middle class. Most important of all, folk architecture was relatively unencumbered by those restricting ambitions which demanded conformity, and which made it virtually impossible for the architecture of the middle class to develop its own original idiom.

Buildings at the folk level were entirely the work of the local carpenter. Like the architect-builder he had access to contemporary architectural handbooks, but unlike his more informed counterpart he had no preconceived ideas or theories about style, nor was he pressed by an ambitious patron to imitate the architecture of the aristocracy. Folk architecture, therefore, like dialects in the speech of the common man, showed a remarkable degree of originality and was richly diversified. Like regional speech, too, it was frequently harsh and awkward; and in the way in which many of the prominent stylistic features of the more fashionable architecture were vulgarized and altered, it was totally uninhibited. Even so, all this gives to folk architecture a remarkable freshness and vitality, and in its own matchless way the architecture of the common man brought to a fitting end the process of stylistic permeation that began in the high courts of aristocratic taste.

English Architecture Around 1600

At the turn of the seventeenth century, English architecture was in a stage of reluctant transition from the late Gothic to the Renaissance. Locked in its island setting, the Gothic survived longer in England than in any other country in Europe. During the second half of the sixteenth century, Renaissance ornamental features made their first hesitant appearance in English architecture; by 1600 they were vying with the Gothic for supremacy. But in spite of these conspicuous inroads the architecture of the Elizabethan and Jacobean eras remained deeply committed to Gothic ideals.

The English Gothic style developed during the thirteenth century as one of many national variants on the great international Gothic of Europe. Just as in France, where the style was born, the English Gothic was essentially ecclesiastical; its glory is found in the great cathedrals. From the cathedrals it spread downward to the folk level of English life, leaving its stamp on the farmer's cottage as well as on the small parish church. Less soaring, less logical structurally, and more decorative than the French, the English Gothic is more severely rectilinear, simpler in massing, and often characterized by large expanses of window. Both structurally and decoratively the English shows greater genius in the use of wood, a peculiarity which reached its most imaginative heights in the wood-trussed ceilings of the late Gothic period. Derived from a long tradition of timber framing, and sustained by the specialized woodworking skills of a nation

FIGURE 6. *Chartham Church,*
Kent, England, roof truss, c. 1300.

of shipbuilders, English trussing methods climaxed during the sixteenth
century in the elaborate hammer beam ceilings of the Tudor Gothic
style.

Quite apart from being used in such outstanding high style examples,
the technique of trussing was common to all types and levels of English
building from early medieval times on.[3] Almost all the small parish
churches, for example, were covered by wood-trussed ceilings rather than
vaults. A splendid early example is the Chartham Church in Kent, built
around 1300 (Fig. 6).

The Renaissance influence that was to shape the character of English architecture around 1600 came from Italy. In the very years when the Gothic was at its height in England, the Italian architects of the Renaissance were evolving a wholly new concept of architecture based upon classic ideals and methods. Their immediate source was the ruins of ancient Rome. Studying, measuring, and theorizing, they took the classical orders, Roman structural methods, Roman concepts of space, and fashioned a powerful new architectural idiom which became a visual embodiment of Renaissance humanism.

Spreading from Italy, the Renaissance ideas slowly penetrated the rest of Europe and by the mid-sixteenth century were making their first important inroads into the Gothic style of Tudor England. Received secondhand, and never completely understood by English builders, the classical forms were used in a purely visual manner as applied decoration. There is no structural logic whatever to this hybrid style. Classical orders, pediments, moldings, and other decorative features were simply attached to what was otherwise a Gothic building. No regard was shown for the proportional discrepancies which naturally resulted from an unhappy union of two completely different proportional systems. The Renaissance forms thus become, in effect, a new suit of clothes which never completely obscured the Gothic body on which it was arrayed.

The Prodigy House

This rich but mixed style reached its most original and most thoroughly English phase in the so-called "prodigy houses" built during the reign of Queen Elizabeth; it came to its end in the stiffer but more refined houses of the Jacobean era.[4] The extravagant Elizabethan mansions, conceived more as show places for entertaining the Queen than as family dwellings, were one of the crowning achievements of the age. Built for an emerging and ambitious landed aristocracy, they were the epitome of high style architecture. The men who designed and built them were master masons trained in the traditions of the medieval guilds. Yet many of the best houses show a remarkable originality in massing and silhouette, and an impressive refinement in detail. This suggests a degree of individual choice and commitment on the part of the designers, which we would be more inclined to expect from the creative architect than from the ordinary work-bound master masons. In fact, the names of some of these designers are known; this, combined with a number of surviving drawings and other documents, indicates that something akin to the architect-builder, if not the professional architect, was slowly beginning to emerge.

An excellent example of the Elizabethan prodigy house is Condover Hall in Shropshire, which was completed shortly before 1600 (Fig. 7). Although it is essentially horizontal in its over-all massing, the projecting and receding sub-components are strongly vertical and are dominated by expanses of perpendicular windows. Grouped chimney stacks and sharply pointed gables break up the outline and tend further to reduce the sense of the horizontal. In all these features the building is thoroughly Gothic.

FIGURE 7. *Condover Hall,
Shropshire, England, 1598.* (*Copyright* Country Life)

At the same time, however, symmetry has taken the place of Gothic asymmetry and Renaissance classical details have been loosely but vivaciously applied as pure pleasurable decoration. This is evident in the engaged columns and pediment which embrace the central door (Fig. 21). The style, therefore, remains a hybrid, fresh and delightful, but inclining more toward the Gothic than the Renaissance.

During the Jacobean phase of this transitional English style, the same principles of massing prevailed, but the verticals were reduced in number and made less urgent by a general strengthening of the horizontals. With less space given over to windows, the walls became more continuous and assertive. Classical details were used with somewhat greater authenticity. The general effect was less animated and more formal, but the hybrid character remained essentially unchanged. This can be seen at Hatfield House in Hertfordshire, built in 1611 (Fig. 8). Especially characteristic in this building are the clustered chimneys, the stepped and curved Flemish gables which crown the central pavilion, and the stone quoined corners.

This elegant style, which reached maturity in the prodigy houses, permeated the whole of English architecture during the late sixteenth and early seventeenth centuries, and in the provincial areas it continued well into the seventeenth century. In towns and villages and across the countryside, structures of all types and at all social levels were built in the same basic language of form. Typical of the low style developments of the period is the Eastbury Manor House, Essex (Fig. 9). It is far less am-

FIGURE 8. *Hatfield House,*
Hertfordshire, England, south front, dated 1611.

bitious than the great prodigy houses, and is more appropriately scaled
to family use than to ceremonial living, but the signs of its stylistic origins
are unmistakable. Although in many ways more awkward than its grand
prototypes, it has the same projecting and receding vertical units, the
same perpendicular windows, the same grouped chimneys, the same irregular silhouette.

Smaller than Eastbury Manor House and even more provincial in character is a small anonymous house in Warwick (Fig. 14). It probably dates
from the late sixteenth century. Here a single horizontal block is cut
vertically in the center by a projecting porch tower, which in turn is
crowned by a high-pitched gable bracketed out from the corners. Originally the house had two mullioned windows of the medieval type instead
of the single double-hung sash windows that now flank the tower on both
the first and the second floors. Engaged to either side of the tower and
to each corner of the main block are the incongruous classical pilasters
of the high Elizabethan and Jacobean styles. This little house—with
features that clearly make it a remote cousin of the prodigy houses—
serves as a useful example of the permeation of the high style ideas to
the provincial folk level.

In the very years that this process was taking place in England, the
first American colonies were established, and it is against this background

FIGURE 9. *Eastbury Manor House,
Essex, England, 1572–73.* (*Copyright* Country Life)

of growth and change in the mother country that we will develop our
story of American architecture. Our critical approach will be at two levels.
At the first level we will consider it as an expression of our national
culture, defining and interpreting those aspects of American building which
are most closely related to the formation and growth of American society.
Here our critical attitude will be as much sociological as architectural. On
the second level we will judge American architecture in the broader context of the European tradition, a tradition in which this country originally
played an integral part and to which it remained inherently loyal throughout the nineteenth century. Here our evaluation will be largely architectural. Using methods similar to those already outlined, we will attempt
to unravel numerous intricate and fascinating problems in style, and above
all, we will seek to discover those areas of creativity which led to a truly
American architectural idiom. This achievement did not happen at once,
nor did it begin at a high creative level. American architecture began in
the wilderness, as a colonial extension of an already established mode of
building.

CHAPTER II

The Atlantic Seaboard
in the Seventeenth Century

Along these lonely regions, where, retired
From little scenes of art, great Nature dwells
In awful solitude. . . .

JAMES THOMSON

Tidewater Virginia

At Christmas time in 1607 a band of hopeful men set sail from England
in three small ships. The following spring they landed on the shores of
the James River in Virginia to establish the first successful English colony
on the soil of North America. No group could have been less qualified
or less well equipped for what lay ahead of them. Made up primarily of
one-time gentlemen, released prisoners, and a handful of practical artisans, they came seeking gold. Instead they found a wilderness so unfamiliar
and so filled with unexpected hazards that a year after their arrival less
than half of the original company still remained alive.

The saga of this pitiful struggle for survival is now part of our national
legend and is well known to all Americans; what is less familiar is the
companion struggle for cultural identity. Like the other adventurers of
their age the first settlers, regardless of their station in life, were men
who had been born and bred in a civilized society. They brought with
them to the Virginia swamps, therefore, certain cultural attitudes, however debased, which included a firmly established image of architecture.
The frontier, however, was a cultural void. Moreover, in its untamed state
it offered resistance to all forms of civilized expression, and whatever refined aspirations and talents the first colonials may have had were overwhelmed by the sheer necessity of keeping alive.

During these first difficult years there was no place for architecture
as an art. As far as buildings were concerned the first need was for
shelter, which was provided by dugouts and crude huts. Some of these
were English types, others were based on the wigwams of the Indians,
but all were meager structures affording no more than scant cover from
the elements.

Civilized men, even in the wilderness, will not endure for long the
absence of the familiar. In a surprisingly short time after the first landings
the Virginia colonials had crawled out of their dugouts and raised, on
the raw surface of the new land, the semblances of a civilized community.

Shortly after 1611, when the arrival of new settlers brought relief to the desperate survivors, modest houses began to appear. By 1615 Jamestown could boast two rows of small two-story half-timbered houses. Only their foundations survive today, but as described in contemporary accounts these dwellings seem to have been similar to the smaller town houses of Tudor England. Although diminutive they were nevertheless built according to traditional methods by English-trained artisans. In their open framing they displayed, in a simple form, the structural and ornamental qualities of provincial English architecture of the late sixteenth century. They represent, therefore, the first tangible impression of English architectural order upon the disorder of the wilderness, and the story of American architecture on the eastern seaboard begins with these simple dwellings.

Since the first settlers of the Virginia Colony formed a community at Jamestown both for protection and for other practical reasons, we might expect that the town, as a way of life, would have set the social and economic pattern for the later growth of the colony. But this was not the case. The method of land apportionment, devised by the Virginia Company in 1618, made it possible for single individuals to accumulate substantial holdings, and almost at once the great plantations, with their vast tracts of thousands of acres, began to take shape. At the same time, West Indian tobacco was introduced to the Virginia farms. This marketable staple ultimately became the basis of the tidewater economy and the principal product around which the plantations were to grow and flourish. Transportation and communication were facilitated by the magnificent navigable rivers of the coastal region. Ships came up these broad waterways to the threshold of each plantation, where they unloaded their goods from London and took aboard the tobacco for England. This traffic kept the colonial planters in contact with the homeland and provided them with a steady source of cultural as well as material nourishment. Consequently, the life of the Virginia planter, although by no means leisurely, afforded him opportunities to assume the posture of an English landed gentleman. This manner of living, which developed around the great plantation houses, had many facets inspired by the landed estates of England. Bound to the crown and church, both by inclination and by royal charter, the Virginia Colony remained more thoroughly English than any other on the entire Atlantic seaboard.

The Adam Thoroughgood House

The early Virginia farmhouses, predecessors of the plantation mansions, were small and unquestionably made of wood. The most workable and useful of all building materials, wood was not only abundant on the frontier, it was also familiar to the colonial craftsmen who had behind them centuries of English tradition in wood structural methods. There was also a ready supply of clay for bricks, and of oyster shells for lime, and as early as 1611 bricks were being made in the Virginia Colony.

FIGURE 10. *Adam Thoroughgood House, Princess Anne County, Va., 1636–40.*

This, combined with the British preference for masonry construction, led to the increasing use of brick as a structural material.[1]

Virginia farmhouses, whether brick or wood, were initially simple structures of one story with a high pitched roof and attic, and a chimney at one or both ends. The smaller dwellings consisted of one room only, the larger ones had two. Some had a central hall. The Adam Thoroughgood House in Princess Anne County is one of the few to survive (Fig. 10). According to most authorities it was built sometime between 1636 and 1640. If this dating is correct, it may be the oldest surviving house in Virginia and perhaps on the Atlantic seaboard.[2] Its builder, Adam Thoroughgood, was typical of the successful colonial farmer. He came to America in 1621 as an indentured servant, and in 1629, the year after he had worked off his bond, he held a seat in the House of Burgesses. By the time he built his house, he had amassed an estate of 5,350 acres.

He emerges, therefore, not only as a prominent planter but also as a person of some civic importance, and his house was probably one of the finest of the period.

The Adam Thoroughgood House is small, but in contrast with the crude shelters of the first years it is a building with distinctive characteristics of style. As restored on the basis of reasonable evidence, it has a simple rectangular plan, and is a story and a half high with two rooms on each floor. The material is brick, laid primarily in English bond. At each end is a tall chimney, the one on the north embedded in the wall, the one on the south projecting prominently and set back in two stages (Fig. 10). Looking at the top of this massive chimney and across the roof to the one at the other end, we can see that, like the group chimneys of Tudor England, the upper portion of each rises well above the ridge line; this is compound in shape with a section projecting toward the center of the house.

FIGURE *11. Small house, Chelmsford, England, late sixteenth century.*

FIGURE 12. *Adam Thoroughgood House,*
Princess Anne County, Va., east façade, 1636–40.

From the east (Fig. 12) the house is seen to have a single door, which
enters directly into the north room, the larger of the two interior spaces
on the first floor. On either side of the door, and opening into each of
the rooms, is a window. Again in a manner reminiscent of Tudor England,
each of these windows is divided by a vertical mullion and a high horizontal bar which cross to form a transom above and a casement below.
As in all medieval windows, the small diamond-shaped glass panes here
were set in lead. In a diminutive way, the general effect is not unlike
that of the expansive windows which we have already seen in the prodigy
houses. There are similar windows on the west side of the Thoroughgood
House. On the north and south, flanking the chimneys, are smaller casement windows on each floor. The door and all window openings are
crowned by segmental brick arches.[3]

The features just described are strongly medieval, but even more so is
the over-all, vertical effect of the house, which becomes apparent when it
is viewed from either end (Fig. 10). This is particularly noticeable at the
south end, where the dominating mass of the chimney rises dramatically

from an eleven-foot base and tapers back through steeply pitched weathering surfaces to the tall slender stack. The top of the stack is crowned by a corbeled cornice of the Tudor type. From each corner of the building,[4] at the low eave line, the end of the roof pitches steeply upward to meet the chimney stack. The resulting confluence of pyramidal shapes creates a decided vertical movement and even though the various components are awkwardly combined, this tapering south end has all the familiar upward sweep of the Gothic style.

Yet there are noticeable intrusions in this predominantly medieval world. Seen from the east, the house appears low and horizontal, in a manner totally unrelated to the Gothic verticality of the ends, and the arrangement of identical windows either side of the door appears symmetrical. Actually, the house is not symmetrical. Because of the irregular plan, the door is not quite on center nor are the windows equally spaced left and right of it. But the arrangement of the windows is so close to reciprocal correspondence that the visual effect is more symmetrical than asymmetrical. It is as though the builder had vaguely in mind the exactly balanced façades of the prodigy houses yet, because of the persistence of the medieval tradition in his experience and training, was hesitant to commit himself wholeheartedly to the idea.

A similar partial commitment to classical ideas is seen at the south end of the house. Here, the horizontal formed by the eave on the east and west sides is carried boldly across the wall and around the chimney by a prominent stringcourse. This not only contradicts the compelling vertical effect of the soaring chimney stack, but when combined with the sloping ends of the roof, this same stringcourse forms a triangle which has all the appearance of a classical pediment. Thus, in its own simple and awkward way, the house displays the same mixture of medieval and classical elements which characterizes the whole of English architecture during the late sixteenth and early seventeenth centuries.

In one sense, these marked stylistic characteristics make the Adam Thoroughgood House something of an anomaly on the Virginia frontier. Although it was built barely thirty years after the first settlement at Jamestown, and thus serves to dramatize the rapidity with which the colonials established themselves in their new environment, it nevertheless creates an image of Old World culture which is alien to the frontier. This incongruity is an inevitable consequence of the whole process of colonization; for wherever civilized men have come into contact with the frontier they have either been destroyed by it or have imposed upon it all the outward manifestations of their native culture, generally with little or no change. This was true in the colonies of ancient Greece and it was no less true in Virginia. As a work of architecture, therefore, the Adam Thoroughgood House cannot properly be evaluated in the context of the frontier. Instead, we must ignore its tidewater setting and see it as part of the evolution of English architecture during the late sixteenth and early seventeenth centuries.

In all its features, as we have just described them, the Thoroughgood

House is a typical small English house of the period. Anonymous and undated small houses like the one in Chelmsford (Fig. 11) still abound in England, especially in those parts of the country from which the early settlers came. They are remarkably similar to the early Virginia farmhouses, and the Thoroughgood House belongs to this group. Except for the color and texture of the bricks, which were conditioned by the peculiar qualities of the Virginia clay, there is nothing whatever, either in style or construction, to set it apart from its English counterpart. The building is, in fact, a superb survival of transplanted English provincial architecture, American by location rather than style. It could hardly have been otherwise. The craftsmen who built it were Englishmen trained in English building methods and ideas. The man for whom it was built was also an Englishman, seeking by association with the familiar to maintain his identity in his new surroundings. If everything else in his environment was strange, his house was steadfastly English.

Because it is English and not American the Thoroughgood House represents, along with other early colonial houses like it, the ultimate permeation and dilution of the high style of the great prodigy houses to the fringes of the British Empire. Only this can account for its curious stylistic features. As we have already seen, evidence of both its Gothic ancestry and an indirect classical influence are unmistakable. Because the Thoroughgood House is folk architecture the deviations from high style are many, and in the process of permeation most of the prominent features of the high style have been blunted and changed. Some have been lost altogether. But the mixture of Gothic and classical form, which is perhaps the most single important characteristic of the high style buildings of the period, remains in the Thoroughgood House fundamentally unaltered, and when viewed in the entire evolution of the style this Virginia farmhouse becomes the end of the line. The expansive creative forces which produced the prodigy houses, and which ultimately permeated every level of English architecture, finally spent themselves on the American frontier.

Seen in the over-all picture of European architecture of the early seventeenth century, the Adam Thoroughgood House emerges as a small provincial English dwelling, of no greater significance than the many small houses in England to which it is so closely related. Yet, in its colonial context it was the center of a vast and productive plantation, comparable in size to the landed estates in England, and when built it was probably among the most ambitious houses in the Virginia tidewater. These are facts of history which cannot be ignored. As the most impressive surviving example of its kind, the Thoroughgood House is a priceless document of early colonial America. Viewed in this light, it takes on a special meaning, a meaning which is to be found first in its antiquity. Its ancient walls, perhaps the oldest surviving in Virginia, are picturesque reminders of the early years, of the slow but inexorable triumph of civilization over the wilderness. They are simple and awkward walls, yet they are tinged with their own poetry, a poetry of legend and folklore, rich, warm, and provocative. But it is the poetry of men and events rather than architecture, and the criteria we use to interpret this poetry should not be confused with the criteria of architectural criticism, nor must age be equated with quality. The Thoroughgood House is neither a great building nor is there anything about it architecturally which can be singled out as peculiarly American. When it was built it was a tiny house on the periphery of the British Empire, casting upon the frontier no more than a blurred and impoverished shadow of the prodigy houses of the homeland. Yet during these same years powerful new forces were already at work in Europe, forces which were to change the whole character of Western civilization. One of the most important manifestations of the impending changes was the spread of European culture to the American wilderness. The Adam Thoroughgood House was part of this great movement. It was built because restless men, driven on by whatever motive, dared to cross the ocean and seek a new life in the unknown. It is as a symbol of this quest that the Thoroughgood House ultimately has meaning.

Bacon's Castle

If the Adam Thoroughgood House was a farmhouse, Bacon's Castle in Surry County aspired to some of the grandeur of a plantation mansion. It was built by Arthur Allen, another successful planter, about 1655 and is one of the most extraordinary survivals of the domestic architecture of Virginia in the seventeenth century. The name Bacon's Castle derives from the fact that the house was seized and used as a garrison by the followers of Nathaniel Bacon during his famous rebellion of 1676. It is thus dramatically connected with the turbulent side of colonial life and has considerable historical as well as architectural interest.

Stylistically, Bacon's Castle is far more advanced than the Thoroughgood House. Where the latter projects a remote folk image of high style tendencies, Bacon's Castle combines, in provincial but more focused terms, several of the most important aspects of English domestic architecture of the late Tudor period. As seen from the south (Fig. 13), the principal mass of the house is a two-story rectangular block with a high pitched roof. Projecting from the center is a vertical tower which rises considerably above the main eave-line before it terminates in a steeply pitched gable. There is a similar tower on the north side. The one on the south housed an entrance hall, called the porch; the one on the north originally enclosed stairs that gave access to the second floor. Such towerlike features are typical of the late Tudor Gothic style, as we have already seen not only at Condover (Fig. 7) and Hatfield (Fig. 8) but also in the small anonymous house at Warwick (Fig. 14). Like the tall tapered chimney of the Thoroughgood House, the towers at Bacon's Castle are strongly vertical and cut through the main horizontal line of the building to create a sharp interruption of the silhouette.

Both the verticality and the irregularity of outline produced by the towers of Bacon's Castle are general medieval characteristics. The treatment of the short, or gabled, ends of the building, however, is specifically Tudor Gothic (Fig. 15). Here the wall is carried above the main roof plane in the form of an elaborate Flemish gable. Beginning at the eave-

FIGURE *13. Bacon's Castle,
Surry County, Va., c. 1655.*

line on corbeled brackets, it rises in alternating steps and curves to a
finial at the top.[5] Projecting from this wall is the bold chimney stack, ten
feet wide at its base, which rises to the level of the eave-line before
it sets back slightly to a simple brick cornice. Soaring above this, and
separated slightly from the wall, are three slender stacks, square in plan,
and set diagonally to the main mass of the chimney. These are entirely
freestanding except at the top, where they are joined by corbeled caps
to form the characteristic Tudor grouped chimney, similar to those at
Hatfield (Fig. 8).[6] Although the entire gable-chimney complex is overwhelming in relation to the rest of the house, it is by far the most
authentic and impressive use of the Tudor Gothic yet to have appeared
in the Virginia Colony.

As in the Adam Thoroughgood House, the interior space of Bacon's
Castle is asymmetrical and only one room deep. Similarly, too, the entrance from the central porch on the first floor gives directly into the
larger of the two rooms: this room was the most important in the house
and its counterpart in medieval houses was known as the "hall." The off-
center plan is typical of the irregular spatial arrangements of the medie-

val house. On the exterior, however, the main, or south, façade of Bacon's Castle (Fig. 13) is symmetrical—its windows equally spaced left and right from the vertical mass of the projecting porch tower. In this it achieved an absolute classical sense of balance, which was only tentatively suggested in the Thoroughgood House.

Also quasi-classical in effect was the original treatment of the window and door openings. On the first floor the windows are headed by segmental arches, on the second they have flat heads and were originally framed in brick with boldly projecting cornices. Today there is no entrance on this side, but an early woodcut shows that originally a door occupied the central position in the tower and had over it a molded brick pediment.

FIGURE 14. Small house,
Warwick, England, late sixteenth century.

Although this pediment had no supporting entablature and columns, as it most surely would have had in a high style English building (see the door at Condover, Fig. 21), the intention is perfectly clear, for the pediment functions, however naïvely, as a typical classical crowning motif to the door. Equally remarkable is the molded stringcourse which separates the first and second floors of the main façade. Although it is not carried around the house, and thus is not permitted to intrude upon the strong verticality of the chimney-gable ends, it is nevertheless an obvious cohesive force in the unity of the symmetrical façade, and in its stress upon the horizontal it is just as classical as the pediment to which it was once

FIGURE 15. *Bacon's Castle,*
Surry County, Va., gable end, c. 1655.

joined. Yet all of these classical elements invade the otherwise medieval
building with the same unabashed directness seen in the prodigy houses.

Bacon's Castle is a milestone in the history of the Virginia Colony,
marking both the social and the economic strengthening of plantation life
in the tidewater region. As the only important surviving house of its period
it is a remarkable document upon which we are forced to rely simply for
lack of other evidence. But whether it was typical of a larger group of
houses now lost to us, or whether, as seems more probable, it was unique
in its day, the house presents a picture of continuing and increasingly
successful efforts toward cultural identification with the homeland. Like
the Thoroughgood House it was a transplanted cultural symbol which
took nothing architectural from its environment except its materials. As the

center of an expanding plantation, however, it fitted serenely into its natural surroundings, with a total sense of belonging, in the same way that the great mansions of England fitted into their environment.

We have already seen that the Adam Thoroughgood House, in its major architectural features, can be identified with a wide body of rural architecture in England. Thus it belongs intrinsically to English folk architecture of the late sixteenth and early seventeenth centuries. Precisely the same is true of Bacon's Castle. Because it is more complex in plan and shows a greater decorative richness than the earlier Thoroughgood House, it reflects a more affluent patronage and a more sophisticated level of architectural taste. But it is a provincial building nevertheless, clumsily proportioned and crude in detail. It is more obvious that Bacon's Castle derives from the prodigy houses than that the Thoroughgood House does. Yet, its direct counterpart in England is to be found not among the great mansions such as Condover and Hatfield, but among the smaller houses such as the one in Warwick already discussed (Fig. 14). Bacon's Castle is more pretentious than the Warwick house, especially in its flamboyant adaptation of the Flemish gable and the grouped chimney. It also aspires more obviously toward a closer identification with high style architecture. But it is in this very obviousness that its provincialism is most vociferously proclaimed. In the prodigy houses of the Jacobean era, such as Hatfield (Fig. 8), the Flemish gable was used discretely as a crowning motif for subordinate vertical units. At Bacon's Castle, however, it encompasses the entire end of the building, where it conspires with the massive chimney completely to dwarf the main block of the house. So incongruously large is this dominating gable that it gives the appearance of once having belonged to a much taller building, from which it was removed and reduced in height, before being applied to its new and totally inadequate setting. Furthermore, there is no tangible relationship in scale between it and the modest pointed gables which once crowned the two central towers (only the one on the north tower still remains). All this creates a drastic contradiction in scale, a contradiction revealing an ambitious but uninformed builder, one whose meager but reasonably accurate knowledge of Tudor detail far exceeded his capacity to unite his various adopted motifs in a coherent design. These drastic deviations from high style practices are the conspicuous marks of provincialism, making Bacon's Castle, in spite of its authoritative Tudor detail, as much a folk style building as is either the Thoroughgood House or the small English Tudor house at Warwick. But like so much folk architecture it has a boldness and vigor which are at once expressive of its vital role in a youthful, expanding planter society and of its more complex function as a symbol of the early colonial struggle toward cultural security.

The Church of England in the Virginia Colony

The charter of the Virginia Company made it mandatory that the Church of England be established as the official one in the colony. It was inevitable, therefore, that a church should be among the first buildings erected. In fact, we know from Captain Smith's own account that efforts were made at once by the original colonists to provide some kind of shelter for religious services. By 1610 they had built a substantial wooden structure twenty-four feet wide by sixty feet long. We also know from the documents that even in this unpretentious building, which could hardly have had more than four walls and a roof, the services were performed with high ceremony. But such commitment to ritual could not be fully gratified by four walls and a roof. It demanded that church buildings of suitable dignity and form ultimately be built in the colony.

Although the liturgy of the post-Reformation church in England was different in many respects from that of the church when it was under the domination of Rome, it still retained certain major features of the Mass. The architectural form of the medieval church, therefore, was still appropriate to the Anglican service. By the time of the first migrations to Virginia not only the great cathedrals but also many of the numerous parish churches of England were being used for Anglican worship.[7] Most of these were either village or country churches and would have been the ones with which the Virginia colonials were most familiar.

Even the smallest of the parish churches had certain characteristics which were essential to both the symbolism and the performance of the Anglican liturgy. Traditionally, the main worship space was long and narrow and oriented east and west. The entrance was at the west end, the chancel with its altar and communion table at the east. In the vast majority of English parish churches the chancel was separated from the congregation; it was a second and somewhat smaller space raised slightly above the floor level of the nave. But in those instances where a single interior space included both chancel and congregation the separation was achieved by a chancel rail or, in some instances, by a rood screen. It was this very simple single-nave type of church (Fig. 16) which provided the model for the earliest of the colonial churches.

In Virginia, an Act of Assembly in 1631 required that wherever a church was either lacking or in bad repair, the inhabitants contribute to the building of a new one. This, together with a growing population, must have provided incentive for an increase in church building. Old records indicate that almost fifty small parish churches were built in the Virginia Colony during the seventeenth century. There may have been more. In any case, the majority were modest structures, reflecting in varying degrees the familiar characteristics of the English parish church.[8] Since life in the Virginia tidewater centered around the individual plantation rather than the town, most were situated by themselves in some convenient location either on the banks of a river or at a crossroads.

St. Luke's Church

Unlike the English churches, which almost without exception were of masonry construction, most of the early Virginia churches were made of wood, and none has survived. But at least three—following more closely the English example—are known to have been made of brick; of these only one, the original Newport Parish Church, Isle of Wight County, remains intact (Fig. 17). It is now known as St. Luke's. Built in 1632 in the Gothic style, it has been recently restored to its original seventeenth-century form. It is the oldest surviving church in America and provides a remarkably complete document of the early church in Virginia.[9]

In every way St. Luke's is a typical English parish church. Its Gothic body and attached tower, its warm brick walls softened by age, stained by seepage, and muted by lichen, stand in lonely isolation amidst a timeless nowhere of luxurious trees. Sometimes seen in shadow, sometimes in sunlight under a veiled luminous sky, St. Luke's creates the compelling illusion of long ago and far away, of East Anglia rather than Virginia, of an English church in a rural English setting. But is this an illusion? Is this not exactly what the men who built the church were trying to create? Away from England by choice, in a new environment with sights, sounds, and smells tantalizingly reminiscent of the England which they had left forever, were they not moved by nostalgia as well as spiritual necessity to create a new England with all the familiar qualities of the old? When it was first built, St. Luke's must have seemed raw and fresh instead of old and venerable as it does today, but as a work of architecture it brought to Newport Parish an image of the Gothic past; yet it did so with certain fascinating twists of style, variations which speak of its colonial authorship as well as its English origin. St. Luke's is a remarkable building with many mysteries and many delightful surprises, a building which belongs as much to the history of the architecture of the Western world as it does to that of early colonial America.

As we approach the church through the shadowed grove of ancient trees which surrounds it we are aware at once of its ancestry in the English parish church (Figs. 16 and 17). The main body of the building is a long rectangular mass with a high pitched roof; a crow-stepped Flemish gable encloses it at the east, a heavily proportioned tower at the west. The building is entirely of brick laid in Flemish bond. On each long side are four round-arched windows divided by brick tracery into two pointed-arch openings of the English lancet type. Between these windows wall buttresses project prominently from the wall, three on each side (Fig. 18). The corners of the building terminate vertically in unadorned turrets, corbeled slightly at their bases. In the east wall is a large lancet window divided by brick tracery into three tiers; the openings in the lower two levels have round heads, those in the upper are pointed.[10] Together these features present an image of a simple but pure and authoritative Gothic style.

The first impression of the tower is that it, too, is basically medieval. The entrance to the porch is a broad round-headed opening with a deep arch which springs from quasi-capitals composed of three slightly projecting courses of brick. In the second story a compound pointed-arch window identical to those on the main body of the church appears on

FIGURE 16. *Parish church,*
Atcham, Shropshire, England.

FIGURE 17. *St. Luke's Church,*
Isle of Wight County, Va., 1632.

each side. All this is decidedly medieval. But then come a number of surprises. Over the door is a strange triangular device, with a widely flaring horizontal base, which is shaped like a classical pediment (Fig. 20). Furthermore, the corners of the tower, to the top of the second story, are set off by brick quoins which are more classical than medieval in design. The third story is still different. Here the quoins give way to pilaster strips, and the windows, instead of being Gothic ones like those in the rest of the church, are simple round-headed openings without any tracery whatever.

It is obvious that the tower of St. Luke's is not, like the body of the church, entirely medieval. To explain this curious mixture of seemingly unrelated elements it is necessary to examine briefly certain aspects of the history of the building and then to relate these facts to the evolution of the Gothic church in England, especially as it affected the small parish church.

The traditional date of 1632 for the beginning of construction of St. Luke's has long been a subject of controversy. During the recent restoration, however, a careful re-evaluation of both old and new evidence gives strong if not conclusive support to this early date.[11] Architecturally, however, a single, precise date here is not particularly important. Historical and technical investigations conducted during the restoration make it almost certain that by 1657 the main body of the building, and the tower to the top of its second story, had been completed. It is equally certain that the quoins were not added to the tower until after 1657, and that the third story was not built until sometime during the last quarter of the seventeenth century. The evolution of the building, therefore, divides itself conveniently into two periods, one before 1657, and one after 1657. We will consider each phase separately, first examining the building stylistically to see what light this might shed upon the issue.

Except for the triangular pediment and the round-arched entrance opening, all the parts of St. Luke's finished before 1657 are in some degree Gothic. In this early part of the church the traceried windows and the wall buttresses are simple but timeless forms of the Gothic style common to small parish churches in all of England. Even the brick tracery, which in its material and simple construction might seem to be a provincial expedient, can be shown to have English precedence. In Essex in particular, where good stone was virtually unobtainable, tracery was constructed of brick in a manner remarkably similar to the treatment of the windows at St. Luke's.[12] The crowstepped gable, too, is an English Gothic device. It was used widely in both Kent and East Anglia during the sixteenth century, and in general was a characteristic feature of small churches of the late Gothic era.[13] Its appearance at St. Luke's, therefore, is completely consistent with English practice and may be considered, along with the windows, buttresses, and small corner turrets, as part of the Gothic idiom.

The interior of St. Luke's is also Gothic (Fig. 19). Although it is entirely restored, the work was done with great care on the basis of thorough research. It probably conveys, therefore, a reasonably accurate image of the original appearance. At the west end there seems to have been a gallery supported on heavy beams which rested in sockets in the masonry. Evidence also indicates the existence of a rood screen and chancel rail so that the traditional division of the church was carried out. But the most important feature of the interior is the trussed ceiling. Here the restoration was based on positive evidence discovered on the tower wall of the nave after the old ceiling had been removed. The restored ceiling, therefore, may be assumed to be exactly like the original. It is a simple truss in which the steep roof rafters are tied together at the middle by collar beams. The framing, however, is not left open to the ridgepole. Between the rafters to the height of the collar beams and then across the collar beams is a recessed plaster ceiling. This seals the interior from the outer roof but does not cover the rafters and collar beams; thus they still may be seen from below. In addition, there are short angle tie beams between the cornice and the rafters and again between the rafters and the collar beams. This

FIGURE 18. *St. Luke's Church,*
Isle of Wight County, Va., east end, 1632.

FIGURE 19. St. Luke's Church,
Isle of Wight County, Va., interior, 1632.

creates a profile down the length of the church which is quasi-elliptical.
The entire structure is stiffened by three massive horizontal tie beams
which cross the church at the cornice level and correspond in their location to the buttresses on the outside wall. This truss is one of the most
thoroughly English Gothic aspects of the building and has its counterpart
in virtually scores of English churches of the Gothic era (Fig. 6).

If the major fabric of St. Luke's is Gothic the triangular pediment
over the door is not. Indeed the pediment is one of the most prominent
classical features of Renaissance architecture. Because of this, the one at
St. Luke's has frequently been cited as evidence for a much later dating of
the church. It has been pointed out that in 1632 a fully developed Renaissance style was still in its initial stages in England itself and it was therefore unlikely that a classical motif such as a pediment should find its way
to colonial Virginia (Fig. 20). But this curious little pediment, with its
spreading cornice, so similar to the one at Bacon's Castle, is not a pure
Renaissance motif. It is rather a pediment of the type which we have
already seen in the high style architecture of England during the very late
sixteenth century, as at Condover (Fig. 21). Its appearance at St. Luke's,
far from being precocious, is in fact a belated use by almost half a century
of a borrowed motif already so adulterated by misuse in a hybrid English
style that nothing remains here of its pure classical form but its triangular
shape. Its use at St. Luke's was not an act of homage to Renaissance

classicism; it was a simple concession to tradition, a naïve application by a skillful, sensitive, but uncritical mason of a familiar device, a device which to him was as much a part of his architectural heritage as the brick tracery he used in the windows.

And so, too, was the arched entrance to the porch, the other feature of the original tower which is conspicuously not Gothic. Here, again, a classical origin is suggested. The round arch was one of the principal features of Renaissance architecture and its appearance at St. Luke's immediately below and together with the pediment has been interpreted as an attempt to classicize the entire entrance ensemble. But there is much more to this arch than its shape, all of it arguing against a classical interpretation. First, it is a very thick, deep arch. Its thickness is the full

FIGURE 20. *St. Luke's Church, Isle of Wight County, Va., door, 1632.*

FIGURE 21. *Condover Hall,
Shropshire, England, door, 1598.* (*Copyright* Country Life)

thickness of the tower wall. Its depth is determined by the bricks which make it up; these have been laid lengthwise along the radials of the arch and are much longer and thinner than the other bricks in the building. Giving the arch a different texture, they set it off from the rest of the wall and thus emphasize its full depth. This effect, together with the broad shadowed inner surface of the arch, creates the appearance of a thick full-bodied structure of great weight and strength. This quality becomes even more apparent when we compare the entrance arch with the much more discrete arches of the windows in the third story. Here the bricks are the same size as those in the rest of the building and are laid short end to the wall so that the arched openings are not as emphatically differentiated from the wall, nor are they as deep.

But it is not the heaviness alone which makes the entrance arch un-classical. The edge of the arch, where the inner curved surface intersects the flat surface of the outer wall, is turned by molded bricks identical with those used to form the tracery in the side windows. This creates the effect of a simple archivolt, a medieval device never used in Renaissance architecture. Moreover, the quasi-capitals, from which the arch springs, project prominently on the inner surface of the entrance opening but remain flush with the plane of the supporting wall, again in a medieval rather than a Renaissance manner. A Renaissance arch, if it were supported by a capital, would show the major face of the capital not to the inner wall but to the outer wall, where it would display itself in a logical visual relationship with the arch above it. The truth is that a heavy arch developed and supported in the way it is at St. Luke's is neither Renaissance nor Gothic. It is rather one of the most thoroughly characteristic devices of early English medieval architecture and dates back to the beginning of the medieval epic, to the Saxon and Romanesque styles.[14] So persistent was this bold, vigorous form of the arch that it appears even in such high style examples of the late sixteenth century as Condover Hall (Fig. 21). There not only the depth of the arch but the slight setback of its face in five receding planes suggests even more strongly than at St. Luke's the archivolt arches of the early medieval style. Envisioned against this background, St. Luke's as it was first completed sometime before 1657 turns out to be a fascinating combination of diverse medieval elements, in character more like a pocket encyclopedia of English medieval architecture than a coherent datable Gothic design.

This charming primitive montage of medieval styles is not without its significance. The very fact that St. Luke's was built at all is important. By the early sixteenth century, following the church-building activities of the late Gothic era, the number of churches in England had reached the point where no more were needed, and with the unrest engendered by the Reformation the incentive for new building ceased altogether. From the mid-sixteenth century, therefore, to the last quarter of the seventeenth, after the great fire of London in 1666 necessitated an extensive church-building campaign, virtually no important churches were erected in England. The small parish churches in particular were already more numerous than necessary. Except for an occasional rebuilding and for modest changes to interiors essential to the new Anglican liturgy, it is doubtful that any totally new country parish churches were built in England.[15] In this light, St. Luke's takes on particular historical importance; for it may very well be one of the last churches built in the direct line of the English Gothic heritage.

Even though St. Luke's is an authentic medieval building it is not stylistically coherent. Ranging as it does from a Romanesque entrance through high Gothic lancet windows to the stepped gable of the late Gothic, it seems to be a capricious play with styles in which several phases of English medieval architecture have intentionally been brought together in the same building. If St. Luke's had, in fact, been begun in Romanesque times, and had subsequently been built in stages over the Gothic era, its mixture of styles would be understandable: this was precisely the way many of the small parish churches of England assumed their hybrid form. But at St. Luke's this was not so. The part completed before 1657 was constructed in a comparatively short length of time and in a single building campaign. The differences in style, therefore, cannot be explained as historical change. They stem rather from a number of conditions, all of them peculiar to the colonial environment.

First, the men who built St. Luke's were not architectural sophisticates.

They were simple carpenters and masons who were totally unaware of "style." Their knowledge of medieval architecture was limited to what they had learned from their respective trades and what they had seen around them in England. Moreover, it seems highly improbable, in view of the virtual cessation of church building in England, that any one of them had ever had much to do with church construction. Through the clergy they were familiar with liturgical requirements, but their actual knowledge of how a church should look was based upon a general and not too well defined image which each remembered from his own personal experience. To them the style of the church was not some particular and sharply focused phase of the Gothic, which might then have been current, but rather a "church" style. Any number of the English churches which might have served them as models could have been built over long periods of time and thus have been mixtures of medieval styles. With their lack of concern about style it would have been perfectly natural for them to build St. Luke's in the same way. Although those master masons who are known to have worked on the high style buildings of England would have been keenly aware of contemporary practices, the provincial English mason would not have been, and the colonial mason who found himself an ocean apart from his native environment would have been even less informed. In fact, it is the very lack of direct communication which accounts for the many fascinating deviations to be found in all folk architecture, and in many ways the innocent mixture of stylistic elements which we have encountered at St. Luke's is its most colonial characteristic.

If the early part of St. Luke's was stylistically naïve, the later changes in the tower were less so. The quoins, which were added shortly after 1657, are common to Renaissance architecture, and were probably intended to supplement the classical effect of the little pediment. On the other hand quoins, used together with basically medieval elements, occur in English architecture as early as the mid-sixteenth century. Since they were particularly prominent in the houses of the Jacobean era (Fig. 8), their appearance at St. Luke's[16] does not represent a radical shift to new stylistic concepts. The third story of the tower, however, does. Here there are no surviving elements of the Middle Ages whatsoever. The corner pilasters and the round-arched windows without tracery are simplified but pure Renaissance motifs which have no parallel in any other colonial church of the seventeenth century. Although the texture and color of the brick afford a continuity of surface which makes the tower a unified whole, the contrast in style with the Gothic part of the church is dramatic. Not only are the third-story windows and pilasters Renaissance motifs, but the wall rectangles within which the windows are contained are more horizontal than vertical. Unlike the Gothic windows in the second story, which are placed at the bottom of a vertical rectangle, those in the third story are positioned slightly above the middle of their containing space. Thus each third-story window is separated from the bottom stringcourse by a space somewhat wider than that above the window. All these proportional relationships are typical of Renaissance design and bring to the tower of St. Luke's a character which was not seen even in England itself until Sir

Christopher Wren rebuilt the churches of London after the fire of 1666 (Fig. 59). Whether there was any direct influence from the Wren churches is not known, but the possibility is certainly very strong. In any case, it is obvious that someone with an active knowledge of the changes that had already taken place in English architecture participated in the completion of the tower.

The shift in style, so emphatically accomplished at St. Luke's, has meaning beyond its immediate architectural connotations. It is also an important manifestation of the changing nature of colonial society. To point this up we need only remind ourselves of what has been said about the earlier architecture of the tidewater area. The Adam Thoroughgood House, as an example of the first half of the century, was a simple farmhouse executed by imported provincial craftsmen in the unrefined but friendly accents of English folk architecture. Scattered through ever-expanding farmlands which but a few years before had been wilderness, houses like this, together with the early churches, became the most important cultural link with the homeland and provided the comforting assurances of the familiar. Bacon's Castle, on the other hand, was more pretentious, reflecting a greater sense of physical security and a more aggressive social ambition. By the time it was built the rough fields had been softened by time and use into a gentle productive countryside. The hardships of the early years were passing into legend and there was time and motivation for reflection upon other things, things that could be acquired from England to build and strengthen both the fact and the image of the English way of life. Bacon's Castle thus aspires toward higher levels of architectural taste by awkwardly assuming, in a provincial folk idiom, some of the outward attributes of high style Jacobean domestic architecture.

And so it was with St. Luke's. Confined by the conservatism of the church to the traditional architectural idiom of the medieval past, and restricted by the general dearth of innovation in English ecclesiastical architecture during the early seventeenth century, the colonial masons and carpenters created their own delightful folk variation of the familiar medieval theme and thus added yet another dimension of Englishness to the rapidly changing face of the tidewater region. This mixed but primarily Gothic image was avidly and uncritically accepted both because tradition said it was right and because it fulfilled the emotional and spiritual needs of the parish.

In contrast, the final addition to the tower of St. Luke's reveals more than unquestioning acceptance. It suggests the presence in the colony of men of increasing cultural preoccupation, of men who were aware of the recent trends in architecture. Who these men were, we do not know; but their very presence in the colony testifies to closer cultural bonds with England, to an expanding and deepening concern for the intellectual as well as the physical life, and to the gradual emergence of patterns of behavior more contemporary with those of the homeland. Although the frontier was to remain a conditioning element in the colonial way of life, its immediate, and in some instances frightening, pressures had been relieved in the Virginia tidewater, and a positive, productive society of civilized men was slowly taking shape. This is the meaning of St. Luke's, for the church not only brought to a close the medieval tradition of the English parish church, but in the precocious third story of the tower formed a prophetic prelude of things to come.

New England in the Seventeenth Century

The architecture of New England, during the seventeenth century, derived from the same sources as that in Virginia. It was English folk architecture of the late medieval period, displaying the same characteristics of style, built with the same structural techniques. Yet it was different. It was different because the land and climate were different, it was different because the men who setttled in New England came from different segments of English society and were motivated by wholly different objectives and ideals. It is one of the ironic facts of history that the small band of Separatists who left England in September of 1620 in the *Mayflower* were destined for the Virginia Colony, but driven by fierce storms far north of their course, they landed instead on the bleak November shores of Cape Cod. The hardships of that first terrible winter took a fearsome toll, but the few who survived remained where they had landed to form the vanguard of the great Puritan migration which began in 1630 with the arrival of the first major contingents of the Massachusetts Bay Company.

The Pilgrims who made up the original Plymouth Colony were religious zealots and came from the lower classes of English society, from the farmers, the laborers, and the artisans. Because of their radical Separatist views they remained an isolated group which had little direct influence on subsequent developments in colonial New England. In contrast, the men who formed the Massachusetts Bay Company came from the landed gentry and commercial classes, from the same circle of Puritans who later provided the leadership for the Cromwellian Revolution. Like the Pilgrims they came to the New World in quest of religious freedom, but unlike the Pilgrims' expedition their own was well planned and thoroughly equipped. The Puritans came to Massachusetts Bay with a formal charter from the King, with abundant capital, and with adequate supplies for the problems that lay ahead. Most important of all, they brought with them the entire administration of their company, and in contrast to the Virginia Colony, which was directed from London, they became at once a self-governing political and religious body, almost totally independent of England.

The original intention of the leaders of the Massachusetts Bay Colony was to carry over into the New World the class distinctions which they had known in England, and to establish an economic system with the great landed estate at its core. But this proved to be impossible. The New England winters were too long and the soil too meager to produce a single staple like tobacco; thus, instead of the plantations, which dominated the southern economy, there developed a system of tightly knit communities. Small self-sufficient farms held in freehold and closely joined together became the mainstays of existence. Both for protection and for efficient management of community affairs it became necessary to "sitt down . . . close togither."

The New England community is one of the remarkable facts of colonial history. It is remarkable not because the idea of the small community was itself new. The village was a familiar and long-established social and economic factor in English life, well known to the Puritans before they came to America. The New England community is remarkable because of its extraordinarily homogeneous character. The English villages had grown over centuries of time and were loosely ordered and random; the New England towns, in contrast, were planned communities placed intact into a virgin wilderness. Each village was built over a short period by virtually the same hands. There were, of course, differences between the various communities, sometimes quite marked. Some of these resulted from the physical circumstances of location, others from the varying social, economic, and political backgrounds of the settlers themselves. Nevertheless, they were all laid out according to a common plan.[17]

The size and specific layout of the individual towns were determined by the system of land apportionment. When a group of settlers wished to form a new town they were granted a parcel of land by the General Court of the Puritan Commonwealth. This became the basis of the town. Within it the land was then divided by common agreement among the individual farmers who held it in freehold.[18] When no more lots were left, no new members were admitted to the community. Instead, new towns were established. The center of each town was the green, or "common." In a prominent position on the green stood the meetinghouse, a unique architectural type which served not only the religious life of the community but the social and civic needs as well. Near the meetinghouse was the parsonage, generally the finest residence in town, and clustered around the green and along the immediately adjacent roads were the other houses, kept close together for common protection but irregularly spaced according to the lay of the land.

The New England communities were homogeneous for yet another reason; the people who formed them had a common, ardent commitment to a high purpose. Whether husbandman, artisan, or Puritan divine, they had all fled England for a land where they might be free to live and worship as they believed. This spirit set the tone of the entire town. Although the conduct of town affairs was frequently marked by sharp differences of opinion, each community was bound together by an individual covenant with God, governed by majority rule at town meeting and completely self-sufficient under an economic system which assured an equitable share to all. Under this system each town gained not only a level of independence from the oppressions of the England which they had left, and curiously still loved, but also an independence from other towns within the colony. In the early days of settlement not even the roads served to join the towns. They were, in fact, first laid out more to provide ready access to the working parts of a town, than to connect one town with another.[19]

The Architecture of New England

Architecturally the individual buildings were as homogeneous as the community itself. Like the early farmhouses of Virginia they were based on English rural architecture of the late sixteenth century. Although the houses varied in size with individual family needs, they were all made of wood. Many of the settlers of the New England towns came from the eastern counties of England, particularly Essex, where wood was the common building material, and the vast majority of the artisans who came with them were trained as carpenters. Furthermore, the forests of New England offered a limitless supply of timber, especially oak and pine, which were highly suitable for building purposes. Throughout the seventeenth century, therefore, the architecture of the New England communities continued to be built of wood. Unlike Virginia—where brick became increasingly important as a building material during the late seventeenth century—New England had few masonry houses: records from the seventeenth century show not more than a dozen. There may have been more, but the total would have been negligible when compared to the hundreds that were built of wood.

In their structural characteristics, the New England houses showed no variation from traditional English practices. They consisted of a heavy wood frame held together by mortise and tenon joints. Generally of oak, this frame was stiffened by angle braces at the corners and by heavy beams called chimney girts which ran completely across the house, abutting the chimney on either side. From these chimney girts to the main girts on either end of the house ran another huge structural member, the summer beam.[20] Within this massive boxlike frame were the lighter vertical studs of the walls and the horizontal joists which supported the floors. For insulation against the weather the wall spaces between the studs were generally filled with a primitive mixture of clay or lime and chopped straw called wattle and daub, or with a rough brick masonry known as nogging. Both were English techniques. At first sun-dried bricks were used for nogging but later kiln-fired ones were employed. The entire structure was protected on the outside by wood clapboards. The interior walls either were plastered over or, as sometimes the case in more elegant houses, were covered with wide vertical wood paneling.

Because so many of the houses of late medieval England were half-timbered, with both frame and fill exposed to the weather, many people have assumed that the early New England houses were constructed in the same way and that the clapboard siding was later developed as protection against the severe New England weather. In those parts of East Anglia from which most of the settlers came, however, a considerable number of the smaller houses were enclosed by clapboards and it seems more plausible that most colonial houses were constructed this way from the very beginning. This assumption gains conclusive support from the extraordinary similarities which exist between surviving wooden houses in England and those in America. This point can be illustrated

FIGURE 22. *Richard Jackson House,*
Portsmouth, N.H., 1664.

by comparing the Richard Jackson House in Portsmouth, New Hampshire
(Fig. 22), with a similar small clapboard house in Essex (Fig. 23).

Just as in the south, the earliest houses of New England were single-
roomed with a large massive chimney at one end. They differed from
those of the south, however, in that the main door opened into a small
entrance way, or "porch," which abutted the chimney. From here, directly
across from the main door, a steep narrow stairs ascended to the loft
or sleeping quarters above, and to the side a door gave access to the
main room, or "hall." In the two-room plan a second room was added
to the other side of the great chimney, with doors opening either way
from the porch. This meant that the chimney then functioned as the
central core of the house, an arrangement which became characteristic
of the seventeenth century in New England and contrasts with the end
chimneys of Virginia. Sometimes the second room was built later than
the first; often the two were built simultaneously. If further space was

needed, a lean-to was attached to the back of the house, where it served as a kitchen. In the latter part of the century, the lean-to was frequently included when the house was built. Those which have been added can generally be distinguished by a slight difference in roof pitch; those incorporated in the house as originally built tended to be continuous with the plane of the roof. But in either case, the short roof plane in the front and the long one in the back gave the house the appearance of a salt box, and it is from this that the familiar "salt-box house" derives its name.

In contrast to Virginia, where not a single wooden house of the seventeenth century still survives, the colder and drier climate of New England has helped to preserve more than seventy examples of the period.[21] Although built according to a common plan and common structural methods, and frequently related by common regional features, no two of these New England houses are exactly alike.[22] Each has its own peculiar character formed by the conditions of location and individual craftsmanship. This diversity has been compounded by additions and changes which have been made to many of the houses as circumstances required, and in modern times the picture has been even further confused by essential but sometimes misleading restoration. Yet with all these regional and individual differences a coherent image of the seventeenth-century New England house emerges, an image which is perhaps most clearly conveyed by the Parson Capen House in Topsfield, Massachusetts.

FIGURE 23. *Clapboard house, Essex, England, late sixteenth century.*

FIGURE 24. *Parson Capen House,
Topsfield, Mass., 1683.*

The Parson Capen House

The Parson Capen House (Fig. 24) is remarkable for several reasons.
First, it is the only house of seventeenth-century New England that can
be dated exactly. June 8, 1683, the date of the raising of the frame, is
carved on the chimney girt in the upper east chamber.[23] In addition,
the house still occupies its original site on a slight knoll immediately
adjacent to the town common and across from the meetinghouse. Finally,
it was built by a second-generation Puritan divine who in every way
epitomized both the colonial New Englander and the community which
he served. The Reverend Joseph Capen was born in Dorchester, Massachusetts, in 1658, was educated at Harvard, and in 1681, at the age
of twenty-three, was called to the pastorate at Topsfield. A year later
he married the daughter of a well-to-do Ipswich family, and in 1683 he
firmly established his position in the community by building his impressive
new house on the green. Parson Capen stayed in Topsfield until his
death in 1725. The story of his life is that of a dedicated preacher,
productive farmer, and dynamic leader in a typical New England town.

The Reverend Capen's house gives vivid reality to this story. Its location on the common and near the meetinghouse makes clear the central role of the parson in the life of the town; its sturdy, forthright construction and practical arrangements speak of the vigorous pattern of life in the New England environment; its simplicity and austerity are the very embodiment of the Puritan mind. All of this unfolds as we approach the house from the common. In the early winter, when the leaves are off the trees, its bold profile dominates the rural setting. At the same time, its sunburned clapboard walls and unrefined surfaces harmonize quietly with the stark gray-brown countryside, making the house a natural extension of the earth upon which it stands. It is like this today with the other houses which surround it all primly dressed in pristine white; it must have been even more earthy in the seventeenth century when all its neighbors shared its roughness, its irregularities, and its textural warmth.

As we approach from the gate, the house is seen to be an ample two-story structure with a high-pitched gabled roof and a massive central chimney. The plan is the two-room type with hall and parlor separated by the chimney and the porch. Narrow stairs ascend from the porch to the second story, and again on to the third. Structurally the house is a superb example of English medieval framing methods. On the main façade the second story overhangs the first; on the two ends the overhang occurs at the attic-floor level, thus enclosing the gable and continuing the horizontal line of the eaves around the house. Sturdy brackets support the overhang on either side of the front door and in the middle of each end wall. The corners, however, are ornamented by carved drops, called "pendills" in colonial times. These and the shaped brackets are the only decorative features on the exterior.

Seen from the outside, the Capen House seems impressively large. Within, however, the effect is small and confining. This is due primarily to the very low ceilings and the enormous size of the summer beams, which seem to press the space downward. Then, too, each of the first-floor rooms is dominated by an expansive fireplace (Fig. 25) which stretches across a major portion of the inner wall. It was these great hearths, together with the sense of enclosure, which provided the warmth and security so essential to life on the New England frontier. This is particularly well demonstrated in the "hall," the room to the right of the entrance porch. Here the fireplace, with its ovens and cooking equipment, occupies more than half the wall, and it was here that most of the family living was centered. Serving both as kitchen and living room, it is a type of room which still survives in many New England farmhouses, and, as its name "hall" testifies, it is an important carryover from the Middle Ages, for in the medieval house the "hall" formed the core of the building. In contrast, the "parlor" of the Capen House (to the left of the porch) was used for more formal entertaining. This type of room, which was common to New England houses, had no direct counterpart in the medieval house. It was rather a product of

FIGURE 25. *Parson Capen House,*
Topsfield, Mass., parlor, 1683.

the changing pattern of social behavior peculiar to British middle-class
society, and was thus directly related to life in the New England community.

As it exists today, the Parson Capen House is the result of extensive
restorations carried out in 1913. We are confronted, therefore—as we
were in our consideration of Virginia architecture—with the ever pressing
questions: How much of what we see here is authentic? How closely
does the present building approximate its original form? In the Capen
House, two significant changes were made at the time of restoration
which considerably altered its character. The first was in regard to the
chimney. Photographs taken before the restoration show a perfectly plain,
rectangular block chimney without clustered sides and ornamental cap.[24]
There may have been no reason to assume that this was the original
chimney, but on the other hand there was no evidence whatever,
structural or otherwise, to indicate that the compound chimney put on
in the restoration duplicated the original one. This new chimney is, in
fact, a reproduction of the one which was on the Hunt House in
Salem.[25]

The other change affected the character of the windows on the principal façade. Structural evidence, as revealed in photographs taken during the restoration, makes it clear that the original windows were not paired vertical frames of the kind that were put on, but rather were horizontal strips of three casements, of the type seen in the Whipple House in Ipswich (Fig. 26).[26] It is important in our evaluation of the house to recognize that these changes make it more elegant than it originally was.

FIGURE 26. *Whipple House, Ipswich, Mass., 1639(?).*

At first glance, the Capen House seems to be a symmetrical building, with the chimney and door forming the fulcrum for equally spaced windows. It would appear as such even if the windows were the original triple casements. Actually, the design is asymmetrical. The parlor, or west room, is slightly larger than the "hall," leaving the chimney closer to the east end of the building. Furthermore, the main door is to the right of the chimney. Although the window groups are lined up vertically and are absolutely identical with one another, the group on the right is closer to the door than is the group on the left.

These irregularities in lateral relationships betray the medieval origins of the style and remind us of the similar arrangement which we saw in the Adam Thoroughgood House in Virginia. Like the Thoroughgood House, the Capen House is completely English throughout and is comparable to numerous wooden clapboard houses of the late Tudor period which still survive in Essex, England (Fig. 23). But again, in the Thoroughgood House, the almost symmetrical arrangement is significant. We know that the classical concept of symmetry was introduced into English domestic architecture more than a century earlier and before 1600 had worked its way down to the provincial level. We have already seen it in Bacon's Castle in Virginia, and it appeared also in a few of the late seventeenth-century houses in New England. Yet in spite of these shifts toward classical form the architecture of seventeenth-century New England, like that of Virginia, remained both provincial and medieval, and houses like Parson Capen's must be seen as fascinating belated survivals of English folk architecture during the late Tudor period.

The New England Community

A comparison between the Parson Capen House and Bacon's Castle is useful in evaluating the differences between the social and economic systems of New England and the South. These two important survivals of the early colonial period are offshoots of the same architectural background in England. They are therefore historically coherent. Yet they are very different. They are different because conditions of climate and available materials dictated that one should be made of wood and the other of brick. But more important, they are different because they were built by men with wholly different attitudes toward life. The southern mansion, in its exaggerated but provincial display of high style manners, aspires toward aristocratic elegance. The New England parsonage, disciplined by the Puritan insistence upon plainness, is shorn of conceit and glorifies itself and its community by its direct and uncompromising acceptance of the simple architectural idiom of rural England. Juxtaposed, the plantation mansion and the New England farmhouse are eloquent witnesses to the wide gulf which separated the Virginia and the Massachusetts Bay colonies in the seventeenth century.

The plantation of the South was a vast self-sufficient agricultural complex which was producing for a foreign market. The plantation mansion, with its dependent utilitarian outbuildings was the center of the complex. Here the social and business life of the farm was carried out under its own regulations and its own management. Political affairs were conducted by representation at the colonial capital; religious activities centered in the parish church, which served numerous plantations in much the same way that the parish churches of England served the landed estates. Except for the colonial capital there was no important community life in Virginia. The plantation mansion thus became both the heart and the symbol of the southern system.

In New England the productive unit was not the single farm but the entire community. No single dwelling was more important than any of the others which clustered around the village green. Although each farmer was self-sufficient in providing sustenance for himself and his family, he held his property in freehold from the town, shared a common pasture with the other members of the community, and at town meeting had a voice in the management of political and civic affairs. The center of this community life, therefore, was not the private dwelling but the meetinghouse. Here the entire town came together and expressed itself in all its affairs, both civic and religious. It was this building, therefore, and not the farmhouse, which became the focal point and symbol of the New England community.

The New England Meetinghouse

The meetinghouse was first of all a house of worship and had its origin in the religious practices of the New England Puritans. In contrast to Virginia, where the preeminence of the Anglican doctrine made the parish church mandatory, the New England colonies were dominated by a powerful Puritan theocracy, to the extent that for most of the seventeenth century the Church of England played no role whatsoever in the religious life of the Massachusetts Bay Colony. Instead, there grew up a system of independent Congregational churches, each formed by an individual covenant and dedicated to the propagation of what the Puritans considered the true religion as revealed through the Word. A Congregational church not only concerned itself with the worship of God, but also exalted sobriety and purity in both the social and the economic affairs of the community. A Gothic parish church, such as St. Luke's, with all its traditional and ritualistic elements, was therefore regarded by the Puritans as "Popery." To gratify their radical Separatist views they developed instead a wholly new concept of church edifice, a simple "four-square" hall. It was called the "meetinghouse" by the Puritans, for even the word "church" they viewed with suspicion.

We recall that in the traditional Anglican church the altar, as a focal point of worship, was located at the end of a long and narrow interior space. It was because the Puritans rejected this orientation that the meetinghouse developed its almost square proportions. The altar was replaced by the pulpit as the center of the service, and to de-emphasize still further the Anglican longitudinal space this pulpit was located in the middle of the long side of the meeting room. The main entrance was on the other long side, opposite the pulpit.

The Old Ship Meetinghouse

The New England meetinghouse was the architectural embodiment of Congregationalism. As a building type, it had no known counterpart in English church history, and it may be viewed as the only original architectural invention of the English colonies. Just one seventeenth-century example of this fascinating building type remains today, the Old Ship Meetinghouse in Hingham, Massachusetts (Fig. 27). It was built in 1681, only two years before the Capen House, but its shape has been considerably altered by additions in 1731 and again in 1755. Although it still retains much of its original character, especially since the restorations of 1930, two significant changes demand attention.

In its present form, the Old Ship Meetinghouse is a rectangular building seventy-three feet long and fifty-five feet wide with an entrance porch on one of the short sides. The pulpit is on the long side to the left of the entrance. This is unusual, for it was customary to have both the door and the pulpit facing one another on the long sides. Originally, however, the building was almost square in plan, forty-five by fifty-five feet,

FIGURE 27. *Old Ship Meetinghouse, Hingham, Mass., 1681.*

so that what is now the short side was then the long side; and the pulpit which is now to the left when one enters the building was then opposite the door on the original long side. It was to keep the location of the pulpit in appropriate relation to the orientation of the interior space that the shift occurred after the building was lengthened. This was more important to the Congregational doctrine than the location of the door in relation to pulpit, and testifies to the determination of the Puritan rejection of Anglican practices. The square shape and general arrangement of the interior space also made the meetinghouse more suitable for its other functions; for it was not only a house of worship, it was also a meeting place for civic affairs.

The other important change in the Old Ship Meetinghouse was in the character of the roof. The original roof was pitched up from all four sides, in the characteristic form of the hipped roof, and terminated in a belfry. It also had in the middle of each side a steep pitched gable which gave the building a more decided medieval character than it has today. Although there is no record of what the original belfry looked like, it is certain that it did not have the delicate proportions and classical scale of the eighteenth-century cupola which now crowns the building. The classical balustrade and porches were also part of the later additions.

The most impressive feature of the Old Ship Meetinghouse is the wood framing that supports the roof (Fig. 28). The principal structural system is a series of three enormous trusses. The 45-foot tie beam, which forms the bottom of each truss, rests on the sturdy vertical posts of the main frame of the building and is stiffened by curved angle braces. From the center of each tie beam rises the main vertical member, the king post. The main triangles of the three trusses, between the vertical king posts and the horizontal tie beams, are closed by concave curved struts. The platform for the belfry is carried on these trusses, which, by means of short braces, also lend support to the main rafter of the roof. The roof trusses are stiffened by longitudinal beams that run through the truss tie beams at right angles; these extend the entire length of the building and terminate in the frame at each end of the room.

    This building is called the "Old Ship Meetinghouse" because the shape of the curved struts resembles the inverted ribs of a ship and local tradition has attributed the construction of the building to ship's carpenters. This seems possible since Hingham was an important center of ship-building activity during the seventeenth century. The curved strut, however, is one of the most common features of English Gothic timber construction, a feature which has its origin in the so-called "cruck"

FIGURE 28. Old Ship Meetinghouse, Hingham, Mass., interior, 1681.

framework, or "bent tree" construction, of the early Middle Ages. This primitive framing method survived in later small cottages and barns, and in a form remarkably like the trusses in the Old Ship Meetinghouse. It also was used for numerous church trusses in England. It seems far more likely that this method, and not the framing method of the shipbuilder, was the source of the Hingham meetinghouse strut, although the two certainly have much in common.

Form and Structure in Seventeenth-Century America

The exposed timber ceiling, whether supported by a truss or by horizontal beams and joists, was a major characteristic of English medieval architecture and was carried over into all colonial buildings of the seventeenth century. In the seventeenth-century houses of New England the dominating feature of the interiors is the great summer beam which abuts the chimney girt and carries the joists of the floor above. Although the summer beam itself was generally enriched by beveled or molded edges, the rest of the ceiling work was unadorned. In some of the rooms, the walls were plastered; in others they were covered with vertical paneling, sometimes left plain, sometimes carved with simple moldings at the joints. Such was the case in the hall of the Eleazer Arnold House in Lincoln, Rhode Island, built in 1687 (Fig. 29). Occasionally, as in the parlor of the Parson Capen House (Fig. 25), the walls and ceilings seem to have been entirely covered with whitewash, although the structural timbers were still left exposed. There are even rare cases where a decorative color was applied to the woodwork. For the most part, however, materials were left in their natural state with all structural elements exposed.

Because of this forthright use of materials, colonial architecture of the seventeenth century has served as a source of both inspiration and affirmation for a comparable development in contemporary American architecture. Exploiting both the structural potential of materials and their visual and textural qualities, American architects today have developed a positive relationship between structure, materials, and form which some have attempted to equate with early American building. The work of Frank Lloyd Wright in particular shows the architect to be responsive to this relationship, and Wright himself expressed his enthusiasm for the seventeenth-century house, which he quite rightly saw as part of the great American tradition. There can be no doubt that there is an affinity here. But there is also a danger that we may over-evaluate the architecture of the seventeenth century and read into it qualities which it does not have; for it is very doubtful that the seventeenth-century builder had any elaborate design program in mind when he left his materials in their natural state. The seventeenth-century builder was an artisan, not a professional architect. Working within the limited technical means at his disposal, he was simply carrying on the formal ideas and structural methods of a building tradition which had come down to him from English architecture of the Middle Ages. This is not to say that the visual appeal of wood, stone, and brick did not evoke a response

FIGURE 29. *Eleazer Arnold House,*
Lincoln, R.I., hall, 1687.

from the seventeenth-century colonial man. It was, indeed, from the natural beauty of materials that the greatest aesthetic enrichment came into his life. But the probability remains that the decision to let the materials speak for themselves was a matter of expedience and habit, and not of design intentions. In Wright's case, however, the specific selection, treatment, and arrangement of materials are rendered in accord with positive aesthetic principles which presuppose a thought process of the most sophisticated kind. It is precisely this which distinguishes the professional from the artisan, which separates the brilliant originality of high style performance from its diluted imitation in the transmuted idiom of the folk style, and American architecture of the seventeenth century was folk architecture from beginning to end.

We have already stressed the importance in the creation of great architecture of both the imagination of the architect and the leadership of enlightened patronage. Early colonial America offered neither the motivation nor the means for either. The creative impulses which brought the colonists to the wilderness in the first place were directed by religious fervor and practical common sense toward the everyday problems of individual and community life. Architecture was thus incidental to more immediate and pressing affairs. To seek in colonial building the beginnings of a new American architecture is to seek the first green of spring while the hills are still frosted with winter's rime. Politically, socially, spiritually, the English colonies on the Atlantic seaboard mark the beginning of a new way of life and a new nation. But confronted with the void of the wilderness, the American settlers, like the colonials of ancient Greece, sought cultural security in the familiar ways of the homeland; and American colonial architecture, far from releasing new forces, kept alive to the last dying flame the transplanted fires of the Middle Ages, which in England itself were already extinct.

CHAPTER III

Sir Christopher Wren
in the Colonial World

*The building is beautiful and commodious, being first
modeled by Sir Christopher Wren, adapted to the Nature
of the Country by the Gentleman there.*
Hugh Jones

The early colonials did not bring with them to the New World the seeds
of revolution in architecture. In England, however, in the very years when
the first contingents of new settlers were arriving in Jamestown, another
group of Englishmen left London for Italy. Unlike the colonial migrations,
which terminated in a cultural vacuum, this journey made its way
through the very heartland of European civilization, and brought enlightened Englishmen into contact with the Italian Renaissance in such a way
as to change the whole course of English architecture, including that of
colonial America. Traveling with the group was an artist of extraordinary
talent, Inigo Jones.[1] Jones began his artistic career as a designer of
theatrical productions for the court, but at some time during his early
years he became interested in architecture, and before going to Italy
he had already served as architect to the Prince of Wales. From the
records of the trip which Jones took in 1613–14, we are able to follow
his itinerary with reasonable accuracy. But more important, he took with
him a copy of Andrea Palladio's *Four Books of Architecture,*[2] in which
he made marginal notes. These notations, brief as they are, show that
he directed most of his attention toward the buildings of ancient Rome,
against which he checked Palladio's plates for accuracy, and resolved
for himself basic questions of proportion and detail. His understanding of
classical principles, therefore, came from firsthand observation of the
monuments themselves and not through the indirect sources which had
provided data for the architects of the prodigy houses.

The ultimate result of Jones's trip was a new architectural style—one
so radically different from the hybrid idiom of the prodigy houses that
it is difficult to see both as the creations of the same cultural climate;
for with the architecture of Inigo Jones, the stubborn persistence of
medieval decorative principles was decisively challenged, and by the time
Bacon's Castle was built in Virginia (c. 1655), English architecture was
rapidly shifting over to its own version of the Renaissance style.

Jones was distinguished from the other architects of his time not only
because of his infinitely greater talent, but also because of his remarkable

powers of synthesis. We have already seen that during the late Elizabethan and early Jacobean eras Renaissance elements were applied as surface ornament to otherwise medieval buildings; in the work of Jones, Renaissance ideas became the very foundation upon which his style was based. In his work, forms were coherently related, rather than superficially combined, in a controlled classical unity. Alert and responsive to the most delicate formal relationships, Jones became the first Englishman fully to grasp both the practical and philosophical basis of Renaissance architecture, and, like his contemporary Shakespeare, he brought to his art the vitalizing forces of a fertile imagination.[3] Moreover, Jones came to architecture not as a mason or carpenter, bound by association with a guild to the traditions of the Middle Ages; he came rather as an artist, whose work in designing for the stage had involved him in endless fascinating problems of both real and illusionistic space. His approach to architecture, therefore, was through a highly developed sensitivity to abstract spatial relationships. For him a building existed more as an aesthetic challenge than as a practical problem in bricks, mortar, and timber. This attitude, together with a refined and reliable taste, made him unique in the England of his day and places him among the great classic designers of Western architecture.

In 1615, shortly after his return to England from Italy, Jones was appointed to the important position of Surveyor of the King's Works.[4] His first commission after the appointment was for Queen's House in Greenwich (Fig. 30). Begun in 1616, it is one of the most remarkable and influential buildings in the whole of English architecture. In every way it was totally unlike the prodigy houses. We remember that in spite of their obvious symmetry and loosely applied classical details, the prodigy houses were dominated by medieval irregularity, a quality engendered by the interlacing effect of tracery, and by the constant shifts in plane created by the towers, the bracketed gables, and the clustered chimney stacks. In a more provincial form, the same lively variety is found in the chimneys, gables, and porches of Bacon's Castle, and in the sharp pointed gables, the overhang, and the open woodwork of the New England houses.

There is not the slightest trace of this medieval vocabulary in Jones's design for Queen's House. The main element of the scheme is a simple rectangular block, self-contained and clearly defined by smooth wall planes. The principal orientation is horizontal, an effect which is emphasized by the continuous line of the cornice and by the balustrade at the top. Above and behind the balustrade rise the chimney stacks. Window and door openings are sharply isolated, incisive, and carefully proportioned with respect both to one another and to the whole. The symmetry is absolute, and authentic classical proportions and details prevail throughout.

Jones's bold yet exquisite reassertion of classical principles in Queen's House marks one of those great creative moments in the history of architecture when a new style is given its first articulate form. The building was not actually completed until 1635, and its originality was not at once understood in England. Shortly after mid-century, however, its

FIGURE 30. Inigo Jones. The Queen's House,
Greenwich, England, 1616–35.

dramatic innovations had permeated most of English architecture and would soon crystallize in the fully developed English Renaissance style. By the late seventeenth century the new mode had reached colonial America and appeared, as we have already seen, in the tower of St. Luke's Church.[5]

But Queen's House not only introduced a new style, it also contained all the elements of a completely fresh concept of domestic architecture, a concept which was responsive to the significant changes taking place in seventeenth-century English society, and which would prove particularly adaptable to conditions in eighteenth-century colonial America. As originally designed, Queen's House was two rectangular blocks connected by a bridge. Although the H-plan which resulted from this arrangement was reminiscent of the Middle Ages, the sharp isolation of the individual blocks had nothing medieval about it; and it was precisely this latter feature, the single horizontal block, which Jones's followers were to exploit as the basis of a new house type.

The independent horizontal block, as an architectural device, was certainly not invented by Jones. We have already seen it in the classical temple, as one of the major characteristics of the architecture of ancient Greece and Rome, and it was later taken up by the architects of the Renaissance. The Italian Renaissance, in fact, was the immediate source of the idea for Jones, especially as he came to know it through both

FIGURE 31. *Roger Pratt.*
Coleshill, Berkshire, England, c. 1650 onwards. (*Copyright* Country Life)

the writings and the architecture of Palladio. During his visits to Italy, Jones must have seen all the existing works of this great sixteenth-century Italian, and the similarity between the individual blocks of Queen's House and such Palladian works as the Palazzo Chiericati in Vicenza has long been recognized.

The isolated block type of house developed in England was very different from its Italian prototype. This is best seen in the first complete example of the type, Coleshill in Berkshire. Built about 1650, Coleshill was primarily the work of Roger Pratt, although Jones seems to have had some connection with the design. In this remarkable mansion all the major ingredients of both the English Renaissance style and the new concept of the house are brought together in a refined and monumental synthesis. The general scheme could not have been simpler. As seen in our illustration (Fig. 31), the isolated horizontal block *is* the house, complete and self-contained. There are no wings, no towers, no courtyards, no interruptions of the horizontal line. A single door occupies the center of the long side, discreetly emphasized as the fulcrum of the design by a bracketed pediment; the windows are incisively isolated against the clean wall and correspond exactly either side of the door. The main block is terminated and contained by quoins at the corners and by a continuous cornice which, together with the stringcourse between the floors, stresses the horizontal orientation. Both the effect of wholeness and the pervasive symmetry are further emphasized by the hipped roof which pitches inward from all four sides to terminate in a balustrade. Rhythmic variety is provided in the triple grouping of the principal windows, a theme which is carried up into the roof by freestanding chimney stacks and by the subordinate stress of the dormers. At the very top the design culminates in the cupola. Details and proportions throughout the building are classical; and in the subtlety with which independent units are related and joined, the building conveys something of the coherent unity of the classical temple.

Simplicity, wholeness, pristine clarity, these are the qualities of Coleshill which confounded the conglomerate medievalism of the prodigy houses and opened the way for a fresh and original flowering of the Renaissance style in English domestic architecture. But that flowering did not occur until the second great architectural genius of the century, Sir Christopher Wren, together with a changing patronage, provided direction · and impetus.

Sir Christopher Wren

Inigo Jones died in 1652, about the time of the completion of Coleshill. Ten years later, Christopher Wren began his first important building, the Sheldonian Theatre at Oxford. Like Jones, Wren came to the profession of architecture from a background different from that of the traditional master masons, who continued, in spite of Jones, to dominate the affairs of building in England during the first half of the seventeenth century. Wren brought to architecture a mind trained in mathematics and astronomy, and from the beginning he showed the same capacity as Jones to think in abstract spatial terms. But unlike Jones, whose vision was limited to the possibilities of the individual block, Wren worked boldly in large spatial systems coherently and dramatically related. Moreover, because of his scientific background and practical ingenuity he had a command of materials and structure which went far beyond the capabilities of anyone of his time and placed him among the greatest architect-engineers in the history of Western architecture. Also like Jones, Wren became Surveyor of His Majesty's Works, and it was in this capacity that he produced his most monumental Baroque schemes (see, for example, Fig. 34). He also did important works outside of royal patronage, and throughout his career was a more prolific and diversified architect than Jones and infinitely more influential.

Jones's role in English architecture had been that of a purifier. His innovations were too abstract to be understood by the traditional-oriented craftsmen of his time, and his influence was not felt until after mid-century, and then only in the work of a handful of followers such as Roger Pratt. Consequently, during his lifetime there is not the slightest hint of his coherent style at the low and the folk style levels. Wren, on the other hand, was a catalyst. Whereas Jones had remained an isolated and relatively obscure artist in the court of James I, Wren was a man of immense and diversified creative power whose name was known internationally before he ever entered the profession of architecture. His productive years also coincided with a period in English history when dramatic social and economic changes were taking place. This provided new and challenging opportunities for the architectural profession as a whole, and during Wren's lifetime, his influence spread through virtually the entire fabric of English architecture. This included colonial America, where his style was to assert itself in two building types in particular, the detached house and the church.

The Detached House

The small detached house was a major contribution of English middle-class society to the history of Western architecture. Like the great country houses of England it stands alone, on its own parcel of land, and is thus distinguished from the small houses of Europe in that the latter were built with common walls. The detached house was conceived in the high style circles of Jones and his followers, and realized in houses such as Coleshill. Here the original mold was cast. It consisted of a simple horizontal block, with the windows on the long side symmetrically arranged around a central door. During the last quarter of the seventeenth century, numerous small but elegant houses based on this simple format were built in most parts of England.

The reasons for this proliferation of the style were not altogether architectural. As we have already seen, one of the most remarkable aspects of the late seventeenth century in England was the depth to which the architectural taste of high patronage permeated the middle-class levels of the economic and social structure. The rapid rise of British commerce had brought new wealth and opportunity to a growing number of merchants, bankers, and tradesmen. Concentrated in London, these men formed a powerful group which became increasingly influential not only in political and social affairs but also in the cultural destiny of the nation. In rural England, a similar middle class emerged, made up of the country squires and of the artisans, tradesmen, and professional men of the small towns. Together they formed a wholly new architectural patronage.[6]

As patrons of architecture the middle class found itself on unfamiliar ground. Traditionally, cultural values had been established by the court and aristocracy, and this new breed of men was neither conditioned nor motivated to challenge this long-standing state of affairs. In matters of taste, therefore, they tended to be acquiescent, accepting without much question the ways of recognized authority. At the same time, however, they were fiercely ambitious. If they were imitative they were aggressively so, and in their emulation of high style precepts they sought and achieved the very best. Consequently their houses, although modest in size, were altogether remarkable for their quality, and in proportions and detail in particular many were comparable to the great country houses of the

FIGURE 32. *Minster House,
Cathedral Close, Winchester, England.*

period. Almost without exception they were simple rectangular blocks with hipped roofs of the type seen at Coleshill. Minster House (Fig. 32), a beautiful small brick dwelling which faces the cathedral close in Winchester, is typical. It is smaller and more simple than Coleshill, is brick instead of stone, but is no less sophisticated in style. Houses of this type were the direct prototype for the domestic architecture of colonial America during the first half of the eighteenth century.

During the years when the small detached house was coming into its own in English domestic architecture, Sir Christopher Wren was at the height of his career. Because of this, a small house of this type is frequently referred to as a Wren-type house. We know from the evidence of Coleshill, however, that Wren did not invent this particular form of house; nor is there any reason to believe that Wren ever designed a small house.[7] Yet the majority of the houses of this period, large and small, have the unmistakable stamp of his style. This is seen in such things as proportion and scale, and in the use of materials, particularly brick and white stone, which were frequently combined by Wren to form rich contrasting surfaces.[8] It is seen most especially in the character of the ornament. Wren's style was a Baroque style, and although there was no opportunity in the simple rectangular block to indulge in complex spatial effects, the ornament was another matter. Window openings in the small houses remained relatively unadorned but the central door became the object of rich decorative treatment. The severe triangular and segmental pediments, which characterized the earlier style of Jones and Pratt, gave way to broken and reverse-curve pediments and to hoods. These were frequently enriched by elaborate foliated carved ornament. It is this ornament in particular which is so characteristic of the work of Wren, especially as it was developed for him by the master carver, Grinling Gibbons.[9]

The Church

Wren's influence on the domestic architecture of colonial America was through the small detached houses of the English middle class. In the colonial church, however, it came directly from the work of the great man himself, through the churches which he built in London after the Great Fire of 1666. This devastating holocaust destroyed most of the old city and took with it eighty-seven parish churches. Wren was charged with the rebuilding, first as a private citizen and after 1669 as Surveyor General.

The task which confronted Wren was immense. First it was necessary to assess the damage and plan the reconstruction. Here was a difficult but challenging opportunity which involved the evaluation and reorganization of space on a monumental scale, and Wren set to work at once. Less than a week after the Fire had been brought under control he submitted to the King a plan which proposed rebuilding the burned city along completely new lines. Except for the location of a few key monuments, such as St. Paul's Cathedral, Wren abandoned the old medieval city with its random narrow streets, and planned instead a new one, laid out on a grid, and crossed by sweeping avenues which converged on major architectural monuments. The destroyed part of the city, however, had been the commercial heart of London, where vested land interests were strong. Because of this, and because a general lack of records made it impossible to establish either exact boundaries or values, Wren's master plan could not be carried out and the city was rebuilt along its original lines.

These complications imposed several limitations on Wren in his program for rebuilding the parish churches. His hope had been to place his churches in prominent positions on ample ground so that each could be seen to advantage. Instead he was forced to work in confined, oddly shaped, and frequently meager sites. To meet this situation Wren approached each church as a separate problem; as a result, of the fifty-one rebuilt no two are alike.[10] But within this variety he sought also to accommodate each interior space design to the contemporary character of the Anglican liturgy. In the majority of the churches he rejected the long narrow nave and deep chancel of the medieval church for the broadly proportioned spaces based upon classical prototype. To enclose and cover these spaces Wren wanted to use classical vault forms; but because of limited funds, it proved impossible to construct them in masonry. At this point his structural inventiveness provided a practical solution. Instead of masonry vaults he used plaster ceilings shaped like vaults and suspended from wood trusses, a technique which he himself had worked out a few years earlier in the Sheldonian Theatre at Oxford. This was a flexible and inexpensive method offering even greater spanning potential than masonry, and with it Wren was able to develop a variety of vaulted shapes, all of which had classical antecedents. In the end he produced a unique spatial solution for each individual church. Because much of the ceiling weight in each case was carried on the roof trusses, he could work with light supporting elements, such as single and coupled columns (Fig. 61). It was also possible to introduce window openings in an imaginative and unusual way. Sensitive to the physical lightness of his method, Wren designed his ornament in a delicate scale appropriate to the eggshell-like plaster surfaces. The results were both original and anti-Gothic, bringing to English ecclesiastical architecture a fresh and vivacious new concept of interior space design.

In both shape and expansiveness the interiors of Wren's London churches were predominantly classical. The exteriors, however, were not. In this regard, Wren's intuitive sense of rightness led him to make an important concession to church tradition. He retained the most characteristic and symbolic features of all Gothic churches, the tower and the spire. This graceful tapering shape, so contrary in its soaring verticality to the horizontal order of classical design, Wren brought into unity with the rest of the church by an imaginative infusion of classical detail. The spires of the London churches vary considerably in quality, suggesting a degree of freedom on the part of the individual artisans who built them. No two are alike, and some, like that of St. Mary-le-Bow (Fig. 66), are among the most exquisitely beautiful objects in the whole of English architecture. The modest size of Wren's London churches, and the fundamental simplicity of his solutions were both appropriate and timely in regard to the conditions in early eighteenth-century colonial America. The church provided for the colonials their most direct contact with Wren's creative genius.

The Wren-Baroque in Colonial America

The name of Christopher Wren is part of the American legend—so much so, in fact, that it would be difficult to enumerate those buildings of early eighteenth-century America (and some even later) which local tradition has ascribed in some way to Wren. This is nonsense, of course, for no architect so deeply committed to the high patronage of court and state would have either the time or inclination to design unimportant buildings on the fringes of the empire. Nonetheless, it is significant nonsense, for it recognizes in its own uncritical way a major and obvious fact of architectural history, that the style of American architecture during the first half of the eighteenth century is wholly and enthusiastically Wren-Baroque developed entirely at the low and folk style levels. It is not necessary that Wren should have designed a single one of these buildings for this to be so. By the turn of the eighteenth century, colonial

FIGURE 33. *Wren Building, College of William and Mary, Williamsburg, Va., 1695.*

America had become an important and rapidly growing part of the British Empire. Moreover, colonial society as it developed in the mercantile centers of the Atlantic seaboard and in the plantations of the South was essentially a middle-class society, not unlike that which was already playing such a significant part in English commercial and political affairs. In architecture, therefore, the current high style of the homeland permeated the colonies in precisely the same way, although at a somewhat later date, as it did the provincial towns and countryside of England itself.

English Renaissance motifs, which were the basis of the Wren style, first appeared in colonial America in scattered works during the last years of the seventeenth century—we have already seen them at St. Luke's Church—but the first coherent example of the Wren style itself was begun in the Virginia Colony in 1695. It is the Wren Building (Fig. 33) at the College of William and Mary in Williamsburg, and not only was it the earliest example of the style in the colonies, but according to one revealing though not conclusive document, the building was designed by Christopher Wren. Writing in 1722, Hugh Jones, the first professor of mathematics at the college, tells us that "the building is beautiful and commodious, being first modeled by Sir Christopher Wren, adapted to the Nature of the Country by the Gentleman there; . . . and is not altogether unlike Chelsea Hospital."[11]

FIGURE 34. *Christopher Wren. Royal Hospital,
Chelsea, England, 1682–89.*

This passage establishes the first and only direct connection between the great Wren and the architecture of the New World. We cannot be sure whether the design was actually prepared by Wren himself or by someone in his office, but Hugh Jones was certainly in a position to know the facts and there can be little doubt that the connection is real enough. In this respect, Jones's reference to Chelsea Hospital is particularly revealing. Comparison of the Wren Building with either of the side wings of Chelsea Hospital (Fig. 34) shows them both to be long horizontal blocks with central pedimented pavilions and with a similar type of fenestration and dormer windows; the cupola over the center of the Wren Building also appears over the main portico of Chelsea Hospital. Beyond these obvious relationships, however, the similarity between the two buildings begins to break down. Where the window openings of the wings of Chelsea Hospital are amply proportioned in

relation to the wall, those in the Wren Building are meager and altogether domestic in scale; where the central pavilion at Chelsea Hospital
is broad and sweeping and embellished with giant Doric pilasters, that
of the Wren Building is tall and narrow and topped by a steeply pitched
pediment which is more medieval than classical in its proportions.
The whole effect of the Wren Building is sharp, brittle, and angular.
Although it is symmetrical and has a cupola and classical details, it still
echoes the provincial medievalism of earlier seventeenth-century buildings
in Virginia, such as Bacon's Castle. It is perfectly apparent, therefore, that
whatever design for the college was submitted by Wren's office, whether
prepared by Wren himself or not, it was drastically modified by the
conditions and limitations of Virginia craftsmanship. Even Hugh Jones was
aware of this when he wrote that the building was "adapted to the
Nature of the Country by the Gentleman there." The important thing
about this building, therefore, is not that it was designed by Wren but
rather that it introduced into the Virginia Colony the major aspects of
his style; and even though the medieval preferences of the local workmen
are apparent in the narrow proportions and angular shapes, the building
represented a radical shift in formal principle and it began a completely
new departure in American colonial architecture.

In 1699, while the Wren Building at William and Mary was still
under construction, the seat of the government of Virginia Colony was
transferred from Jamestown to Williamsburg and an entirely new colonial
capital was laid out. This created an opportunity for planning and building
on a scale and quality level which had no precedence in the New World.
Although Williamsburg was the fourth planned town in the colonies it was
in many ways the most ambitious, and with its grid arrangement of streets,
and long spacious avenues terminating at important architectural monuments, it was a typical Baroque plan, not unlike Wren's plan for the
rebuilding of London. At one end of the principal avenue stood the
Wren Building; at the other, almost a mile away, was the Capitol
(1701). Extending at right angles from the main avenue was the Palace
Green, a wide spacious strip of lawn, flanked by boulevards and terminating at the Governor's Palace (1706). Like the Wren Building, both the
Capitol and Palace were in the Wren-Baroque style. The buildings, as
they exist today, are complete restorations, thus cannot be judged in the
same way as authentic examples of the period. But as illustrated in an
eighteenth-century engraving, which formed the basis of the restoration,
they show the same simple massing, provincial awkwardness, and strongly
vertical proportions as the Wren Building. Yet, in spite of their provincial
character, as a group they represent a coherent stylistic statement at a
level of taste which was more sophisticated and contemporary than that
of the simple folk buildings of the seventeenth century.

Because the name of Wren was associated by a document with the
building of the college, efforts have also been made to ascribe to him
the Capitol and the Governor's Palace; and both the advanced stylistic
character of the buildings and the fact that the new capital at Williamsburg was a government project approved by the Crown suggest the high

probability that the two later buildings were, indeed, designed in London. As in the case of the college, the question of whether or not Wren was actually the designer is not important. Because of their provincial character, the Capitol and the Palace are much more closely related to the lesser buildings of England such as Minster House (Fig. 32) than to any of the works of Wren. The new Wren-Baroque idiom, introduced into the colonies at Williamsburg, was that of the English middle class even though in its colonial setting it represented the highest level of achievement yet seen in the New World. Thus the shift from the late medieval to the Wren-Baroque style was not the only change in colonial architecture which was initiated at Williamsburg. Equally important was the upward trend in the level of taste—from the folk style architecture which inspired all American colonial architecture of the seventeenth century to the low style architecture of the middle class.

The Detached House in Virginia: Westover

The growing social and economic status of the Virginia Colony which made necessary its elegant and fashionable capital also led to new attitudes toward the plantation house. Thrown into shadow by the monumentality and elegance of the capital buildings, even the more ambitious houses such as Bacon's Castle seemed woefully old-fashioned, and in order to reassert their prominence the tidewater planters sought, in houses of their own, to emulate the Governor's Palace. Among the most influential and ambitious of these planters was William Byrd II; his plantation house, Westover, which he built between 1730 and 1734 (Fig. 35), was the first in the region to surpass the Governor's Palace in sophistication and grace.[12] Byrd was a second-generation colonial, born on the banks of the James River in Virginia, but he received his education in England, where he moved in the world of high fashion, and counted among his friends distinguished members of the English gentry and nobility. Although he was a dedicated farmer who gave much of his time to the active management of his estate, he also played a significant role in both the political and cultural life of the Virginia Colony.[13] He sat in the House of Burgesses, was a member of the King's Council for thirty-seven years, and for three long periods of his life held a diplomatic post in London as the official agent for the Virginia Colony. To sustain his interest in cultural affairs he assembled at Westover a library of almost four thousand volumes.

This was the man who built Westover and the house is the essence of the man. Serene, gracious, and thoughtfully conceived, it is the most beautiful of the tidewater mansions and one of the most thoroughly English houses extant from eighteenth-century America. Unlike the Governor's Palace, which is entirely restored, Westover survives in virtually original form and provides us with a revealing and characteristic document of the period. Situated on the north bank of the James, about twenty-five

FIGURE 35. *Westover,*
Charles City County, Va., c. 1730–34.

miles from Williamsburg, and at a point on the river where the stream
begins to broaden for its final reach to the sea, this magnificent house
formed the social and administrative heart of a vast plantation of over
two hundred square miles. In colonial times the main approach was from
the river and the house is oriented in this direction. Today, however,
it is reached from the north across ample stretches of cultivated plantation
land. The house itself lies amidst a parklike cluster of giant tulip trees
and is guarded on the north side by a superb English wrought-iron gate
and fence. This splendid ornamental feature, with its delicate and gracefully rhythmic foliated top, was made in London and not only provides
an authoritative and appropriate introduction to Westover, but in its sheer
elegant beauty it also anticipates the character of the house. For Westover,
if nothing else, is an elegant house, much more so, in fact, than any of
those at Williamsburg; and in quality, it is absolutely comparable with
the best small houses of England that were built during the age of Wren.

In our illustration (Fig. 35) we see Westover from the south. Here
we recognize at once the simple rectangular block with level cornice line
and high pitched roof, so characteristic of the small detached house of
the Wren-Baroque period. The wings which now connect it to its dependencies are later additions; originally it stood as a thing complete in
itself. Because it is seven bays wide rather than five, it is more horizontal
than the Governor's Palace and therefore more classical in its proportions.
The planes of the hip roof, too, although steeply pitched, are not as
steep as those of the Governor's Palace, and the general effect of stability
and serenity is greater here than in the more soaring earlier house.

This is true in spite of the extremely tall chimney stacks which rise to a height slightly above the ridgepole.

The exterior of Westover is quietly elegant. Within the simple main block, the windows are gracefully proportioned, slightly on the tall side. This provides an element of tension between the emphatic horizontality of the house itself and the vertical movement of the window bays, a tension that is enhanced by the delicately tapered gauged bricks which form the segmental arches over the windows and by the upper sashes which are curved to correspond to the arches. But as though to resolve this tension, as the windows approach the horizontal cornice, those on the second floor are slightly smaller than those on the first. This subtle gradation is achieved through a reduction in height of each of the individual panes rather than through a reduction in the number of panes in each window. In the roof an equally delicate rhythmic refinement is found in the way the shingles are laid. The amount of surface exposed to the weather in each line of slate is graded from wide at the bottom to increasingly narrow toward the top.

The Baroque character of Westover is seen in its rich surface treatment and its elaborate ornamental features. The walls are made of a warm red-orange brick, rather deep in tone, and laid in Flemish bond. The individual bricks are small in relation to the ample size of the house, and thus add to the animation produced by the alternating pattern of the Flemish bond. In contrast to this, the segmental arches over the windows are made of long, thin gauged bricks of a slightly more orange color and smoother surface. These are laid with tighter joints than those in the horizontal courses of the wall, and are shaped as voussoirs, tapering toward the center of the arch. The effect is not only a discreet change in texture and color, which heightens the vivacity of the wall surface, but the delicate taper of the voussoirs adds another element of grace to the over-all character of the building.

Poised against this beautiful surface, in the center of each façade, is a splendid entrance motif carved in Portland stone (Fig. 36). Here, all the contained decorative promise of the warm brick walls is released in a gentle burst of Baroque enthusiasm. In both doorways the pure clean off-white of the stone contrasts dramatically with the brick, bringing each motif into prominence and giving lively emphasis to its sculptural three dimensionality. The carving is not extravagant, yet it is rich, refined, and competent and in its qualities of movement it is emphatically Baroque. At the same time, it is restrained and therefore thoroughly English. This, together with the fact that the doorways are of Portland stone, makes it reasonably certain that they were made by a London craftsman and imported to Westover along with the superb wrought-iron gate which guards the entrance to the mansion.

The doorways at Westover were certainly among the most sophisticated and classically correct yet employed in the colonies. The one on the north front has two finely proportioned Corinthian pilasters which support a full entablature and segmental pediment. The one on the south, or river,

FIGURE 36. *Westover,*
Charles City County, Va., river front door, 1730–34.

FIGURE 37. *William Salmon. Design for a door.*

front is more elaborate. In this case the order is Composite and the pediment is a broken swan's-neck type, its reverse-curve raking cornices terminating in richly carved rosettes. In the center, between the rosettes, is a pineapple finial, symbolic of hospitality. Each doorway seems to have been derived from a plate in a book entitled *Palladio Londonensis*, published by William Salmon in 1734 (Fig. 37), the year in which Westover was brought to completion.[14] Actually, they were a type common to English houses built a quarter of a century earlier, and this timely publication may have served to remind Byrd of his own years in London and of the many similar doors which must have attracted his attention there. For William Byrd never forgot London, even in the remote setting of his beloved plantation. His deep affection for the English way of life and his pride and ambition as an English gentleman made it inevitable that he should attempt to create at Westover a house of the highest quality and in the latest English fashion.

The interior spatial organization of Westover is no less English than the exterior. In this respect the first thing which attracts our attention is the asymmetrical plan (Fig. 38). In contrast with the obvious symmetry of the two façades, the rooms on the first floor vary in size and orientation, and the hall is off-center. This unbalanced arrangement, which is completely anticlassical, might seem to be the whim of the provincial builder. But this is not the case. The asymmetrical plan was common to many of the small houses of the period in both England and the colonies and was actually a survival of late medieval planning methods. Westover, therefore, is neither unique nor particularly provincial in its off-center arrangement.

FIGURE 38. *Westover,*
Charles City County, Va., plan, c. 1730–34.

The decorative treatment of the interior of Westover is not so coherent as that of the exterior. The first-floor rooms are paneled from floor to ceiling, but for the most part this paneling is awkwardly proportioned and sometimes curious in its use of classical detail. This is because it was the work of local craftsmen, probably Negro slaves employed on the plantation. In contrast the beautiful mantel pieces were probably made in London and brought to Virginia by Byrd along with the exterior doors. Some are marble, others are wood, and all are richly carved in the extravagant interior style of the Wren period. The wooden ones in particular are reminiscent of the work of Wren's great wood carver, Grinling Gibbons. Also of imported quality is the elaborate plaster ceiling ornament which graces the hall and drawing room on the first floor (Fig. 39). Arranged in sweeping reverse-curve patterns, the delicate scrolls and foliated motifs show the strong influence of the French Rococo, a taste prominent in English interior decoration during the first half of the eighteenth century. This decorative work must also have come from London, in precast form; like the fireplaces, it has an ornate elegance that is decidedly out of character with the more austere and awkward simplicity of the paneling.

The most harmonious room at Westover is the hall (Fig. 39). Here the spacious stairs ascend along the west wall in a long sweeping reach and then break back in two short flights to the second floor. In this room the paneling is much simpler than in the others and together with the chair rail is finely scaled so that it is consistent with both the delicate mahogany balustrade and the fragile rococo ornament of the ceiling. This type of monumental stairway became a favorite device for the eighteenth-century colonial house, and the one at Westover, on many social occasions, must have provided a dramatic and gracious means of entrance for the beautiful Evelyn Byrd.[15]

The Detached House in New England

Westover was unquestionably the show place of tidewater Virginia in the colonial era; however, it may be taken as typical of a number of the mansions built there during the first half of the eighteenth century. Although they vary in plan and specific detail, they have many things in common, and all reflect the major stylistic characteristics of the smaller English house of the Wren-Baroque period.[16] This tendency toward stylistic unity was not limited to Virginia. It was found in all the colonial clusters of the eastern seaboard from the Carolinas to New England, thus minimizing the marked regional differences of the seventeenth century, and imparting a greater formal coherence to colonial architecture as a whole. This was perhaps less noticeable in the plantation society of the South than it was in the coastal communities of New England, where a greater change in colonial society led to a correspondingly greater change in the character of the architecture. Here the austere Puritan caste of the closely knit seventeenth-century communities was mellowed by a growing aristocracy of merchants and British government officials, so that social pretensions, which had been mollified by the Separatist attitudes of the early colonial years, became as assertive as those in the South, and the right kind of house became essential as a symbol of material success. To this end, the Wren-type house, the supreme creation of British middle-class society, was as useful to the New England merchant as it was to the southern planter.

The MacPhaedris-Warner House

One of the earliest Wren-type houses in New England was the Mac-Phaedris-Warner House in Portsmouth, New Hampshire (Fig. 40), built

FIGURE 39. *Westover,*
Charles City County, Va., hall, 1730–34.

between 1718 and 1723. Its walls, laid in Flemish bond, represent one of the first important uses of brick in eighteenth-century New England. Although brick did not become common in New England coastal towns until after 1800 (it dominated southern architecture throughout the eighteenth century), it was used for a number of the more elaborate houses, and its appearance in Portsmouth in 1718 was due in part to the fact that the small detached houses of England were themselves entirely masonry construction, and the most effective way to imitate them was to build in brick. Not many New England houses achieved this distinction in the eighteenth century, but those like the MacPhaedris-Warner House that did were all the more conspicuous because of it.

FIGURE 40. *MacPhaedris-Warner House,*
Portsmouth, N.H., 1718–23.

Unlike the plantation houses of the South, which were surrounded by lawns and great trees, the MacPhaedris-Warner House is directly on the street and in the center of town. In its architectural features, however, it has much in common with the southern plantation houses. The central door has a heavy segmental pediment carried on Corinthian pilasters, a type of door motif which we have already seen to be common in England during the late seventeenth century, and one which we have also encountered in a more elegant form at Westover. But the Portsmouth door is made of wood rather than stone. In other respects, too, the design of the Portsmouth house is not as coherent as Westover's. As originally built, the Warner House had two parallel gabled roofs which were later raised to a gambrel. To this were added a balustrade and a cupola. The roof plane is broken by heavily scaled dormer windows with alternating triangular and segmental pediments. All these features, dormers, balustrade, and cupola, are reminiscent of the great English house Coleshill but the effect here is cramped and awkward. The Portmouth house also lacks the refined soaring elegance we saw at Westover.

One aspect of the MacPhaedris-Warner roof is of particular interest. Both end walls extend slightly above the roof to form a raking parapet, a characteristic feature of English houses of the same and earlier periods. But on the north end, tall twin chimneys, connected by the plane of the wall, rise from the parapet to a point high above the roof. Although this treatment of the end chimneys is also English, the builders of eighteenth-century New England gave it a special largeness and dignity and it was used with increasing frequency in New England town houses. In the early nineteenth century, especially in the seaport towns, chimneys of this nature were to become as common as the brick walls themselves.

The Wentworth-Gardner House

We have just said that the MacPhaedris-Warner House, because it was brick, was unusual for its time and place. More characteristic of the average New England house of the eighteenth century is the later Wentworth-Gardner House, built in 1760 and also in Portsmouth (Fig. 41). In outward appearance it is a typical detached house of the kind we have already observed in both Virginia and England. Its rectangular massing and hipped roof are reminiscent of Westover; the same features, plus its quoined corners, make it strikingly similar to a late seventeenth-century small house in Stamford, Lincolnshire, England (Fig. 42). Yet, unlike its predecessors, it is made of wood, not brick or stone. To give it the appearance of stone, however, the matched boards of the façade are cut in imitation of rusticated masonry. The sharply projecting quoins are also of wood. This attempt to simulate the effects of stone was carried even further by the use of color. The wall was originally painted a neutral yellow, similar to that which is on it today. In fact, contrary to popular opinion, most of the wooden houses in New England before the Revolution were not painted white. Browns, dull reds, grays, and neutral yellows are mentioned in contemporary documents and referred to as "stone" colors, indicating an obvious association with masonry.[17] In some instances, sand was mixed with the paint to give it a stonelike texture. As in the Wentworth-Gardner House, however, trim and other decorative elements were generally painted white.

Although smaller than Westover, the Wentworth-Gardner House is even more pretentious, especially in the abundance of its ornamental detail. The present door is a modern reconstruction, and evidence found at the time of the restoration seems to indicate that the original had a swan's-neck pediment.[18] This suggestion is strengthened by the fact that a number of other houses in Portsmouth had doors of this type, and we can judge from the one on the Richard Shortridge House, built in 1770 (Fig. 43), what the Wentworth-Gardner door may have been like. Judged on the basis of the rest of the house, it must surely have been an elaborate door ornamented in the best Wren-Baroque manner.

The interior of the Wentworth-Gardner House is one of the most extravagant in eighteenth-century New England. A large central hall is paneled from floor to ceiling, with regularly spaced Ionic pilasters, and a full entablature with a heavy and richly carved modillion cornice. The principal rooms, which are absolutely symmetrical around the central hall, are similarly paneled. But the decorative showpiece of the house is the mantel in the southeast parlor (Fig. 44). Flanked by full height Corinthian pilasters, it has a deep frieze on which are decorative swags of fruit and flower motifs, carved in a manner that is reminiscent of the

FIGURE 41. *Wentworth-Gardner House,*
Portsmouth, N.H., 1760.

FIGURE 42. *Till House,*
Stamford, Lincolnshire, England, 1674.

FIGURE 43. *Richard Shortridge House, Portsmouth, N.H., door, c. 1770.*

FIGURE 44. *Wentworth-Gardner House, Portsmouth, N.H., southeast parlor, 1760.*

elaborate sculptural panels of the great wood carver of the Wren-Baroque period in England, Grinling Gibbons (Fig. 91a). Seen here in Portsmouth, however, this work is half a century out of fashion and there is nothing original about it nor, indeed, about any other part of the house. Its excessively eclectic elements are English in every respect. What is of historical interest, however, is the presence in Portsmouth in 1760 of a significant group of craftsmen capable of such high level production. For there are no imports here, as there were at Westover. The decoration of the house, which tradition says required eighteen months to complete, was entirely the work of local craftsmen. But this is as we would expect. In contrast to the plantations of the South, with their widely scattered and sharply localized building activity, the growing New England coastal towns were thriving centers of opportunity for woodworking craftsmen of every kind: carpenters, shipwrights, cabinetmakers, as well as wood carvers. Thus the extravagant taste which the Wentworth-Gardner House displays—and there were many other houses like it in New England—reflects not only an ambitious patronage, but also an emerging group of self-confident wood carvers whose craft was rooted in a long-established English tradition.

Mark Hunking Wentworth, who built the Portsmouth house as a wedding present for his youngest son Thomas, was a figure in New England comparable to William Byrd in Virginia. As a wealthy merchant he was prominent and influential in Portsmouth society, and through his business connections he maintained close ties with England. Moreover, his brother, Benning Wentworth, was the first Royal Governor of New Hampshire, and his oldest son John, the second one. Mark Wentworth represents in New England, therefore, a different kind of colonial from Parson Capen and his Puritan flock who made up the town of Topsfield in the seventeenth century. Anglican by persuasion, and through business associations and family ties decidedly pro-British, he was as much impelled to emulate the best middle-class English architecture as William Byrd had been. But the New England colonial temperament was less cavalier than the southern. Manners in the rough-and-tumble of New England commerce were cruder, ambitions were more violently assertive; for in the New England coastal communities there was still something of the frontier to blunt the migrating patterns of English culture.

The overabundance, the pretentious elegance of the Wentworth-Gardner House make it a more provincial work than Westover. Mark Wentworth was not as well informed about English architecture as William Byrd, who spent much of his life in London, nor were the influences on his house as direct as those at Westover. It is not surprising, therefore, to find numerous awkward touches such as the modillioned cornice which overlaps the headers of the second-story windows on the façade, and the disturbing conflict in scale between the thin window pediments and the heavy quoins. There is also the lack of any coherent relationship between the imitation stone on the façade wall and the clapboards on the sides. When viewed in the context of eighteenth-century Portsmouth, the Wentworth-Gardner House reflects a knowledgeable taste and a high level of cultural aspiration; nevertheless, it was fifty years behind the times. There is something almost frenetic about its lack of unity, its lavish decoration, its unabashed effort to make wood look like stone. But then Wentworth's objective was not to create new architecture expressing a new way of life in a new and exciting environment, it was rather to bolster up his position as a prominent English colonial with appropriate symbols from the accepted authority of his traditional past.

The Detached House: Its Folk Phase

The final chapter of the small detached house of the Wren-Baroque period was not written in the seaport towns of New England, nor in the plantation houses of tidewater Virginia. For the ultimate dissemination of the form we must turn, rather, to the New England back country, to those offshoot communities which appeared on the frontier as the expanding colonial civilization pushed into the wilderness. At the turn of the century, when the Wren-Baroque style was first introduced in colonial Williamsburg, the New England frontier had reached the upper Connecticut Valley, where it stood poised on the eastern slopes of the Berkshire plateau. Here the ideals of communal living established in the Congregational villages of the seventeenth century remained in force and the concepts of the house and the meetinghouse continued to set the character of the town.

The outpost community in this inland thrust was Old Deerfield, Massachusetts. Bypassed because of a shift in highroads, and untouched by the nineteenth-century industrialism which totally engulfed many New England communities, Old Deerfield survives today virtually intact, with its history as a town clearly written in its architecture. Although somewhat distorted by overzealous restoration, and by the importation of buildings which were never there in the first place, Old Deerfield remains, nevertheless, a priceless microcosmic image of early American architecture. As a document of American history it ranks with such significant survivals as Newport and Salem.

It was in communities like Old Deerfield, removed from the temptations of direct English influence, and free from the overriding ambitions of a competitive merchant aristocracy, that the first true spirit of independence in American architecture emerged. Although the houses in these towns display an astonishing richness in detail comparable to that found in the seaboard communities, they are, at the same time, relatively unencumbered by those stultifying restrictions imposed by too much book knowledge and by the uncompromising compulsion to imitate contemporary fashions in the mother country. In the isolation of the frontier, the enchantments of London lost some of their intoxicating effect. Although the craftsman probably worked from the same books that were popular on the Atlantic seaboard, he remained uninhibited by the drive for conformity and was thus free to exploit his own imagination and his own peculiar skills. We will not find in these communities a rebellious spirit in architecture, nor will we find a spirit of innovation or reform. We will find, rather, a primitivism inherent to the frontier, a reworking of the classical details through a more personal relationship between the wood, the tool, and the hand. In a magnificent door from Hadley, Massachusetts, in the Connecticut Valley, the tobacco leaf replaces the classical acanthus leaf in the Corinthian capital (Fig. 45) and imparts a new sense of growth and immediacy to the overformalized lifelessness which centuries of reworking had imposed upon the brilliant invention of the ancient Greeks. All this we find in abundance in Old Deerfield.

The bold and simple spirit of seventeenth-century New England was carried well into the eighteenth century in the earliest houses of the frontier communities. Such was the John Williams House in Old Deerfield, built during the years 1706–7. An old painting shows that it originally had a framed overhang in front, a grouped central chimney, and a plain door with single casements on either side. In 1756, however, it was considerably rebuilt. As it exists today, it is a simple rectangular block with a pitched roof (Fig. 46). The central chimney has been replaced by two symmetrical interior chimneys and the overhang eliminated. In the center of the main façade is a richly carved door motif with a swan's-neck pediment. Two ranges of windows are grouped symmetrically, and those on the lower floor are topped by simple triangular pediments. In proportion to the wall, the windows are small, the door large. The weathered clapboards and austere simplicity give the house a strong seventeenth-century character. On the other hand, the symmetry of the façade, the classical details, and, most especially, the elaborate Baroque door identify it with the eighteenth century.

FIGURE 45. *Porter House,*
Hadley, Mass., door, c. 1757.

FIGURE 46. *Williams House,*
Old Deerfield, Mass., 1706–7.

FIGURE 47. *Williams House,*
Old Deerfield, Mass., door, 1756.

The vigorous folk art character of the Williams House is best seen in the door (Fig. 47), especially when compared to the river door at Westover (Fig. 36). The basic Baroque motif is the same in both doors, pilasters supporting an entablature and a broken swan's-neck pediment. Beyond this, however, the two have nothing in common. Like its predecessor in Hadley (Fig. 45), the Deerfield door is made of wood instead of stone, and has none of the sculptural largeness of the one at Westover. Instead it is thin, flat, and small in scale, so that in spite of its greater complexity it is in reality less Baroque. The effect is agitated and sharp with many competing small elements such as the finely cut rustication and the numerous thin moldings. The arrangement of the pilasters in two planes complicates the image even further by creating the curious illusion that one is seeing double. Although the basic forms here are classical in origin there is really little else that is classical about them. Throughout the design are the delights of an uninhibited free handling, and in the animated frontier works like this one we find the first hints, even though they are at folk art level, of an emerging American artistic temperament.

The Wren-Baroque style reached the limits of its permeation in the buildings of the colonial frontier. Houses such as the Williams House represent a type which became ubiquitous in the New England hinterland during the eighteenth century. Its rectangular block with a single pitch roof was the least complicated to build, its simple shape best suited to the classical taste of the era; and it could be adorned or not without changing its fundamental character. There are many houses of this type in Old Deerfield; the Mulberry House (1752) is a particularly fine example (Fig. 48). The steep pitched roof and gable ends of this house are shadowy

FIGURE 48. *Mulberry House,
Old Deerfield, Mass., 1752.*

reflections of seventeenth-century building ideas, but the details, although rendered in the local vernacular, are classical throughout.

The more ambitious houses of rural New England remained more faithful to the Wren-Baroque principles. A fascinating example is the Old Manse in Old Deerfield, built by Joseph Barnard in 1768 (Fig. 49). There are no seventeenth-century survivals in this house. Instead it is a magnificent provincial transformation of the type already seen both at Westover and in the Wentworth-Gardner House. Its rectangular façade, its double-hipped roof and quoined corners, and its segmental pedimented door are all features of the Wren-Baroque style. But the house has a largeness and vigor which contrast it with its more urbane counterparts on the seacoast, and the handling of classical details is anything but correct (Fig. 50). The fluting on the door pilasters, for example, is shallow and crudely carved and the meager Doric capitals are a gross debasement of the classical form. Instead of using the classical echinus, the character of which was easily available in handbooks, the builder chose to combine a number of simple cornice moldings, all of which could have been cut with the planes at hand in his molding kit. Such drastic misconstructions of the classical forms, the fruit of limited tools and skills, provoke a primitive awkwardness

FIGURE 49. *Old Manse,*
Old Deerfield, Mass., 1768.

FIGURE 50. *Old Manse,*
Old Deerfield, Mass., door, 1768.

which is natural to all folk art. Remote from the sources and less coerced by ambitious demands for conformity, the frontier craftsman-builder could permit the tool and the hand to modify the book in any way suiting his own skills or fancy.

The Joseph Stebbins House, built in Old Deerfield about 1772, is another splendid example of provincial individualism (Fig. 51). The fine door is flanked by pilasters and crowned by an ornate entablature and deep segmental pediment. These and the quoined corners are familiàr Wren-Baroque forms, but in the crudely carved Ionic capitals, the refined harmonies of the classical idiom are made ungainly by the stumbling uncertainties of a harsh Yankee accent.

The Stebbins House has another feature peculiar to the colonial version of the Wren-Baroque. This is the gambrel roof, a commodious treatment of the third-floor space, which originated in England but later became typical of many New England houses.[19] As developed in England, the gambrel roof butted against masonry wall parapets which, when combined with chimney stacks, obscured the end profile of the roof; we have seen this arrangement in the MacPhaedris-Warner House. In the wooden houses of New England, however, the gambrel roof took on a different character. Utilizing standard techniques of frame construction, the local carpenters permitted the roof plane to overlap rather than abut the end wall, and then dressed the resulting overhang by carrying a raking cornice across the entire double-pitched gable. This clearly defined the upper floor spaces and gave the house those qualities of largeness and dignity so characteristic of its type. Numerous such houses were built during the eighteenth century, and many still grace the streets of the earlier New England towns.

The New England Town House

In the eighteenth century, New England was more and more differentiated from the South, not only by its community life but also by the predominance of its aggressive mercantile middle class. Whereas life in the South continued to center around the great plantations, that in New England clustered in the towns. Beginning in the late seventeenth century, the economy of New England shifted gradually from purely agricultural pursuits to commerce, shipping, and the extractive industries. The coastal communities became the centers of activity, and as the economy expanded, they grew from small villages into raw and boisterous towns. By the middle of the eighteenth century, Boston was one of the largest and most flourishing seaports in the British empire and in its waterfront area had much of the character of London itself.

Domestic architecture in the New England coastal towns developed accordingly. The detached house, which by its very nature demands a certain amount of space around it, was not entirely suitable in close quarters, nor did it convey the proper image of the town. As a result, another type of dwelling, the English town house, appeared in Boston during the last years of the seventeenth century. For the origins of the

FIGURE 51. *Stebbins House,*
Old Deerfield, Mass., 1772.

English town house of the late seventeenth and early eighteenth centuries,
we must go back once more to the years of Inigo Jones, to the building of
the first of London's formal squares, Covent Garden. This early town planning project was begun in 1630 and Jones seems to have played an active
role in the design. Similar undertakings followed on Great Queen Street
in 1637 and at Lincoln's Inn Fields in 1640. These projects were but the
beginning of major land developments which took place on the fringes of
London and reached their heights during the last quarter of the seventeenth
century in the speculative housing schemes of Nicholas Barbon.[20]
    All of this urban growth was taking place in England at the time when
Boston was emerging as a seaport town, and its influence was directly felt
in that town about 1688 with the building of the Foster-Hutchinson
House. It no longer exists, but seems to have been the first fully developed English town house in the colonies; it may also have been the first
American house completely in the Renaissance style. With its three-story
façade, its crowning balustrade, and its Ionic pilaster, it was strikingly
similar to Lindsey House, one of the most important units of the Lincoln's
Inn Fields development. Three-story façade-type houses like Lindsey House
could be built independently or they could be joined to their neighbors
by common walls, and during the eighteenth century they became stand-
ardized in urban London. Although it would be some years before houses
in Boston would need to share a common wall, the potential was there;
and the fragmentary remains of the Thomas Savage House, built on Dock
Square in Boston, 1706–7, indicate that this type was well established

FIGURE 52. *Royall House,*
Medford, Mass., east façade, 1733–37.

fairly early in the century. By the time of the Revolution three-story
town houses were common to all coastal communities.

The Royall House

The Royall House in Medford, Massachusetts, is typical (Fig. 52). It
was originally built in the late seventeenth century as a two-and-a-half-
story brick house one room deep.[21] But in two stages, occurring 1733–37
and 1747–50, it was drastically rebuilt by Isaac Royall, a successful New
England rum merchant. In the first stage, it was enlarged in depth to two
rooms, and the east front was raised to a full three stories. The end walls
were continued in brick and they culminated in two symmetrical chimney
stacks connected by a parapet. This chimney treatment is the same as
that already encountered in the MacPhaedris-Warner House in Portsmouth.
The end walls of the Royall House were left unadorned and are penetrated
only by tiny windows at the upper floor levels. In their stark simplicity, they
could very well be common walls, shared with adjoining houses on
either side. All ornamental richness is concentrated on the front and
garden façades.

The east, or main, façade is a clapboard wall with a modillioned cornice and quoined corners rising through the full three stories and applied over the old brick. The window openings have elaborate molding surrounds and are connected vertically by spandrel panels projecting slightly from the wall. Painted white, the windows and the spandrel panels together form tall vertical strips which contrast with the gray of the clapboard. Similar vertical effects were achieved in many of the English town houses, such as the Fitzwilliam House, Cambridge (1727), by using contrasting colors of brick (Fig. 53). The fully rusticated door motif has Doric pilasters and a wide projecting cornice. Although the proportions are awkward and the rendering of classical details naïve, the over-all effect is self-consciously elegant.

Ten years later a façade with more sophisticated detail was added on the west (Fig. 54). Here, instead of clapboards, matched boards were cut to imitate stonemasonry; and instead of quoins, tall thin Doric pilasters were used on the corners. Above the windows on the first two floors are classical pediments, and the door has a delicately proportioned segmental pediment supported on Ionic pilasters. In spite of the greater classical correctness of the individual parts, certain aspects of the new façade are clumsy, such as the narrow crowning cornice which rests so uneasily on the corner pilasters; similarly, the scale and detailing of the decorative elements is so out of character with the more archaic east façade that it is difficult to relate them as parts of a coherent whole. The building thus remains delightfully provincial, an incoherent and arbitrary coalescence of diverse elements, dominated by the presumptuous grandeur of the simulated stonemasonry.

FIGURE 53. *Fitzwilliam House,*
Cambridge, England, 1727.

The rich and elaborate interiors of the Royall House date from 1750, the time of the second enlargement. Like those in the Wentworth-Gardner House, its handsome rooms make it one of the most ambitious dwellings of the period. The living room on the first floor and the great chamber on the second floor received special attention. Both are paneled from floor to ceiling, with door openings and corners defined by full height pilasters— those in the living room are a very elegant Doric with delicately carved and molded capitals; in the great chamber (Fig. 55) they are Corinthian, and are painted in imitation of grained marble. This attempt to simulate in paint the visual appearance of a luxury material was prompted by the same motives which led Isaac Royall to imitate masonry in wood on the west front of his house, and since there are any number of similar instances in eighteenth-century colonial architecture, it might seem that we are confronted here with a peculiarly American characteristic. But this is not entirely the case. Although the imitation of stonemasonry in wood was largely American, the imitation of different materials through painting was not. "Imitation painting" was extremely common in the less expensive houses of England itself, particularly during the late seventeenth and early eighteenth centuries. It was also employed in one of the most English buildings in the colonies, the Capitol in Williamsburg.[22]

Isaac Royall was an ardent Loyalist who fled the colony at the time of the Revolution, and like William Byrd and Mark Wentworth, he never considered himself anything but an Englishman. Like them, too, he was an Englishman on the fringes of the empire, striving in every way he could to identify with the homeland. His uninhibited acceptance of imitative techniques was therefore an act of provincialism rather than Americanism, and it points up sharply the basic Englishness of American colonial architecture. In spite of its awkwardness and the limitations imposed by its wooden fabric the Royall House was a typical English town house; and like Westover and the Wentworth-Gardner House, it was Wren-Baroque in every respect.

The Wren Church in Colonial America

So far we have concerned ourselves primarily with the permeation of the Wren-Baroque style in the domestic architecture of the American colonies. As we have seen, the influence of Wren in this area was broad and nebulous, coming to the colonies from a variety of sources none of which directly related to the great man himself. Wren's London churches, however, were all small parish churches, thus, like the detached house, immediately adaptable to the colonial situation; but contrary to what happened in the case of the detached house, Wren's influence on the colonial churches of the early eighteenth century was both direct and powerful.

The earliest church in the colonies to reflect this influence was the Bruton Parish Church in Williamsburg (1711–15). Built of brick, it has round-headed windows and classical details directly contrasting with the Gothic forms of St. Luke's a few miles away; and on the interior, instead of an open truss, it has a flat suspended plaster ceiling surmounting

FIGURE 54. *Royall House,*
Medford, Mass., west façade, 1747–50.

a broad coved cornice. Although this suspended ceiling and the classical details reflect the influence of Wren, the cruciform plan of the church does not. In his London churches Wren abandoned medieval plan concepts almost entirely in favor of his own expansive and classically oriented space. The Bruton Parish Church, therefore, is similar in manner to the Wren Building at the College of William and Mary, being a mixture of drastically simplified Wren forms with a persistent and conservative survival of medieval ideas.

Except for Bruton Parish, there were no Wren-type churches built in the South during the first half of the eighteenth century. In New England, however, Wren's London churches exerted a considerable influence. In view of the strongly Congregational nature of the New England religious community, this might seem contradictory, for Wren's churches were all Anglican. Moreover, a review of New England church buildings during the first half of the eighteenth century indicates that the traditional four-

FIGURE 55. *Royall House,*
Medford, Mass., great chamber, c. 1750.

square meetinghouse, as developed in the seventeenth century, remained the most important type. This was especially true in the new, offshoot communities that sprang up along the ever-expanding frontier. The tradition was so persistent, in fact, that one of the earliest eighteenth-century Anglican churches built in New England was in the form of a meetinghouse. This was St. Paul's Church in Narragansett, Rhode Island (Fig. 56). It was built in 1707 and later moved to Wickford, where it now stands. Except for the large round-headed windows on the first floor, and the broken segmental pediment over the door, the building is thoroughly domestic in character and seems more like a detached house than a church. In the New England hinterland, where men like Jonathan Edwards preached a fierce Puritan doctrine in violent opposition to the growing Anglicanism of the coastal towns, the meetinghouse persisted as long as the frontier made it possible to organize towns similar to the first New England communities. The meetinghouse in Rockingham, Vermont (Fig. 57), for example, was built as late as 1787, at a time when a wholly new architectural climate was already apparent in the coastal towns.

In spite of the persistence of the meetinghouse, two important churches were built in Boston in the 1720's, both derived from the churches of Wren in London. Several factors account for this. The first was a government decree in 1684 which canceled the original Massachusetts Bay charter. A series of events followed which led in 1691 to the rechartering of Massachusetts as a Royal Colony similar to Virginia. This paved the

FIGURE 56. *Old Narragansett Church* (*St. Paul's*), *Wickford, R.I., 1707.*

FIGURE 57. *Rockingham Meetinghouse, Rockingham, Vt., 1787.*

way for the establishment of the first Anglican parishes in Boston: King's Chapel in 1686; and later, to accommodate the growing Anglican community in the North End, Christ Church in 1723.

The other factors were those already stressed as important in the development of colonial domestic architecture, the increasing prosperity of Boston, and the emergence of an affluent and ambitious merchant class. As an economic and social group they had become the exact colonial counterpart of the ruling middle class of London itself. Their prosperity, combined with the more aristocratic character of the society centered around the new Royal Governors, ordained an elegance and dignity of architectural expression which the simple meetinghouse could not provide. In the same way that these ambitious merchants turned to England for their houses, so too they turned to the London of Christopher Wren for their new churches.

Old North Church, Boston

The first church in the English colonies to assume the fully developed character of a Wren church was Christ Church in Boston. Known also as "Old North," it was built in 1723 for the second Anglican parish in the city (Fig. 58). The building was designed by William Price, a Boston print dealer who must have had information about the Wren churches, for in all its major aspects, Christ Church is simplified Wren. The main body of the building is a rectangular block with a pitched roof and two ranges of round-headed windows. Domestically scaled and without ornamentation, it is not unlike the earlier meetinghouses. On the east end, however, is a small semicircular apse; on the west is an attached tower rising well above the ridgeline of the roof and terminating in a graceful spire. The body of the church and tower are brick laid in Flemish bond, the spire is wood.

The most distinctive Wren features of the exterior are the tower and spire.[23] Both can be traced to Wren churches in London. The tower is remarkably similar in proportions, in the location of its stringcourses, and in the positioning and shape of the window and door openings to St. James, Garlickhythe (Fig. 59); the model for the spire may have been St. Lawrence, Jewry, although the relationships here are less direct. The colonial treatment of these basic motifs, however, is very different from that of their London prototypes. All ornament in the tower has been stripped away so that the brick surfaces seem excessively flat and altogether devoid of that sense of weight which is produced by Wren's stone walls. The spire, too, because it is wood, is leaner and more finely drawn, as though it were inspired by a print rather than an actual stone spire of a Wren church. And then there is the primness, the neat way in which windows and doors are cut into the walls and the rather stiff vertical quality which somehow belongs more to Puritan Boston than to the London of Wren.

The interior of the church (Fig. 60) is a simple rectangular space of rather classic proportions, which is oriented longitudinally by the aisles which separate the box pews, and by the range of piers which support the side balconies. This orientation terminates in the apse and gives the church its traditional direction toward the altar. The plain plaster ceiling above the balcony is a series of cross vaults supported on entablatures which

FIGURE 58. *Christ Church* (*Old North*), *Boston, Mass., 1723.*

FIGURE 59. *Christopher Wren. St. James, Garlickhythe, London, c. 1680.*

FIGURE 60. *Christ Church* (*Old North*),
Boston, Mass., interior. 1723.

abut the outer wall at one end and are carried by the piers at the other.
Between these cross vaults and running longitudinally toward the altar is
sprung the elliptical vault of the main ceiling itself. Most of the weight
of this plaster ceiling structure is carried by suspension from the main
trusses of the roof, and both structurally and as a spatial concept it can
be traced directly to the Wren London interiors, particularly St. James,
Piccadilly (Fig. 61). Missing altogether, of course, in favor of an austere
simplicity, is the elegant and expressive plaster ornament of Wren, and in
the Boston church such classical details as the piers and entablatures are
awkwardly shaped and proportioned.

Trinity Church, Newport

The theme developed in Christ Church, Boston, was picked up almost immediately by another of the oldest Anglican congregations in New England, Trinity Church in Newport, Rhode Island (Fig. 62). This church was begun in 1725 and the main body was completed by 1726; the spire was designed in 1726 but not finished until 1741. Except for the spire, which is almost an exact replica of the one on Christ Church, Trinity Newport is a simplified and somewhat clumsy wooden version of the Boston church. Its designer-builder was a local craftsman by the name of Richard Munday. His direct connection with Christ Church is certain, for one of the founders of Trinity was the same William Price who was said to have designed the Boston church.

As originally built, Trinity Newport was only five bays long and thus very similar in its proportions to the traditional four-square New England meetinghouse. In 1762, however, it was lengthened by the addition of two bays, and the resulting longitudinal orientation makes it very similar to its Boston model. On the other hand, it differs in that the lateral cross vaults of the aisle bays are lifted to the level of the main vault, thus forming a system of quasi-groin vaults. Just as in Christ Church the entire ceiling is suspended from the trusses of the roof. For the most part, the molding profiles of Trinity are even less classical than those of Christ Church and the proportions are very much more awkward. The top window in the tower, for example, is jammed up tightly under the cornice, leaving excessively wide spaces between the windows below. Many of the decorative features, too, have a strange archaic quality. This is readily seen in the north doors (Fig. 63). Over each is a heavy segmental pedi-

FIGURE 61. *Christopher Wren. St. James, Piccadilly, London, interior, 1680–84. Burnt 1941; restored 1952.*

FIGURE 62. *Richard Munday. Trinity Church,*
Newport, R.I., 1725–26. Spire finished 1741.

ment which is broken abruptly toward its center by an angular shift
downward which forms an inverted semicircle. Although in the shadowy
background of this clumsy pediment is the broken segmental pediment
of the Wren-Baroque door, the effect at Trinity is both unorthodox and
capricious, and contrasts curiously with the taut elegance and classical
correctness of the spire. It is obvious from this that Munday's own taste
was marked by vigor rather than grace, and that his spire at Trinity, one
of the loveliest in New England, owes its fine quality to its derivation
from the original spire of Old North.

Old South Meetinghouse, Boston

Both Christ Church and Trinity were built for Anglican congregations.
Their affinity with the London churches, therefore, was spiritual as well

as architectural. By contrast, the first important Congregational meeting-house built in Boston in the early eighteenth century, the Old Brick Meetinghouse, continued the established meetinghouse form as we have already seen it in the Old Ship Meetinghouse at Hingham. Erected in 1713, the Boston Meetinghouse was made of brick, had classical details, and was topped by a classical cupola. But its plan was almost square, with the entrance on the long side. The building no longer exists.

In 1729, a Congregational meetinghouse of a very different character was begun in Boston. Now known as Old South Meetinghouse, it was built by one of the most radical congregations in New England. The history of Old South is a stormy one; and fulfilling its function as a meetinghouse it played an important role in civic and political, as well as religious affairs. Some of the most significant meetings leading to the Revolution were held in this building. It is therefore of immense historical importance.

Old South is a characteristic meetinghouse (Fig. 64). It is almost square in plan, is two stories high, with the main entrance on the long side. The interior in its original form was also typical, with a high pulpit opposite the door, and a gallery on the other three sides. The main orientation of the interior space, therefore, was across the width of the church. At the west end, however, and in absolute contradiction to this lateral axis (Fig. 65), is a tall attached brick tower which culminates in a soaring wooden spire one hundred and eighty feet high. Thus, while the interior retained its traditional meetinghouse character, and its function as a center

FIGURE 63. *Trinity Church, Newport, R.I., door, 1725.*

FIGURE 64. *Old South Meetinghouse, Boston, Mass., 1729.*

FIGURE 65. *Old South Meetinghouse,*
Boston, Mass., 1729.

FIGURE 66. *Christopher Wren. St. Mary-le-Bow,*
Cheapside, London, England, 1670–77.

of political as well as religious controversy, the exterior took on all the appearances of a Wren-type Anglican church. For Old South, except for its side entrance and the fact that it had no apse in the east end, is identical in its outer form to Old North Church, and its steeple is similarly derived from the Wren churches of London. With its open colonnaded belfry, the design is reminiscent of one of Wren's most beautiful works, the steeple on St. Mary-le-Bow in London (Fig. 66).

Old South was a meetinghouse and continued to function as such. But in a changing Boston it was much more than that. In spite of their Puritan background, the Boston merchants who made up the congregation of Old South were ambitious and highly competitive; and since their meetinghouse was as much expressive of their material success as it was of their spiritual strength, it was unthinkable to them that they should be outdone by their Anglican neighbors. The attitude which condoned a return to traditional symbols such as the spire, once so fiercely rejected, was not so much a fundamental change in religious conviction as an assertion of personal and civic pride, a pride born in the competitive world of trade and fired by the pretensions of a wealthy pro-British society. The spire of Old South was as much a symbol of success as was the imitation stonemasonry of the New England houses.

The Wren Church in the Hinterland

The influence of the Wren-type church was not limited to the large cities like Boston. Just as in the case of the small house it reached its final and most original form in the small communities of the New England hinterland. Once established at Old South, the meetinghouse form, combined with a Wren-inspired tower and steeple, appears in numerous variations throughout inland New England. The Congregational Meetinghouse in Farmington, Connecticut, is typical (Fig. 67). Built as late as 1771, it is made of wood rather than brick, as were all the country churches of the eighteenth century. The main body of the building is a characteristic meetinghouse with its entrance on the side (the present Greek Doric portico is a much later addition). The delicate but simplified octagonal two-stage belfry and spire are obviously inspired by Old South Meetinghouse in Boston, and are thus a remote provincial survival, dating from the years immediately preceding the Revolution, of St. Mary-le-Bow in London.

The Wren-Baroque in Public Buildings

Further manifestations of the Wren-Baroque style are to be found in a few of the government buildings of eighteenth-century colonial America. We have already touched on this briefly in our discussion of colonial Williamsburg. But during the first half of the century other colonial capitols were built and of these one of the most important is the Old State House in Philadelphia, generally known as Independence Hall (Fig. 68). This mecca of American history was designed by Andrew Hamilton and begun in 1731, although it continued under construction for a con-

FIGURE 67. *Congregational Meetinghouse, Farmington, Conn., 1771.*

siderable period of time; the wood tower and spire were not finished until 1753. Built of brick, the main body of the building is a two-story rectangular block completely domestic in scale and character. In fact, there is little to distinguish the north façade from those of the houses of the period except its length and the rectangular panels of marble between the windows of the first and second floors. The latter feature is a decorative device common to English civic architecture of the Wren-Baroque period. The south front is dominated by an enormous attached brick tower which rises above the three central bays. Topping this tower is the wood steeple rising in two square stages to an octagonal belfry, which in turn is topped by a small cupola and spire.[24] The building as a whole can be distinguished from a church only because the tower

FIGURE 68. *Independence Hall, Philadelphia, Pa., 1731.*

is placed in the center of the long side rather than on the west end. On the interior the rich wooden paneling and applied classical ornament are inconsistent in scale with, and somewhat heavy for, the small rooms they decorate. Nevertheless, the entire building has the stamp of bookish authority and in some respects it is one of the most authentic English buildings surviving from the eighteenth century.

Far more provincial and at the same time more original is the old colonial Capitol building in Newport, Rhode Island (1739–41). Known as the Old Colony House, this delightful building (Fig. 69) was designed by Richard Munday, the same architect-builder who was responsible for Trinity Church in Newport. The Old Colony House, however, is a much

FIGURE 69. *Richard Munday. Old Colony House, Newport, R.I., 1739–41.*

more interesting building than Independence Hall. Compared to the Philadelphia building, with its quite proper and authoritative Englishness, Munday's Colony House is a boisterous provincial. Whereas the design for Independence Hall was prepared by a gentleman-amateur and is, despite some inconsistencies, self-consciously correct in detail, the Old Colony House was designed by the man who built it; and in this man we encounter the first recorded architect-builder in the colonies during the first half of the eighteenth century. Munday was a carpenter by trade who through his own talents and initiative gained a reputation as a designer; and the freshness and imaginative quality about his work, however naïve it may be, are impossible to find in the more sterile correctness of Independence Hall.

The Old Colony House was distinguished in Newport by the fact that it was brick. During the first half of the eighteenth century Newport was a town "all of wood" and Munday's use of brick and sandstone masonry not only appealed to the uncommonly luxurious taste of that affluent seaport town,[25] but introduced into America certain Baroque qualities of texture and color that were unmatched in any other colonial work. Munday's brick walls, laid in Flemish bond, are enlivened by red sandstone quoins and rusticated trim. Over the windows are rusticated segmental arches with prominent keystones, and, just as at Westover, the tops of the wooden window casings are curved to fit these brick arches. So that they may correspond in shape to the windows below, the wooden cornices over the dormer windows form similar segmental arches beneath the bolder curves of their pediments. All this is as vigorously Wren-Baroque as it could possibly be. So, too, is the entrance motif. Made of wood and painted white, it rises through the full two stories of the building and has a balcony on the second floor. The entrance door itself, approached by a series of stone steps, is flanked on either side by a Corinthian pilaster; the balcony door above is shorter and has glazed lights, and the pilasters have thicker proportions than those on the first floor. The whole is crowned by a broken segmental pediment with elaborately carved scroll ends between which is a gilded pineapple finial. The effect is extravagantly rich and elegant.

The Old Colony House is also charmingly provincial. Breaking the roof on the main front is an awkwardly proportioned truncated pediment which contains a clock framed by an octagonal surround of red sandstone in a quoin-like pattern. Flanking this are two oculus windows similarly framed; together the clock and windows are crammed awkwardly into the pediment. The building is a strange mixture of formal correctness and primitive vigor. Certain elements, such as the entrance and the balcony, suggest sophisticated sources; others, such as the pediment and the arched dormer windows, are vigorously individual with little regard for classical proportions or authentic rendering of detail.

The same mixture is found on the inside (Fig. 70). The principal rooms are paneled from floor to ceiling: in the Senate Chamber, corners are framed by Corinthian pilasters and the paneling in the overmantel has an elegant reverse-curve top. Although the details here are less extravagant than the polychrome sculptural surfaces of the façade, they are none-theless Baroque, and at the same time filled with delightful unorthodoxies, especially in the curious shifting scale and the nonclassical combinations of moldings. Munday has drawn heavily on the Wren-Baroque but the actual character of his forms has been determined as much by his own skills and by the limitations of the tools he had available as by the books which served as his sources.

The Old Colony House is a fine example of the colonial Wren-Baroque at its best. As in the houses of the New England country towns, the work is sufficiently unrestrained by constricting pretensions to permit a free exercise of the artist's imagination. Even though the building captures the spirit of the Wren-Baroque better than any other of its period, it does so with a zest and originality that make it at the same time un-English. If there are any qualities in colonial architecture of the eighteenth century which can be said to be peculiar to the American environment and the American temperament, they are the qualities of abundance and vigor so conspicuously in evidence in the Old Colony House. With its roots in the homeland but its fabric in Newport, it is a fascinating document of both the bustling energy and the cultural aspirations of a prosperous seaport town.

FIGURE 70. *Richard Munday. Old Colony House, Newport, R.I., Senate Chamber, 1739–41.*

CHAPTER IV

Gibbs and Palladio
in the Colonial World

*Buildings of all Sorts and Dimensions are undertaken and
performed in the neatest Manner, (and at cheaper rates)
either in the Ancient or Modern Order of Gibbs' Architect.*
JOHN ARISS

English Palladianism

George I came to the throne in 1714, and most of the eighteenth-century
colonial buildings we have discussed so far were built after that date. It
would seem logical to assume, therefore, that they are Georgian. Moreover, it is precisely this term which is most commonly used to define
eighteenth-century colonial architecture, used to the point, in fact, where
in American vernacular speech it has come to include all buildings that
have quoined corners, pediments, and engaged pilasters. Quoins, pediments, and pilasters are, it is true, characteristic of one phase of Georgian
architecture, but the Georgian era ran from 1714 until 1830, when
George IV died. During these years, English architecture underwent many
changes of style, and at the end had forsaken quoins and pediments
for the crockets and finials of the Gothic. Actually, the word "Georgian"
is a dynastic, not a stylistic, term, and when applied to architecture we
will use it only in the dynastic sense. We saw in the previous chapter,
for example, that colonial architecture during the first half of the eighteenth
century, even though it was built in the Georgian period (and has been
persistently called "Georgian"), was actually Wren-Baroque. We saw
further that this same style persisted in the New England hinterland
down to the time of George III and the Revolution. Calling these buildings
"Georgian," therefore, completely distorts their relationship with the English architecture from which they derive. Nevertheless, the term is too
much a part of the American architectural vocabulary to be ignored
altogether, and to understand the change in style that did occur in the
colonies after 1750 it is necessary to examine the whole question of
"Georgian" in some detail.

English Baroque architecture, first formulated by Wren, reached its climax in the work of three younger men, Nicholas Hawksmore, John Van-
brugh, and Thomas Archer.[1] In contrast to the elegance of Wren, their
style was heavy and vigorous and was centered primarily in monumental
works for the aristocracy and court. The work of these men therefore
had no influence in the colonies. It represented, however, the last phase

of the official architecture of the Stuart era, and as such, became the principal target of attack for the proponents of a new taste in architecture. This change in attitude found its greatest support in the Whig aristocracy, whose anti-Stuart sentiments brought them into violent opposition to the work of Wren and the other Baroque architects. Known as the "Palladian movement," it was a reaffirmation of classical principles, particularly as found in the work of Inigo Jones and Palladio. This style was the first phase of Georgian architecture and was totally different from that of Wren and his followers.

The Palladian movement was initiated by two significant books, Colen Campbell's *Vitruvius Britannicus* and an English translation of Palladio's *I quattro libri dell' architettura*.[2] Both were published in 1714, at the very beginning of the Georgian era. The first contained a series of plates illustrating classical buildings in England, and among the works featured were several by Inigo Jones. The second was a new edition of Palladio, with the plates drawn by an Italian, Giacomo Leoni, and the English translation by Nicholas Dubois. These publications provided both the architectural data and the theoretical basis of the Palladian movement; enthusiastic support came from the aristocracy, especially in the active participation of Richard Boyle, Lord Burlington, whose patronage not only gave authoritative sanction to the new style, but whose own architectural works helped to shape its formal destiny. Closely associated with this influential young nobleman were Colen Campbell, the author of *Vitruvius Britannicus,* and another architect, William Kent. Together, these three formed the creative core of Palladianism, and the theoretical principles embodied in their work were to dominate English architecture for forty years.

English Palladianism was a quest for absolutes and can thus be identified with the Age of Reason. Stylistically, its premise was the purity and separateness of each individual unit of the design. This can be seen in one of the great works of the period, Holkham Hall (Fig. 71), designed by William Kent and begun in 1734. Here the wall planes are flat and tautly drawn against sharp corners, with doors and windows cleanly cut and isolated one from the other. The various block units are symmetrically poised and are joined by straight connecting blocks similar to those found in the plates of Palladio (Fig. 72). Classical details and proportions are all rendered strictly according to the Palladian doctrine. Self-consciously correct, the style as embodied in this building is theoretically conceived in rigid geometric terms and is militantly antagonistic to the more expansive richness of the Wren-Baroque.

Both in its monumentality and in its commitment to principle, English Palladianism was a logical style for the aristocracy and the court of George I. But for these same reasons it had only indirect influence in the colonies. We have already found this to be true in the case of the Wren-Baroque, where colonial architecture took its inspiration not from high style circles but from the lesser low style buildings of the middle class. Similarly, in the case of Palladianism, we must turn to the wider proliferations of the style to evaluate its impact upon the architecture of eighteenth-century America.

FIGURE 71. *William Kent. Holkham Hall, Norfolk, England, begun 1734.*

FIGURE 72. *Andrea Palladio. Design for a villa.*

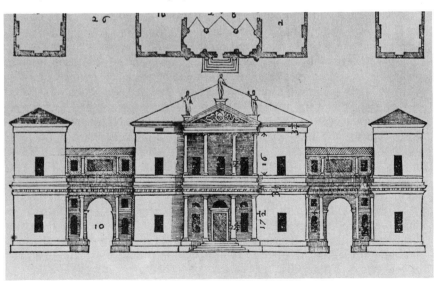

Gibbs and Palladio in the South

The Palladian ideas were communicated to the colonies primarily through books. Following *Vitruvius Britannicus* and the English translation of Palladio, several other publications appeared which took up the theme, and many made their way to America. Of these the most important was James Gibbs's *A Book of Architecture*, first published in London in 1728. Frankly intended as a pattern book, it was both conservative and simple, was illustrated with magnificent plates, and appealed at once to the colonial taste.[3]

The precise nature of the influence which Gibbs's book exerted on colonial architecture can best be explained by a careful analysis of the plates themselves. In those devoted to domestic architecture, Palladio's principles of extended symmetrical plan and unit massing are conspicuously in evidence (Fig. 74). Many of the houses shown are of the villa type with a dominating central component and symmetrical dependencies connected by straight or quadrant (curved) passages to form an open forecourt. At the same time, however, an equal number of Gibbs's domestic plans are of the simple rectangular block type so characteristic of the age of Wren (Fig. 87). Furthermore, the majority of the façades shown have little to do with English Palladianism (Fig. 76). In all of them, Gibbs shows a preference for such ornamental features as quoins, heavy rustication, pilasters, and balustrades, all of which were anathema to the Palladians and tend to give his illustrations a Baroque richness which is more akin to the style of Wren than to the severity of the strict Palladian doctrine.

This aspect of Gibbs's book can best be visualized by comparing his plates with those in the original edition of Palladio's *I quattro libri dell' architettura* (Fig. 72).[4] As demonstrated by these plates, Palladio's approach to architecture was through two-dimensional considerations. He was concerned with proportion and profile, both of which could be achieved with the outline drawing. His plates, therefore, are abstract linear schematics, which convey only the most essential aspects of dimensionality and outline. His only means of separating the plane of the wall from the plane of the paper is a crude crosshatching, used to indicate areas in shadow; wall openings are rendered as very dark gray or black. The effect of this is to isolate the various components of the façade and to intensify their separateness one from the other. It was precisely these qualities of exact dimensional definition, rigid balance, and staccato accentuation of the parts—more apparent in Palladio's illustrations than in his actual works—that were exploited by the English Palladians.

In contrast to the flatness of Palladio's plates, those of Gibbs are elaborately three-dimensional (Fig. 76). Not only do they show a preference for richer ornamentation, but the engravings themselves are executed with infinitely greater variety. The complex projection and recession of the structural and decorative elements are brought to life by a sophisticated use of light and shade, and through subtle changes in the direction and character of the engraved line, distinctions are made between different qualities of surface and texture. Thus the plane of the wall is no longer identified with the plane of the paper, and the image takes on some of the weight and density of the buildings themselves. It was these very qualities, rooted as they were in Baroque illusionism and in the older style of Wren, which kept Gibbs from being a full-fledged Palladian; and because of the popularity of his books in the colonies, it was these same qualities which directed American architecture toward a form of Palladianism that never completely disassociated itself from the Wren style of the first half of the century.

Mount Airy

Palladian formalism is most apparent in the domestic architecture of the South during the third quarter of the eighteenth century. This is precisely as we would expect. The villa-type house, with its spreading symmetrical plan and attached dependencies, was a natural form for the great plantations, and after 1750 a group of them appeared in the South.[5] All were symmetrically planned with attached dependencies and all were derived from the books. Of those which still survive, the most impressive is Mount Airy (Fig. 75) in Richmond County, Virginia (1758–62). Built of dark brown sandstone with light colored limestone trim, it is one of the rare examples of eighteenth-century stonemasonry in the South.

The designer of Mount Airy is not known for certain, but the name of John Ariss, a native Virginian who seems to have gone to England to study architecture, has sometimes been associated with the building. Although Ariss's connection with Mount Airy is purely a matter of scholarly conjecture, his activity as an architect is firmly established by a notice in the *Maryland Gazette* of May 22, 1751. Moreover, in this same notice he advertises himself as capable of designing "either in the Ancient or Modern Order of Gibbs' Architect," and thus establishes the first documentary suggestion that Gibbs's book had reached the colonies.[6] In any case, his *A Book of Architecture* and another closely related volume, Adam's *Vitruvius Scoticus,* published in Edinburgh in 1750, are conspicuously the source for Mount Airy. The plan and the river front are derived from the former (compare Figs. 73 and 74; 75 and 76), the north front from the latter.

Following its Gibbsian prototype, the plan of Mount Airy is entirely Palladian (Fig. 73). The main block is a rectangle, more squarish than classical in proportions, with a central hall set rigidly on axis. Symmetrically placed and connected to the house by quadrant passageways are two identical dependencies. The approach to the house, therefore, is through a forecourt, and the main entrance is gained by a flight of steps leading to an open loggia which in turn forms the lower part of a slightly projecting central pavilion. From the outstretched arms of the dependencies to the assertive central thrust of the main hall, the space is controlled and center-oriented. The absolute symmetry directs all movement toward the main axis so that the observer is given no choice as to where he will look or how he will enter; nor are there any surprises in

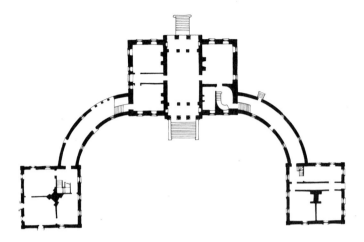

FIGURE 73. *John Ariss.*
Mount Airy, Richmond County, Va., plan, 1758–62.

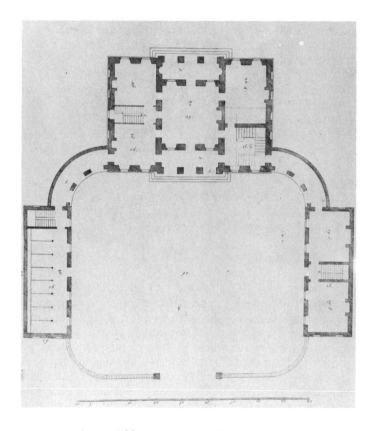

FIGURE 74. *James Gibbs. Design for a house.*

store for him on the inside, as there were at Westover. Once he gains entrance to the building he finds the major divisions of interior space are precisely as they were proclaimed to be by the façade; boldly differentiated pavilions on both fronts announce the dominating central hall; rooms correspond left and right. Instead of the asymmetrical caprices of many of the earlier houses a new formalism governs the design.

Quite in contrast to the rigid Palladian plan of Mount Airy is the warm and elaborate treatment of surface and detail to be found in the two façades (Fig. 75). The two pedimented pavilions are light cream-colored limestone, laid up with heavily rusticated joints against the dark brown sandstone of the walls. The stringcourse, quoins, and window surrounds are also of light sandstone and together with the pavilions create a sculptural and coloristic effect which is exactly the opposite of the smooth masonry surfaces and cleanly cut corners of high English Palladianism (compare Fig. 71). These decorative qualities of Mount Airy are entirely Gibbsian; the south façade comes directly from a plate in Gibbs's book (Fig. 76), except that it has been shortened at either end by one bay. More than that, the use of contrasting materials is also suggested in Gibbs's plate. By subtle variations in the hatching the English architect has made the pavilion seem lighter in tone than the walls, and the builder of Mount Airy has translated this pictorial suggestion of color literally by using two kinds of stone in the building.

In Mount Airy we encounter a new colonial style. Because it is more Gibbsian than Palladian, it still retains many of the visual qualities of the earlier Wren-Baroque, and therefore it was attractive to the conservative taste of the mid-century Virginia planters. For them the buildings of the first half of the century displayed a reassuring venerability and began to assume many of the characteristics of an architectural tradition which they regarded as much their own as British. At the same time, the new mode offered qualities of monumentality which were more in keeping with the changing tenor of life than the relaxed informality found so frequently in the earlier style. As the frontier passed into legend an increasingly aristocratic social order developed, and the new Gibbsian style catered to its taste. This style, too, and not the Wren-Baroque of the first half of the century, introduced into the colonies the first authentic version of what can properly be called colonial "Georgian" architecture.

Carter's Grove

Unfortunately, the interiors of Mount Airy were destroyed by fire in 1844 so we have no way of knowing what they were like. There still exists at Carter's Grove (1750–53) in Virginia, however, a splendid interior of comparable date which we may take as characteristic of the new colonial style. The brick exterior of this house has qualities of simplicity that make it not unlike the earlier houses in Williamsburg. The elaborate interior, therefore, comes as a surprise. The magnificent wood paneling of the first-floor rooms is the finest in any southern colonial mansion. Not only is it superbly executed but it is done with an authenticity of classical proportion and detail which we have not seen before in colonial America. It is therefore correct as well as beautiful.

FIGURE 75. *John Ariss.*
Mount Airy, Richmond County, Va., 1758–62.

FIGURE 76. *James Gibbs. Design for a house.*

The most impressive room is the entrance hall (Fig. 77). Slightly rectangular in plan and oriented the length of the house, it is entered through a central door with a window on either side. The basic arrangement therefore, like that at Mount Airy, is absolutely symmetrical. The walls are paneled throughout, with all openings, except the windows, framed by Ionic pilasters; a full entablature encircles the room. Opposite the main door and on the central axis of the building is a broad elliptical arch which sweeps almost the entire length of the room and serves as a visual frame for the stairs behind it. The stairs ascend in a long initial flight and then turn back in two short flights to the second floor. The paneling is pine throughout; the stairs, wall dado, and the balustrade, however, are walnut. As it exists today the pine of the paneling is in its natural state, muted to a dark honey color by the oil from the paint which covered it for two centuries. Since the removal of the paint the only treatment of this lovely surface has been wax, and it is incomparably beautiful; it must be kept in mind, however, that originally the woodwork in all the rooms was painted. Only the walnut of the stair ensemble, because of its dark and rich quality, was left natural to contrast with the painted paneling.

Not only the hall but the entire plan of Carter's Grove is symmetrical. Like Mount Airy's, therefore, it is more formal than the off-center arrangement of Westover. In addition, the authentic classicism of the woodwork makes a more coherent design than did the curious combination of provincial awkwardness and imported elegance which gave us such delight at Westover. The style, however, is as much Baroque as Palladian. Many of its features are directly traceable to the small and more conservative English houses of the early Georgian period which, like their colonial counterparts, refused to forsake the decorative richness of the Wren-Baroque for the more severe and cerebral Palladian style. This may be seen by comparing the arched opening which separates the stairs from the main entrance hall at Carter's Grove to an almost identical treatment at Frampton Court, a small English house in Gloucestershire built between 1731 and 1733 (Fig. 78). Both the quality and stylistic coherence of Carter's Grove suggest the probability that here, just as at Westover, some of the decorative elements were imported from London; and it is known from documents that an English carpenter, Richard Bayliss, was brought to Virginia to carry out the woodwork. Within the limitations of the colonial environment both Mount Airy and Carter's Grove were as English as it was possible to make them, for in spite of the sense of independence that was beginning to assert itself in other areas of colonial life social and aesthetic attitudes were more than ever governed by English cultural values.

Other Palladian Influences

All the more important houses built throughout the colonies after 1750 exhibit in varying degrees the greater formality, the more authentic treatment of classical detail, and the continued sculptural richness of the Gibbsian style. During these same years in the South, however, a few houses

FIGURE 77. *Carter's Grove,*
James City County, Va., hall, 1750–53.

FIGURE 78. *Frampton Court,*
Gloucestershire, England, hall, 1731–33. (*Copyright* Country Life)

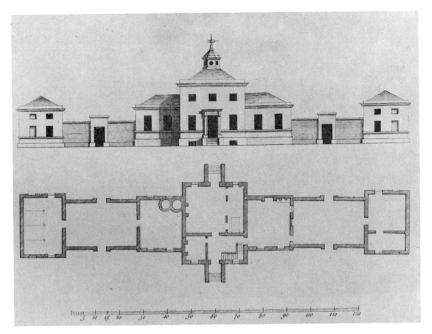

FIGURE 79. *Robert Morris. Plan for a villa.*

appeared which showed a more direct Palladian influence. They were consequently more akin to the high Palladian style of Lord Burlington and his circle. This variant on the English style was brought to the colonies by yet another architectural handbook, Robert Morris's *Select Architecture,* published in 1757. This book not only presented schemes which were closer in character than those of Gibbs to the great English Palladian mansions such as Holkham Hall (compare Figs. 71 and 79), but also like Gibbs and Adam showed houses sufficiently small in size to be within the limits of colonial resources. Morris's book seems to have made its way to tidewater Virginia by the mid-sixties and to have had direct influence on a few of the later mansions in the area.[7] Of these, Brandon (c. 1765) in Prince George County is by far the most interesting (Fig. 80). Both the plan and general massing of this house come directly from a plate in Morris's book and show the extended symmetrical grouping of contrasting blocks so typical of English Palladian arrangements (Fig. 81). Moreover, Brandon is stripped of the Baroque ornamentalism just observed at Mount Airy. The walls are clean with openings sharply cut, and although the scale is smaller and the brick surfaces more animated than the dressed stone walls of high English Palladianism, Brandon has the separateness of parts and staccato accents so characteristic of the Palladian houses (compare Fig. 71).

In a few isolated instances, the published works of Palladio himself had influence in the southern colonies. One of the most important surviving examples is the Miles Brewton House (1765–69) in Charleston, South Carolina (Fig. 82). Here we are confronted with a single block, rather square in proportions, with a hipped roof and freestanding two-story portico of exquisitely beautiful and correct classical design. This motif, so unlike

FIGURE 80. *Brandon,*
Prince George County, Va., c. 1765.

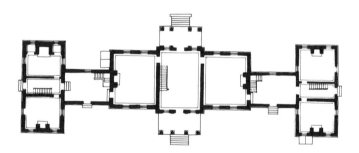

FIGURE 81. *Brandon,*
Prince George County, Va., plan, c. 1765.

the horizontal block of the Wren-type house, was inspired not by an English book source, or by an existing English Palladian building, but by a plate in Palladio's *I quattro libri dell' architettura* (Fig. 72). Here, again, the scale in the Palladian plate is sufficiently modest to be adaptable to a colonial house, and even in the contrasting materials of brick and painted wood, something of the pure geometric simplicity of the Palladian concept is preserved.

Houses like Brandon and the Miles Brewton House, because of their relationship with English Palladianism, were unusual even in the South. Yet in spite of their precociousness, they are almost half a century out

FIGURE 82. *Miles Brewton House,*
Charleston, S.C., 1765–69.

of date when compared to Palladian buildings in England. More than
that, they are Palladian by reference rather than in conception. Those
characteristics which mark them as Palladian, far from being inspired,
were in fact direct quotations from the books; and the closer they followed
the books the more erudite but less original they became. The style of
the second half of the century was in every respect more bookish than
that of the first half, and although this led to a greater stylistic uniformity
throughout the colonies, it did so at the expense of that appealing freshness which we have discovered in the more provincial but less inhibited
buildings of the earlier years.

Gibbs in the North

After mid-century, in the cities and coastal communities of New England
the more ambitious houses began to reflect the Gibbsian version of English
formalism. But here there is not the slightest hint of either the extended
plan or the alternating block units of the Palladian scheme. Instead, the
most conspicuous changes came in the façades, which took on a certain
monumentality through the use of the projecting pedimented pavilion and
pilasters. Both inside and out, classical details were rendered with greater
authority, and, as happened in the South, books were the principal source
for the new style. At the same time, however, the houses of New England

clung more tenaciously to many of the older ideas than the houses in the South. Built for an urban rather than an agrarian society, they also remained more narrow in scope. Nowhere in New England is there a surviving example from the eighteenth century of a spread-out Palladian complex with central unit and attached dependencies. Instead, the simple rectangular block and the three-story town house remained characteristic of even the largest dwellings. Moreover, the continued predominance of wood not only imposed its own qualities on the classical forms but also impressed a definite regional stamp upon the New England houses.

The John Vassall (Longfellow) House in Cambridge, Massachusetts (1759) is typical (Fig. 83). Made of wood with clapboard siding, it is a characteristic horizontal block with a symmetrical façade and a low hipped roof crowned by a balustrade. Instead of the plain wall of the earlier houses, however, there is a central pavilion topped by a pediment and framed by two giant pilasters. Similar pilasters are used at the ends of the façade. All these give the house a decided Gibbsian flavor. Yet there is little new here. In fact, as a formal concept, the house retains all the basic elements of the detached house of the Wren-Baroque era. The stylistic change which has occurred, so characteristic of most New England houses after 1750, is not in fact a change in basic form. It is rather a shift toward more classical proportions and a more authentic rendering of classical detail, all of which came directly from architectural handbooks, such as the one by Gibbs.

FIGURE 83. Vassall (Longfellow) House, Cambridge, Mass., 1759.

The same can be said of the houses in the middle colonies. One in particular which exhibits the same fundamental character as the Vassall House is Mount Pleasant (Fig. 84) in Fairmount Park, Philadelphia (1761–62). It, too, is a rectangular block with a pedimented central pavilion and a hipped roof crowned by a balustrade. At the same time it is more decoratively lavish than the Vassall House, and is masonry rather than wood. Almost without exception the finer houses in the vicinity of Philadelphia were either brick or stone and thus are more heavily scaled and sculptural than the finely drawn wooden houses of New England. Actually, the walls of Mount Pleasant are rubble masonry covered with a very light and neutral red-orange stucco incised to imitate dressed stonemasonry; the quoined corners and stringcourse are brick. This creates a contrast in surface quality which is reminiscent of the two colors of stone used at Mount Airy. To supplement this basically pictorial quality a heavily molded Palladian window appears in the center of the tall and narrow pedimented pavilion, and the door surround is richly adorned with Doric pilasters, full entablature, and pediment. Overriding all this is a symmetrical plan developed around a dominating central hall. Equally spaced on the garden side are two identical detached dependencies. This scheme of course is predominantly Gibbsian, but the general effect is of excessive abundance, so much so in fact that the house seems overburdened by the sheer weight of its ornament. With its twin dependencies and isolated location on an enormous tract of land, it has a certain kinship with the mansions of the South, but in its material extravagance it belongs to the aggressive world of the man who built it, the Scottish privateer and sea captain, John MacPherson.

Mount Pleasant and the Vassall House typify the more ambitious houses of the North during the third quarter of the eighteenth century. Quite apart from the symmetrical plan and the more authoritative handling of the classical details, that feature which distinguishes them most emphatically from the style of the first half of the century is the pedimented pavilion. Although this device did not make its way to the colonies until after mid-century, when it was introduced by such books as Gibbs's *A Book of Architecture* (Fig. 87), it was used often in England in the small detached houses of the Wren-Baroque. A superb example is The Moot, Downton, Wiltshire, built about 1700 (Fig. 85). The fact that the pedimented pavilion appears so often in Gibbs, therefore, is one of the several links with the past which made him so readily acceptable to the colonials. As used in the colonies the pedimented pavilion proved to be more an enrichment of the established mode than a break with it, and both the popularity of the pavilioned façade and its derivation from the Wren-Baroque did much to assure that the more distilled and severe style of the Palladians would have no influence upon the architecture of the North.

The Jeremiah Lee Mansion

Perhaps the most interesting example of the persuasive appeal of the pedimented pavilion is to be found in the Jeremiah Lee Mansion in Marble-

FIGURE 84. *Mount Pleasant, Fairmount Park, Philadelphia, Pa., 1761–62.*

head, Massachusetts (1768). This is a typical New England town house built immediately on the winding, narrow main street of one of the most fascinating coastal communities on the Atlantic seaboard (Fig. 86). Its three stories identify it at once with such earlier houses as the Royall House in Medford (Fig. 52). Yet is it a characteristic town house form? The English town houses of the early eighteenth century, like the Fitzwilliam House in Cambridge (Fig. 53), showed a three story vertical wall to the street with the roof screened behind a parapet.[8] The English town houses of mid-century continued this basic form. The Lee Mansion, however, does not. Instead, it takes the familiar Wren-Baroque-Gibbsian formula (Fig. 87), makes it three rather than two stories high, and in order to maintain the horizontal orientation it widens the house by one bay on each side. Although the house is entirely of wood, the main walls are cut in imitation of rusticated stonemasonry, and the four corners are quoined (Fig. 86). The hipped roof has a rather flat pitch in a manner

FIGURE 85. The Moot,
Downton, Wiltshire, England, c. 1700.

FIGURE 86. Lee Mansion,
Marblehead, Mass., 1768.

FIGURE 87. *James Gibbs. Design for a house.*

characteristic of the Gibbsian style and terminates in a simple octagonal cupola, a device frequently found on small English houses of the period.[9] The most monumental feature of the façade is the pedimented pavilion. The widely spaced bays give it sufficient width to maintain its classic proportions; and to emphasize its centrality, a shallow porch projects from the wall with freestanding Ionic columns, full entablature, and pediment. This is one of the earliest examples in New England colonial architecture of the freestanding entrance portico, a feature which was to become a hallmark of the great town houses of the New England coastal communities during the last quarter of the eighteenth century. Exquisitely and correctly proportioned, it adds to the classical effect of the central pavilion and cupola, making the Lee Mansion more formal but at the same time less spontaneous than the Royall House with its vigorous but awkward façade (Fig. 52).

All these characteristics bear directly upon the man who built the house. Jeremiah Lee was probably the greatest import-export merchant in the colonies before the Revolution,[10] and his house, as a symbol of success, was one of the most pretentious and costly in New England. The façade proclaims this from its domineering position on the narrow street. The climax, however, comes in the interior. Extravagantly adorned with paneling, carving, and imported wallpapers from England, the inner arrangements culminate in the elegant banquet room on the first floor (Fig. 88). This spacious chamber is paneled from floor to ceiling in what seems to be dark English oak. Dominating the composition is an elaborate fireplace (Fig. 89) framed in white marble and flanked by richly carved consoles; above is a carved overmantel with ornate garlands and swags. This entire

FIGURE 88. *Lee Mansion,*
Marblehead, Mass., banquet room, 1768.

motif was taken from a mid-century English pattern book, Swan's *British Architect* (Fig. 90), and the vigorous carving, in its crisp interlocked and curvilinear forms, has many of the qualities of the luxuriant foliated style of Grinling Gibbons (Fig. 91 a, b).

Compared with the extraordinary virtuosity of Gibbons's work, the panel in the Lee Mansion seems meager and lifeless. But the basic characteristics of the Wren-Baroque style are there nevertheless, and when placed beside other colonial wood carving its quality appears unusually high. In this respect it is comparable to the slightly earlier, carved fireplace panel in the Wentworth-Gardner House (Fig. 91 c), but like that work too it is totally without invention and testifies only to the greater skill of the mid-century colonial craftsmen. Furthermore, when it was made it was many years out of fashion, for Grinling Gibbons, whose style it imitates, died almost half a century before the Lee Mansion was even begun. In sum, the Lee mantel adds but yet another patch to the time-worn cloak of conformity which wrapped the architecture of the mercantile North in its protective authority.

With all its dignified elegance the banquet room in the Lee Mansion is not only imitative, it is also brashly pretentious. Because of their dark color and grain our first impression is that the walls are made of English oak. But this is an appearance only. In truth, the wood is not a hard wood at all. Instead it is a lowly pine, made to look like oak by skillfully painted imitation graining. The semblance of a costly material was thereby imparted to the interior in the same way that the qualities of stonemasonry were carved and painted on the wooden façade. We have come to recognize

FIGURE 89. *Lee Mansion,*
Marblehead, Mass., mantel, 1768.

this imitative technique as a mark of provincialism not only in colonial architecture but also in much of the lesser architecture of England itself. The earlier Royall House is a notable colonial example, and the Lee Mansion adds nothing to this well-established practice. As a work of architecture, however, it differs from the Royall House in its greater formality and classical correctness. In its more sterile bookishness it lacks the vitality of the earlier example, and its pretentiousness, therefore, is even more conspicuous. But to Jeremiah Lee his splendid mansion, with all its chicanery, was the ultimate embodiment of his status as both a cultured English gentleman and an aggressive merchant, and the image of self-assurance which it presents is matched only by the superb full-length Copley portraits of himself and Mrs. Lee which once graced the walls of the mansion.[11]

FIGURE 90. *Abraham Swan. Design for a fireplace.*

Gibbs and the Colonial Church

The influence of James Gibbs on American colonial architecture came not only from his books but also from one of his greatest works, the Church of St. Martin-in-the-Fields in London (1726). St. Martin's (Fig. 92) is obviously derived from Wren's London churches. Yet it is also quite different. All the Wren churches, even the larger ones such as St. Bride, Fleet Street, have a quality of intimacy and smallness about them, which is experienced primarily through the master's refined sense of scale. St. Martin's by contrast is a monumental church. Although the main body is a simple rectangular block, the walls are richly ornamented with heavy but rather strict classical forms, including colossal pilasters which range each side between the windows and are coupled in the corner bays with engaged columns. The tower with its spire rises directly from the main body of the church and is fronted by a freestanding colossal Corinthian portico. This monumental templelike front, used so often by the English

FIGURE 91. (*a*) *Grinling Gibbons. Holme Lacy,
Herefordshire, England, one half oak swag.* (*Copyright* Country Life)

FIGURE 91. (*b*) *Lee Mansion,
Marblehead, Mass., mantel detail, 1768.*

FIGURE 91. (*c*) *Wentworth-Gardner House,
Portsmouth, N.H., mantel detail, 1760.*

FIGURE 92. *James Gibbs. St. Martin-in-the-Fields, London, England, 1726.*

Palladians, does not occur in a single Wren church, not even St. Paul's, and it imparts to St. Martin's a quality of authoritative classicism that is quite in contrast with the free and more imaginative use of classical forms found in the work of Wren. On the other hand, St. Martin's has none of the austere geometry of the high Palladian style. The church is, in fact, a magnificent synthesis of Wren's Baroque richness and the more severe classicism of the Palladians, and in its exploitation of the Wren-type church, it became both adaptable and attractive to the colonial church builders.

The same is true of the interior (Fig. 93). Here, the quality of poised space, first conceived by Wren in his London churches, was stretched to new heights of expansiveness. The effect was achieved through sweeping intersecting vaults, tenuously balanced on tall, slender columns. The visual impact of this dynamic yet delicate combination is even more startling when we consider the structural system. Obviously, no stone or wooden column on the face of the earth could support masonry vaults of such magnitude, yet they remain easily aloft. It is precisely at this point that the genius of both Wren and Gibbs is revealed, for these vaults, like

FIGURE 93. *James Gibbs. St. Martin-in-the-Fields, interior, 1726.*

those of Wren, are not stone but are wood and plaster suspended from the great roof trusses. The taut, rhythmic shapes are lightened in appearance by the delicate scale of the applied ornament, but at no time is the continuity of surface interrupted. The effect is voluminous, as though the vaults were made of flexible substance and were held aloft by the pressure of the space itself, in the same way that the air pushes up into the blossom of a parachute. Like a fine piece of machinery, the design is intricate but controlled, and in its studied completeness combines lightness with grandeur, elaborate ornament with substantial structure. It is both theoretical and inspired, and because it embraces so many dimensions of eighteenth-century English architectural thought, it is probably the most thoroughly "Early Georgian" building in England.[12]

The success of St. Martin's was deserved and immediate; the colonists knew this church not only by reputation but also through reproductions, for it was richly and fully illustrated in Gibbs's *A Book of Architecture* by a series of plans, sections, and elevations that showed several preliminary schemes as well as the final design (Figs. 93, 98).

Christ Church, Philadelphia

The first direct influence of St. Martin-in-the-Fields on colonial church architecture is found in Christ Church, Philadelphia (Fig. 94). Built in the Quaker capital for an expanding and affluent Anglican congregation, it was begun in 1727 as a Wren-type church with a simple square

FIGURE 94. *Christ Church,
Philadelphia, Pa., 1727, spire, 1754.*

tower. Construction was carried further during the thirties, however, and by 1744 the main body of the church had been completed. This part of the building seems to have been designed by a gentleman-amateur, Dr. John Kearsley, but the spire was not completed until 1754 and is the work of another hand.

In its final form, Christ Church is more closely related to Gibbs's St. Martin-in-the-Fields (Fig. 92) than to the Wren churches. The heavy massing, the double tier of arched windows separated by pilasters, the full entablature crowned by a balustrade, and most especially, the wooden spire and the enormous Palladian window in the east end are all conspicuously derived from Gibbs's church. The interior (Fig. 95) was also inspired by St. Martin's (Fig. 93). Widely spaced Doric columns resting on pedestals are topped by full entablature blocks; these support wide longitudinal arches, which in turn carry a flat plaster ceiling. The side balconies are now separated from the columns but were once further forward so that they were engaged, just as they are in the London church. Both in scale and effect, the great Palladian window, which fills the entire chancel wall, is also remarkably similar to Gibbs's design. Although mixed in style, sometimes clumsily proportioned and filled with strange contradictions in scale, Christ Church was the most advanced and completely English church in the colonies.

FIGURE 95. *Christ Church,*
Philadelphia, Pa., interior, 1727.

St. Michael's, Charleston, South Carolina

After 1750 all important city churches built in the colonies were patterned
after St. Martin's. St. Michael's, Charleston, South Carolina (1752–61)
is one of the most monumental (Fig. 96). Anonymously designed,[13] it is
simpler in detail and more consistent in scale than Christ Church, Philadelphia. The main body of the church is brick covered with stucco; the
steeple and portico are wood. Although no part of the church can be
directly related to a book source, the building is Gibbsian throughout, and
many of its parts are reminiscent of plates in *A Book of Architecture.*
Its freestanding Doric portico is the first of its kind in the colonies. The
rusticated tower, instead of being attached as in the earlier Wren-type
churches, rises from the main auditorium block, as it did at St. Martin's,
to culminate in a massive steeple comprised of three octagonal stages, the
uppermost of which is an open belfry topped by a spire. This, together
with the portico and the horizontal weight of the main body of the auditorium, make the church similar in massing, though not in detail, to the
Gibbs church.

FIGURE 96. *St. Michael's Church,*
Charleston, S.C., 1752–61.

The First Baptist Meetinghouse, Providence, Rhode Island

The most important church built in New England in the years immediately preceding the Revolution was the First Baptist Meetinghouse in Providence, Rhode Island (Fig. 97). Built during the years 1774–75, it was also directly influenced by Gibbs. The design was provided by Joseph Brown, a wealthy Providence merchant and brother of the Moses Brown who was later to play a significant role in the early industrial developments of America. A member of the faculty of Rhode Island College (later Brown University), Joseph Brown was a typical native-born gentleman-amateur of the eighteenth century.[14] Like Christopher Wren before him, he was a mathematician and astronomer who brought to his designing a mind trained in abstract space relationships. Brown did not, however, have the sophisticated command of structure which had enabled Wren to achieve such an immense variety of spatial solutions in his London churches. Brown, in spite of his mathematical background, and in typical colonial manner, drew his ideas from books and relied on the builder to carry them out.

FIGURE 97. *First Baptist Meetinghouse, Providence, R.I., 1774–75.*

Structurally Brown's church is typical of New England in that it is completely a frame building with clapboard siding and quoined corners. Again reflecting its New England meetinghouse ancestry, it was originally square in plan. A pedimented pavilion projects prominently from the main façade and forms the base for the steeple. The windows are the plain round-headed type, and in the center of the upper story of the pavilion is a Palladian window. There is a similar one on the opposite end of the church. Otherwise the main body of the building is unadorned. In contrast to the rather austere simplicity of the building itself the entrance is framed by a freestanding pedimented Doric portico (Fig. 99). Topping the whole is a superbly proportioned and elaborately ornamented spire, which is totally unrelated, in both scale and quality, to either the building or the portico.

The disturbing lack of coherence in Brown's design betrays his amateur methods; for Joseph Brown was not an architect, he was a college professor who owned a copy of Gibbs's *A Book of Architecture*. In approaching the design he did not see the church as a unique spatial and structural problem to be resolved in coherent interrelated terms. Instead, he opened Gibbs's book to certain selected plates and directed his builder to accommodate them to the building on a part-to-part basis. The tower, for

FIGURE 98. *James Gibbs. Proposed steeples for St. Martin-in-the-Fields.*

example, was taken almost line for line from one of the rejected designs for St. Martin's which Gibbs illustrated in his book (Fig. 98). A Boston master carpenter, James Sumner, was brought to Providence to execute the design in wood, and the only important change which he made was to eliminate all carved ornament except the strictly architectural features. Otherwise the rendering is authentic and careful, and presents a reasonably accurate image of the engraved plate. Moreover, an early description tells us that the spire was originally painted in imitation of grained stone, making it even more like the original.[15] But Gibbs designed his tower to surmount a colossal Corinthian portico (Fig. 92). Brown used instead a small one-story portico, taken from another plate in *A Book of Architecture* (Fig. 100), a portico intended by Gibbs for a very much smaller church, his design for Marybone Chapel. In Brown's unhappy union of steeple and portico there is no relationship in scale between the two. Nor does either, in turn, relate to the commonplace clapboard siding of the main body of the church.

FIGURE 99. *First Baptist Meetinghouse, Providence, R.I., portico, 1774–75.*

FIGURE 100. *James Gibbs. Marybone Chapel, façade.*

The interior is more consistent (Fig. 101). As it exists today, there are two rows of single Doric columns which carry an elliptical ceiling and groin-vaulted gallery bays. Cutting through the columns on both sides is a balcony. This arrangement is a simplified version of the interior of Marybone Chapel, as illustrated in Gibbs's book. All the architectural details also, come from Gibbs. The broad elliptical vaults, although devoid of any decorative ornament, are delicately poised on the slender Doric columns. The effect, though austere, is soaring and voluminous, and in a diminutive way suggests something of the dynamic spatial sweep of St. Martin's (compare Fig. 93). The First Baptist Meetinghouse is one of the loveliest eighteenth-century churches in America, yet with all its quiet dignity it is not a unified design. It is rather a series of quotations "performed in the neatest Manner" and owes its many delights not to Joseph Brown but to James Gibbs, architect, and to the very special skills of James Sumner, carpenter.

The Architect in Eighteenth-Century America

We have already emphasized that the professional architect, whose life was given over to the creation of buildings at the conceptual level, had no place in colonial society. Men like Jones, Wren, or Gibbs would have found neither motivation nor patronage in the provincial attitudes and

FIGURE 101. *First Baptist Meetinghouse,*
Providence, R.I., interior, 1774–75.

economic limitations of the frontier. Instead, most colonial buildings were
not designed at all, but were simply built by local craftsmen who worked
with available materials and skills in the established English tradition. For
specific details they relied upon their architectural handbooks. But the
way in which each craftsman interpreted these books was conditioned by
his own capabilities and limitations, and by the degree of informed experience which motivated his patron. A few, such as Richard Munday of
Newport, showed genuine qualities of originality and in many ways performed the functions of the architect. Nevertheless, they were designers
more through environmental necessity than professional choice, and their
primary commitment remained to the mechanics and details of construction.
Because of this dual character, they may properly be described as archi-
tect-builders.

Occasionally designs were prepared by individuals who had nothing
directly to do with the actual construction. This was almost always the
case in the more ambitious and formal structures such as churches and
public buildings. This type of designer we have already identified as the
gentleman-amateur, a phenomenon of the eighteenth century both in England and America. He was generally a man like Joseph Brown who,
through background and experience, had acquired some knowledge of
architectural matters, and whose position in society gave his opinion the
weight of authority.

By 1750, the majority of the colonial "architects" had been born in the colonies, and although the gentleman-amateur, because of his cultural pretensions, consistently strove for a more authentic image of English architecture than did the architect-builder, the work of both was marked by a decided provincialism. As the century progressed, however, the opportunities afforded by the colonies attracted a number of Englishmen with wider ranges of knowledge and technical competence. Although none came with all the qualifications of a professional architect, they had all gained their knowledge firsthand; and they introduced into the colonies a more up-to-date form of English eighteenth-century architecture. Through the work of two such English immigrants colonial architecture of the eighteenth century reached its most mature phase. The first was the gentleman-amateur Peter Harrison, of Newport, Rhode Island, the second was the builder and wood carver William Buckland, of Annapolis, Maryland.

Peter Harrison

The name of Peter Harrison is one of the most prominent in colonial architecture: even in his own day, his accomplishments were widely acclaimed, and no subsequent generation has ever seriously questioned his superiority in the field. In recent years he has been elevated to the distinguished position of America's first professional architect.[16] There is much to be said for this recognition. Not only was Harrison responsible for more documented buildings than any other man of his generation, but his work displays an advanced formal correctness that no colonial builder had yet achieved. He was also proficient in various skills directly or indirectly related to architecture. He had sufficient knowledge of shipbuilding to supervise the fitting out of his own vessel, he prepared plans for strengthening the defense installations of Newport Harbor, he designed a lighthouse, and he mapped the town and harbor of Newport. All of these activities presuppose considerable skill as a draftsman and at least a basic knowledge of engineering.

Harrison's active and continuing interest in architecture was in part an attribute of his time. In the eighteenth century, some knowledge of the subject was expected of a gentleman, and as an aspiring young merchant Harrison made a conscious effort to keep himself informed in the field.[17] From his many trips to England as captain of a ship, he brought back a careful selection of the most recent books on architecture, and these ultimately formed part of an architectural library[18] equalled only by that of William Byrd at Westover.

Harrison was also drawn to architecture by background and temperament. Born in Yorkshire, where he saw the Palladian style of Lord Burlington and William Kent at its best, he was ardently Anglican by persuasion, and a dedicated Englishman in both sentiment and manners. Yet with all this he was not a "professional architect," and to think of him as such is to misunderstand the role of the architect in colonial America. Harrison never received more than a token gift for his designs and, except for occasional supervision, never actually participated in the construction

FIGURE 102. Peter Harrison. Redwood Library, Newport, R.I., 1748–50.

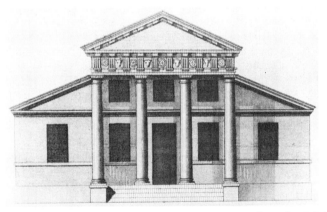

FIGURE 103. Edward Hoppus. Headpiece to Fourth Book of Palladio, 1736.

of his buildings. His principal occupation was that of a merchant and sea captain, and in the later years of his life, he became a Collector of Customs for His Majesty's Government in New Haven. Architecture was his principal avocation, never his vocation, and by experience and inclination he was the very epitome of the gentleman-amateur. An evaluation of his work can only be meaningful if this important distinction is kept in mind.

The first building designed by Harrison was the Redwood Library in Newport, Rhode Island (1748–50). As a building type, it was one of the first of its kind in the colonies and in style it had no counterpart in America (Fig. 102). As originally built,[19] it was a simple rectangular block with a low pitched roof. The main entrance was on the short rather than the long side and was preceded by a monumental Doric portico raised on a podium. We recognize this at once as the classical temple form, and its appearance in the Redwood Library has been proclaimed as the first in the colonies and one of the earliest in English architecture. But the temple form as used here by Harrison is not pure. Extending from the center of each side is a low shallow wing whose pitched roof and level cornice create the effect of a second and lower pediment. This curious winged front was taken by Harrison directly from an English translation of Palladio published in London in 1736 (Fig. 103). Thus the idea is strictly Palladian in origin and cannot be construed as a conscious adaptation of the classical temple. This is an enormously significant point, for the new styles which were to emerge during the first fifty years following the Revolution were largely inspired by the architecture of the ancient world rather than by Palladio, and Harrison's overt application of a Palladian front must in no way be confused with this later Neoclassicism.

Harrison's methods and objectives are both perfectly clear in the Redwood Library. In working up his design, he relied entirely on the books. Not only did the basic form of the building come from Palladio, but every important feature of the detailing can be traced to some book in his possession.[20] Furthermore, in transposing various elements from the books he permitted himself little deviation from the models either in proportions or detail. He was also conscious of the fact that Palladian architecture was conceived in stone and he did everything within the limits of local techniques and materials to achieve this effect. The outer walls of the Redwood Library were worked in pine plank cut in imitation of rusticated masonry; they were then painted brown, sand having been mixed with the paint to create the texture as well as the color of stone. Harrison was the first colonial designer to go to such extremes of deliberate imitation, and with his firsthand knowledge of English building, plus the number of books which he had in his library, he achieved a more rigid adherence to academic principles than the colonies had yet known.

Since the direct adaptation of a Palladian motif in the Redwood Library makes it the earliest example in the colonies of theoretical Palladianism, some critics align Harrison with the Palladian movement of Lord Burlington and his followers. Although this assumption is implicit in Harrison's methods, it needs careful qualification, for in a very important sense his quotation from Palladio has nothing to do with high English Palladianism. It is true as we have already seen that Burlington and Kent developed their ideas on Palladian doctrine, but they also brought to their work a higher philosophical reasoning which gave it a largeness and geometric purity which was uniquely its own. There is none of this in the slavish and meager adaptation of Harrison. In fact, it can be said that

FIGURE 104. *Peter Harrison. King's Chapel, Boston, Mass., 1749.*

Harrison's loyalty was to the books and not to English Palladianism, for certain parts of the Redwood Library can be traced to non-Palladian sources; moreover, in his second and most important work, King's Chapel, Boston, he turned for inspiration entirely to Gibbs rather than Palladio.

King's Chapel (Fig. 104) was designed in 1749 and was opened for services in 1754. The main body of the church is a rectangle with a hipped roof and has an upper range of high, round-headed windows above shorter ones with segmental arched tops. This system of fenestration comes directly from Gibbs's design for Marybone Chapel, as illustrated in *A Book of Architecture*. Originally Harrison's church was to have been erected entirely in Quincy granite, but only the body of the church and the tower were finished in this material. The colossal Ionic portico is wood and was not completed until some time between 1785 and 1787. It was designed by Harrison, however, and is thus the earliest intended colossal portico on any church in the colonies.[21] In addition, King's Chapel was the first American church to be built of stone.

Harrison also intended a lofty spire in stone. Although it was never built, drawings for it were still in existence in 1784, and a contemporary description suggests that it was remarkably similar to that on St. Martin-in-the-Fields. The magnitude of Harrison's scheme posed many problems which were beyond the limited skills of colonial masons, and to help bring it to completion he solicited aid from the famous Ralph Allen of Bath, England. The latter responded by offering to donate all the "Bath Stone" required for the building, and to supply the skilled stonecutters necessary to work it. Unfortunately, this magnanimous gesture was never fulfilled.

The interior of King's Chapel (Fig. 105) is also reminiscent of St. Martin's. Two rows of columns support a range of plaster groined vaults above the galleries on either side of the church. These in turn carry a flat ceiling down the center. At the end, behind and above the altar, is a Palladian window. All these are basic ingredients of St. Martin's. Furthermore the Corinthian columns are superbly proportioned, and like the block entablatures which top them, are executed with impeccable attention to detail. As decorative elements they are both authoritative and exquisitely beautiful. At the same time, there is something quite wrong with Harrison's scheme. Because the main portion of the ceiling is flat and set off from the groined vaults in the lateral galleries by a bordering cornice, it seems to press down into the space of the room and therefore lacks altogether the lofty suspended quality of Gibbs's design. Moreover, except for the coupled Corinthian columns, the rest of Harrison's interior is relatively unadorned; thus the columns, in all their classical elegance, stand out in large and isolated splendor. Even though these columns were copied with great care from one of Gibbs's books, their effect is overpowering and excessively ornate. Harrison had a similar book source for all the decorative features in King's Chapel and because of his tenacious adherence to the specific characteristics of each, it is difficult to see them as related parts of a whole. The design, indeed, lacks coherence. Yet in the America of its day, King's Chapel introduced a new level of architectural sophistication and helped to establish more firmly than ever the role of the gentleman-amateur architect in colonial society.

FIGURE 105. *Peter Harrison. King's Chapel, Boston, Mass., interior, 1749.*

FIGURE 106. *Peter Harrison. Touro Synagogue,
Newport, R.I., 1759–63.*

His last two works, the Touro Synagogue and the Brick Market, both
in Newport, make it clear that Harrison's bookish methods continued
to the end of his career. The Synagogue (1759–63) was the first Jewish
house of worship built in colonial America. Although the exterior is
excessively plain, the interior (Fig. 106) is generally regarded as one of
the masterpieces of the colonial eighteenth century. In every way it is an
appealing and gracious room, and to the degree that it captures the
quality and spirit of English architectural ornament, it is an extraordinary
work. Yet there is hardly a piece of original design in it. Everything
from the general scheme to the details can be traced not to one but to
several book sources.[22]

Not only is the Touro Synagogue without invention, but its meticulous
propriety and elegance defeat its purpose as a house of Hebrew worship.
This was not altogether Harrison's fault. When asked by Congregation
Jeshuat Israel to design a building for them, he found himself confronted
with a problem for which there was no established architectural solution.

This was so not only in the colonial environment, where no synagogue had ever before been built, but it had been true throughout the history of the Hebrew people. The ancient Hebrews had been nomadic tribes whose culture revealed itself most expressively in the majestic poetry of the Psalms, not in buildings, and they left behind them no architectural heritage whatsoever. Wherever they have gone the Jewish people have embraced as their own the architecture which they have found around them. So in Newport in 1759 a small band of Sephardic Jews accepted Harrison without question, and he in turn responded in the only way he could, by quoting from his books in the best Protestant middle-class English manner. It is true that certain inflexible demands were placed upon him by the nature of the Jewish service. In the center of the worship space he placed a raised table surrounded by a heavy balustrade; this was for the reading of the law. Around the perimeter on the main floor were seats for the men; immediately above on three sides of the room was a balcony for the women. The twelve columns which supported this balcony symbolized the twelve tribes of Israel. On the east wall Harrison provided an elaborate architectural setting for the Ark of the Covenant. All this was prescribed for the designer by Isaac Touro, who had recently arrived in Newport from the Rabbinical Academy in Amsterdam, and Harrison met the demands with ease and grace. He did so, however, entirely within the limits of a well established colonial worship space; for the squarish plan and balcony arrangement of the Touro Synagogue vary only slightly if at all from that found in countless eighteenth-century meetinghouses throughout New England.[23] To be sure, there is a certain ingenuity about the manner in which the ritualistic furnishings are fitted into this space, and the detailing is exquisitely correct. In this room, too, Harrison's sense of scale is more coherent than in any other building he designed. Yet the atmosphere is one of pretentious refinement, many times more appropriate to the elegant dialogue of a Restoration comedy than to the dark brooding intonement of the Hebrew service. Historically the Touro Synagogue is one of the most important eighteenth-century buildings surviving in America; architecturally it is one of the least original.

The Brick Market (1761–72), which followed Touro Synagogue, was not only Harrison's last work but also his most rigidly academic (Fig. 107). Since the requirements for a market house demanded an open first floor, he chose for his model the new gallery of Somerset House, a sophisticated English Renaissance work of the seventeenth century attributed to Inigo Jones. His source was a plate in Colen Campbell's *Vitruvius Britannicus* (Fig. 108). Harrison took over intact the entire structural and rhythmic scheme of the English model. His building is made of brick, laid in common bond in the basement story and in Flemish bond in the upper two. As in Somerset House, the lower level here is an open arcade, but because he was working in brick rather than stone, Harrison eliminated the rustication. He maintained the stringcourse, however, at the level where the arches spring from the piers, and the rhythmic pattern is identical to that of the English model. Again, as at Somerset

FIGURE 107. *Peter Harrison. Brick Market,*
Newport, R.I., 1761–62.

FIGURE 108. *Somerset House, London, England, river front.*

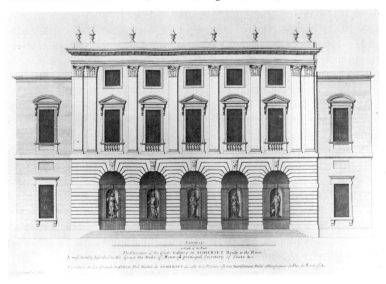

House, the second-floor windows are rectangular with alternating triangular and segmental pediments; those on the third floor are square with simple surrounds. Between these are pilasters of wood, coupled at the corners, and carrying a full entablature. The decorative features in Harrison's scheme are simpler than those in Somerset House, and the order has been changed from Corinthian to Ionic, but even these modifications were drawn from Gibbs's *Rules of Drawing;* and the use of brick and white wood, which might seem to make the building more colonial than English, was, in fact, a combination of materials fairly common in England, and in some ways it tends to emphasize rather than minimize Harrison's overt adaptations.

Harrison's doctrinaire methods and stanch royalist sentiments are nowhere better summarized than in this completely derivative and thoroughly English building. In everything that he designed, he sought to capture both the character and the spirit of his native architecture; and in this attitude he enjoyed the unqualified support of his patronage, for the praise accorded him in his day leaves no doubt that he gave to his contemporary colonials, including Congregation Jeshuat Israel, precisely those qualities of Englishness which they were never able to attain from his American-born rivals. Because Peter Harrison put his designs together in pieces from the books, and because he remained largely aloof from the actual building procedures themselves, he never attained that quality of organic unity which is so essential to fine building. Throughout his career, his work remained a pattern-book architecture, an indecisive miscellany of skillfully rendered quotations whose rigid adherence to source left no room for those vigorous personal statements so conspicuous in the work of Munday.

William Buckland

In the work of William Buckland we find no such separation of part from whole. Like Harrison, he was English-born, but his background and training were altogether different. Apprenticed at the age of thirteen as a cabinetmaker'and carpenter, he was brought to the Virginia Colony in 1755 as an indentured servant to design and execute all of the interiors of Gunston Hall, George Mason's house in Fairfax County.[24] At the completion of this work in 1758, he was released from his indenture and left free to exploit his knowledge and skills. He continued to work as a designer, wood carver, and builder, first in Virginia and then, after about 1770, in Annapolis, Maryland. In the four remaining years before his untimely death in 1774, he was the master of a sizable workshop and was responsible for the design and execution of several houses in the Annapolis area. Of these, the Hammond-Harwood House (1773–74) in Annapolis is the finest (Fig. 109).

This remarkable house is a recognized colonial masterpiece. Designed for a young lawyer and planter, it is particularly notable for its complex five-part plan and its magnificent interiors. The main body of the house is a simple rectangular block with hipped roof and slightly projecting

FIGURE 109. *William Buckland. Hammond-Harwood House, Annapolis, Md., 1773–74.*

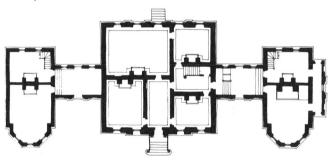

FIGURE 110. *William Buckland. Hammond-Harwood House, Annapolis, Md., plan, 1773–74.*

pedimented pavilions on both the street and garden sides. Symmetrically arranged either side of this main section is a rectangular two-story unit with a polygonal front. Each of these is turned at right angles to the main longitudinal axis of the house, and is joined to the central unit by a one-story wing. Attention is focused on the center of the façade by the second-story window which is carried on wooden brackets and has a classical surround with full entablature. All the other windows are widely spaced and are cut cleanly into the wall without surrounding decoration of any kind. The main door is framed by engaged Ionic columns with entablature and pediment and is one of the most chastely designed and exquisitely carved ornamental features in eighteenth-century American architecture.

In the plan of the Hammond-Harwood House (Fig. 110) we recognize at once the extended multiple-unit arrangement already seen in several other houses of the period, notably Brandon (Fig. 81). We recognize, too, the geometric clarity of the various components, the inward and outward movement of the blocks as they alternate symmetrically from large to small and back to large around the central axis, and the staccato isolation of the window and door openings. All of these are strictly Palladian. But unlike Brandon with its seeming smallness, Buckland's design has qualities of largeness and solid dignity which reveal not only awareness of high English Palladianism, but also a genuine feeling for its more sophisticated aspects. The Hammond-Harwood House, more than any other building in colonial America, captured something of the monumental style of Lord Burlington and his followers.

A careful study of Buckland's work also makes it clear that, like Peter Harrison, he owned a substantial number of English architectural handbooks and relied on them constantly for ideas.[25] His adaptations, however, were never as direct as Harrison's, and specific relationships are much more difficult to find. Where Harrison's approach was that of a gentleman aspiring toward correctness, Buckland's was that of an artist and craftsman giving free reign to his own imagination. This is apparent immediately in the bold massing and impeccable proportions of the exterior of the Hammond-Harwood House. It is revealed with even greater clarity in the ornamental features of the building. The door motif (Fig. 111), for example, is easily traceable in its general form to a mid-century English architectural handbook. But the sheer beauty of shape and proportions, the consistent scale, the buoyant, graceful rhythms of the foliated ornament, and the consummate skill with which it is executed are not found in any book. These are the fruits of an original and poetic mind which found exquisite delight in the smallest part, but never lost sight of the whole.

These same qualities are found in even greater proliferation in the interior. In the dining room (Fig. 112), for example, the fireplace and overmantel motif can be traced to Abraham Swan's *British Architect*,[26] but the similarity is in basic form alone. Buckland's imaginative and gracious treatment of the ornament is warmed throughout .by an inexhaustible delight in the variety and beauty of natural forms. Unlike Harrison's pure but sterile ornament, which was executed according to his designs by another hand, the carving of William Buckland pulsates with a vitality born of the master's complete identification with the whole creative process. Buckland not only understood all the material qualities of wood, but, through his innate sense of form and his superior manual skill, was able to shape it toward a new formal destiny which was neither wood nor flower, but rather an offspring of the artist himself. Delicately carved, impeccably scaled, and moved by a sprightly elegant rhythm,

FIGURE 111. William Buckland. Hammond-Harwood House,
Annapolis, Md., door, 1773–74.

Buckland's ornament was the closest thing in the colonies to the Rococo of Europe, and for sheer virtuosity alone it was not to be matched in colonial America until a generation later in the work of the Salem wood carver, Samuel McIntire.

Both Harrison and Buckland were Englishmen by birth, and the sophisticated quality of their work may be attributed to an understanding acquired through their familiarity with the very best in English architecture. No colonial-born architect could match this advantage. This they shared in common, yet their work is very different. The explanation lies in their respective backgrounds and motivation. Although Harrison had both the skill and aesthetic judgment necessary to qualify him as an architect, the designing of buildings was not his principal occupation. He was a gentleman-amateur whose working methods were exactly the same as those of the Providence-born Joseph Brown. His work was more knowledgeable than Brown's because of his firsthand experience with English architecture and possibly because he had a wider range of architectural handbooks to serve him as models.

William Buckland was trained as a joiner and wood carver, and it was his talent and skill in this field which brought him into prominence in eighteenth-century American architecture. He not only designed buildings, but also ran a joiner's shop; in addition, he was actively engaged in supervision of construction and in the execution of architectural detail. For this work he received full compensation. Buildings were not something which he did in his spare time; they occupied the whole of his time

FIGURE 112. *William Buckland. Hammond-Harwood House, Annapolis, Md., dining room, 1773–74.*

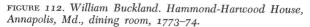

and creative energy. His working methods were similar to those of Richard Munday of Newport, and he therefore belongs to the same category of architect-builder; but the sophisticated quality of his work, when compared to the primitive boldness of Munday, marks the difference between the colonial and the English-born craftsman.

The popular image of colonial America in the eighteenth century is that of a dynamic and productive period in which heroic deeds were performed and the ingredients of modern American democracy were crystallized in thought and action. It is also viewed as a period of high cultural attainment; accordingly we are urged to understand the architecture of the period as an original style, peculiar to the colonies, and as fundamental to the development of American architecture as the *Mayflower Compact* was to the evolution of American political thought. Even though, as we have already seen, this was not the case, the idea is deeply rooted in the American legend. The degree to which it has permeated popular thought may be seen in the amorphous use of the word "colonial." It is used to describe any house that is painted white and has green shutters, or any piece of pine or maple furniture stained with an appropriate "Early American" color; and there is hardly a town in the country that does not have a subdivision of white boxes known as "Colonial Village." But this cult of the colonial is also manifest in a more authoritative and persuasive form: in the growing tendency to retrieve through restoration the image of the colonial past. A consummate example of this is Colonial Williamsburg. Here the visual semblance of eighteenth-century colonial society has been reproduced with remarkable fidelity at a fantastic cost. Moreover, it is presented in such a way as to convey the impression that here are to be found all the roots of modern American culture.

There is no doubt about either the fascination or the importance of Williamsburg. As a colonial capital it was the scene of some of the most important events in American history. It is thus a significant monument to our struggle for independence, and is worthy of being preserved. In terms of cultural history, however, the fact remains that it was the most thoroughly British segment of the eighteenth-century Atlantic seaboard; and its architecture, far from forming the basis of a new American style, represents the last flowering of the Wren-Baroque. It was this very British character which in part led Thomas Jefferson to denounce some of the Williamsburg buildings as "rude, misshapen piles which, but they have roofs, would be taken for brick kilns." It also inspired him, immediately following the Revolution, to propose a bill in the Virginia legislature which called for the moving of the capital from Williamsburg to Richmond. This bill was passed and Williamsburg was left to fall into ruin until the recent restorations brought it back to life as the mecca of the modern cult of the colonial.

Generally overlooked in the popular evaluation of eighteenth-century colonial architecture is motivation: what prompted men to build the way they did? Conservatism in artistic matters and a tendency to continue the traditional idiom are natural ingredients in any colonial society. This was particularly true in the American colonies, where close commercial ties were constantly maintained with the homeland, and where an ever-expanding frontier attracted a continuing flow of immigrants. Even in the urban centers along the Atlantic seaboard the residual elements of the raw frontier were still very much in evidence, and the attitudes which were formed thereby left little room for originality in architecture. The motivations of the eighteenth century, therefore, were basically the same as those of the seventeenth, and differ only in that they aspired toward higher and more up-to-date levels of architectural taste.

The changes in style which did occur were brought about largely through changing economic and social conditions. Increasing affluence led to a more discriminating patronage, and ambitions could only find fulfillment in the monumentality and elegance of the English Renaissance style. Nothing in the colonial environment offered equivalent possibilities. Men like Harrison and Buckland were familiar with current architectural developments in England. With the colonial patron, they made every effort to shape available materials into the image of English architecture. Their work is tasteful and authoritative, and is rendered with a fine sense of proportion and detail. Sometimes, as in the case of Buckland, it is enriched by a remarkable personal sensitivity; more often, in the frontier areas, academic formula was forgotten and the classical forms were warmed and enlivened by the uninhibited outpourings of the local craftsmen. But for the most part colonial architecture was imitative from beginning to end. Even the work of men like Buckland points no new directions, seeks no solutions which cannot be sustained by established tradition. Colonial society was totally devoid of that cultural curiosity which drives men to seek new architectural forms expressive of themselves; and colonial architecture, with all its visual delights and sentimental appeal, represents the end of a long and venerable tradition, not the beginning of a new one. Invention in American architecture was to be the prerogative of the nineteenth and twentieth centuries.

CHAPTER V

Other Colonial Manifestations: Baroque Transformations in the American Southwest

"Anybody might have found it, but—
His Whisper came to Me."
PADRE EUSEBIO FRANCESCO KINO

Both the practical and the theoretical impetus which initially shaped the cultural destiny of the United States came from England. Almost without exception the men who provided the leadership and made up the great body of the citizenry in the colonies of the eastern seaboard were Englishmen. They spoke the same language, and in spite of differences imposed by regional conditions, they thought and behaved in a similar manner; and those things which they fashioned to make life more livable had a character and quality which came directly from England.

This does not mean that other European nations did not establish colonies in North America. They did, and the architecture which they brought with them is part of the story. Some of these settlements, like the German and the Swedish, remained isolated cultural microcosms and are of local rather than national interest.[1] The colonizing efforts of Holland, however, were considerably more extensive, and Dutch holdings were ultimately to reach from Manhattan Island up the Hudson River as far as Albany.[2] Yet less than half a century after their first settlements in New Amsterdam, the Dutch were brought under British domination and so they, too, had little more than local effect on the subsequent cultural development of the nation. The provincial buildings which they scattered along the Hudson Valley and in the adjacent areas of New Jersey and Long Island are primarily important to the history of American architecture as rural survivals of the early international struggle for possession of the continent. Only the so-called "Dutch colonial house," with its sweeping gambrel roof, was to exert any influence on later American building. This type, which was as much Flemish and English in origin as it was Dutch, was moderately popular in the "colonial revival" of the early twentieth century.

In contrast to the quiet rural character of Dutch colonial buildings, the architecture of the Spanish settlements was dramatic; for it introduced into America the only authentic colonial version of the exuberant and lavish Catholic Baroque. Although the colonial phase of this European Baroque style reached its most elaborate form in Mexico during the eighteenth century, fascinating provincial variants are to be found in the missions and mission churches of the American Southwest. Here, the extravagant Baroque idiom was transformed by the techniques of the native Indians into a wholly new and original style.

To fix this movement in time, we must remember first that New Mexico, the forty-seventh state to be admitted to the Union, was settled by the Spanish at the same time as the first English colony at Jamestown. The colonization of the American Southwest was actually the last phase of a century of exploration and conquest which brought under Spanish domination one of the most far-reaching empires in the annals of the human race. Following dreams of gold and glory, and seeking to spread the Christian doctrine, the Spanish conquistadors and monks hacked their way through the whole of Central and South America; and before the establishment of the first English settlements on the Atlantic seaboard they had explored the entire southern section of the United States from Florida to California. The gold and glory never materialized for the Spaniards in the American Southwest, since the barren reaches of the area yielded no material treasures. On the other hand, the Southwest did offer fertile fields for spiritual conquest. The Pueblo tribes, which occupied the whole area of the upper Rio Grande, were sedentary people who lived in primitive villages and made their living from the soil. Peaceful and receptive, they proved susceptible converts to the Christian faith. In the late sixteenth century, therefore, when the Spanish settlements in Mexico reached the Rio Grande, the conquest of the Pueblos became feasible and the colonization of the upper Rio Grande in what we now know as New Mexico began.[3]

The Spanish colonization of the Southwest was essentially a missionary movement. Franciscan friars made their way into the Pueblo villages to establish missions, to heal the sick, to instruct in reading and writing, and to introduce European methods of cultivation. By 1626, they had built forty-three churches in the region of present-day New Mexico and had converted some thirty-four thousand Indians to Christianity. Civil authority was also established, but its rule was marred by cruelty and exploitation. The oppressions which the civil and military leaders imposed were sometimes met by fierce opposition from the friars and by open revolt on the part of the Indians. The governors and soldiers, therefore, remained apart from the communal and mission life, and their role in the development of the architecture of the region was negligible.

The mission buildings of New Mexico present a remarkable fusion of European and indigenous ideas. The most ambitious among them were the churches. These, of course, were planned by the friars; and since the Catholic doctrine had requirements with respect to church form, the missionaries sought to retain as many traditional features as possible. Drastic limitations were imposed by the new environment, however, and in the end many aspects of the churches—their shape, texture, and color, as well as their structural character—were determined by the Indians who built them. The fact that New Mexico churches were built by the Pueblo Indians gave them qualities of primitivism which made them totally unlike the colonial churches on the eastern seaboard. Although many of the early English buildings were of necessity crude, they were built by men trained in a long tradition of highly developed skills using sophisticated tools, and in appearance they conveyed something of that tradition.

There was none of this in the New Mexico churches. The Pueblos, in spite of the fact that they lived in communities, were still a primitive people; and like all primitive men they used materials without pretense in the simplest possible way. Thus, when called upon by the Spanish monks to build their churches, the Pueblos relied entirely on those materials most common to their culture—adobe and wood; and these they worked with only the crudest tools in a bold and primitive way. Although the friars might have preferred to build with more permanent and impressive materials, they had no choice. The Indian population and its natural resistance to change, the meager economy and inhospitality of the land, the primitive nature of frontier society, all these precluded the possibility of sophisticated building techniques, even though more permanent materials, such as stone, were readily available.

Of the native materials, adobe was the most characteristic of the region. Used in the majority of semiarid countries since prehistoric times, it consists of clay soil mixed with straw or manure and shaped into bricks by means of a wooden mold. These bricks are dried in the sun and then laid up in walls with mud as a mortar. The surfaces of the walls are covered with a wet mixture of clay, which is smoothed by hand. Adobe is an ideal material for hot, dry climates. Because of its dry, porous nature it is highly effective as insulation. Moreover, it has considerable strength, and although susceptible to weather erosion, it is easily and cheaply repaired.

The Pueblos, who were distinguished from the nomadic tribes by their villages, used adobe for most of their building.[4] Their huge communal dwellings (Fig. 113), which were piled up in ascending terraces, sometimes reached to the height of four and five stories. Because they were adobe, these complex housing units were characterized by bold but irregular massing, by walls which taper in slightly toward the flat roofs, and by the almost total absence of windows. They were devoid of ornament of any kind; surfaces were rough and corners were round. The roofs were supported on closely spaced logs embedded in the top of the wall. Intermittently these logs were permitted to project beyond the wall to form one of the most characteristic features of Pueblo construction. A mesh of light poles and brush laid athwart the beams carried the adobe roof. The outer walls were extended above the roof as a low parapet, and for drainage the roof was pitched slightly toward an outside waterspout.

These primitive dwellings were the indigenous architecture which the Spanish found when they arrived in the Pueblo country. The influence of the Indian techniques was felt at once in the first important building which the Spaniards erected in colonial America, the Governor's Palace

FIGURE *113. Taos Pueblo,*
Taos, N.M.

at Santa Fe (Fig. 114). Built between 1610 and 1614, it has low massing, plain slanting walls, projecting roof and beams, and warm sunburned color, all of them Indian features. In contrast, the long, cloister-like loggia which fronts the building is Spanish. Here, the flat adobe roof rests on a continuous wooden beam which is supported by a range of round wooden posts topped by crudely carved brackets. The regular rhythm of these posts imparts a degree of visual order which was unknown in the Pueblo villages, and thus asserts its European origin. But the general workmanship is that of the primitive Indian, and everywhere the strict imposed order of the loggia is warmed by the earth-bound roundness of the adobe.

San Estevan, Acoma

Adobe has a natural quality of largeness, and under the guidance of the Franciscans this quality was exploited to the utmost, particularly in the mission churches where simple largeness became monumentality. Among the earliest and most impressive of these is the Church of San Estevan in Acoma, New Mexico (Fig. 115). Situated high on a mesa overlooking the surrounding desert, and immediately adjacent to the ancient pueblo, it occupies one of the most spectacular sites in the Southwest. It was begun about 1629, but all materials had to be carried from considerable

FIGURE 114. Governor's Palace,
Santa Fe, N.M., 1610–14.

FIGURE 115. San Estevan,
Acoma, N.M., c. 1629–c. 1642.

distance up the steep, rocky trail to the mesa top, and actual construction was slow. It was not completed until about 1642. San Estevan is adobe throughout, and in the upper portions, where the protective surface has eroded, the adobe bricks are clearly visible.

The façade is a severe slanting surface broken only by a small central window and a door. It is flanked on either side by boldly projecting square towers which taper slightly toward blunt tops. The two belfries have rectangular openings. Attached to the north side, around an open patio, are the low walls of the *convento,* or living quarters, which faintly recall the cloisters of medieval Europe. These walls, the heavy flanking towers, and the long mass of the nave, which narrows toward the altar, are all traditional features of the Catholic church. But the construction and quality of San Estevan are not. The thick walls with rounded corners, and the rough irregular surfaces speak of the primitive hands of the Indians. Forms are no more refined here than they were in the Pueblo villages. Yet these same qualities of largeness and roughness, when combined with the symmetry dictated by the friars, assumed a new and imposing dignity; on the other hand, the time-worn European forms were given a new life by the fresh and uninhibited vitality of the Indian techniques.

The European ideas came into the American Southwest from Mexico, but the original source was the architecture of Spain. The twin-tower façade of San Estevan is a case in point. The origin of the twin-tower façade can be traced back in the history of the Christian church to medieval times when it was used in the great cathedrals for both its emotional appeal and its symbolic connotations. Although partially superseded during the High Renaissance by the dome, it never completely lost favor and by the turn of the seventeenth century it was a major characteristic of the larger churches of Spain and Mexico. Because of the dramatic visual possibilities of the twin-tower scheme it was particularly compatible with the intensely emotional religious attitudes of the Spanish. This combined with their taste for elaborate, colorful surfaces—a taste no doubt engendered in part by the ancient Moorish domination of Spain—caused the twin-tower façade to become the focus of extravagant ornamentation, a practice which reached its most ebullient phase during the eighteenth century in Mexico, and which, as we shall see, was to have its effect on the later churches of the American Southwest.

There is nothing of this yet, of course, in the unadorned towers of San Estevan. Built in the early seventeenth century, in the very years when Spanish architecture was itself cast in a severely classical mode, the little New Mexico church has a rectilinearity and breadth of proportion, even in the squared-off towers, which proclaim a classical rather than a Baroque heritage. Indeed it is reminiscent of the first great Mexican cathedrals, of which the Cathedral of La Asuncion de Maria in Mexico City is typical. This complex church was begun in the late sixteenth century, when strong Renaissance tendencies still prevailed in the architecture of Mexico, and the horizontal emphasis and short towers of San Estevan are a remote reflection of this fact.

Unlike its contemporary, St. Luke's in Virginia (Fig. 17), which
brought to America the last shadow of the authentic Gothic line of descent,
San Estevan is one of the first classically inspired buildings in the colonies.
This comparison is informative, for not only was the Protestant taste of
the English colonies conservative, but the Renaissance came to England
more than half a century later than it did to Spain, and San Estevan,
in spite of its rough, primitive character, was a more modern building
than any on the eastern seaboard. So, too, in its fanatic zeal the Spanish
Counter Reformation was more aggressive than the restrained Anglicanism
of tidewater Virginia. Only in the radical Separatist atmosphere of the
seventeenth-century New England communities were the creative forces
of the Reformation to manifest themselves in original architectural form.
The New England meetinghouse, with its overt rejection of all emotional
and symbolic elements, stood as a militant challenge to both the English
parish church of the South and the Catholic mission of the Southwest.

San Jose, Old Laguna Pueblo

Another revealing mission in the New Mexico field is that of San Jose in
Old Laguna Pueblo (Fig. 116). The mission itself was founded in 1699

FIGURE 117. *Augustinian Church,
Acolman, Mexico, façade, 1560.*

FIGURE 118. *San Jose,
Old Laguna Pueblo, N.M., ceiling.*

and the church was completed in 1706, but in spite of the fact that it is later than Acoma, it actually represents a less advanced style. This is seen first in the façade, which is a perfectly plain wall without flanking towers. It is more vertical than San Estevan and rises above the flat roof of the main body of the church as a bell screen, which is shaped like a stepped gable with small flanking turrets on either corner. Two symmetrical rectangular openings contain the bells.

Both the freestanding bell screen and the turrets are familiar features of Mexican monastic architecture of the sixteenth century. The severe vertical façade of the Augustinian Church at Acolman is typical (Fig. 117). It was built in 1560, and with its bell screen and turreted parapet it is remarkably like San Jose. But where the Mexican church has a handsome sculptural portal, the one at Old Laguna is totally devoid of ornament. As at San Estevan the European-Mexican forms have been drastically simplified by the primitive Indian building technique. Here the walls are made of rough field stone rather than adobe brick, but the stones are laid with adobe mortar and are covered with adobe plaster, so the visual effects are exactly the same. Corners are rounded, and in the relentless raking sunlight of the high country the surfaces not only look rough but also seem to undulate in gentle irregular waves.

On the interior, San Jose is one of the most rewarding churches in the Southwest. The nave is a long narrow rectangular space oriented toward the altar. Its origin in the Christian churches of Europe is obvious enough. The construction, however, and the treatment of the side walls are entirely the work of the Indians. In the ceiling (Fig. 118), which is characteristic Pueblo construction, the heavy crossbeams, or vigas, are simple logs supported by crudely carved wooden brackets which in turn are embedded in the stone and adobe walls. The thin cedar poles which actually carry the adobe roof are laid diagonally across the main beams in a herringbone pattern, a technique dating back to the earliest days of Pueblo culture. The vigorous alternating directional effect which this creates is accentuated even further by the fact that the diagonal poles are painted in broad bands of red, yellow, white, and black. Both aesthetically and symbolically this eccentric rhythm is in direct conflict with the traditional character of the nave; for not only does this lateral movement contradict the main directional thrust of the nave toward the altar, but also, through its angular oscillation, it denies the basic symmetry of the space by obliterating any possible reference in the ceiling to the central longitudinal axis.

Equally bold, and equally un-European are the mural decorations which line the walls of the nave (Fig. 119). Running down each side at dado height is a continuous band of symbolic images, some curved and some terraced and angular like great mounds of earth and rock, but all derived from Pueblo mythology. They are drawn in abstract patterns of earth colors and black against the white walls, and in their dynamic accented rhythms they are the exact counterpart in applied painted decoration both to the undulating pattern of the ceiling and to the stark primitive shapes of the building itself.

FIGURE 119. *San Jose,*
Old Laguna Pueblo, N.M., Indian wall painting.

The chancel of San Jose is formed by a slight inward break in the angle of the side walls and is separated from the nave by a simple chancel rail of crude balusters. These are cut in profile rather than turned and are painted in contrasting colors. At the end of the chancel and filling the entire wall behind the altar, is a primitive reredos (Fig. 120). Partly architectural and partly painted, it is totally different in both concept and technique from the Indian wall paintings and bears instead a direct relationship with the great altar screens of the Spanish Baroque era, especially those in colonial Mexico (Fig. 142). The lower section is divided into three vertical panels by four spiral columns carved in full relief. The rest of the surface is painted and further divided into panels by bands of floral, geometric, and architectural ornamentation. In the central panel, at the top, is a large painted image of the Holy Trinity; between the columns in the lower section are St. Joseph with the Christ Child in the center, St. Francis on the left, and St. Agatha on the right. The color is strong, with reds, yellows, greens, and blues predominating.

The reredos at San Jose, although unusual in New Mexico, is typical of a group found elsewhere in the mission churches of the Southwest. Because of the crude manner in which they are executed, these remarkable altar screens have long been considered the work of the Indians, produced under the guidance of Spanish priests. In the New Mexico churches the use of adobe and the close similarities in form with the buildings of the Pueblo villages leave no doubt as to Indian workmanship. An analysis of the altar screens, however, reveals no such affinity with the indigenous artistic idiom of the Indians. This is best illustrated by a stylistic comparison between the altar screen and the nave paintings in San Jose at Old Laguna (Figs. 119, 120). The Indian paintings are flat, simple, geometric, and they are large in scale. The various mythological symbols are conceived entirely in the abstract and are arranged in a random running band along the length of the wall. By contrast, the design of the reredos is symmetrical and is compartmented with major vertical and horizontal divisions. The columns rest on pedestals and carry individual entablature blocks which terminate in spiral finials. The corners of the top panel are cut off by reciprocal diagonals which create the effect of a truncated pediment. In the reredos too, the human figure, which is conspicuously lacking in the Indian murals, is the principal pictorial motif. Although crudely drawn, the figures show some understanding of human proportions and anatomical detail. Furthermore, the figures fill the panels in which they are placed, and the primitive drawing makes bold suggestions of a complex three-dimensionality.

In spite of its provincial awkwardness, the San Jose altar screen is conceptually humanistic and European, and shows not the slightest vestige of Indian primordial simplicity. In view of this, it seems impossible to associate the work with either Indian craftsmanship or Indian aesthetic principle. In fact, recent research has produced sufficient evidence to make it certain that these elaborate pieces of church furniture were the work of Spanish-American artists and not of the Indians.[5]

FIGURE 120. *San Jose,
Old Laguna Pueblo, N.M., reredos.*

Because of the varying role of the Indian in the Spanish colonial churches, the word "primitive," as applied to these buildings, raises certain questions. As used in art criticism, the term sometimes denotes the beginning of a stylistic evolution and implies a distortion of the norm in favor of exaggerated simplification rendered by narrow technical means. In such works the complex world of visual reality is transmuted into a system of abstract symbols in which shape is seen as outline and mass as flat pattern. It is precisely this view of the world that is evoked by the art of the Pueblo Indians. Seen in the over-all evolution of Western civilization, their architecture and their artifacts are but rude beginnings whose natural destiny was sealed forever by the Spanish conquest. The term "primitive," therefore, applies exactly to the visual character of the mission churches of New Mexico, whose rough adobe walls and log ceilings reduced to the level of primal simplicity the complex formal order of Spanish Baroque architecture.

When the term "primitive" is used to define the altar screens, no such conclusive meaning can be found, for the style of the altar screens is by no means simple. If we consider only the obvious deviations from the norm—the crude drawing and the reductions of the Baroque spatial involvements to a language of outline and flat pattern—then we are indeed confronted by the inarticulate gropings of a "primitive" artist. The term, in fact, is frequently used in precisely this sense. In the general evolution of style, however, a lack of knowledge and technical skill is not necessarily a symptom of primitivism. It can indicate termination as well as origin, disintegration as well as growth. This is certainly true in the case of the altar screens, for here we are not confronted with the beginning of a style but rather with its end. These ancient paintings represent a passive acceptance of long-established and familiar conventions, a peripheral effusion of style in which the luxuriant, profuse forms of the Spanish Baroque have been brought down to the level of folk art. Those crudities in execution, which have led some critics to deny that the altar pieces could have been made by "Christians" and to attribute them instead to the "primitive" Indian, are no more than the inevitable consequences of provincial craftsmanship under the conditions of a frontier society. Like St. Luke's Church in Virginia, the Spanish-American altar pieces do not belong to the early stages of an indigenous American art form, but rather to the last colonial attenuation of an European style, in this case the Spanish Baroque.

St. Francis of Assisi, Ranchos de Taos

Primitive Indian building materials and methods continued to dominate the form of the mission churches of the New Mexico field for the rest of the Spanish colonial period. The rude but massive adobe walls of the church in the St. Francis of Assisi Mission at Ranchos de Taos (Fig. 121), built as late as 1805–15, show no marked advance over the seventeenth- and eighteenth-century churches. Currently surrounded by dilapidated and meager buildings which detract from its wonder, the austere, simple church

FIGURE 121. St. Francis of Assisi,
Ranchos de Taos, N.M., apse end, 1805–15.

is nevertheless immensely moving. It is situated on a high plateau more than nine thousand feet above sea level. With blue-shadowed stony peaks towering to thirteen thousand feet on one side, and with an endless sloping stretch of piñon-studded tableland on the other, it grows from the earth like the mountains that rise to frame it, and scatters the hard light of the high country from the molded surfaces of its earthen walls. It models the space around it. The symmetrical towers (Fig. 122) of the main façade are supported by enormous, clumsy buttresses; a similar massive buttress presses against the end wall of the sanctuary. At the lateral extremities strange curved buttresses, shaped like beehives, wrap themselves around the corners. The church also has wide transepts which rise slightly above the roof level of the nave. Seen from the west end, the bold tapering masses, unbroken by window openings, pile up into an impressive complex of rough, warm surfaces which seem to have been molded from the clay itself rather than built up with bricks.

Only in the bell towers, with their round-headed openings, in the general symmetry of the façade, and in the cruciform plan (Fig. 123) do the traditional forms of the Christian church assert themselves at Ranchos de Taos. The rest of the building is dominated by the simple architectural language of the Pueblos. The innate monumentality of adobe construction, which we have already referred to, is nowhere better epitomized than in the crude but massive walls of this mission church. Enormous

FIGURE 122. *St. Francis of Assisi,*
Ranchos de Taos, N.M., façade, 1805–15.

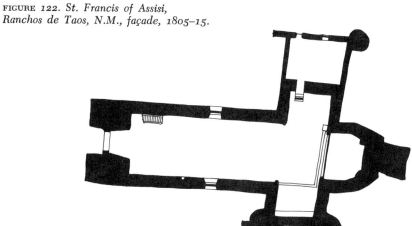

FIGURE 123. *St. Francis of Assisi,*
Ranchos de Taos, N.M., plan, 1805–15.

in scale and either flat or curving outward, they are totally devoid of projections or undercuttings. From the façade to the chancel buttress, the malleable clay has yielded to the pressure of the human hand, more in some places than others, but always amassing slowly upward and inward to embrace the inner sanctuary with the essence of the earth itself.

On the interior of Ranchos de Taos, which forsakes the drama of its setting for the mystery of the Mass, the hand of the Spanish priest is more in evidence. Although the walls and the great brackets supporting the crossbeams are still the work of the Indians, the long, narrow, dimly lit nave culminating in the altar is conceptually European. Even more so is the manner in which the transept and altar are lighted (Fig. 124). The transept roof is higher than that over the nave; in addition the nave ceiling lowers slightly as it moves toward the transept. The effect is of a gradual closing down of the shadowy nave as it approaches the altar. Immediately beyond, in the crossing, light from a hidden source floods the transept and the sanctuary (Fig. 125). This thoroughly Baroque technique of indirect lighting was made possible by inserting windows in the higher transept wall at the crossing where it passed above and at right angles to the nave. This particular method of lighting seems to have been peculiar to the churches of the upper Rio Grande.

The repoussoire effect of dark against light achieved at Ranchos de Taos was one commonly used by European Baroque artists for developing dramatic spatial contrasts, and it reached its most spectacular heights in the Trasparente in Toledo Cathedral, Spain.[6] In Baroque churches, the effect was generally accomplished by windows in the drum of the central dome. But since the Pueblo Indians never mastered the techniques of vaulting, the Spanish priests resorted to the simple but effective solution of the hidden lateral window. Even in some of the churches without transepts, the roof was raised immediately in front of the sanctuary to permit the insertion of such a window. The effect of an indirect light source was dramatic, playing deliberately on the emotions, and its use in the New Mexico churches was one of the most important manifestations of the Catholic Baroque in American colonial architecture.

The stark, elemental masses of Ranchos de Taos (Fig. 121), brought into bold relief by the fierce New Mexico sun, have led several critics to compare the building to contemporary abstract sculpture. Extremely important in creating this impression are the slight irregularities which disturb the fundamental symmetry of the building and give it an assertive, dynamic character. This affinity with modern sculpture is fascinating and real, but in evaluating the building as a work of architecture, it should not be given undue importance. For those visual qualities which give the church its "modern" look are the same which make it primitive. In modern sculpture, the irregularities of form are deliberate, in the adobe churches of the Rio Grande they were accidental—no more a part of a conscious design intention than was the stress upon the natural qualities of materials which we observed in the seventeenth-century New England house. A piece of modern sculpture is fashioned by a sophisticated creative artist with highly developed manual skills; the walls of the mission churches were built by primitive Indian women; and in spite of certain obvious similarities, the results could hardly be farther apart in either quality or intentions.

The analogy between the mission churches and sculpture is more rewarding if it is pointed not toward the modern world but toward the world of the Indians themselves. One of the most ancient forms of sculpture and the only one used by the Pueblos was pottery: in its elementary shapes it is similar to their architecture, and the actual techniques of pottery and adobe are essentially the same. Both are made of malleable clay wrought

FIGURE 124. St. Francis of Assisi,
Ranchos de Taos, N.M., detail of elevated crossing, 1805–15.

FIGURE 125. St. Francis of Assisi,
Ranchos de Taos, N.M., window in elevated crossing, 1805–15.

into shape by the human hands, and considered in terms of materials and structure, an adobe building is little more than an enormous pot. Coarse clay molded by the human hands without tools does not lend itself to delicate and intricate development, and in primitive hands, undirected by high and formal concepts, it remains outward-curving and bulbous, elemental and crude. It is precisely because of this that no ornamental elaboration of surface other than painting is to be found in the mission churches of New Mexico.

The Missions of Texas and Arizona

There can be no doubt that the Franciscan friars who established the missions on the upper Rio Grande in New Mexico would have preferred the expressive extravagance of their native Spanish Baroque. Since they relied entirely upon the Indians for the construction of their churches, however, this was impossible. Only on the interiors and in the altar screens do we find blurred suggestions of the unrestrained and florid European style. In the mission churches of South Central Texas, however, the situation was different. Here there were no communal Indians with developed building crafts of their own. Instead, it was necessary to bring in skilled artisans and to use the Indians for only the most rudimentary labor. As a result, the Texas churches were more European in character than were those in New Mexico.

The Alamo

Many missions were established by the Spaniards in South Central Texas, but the most important ones are a group of five clustered in the vicinity of San Antonio.[7] Of these, the most famous is the Alamo (Fig. 126), a building which played an enormously significant role in the history of

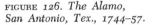

FIGURE 126. The Alamo, San Antonio, Tex., 1744–57.

FIGURE 127. The Alamo,
San Antonio, Tex., detail of door, 1744–57.

Texas. Begun in 1744, it was not finished until 1757. Unlike the churches
of New Mexico, it was built of stone and the main body of the church
was roofed by a barrel vault and dome. It also had symmetrical towers
flanking the façade. Five years after it was completed the vaults and
towers collapsed, and all that survives today are the walls and the façade.

The principal differences between the churches of Texas and New Mexico may be clearly seen in the Alamo. In the central portion of the façade
we recognize at once the remains of a stepped and curved gable not unlike the one at San Jose in Old Laguna, and like Acoma and Ranchos de
Taos it had flanking towers; but since the building is made of stone and
not adobe, it has a greater exactness of form, with all wall openings
crisply defined. It also has a more complex three-dimensional quality. The
main door (Fig. 127) is flanked by two concave niches between pairs
of spiral columns, and the whole is topped with a full entablature. This
sculptural treatment, cutting into and projecting out from the wall, would
have been impossible for Indian craftsmen working in adobe, but it posed
no special problems for the Spanish-American sculptor working in stone.
Although somewhat clumsy in execution, the façade of the Alamo brings
to the frontier several significant aspects of Spanish architecture, especially as it was developed in colonial Mexico.

We shall turn again to the church at Acolman for comparison (Fig.
128). The single arched opening flanked by paired engaged columns is
a compositional device which occurs in numerous Mexican churches, and

FIGURE 128. *Augustinian Church,*
Acolman, Mexico, detail of door, 1560.

although the Alamo has no figural sculpture it does have niches between
the columns, and at the bottom of each is a pedestal which may have
been intended for sculpture. In contrast to the ornamental elaboration of
the Acolman portal that of the Alamo is relatively simple and severe. Yet
for its provincial setting it has a considerable plastic richness, especially
in such individual parts as the spiral columns, and in the sharp interlacing
linear ornament which rests loosely on the surface of the wall. This ornament, which breaks in lacelike patterns around the niches and the door,
is particularly Spanish. No clear necessity seems to determine either its
character or its location. It is neither organically related to structure, as
in Gothic architecture, nor is it systematically part of a total harmony,
as in the architecture of the great classical periods.[8]

   This independent applied decoration may be traced back to the intricate interlace ornament introduced into Spain during the years of Moorish
domination. It first became significant in Spanish architecture with the
development of the Plateresque style of the early sixteenth century. It is
called Plateresque because of its resemblance to the art of the silversmith.
In characteristic work of this period, the ornament is organized in isolated
clusters without regard for the unity of the whole, so that these clusters
seem to be suspended against rather than coherently a part of the wall.
It is this type of ornament which is so vividly displayed in both Acolman
and the Alamo.

   During the late seventeenth and the early eighteenth century, this principle of isolation was vitalized by an infusion of Baroque exuberance. The

decorative clusters became more expansive, both in size and in three-dimensional complexity. Structural elements were interrupted, fractured, and separated by a convulsive proliferation of garlands and swags, of foliation, fruit, and drapery; forms projected and receded, passed into shadow and back into the light in swelling, sensuous rhythms (Fig. 135). Although each of these fantastic islands of exaggerated sculptural richness was within itself organized according to the classical principles of symmetry and order, it was at the same time set against a plain wall of an entirely different texture and color, so that both its isolation and its extravagance were heightened by contrast. For sheer sumptuous beauty, Spanish decorative sculpture of the Baroque era is· matched in Europe only in the eighteenth-century churches of Bavaria.

The most extreme limits of this style were not reached in Spain itself but in colonial Mexico. Somewhat less undulating and three-dimensional, the ornamental involvements were frequently sharper and more florid, and the individual decorative clusters more profusely applied. As in Spain, entrance portals received the most prolific treatment, but towers and window openings were also copiously adorned. Characteristic of the style at its height is the mid-eighteenth-century church of Santa Prisca y San Sebastian in Taxco (Fig. 145). This fantastic church is one of the most arresting in the world. Built between 1751 and 1758, and paid for by a rich mining magnate, Jose de la Borda, its rose-colored walls and towers rise high against the mountain skies in a sparkling crescendo of sculptural outpouring. As an extravagant Baroque performance, nothing comparable in quality would appear in the American Southwest. But as a church type, tall in proportions and with convulsive ornament set against simple walls, it epitomizes the Mexican parish churches of the eighteenth century, and these would leave their mark emphatically on the American mission churches.

San Jose, San Antonio

Various provincial manifestations of this exuberant phase in Spanish Baroque architecture are found in the mission churches of Texas. Of these, by far the most aspiring was the church of San Jose y San Miguel de Aguayo in the mission valley near San Antonio. The mission itself was founded in 1720 by Fray Antonio Margil, one of the most courageous Franciscan pioneers, and was dedicated to the Marquis of San Miguel de Aguayo, then Governor of Texas. The church was begun in the same year and finished in 1731. The mission complex forms an enormous quadrangle embracing approximately eight acres and is completely enclosed by buildings and walls. It has been recently restored and is superbly maintained in such a way as to convey much of what it once must have been.

The church of San Jose (Fig. 129) is the most authentic surviving example of the European Catholic Baroque in America. Seen on a sunlit afternoon through the gray-green lace of the mesquite and flowering acacia trees, its bold planes and vivacious sculptured masses seem suspended in a flood of gold and violet light. Yet it has weight and density. The

FIGURE 129. *San Jose y San Miguel de Aguayo,*
San Antonio, Tex., 1720–31.

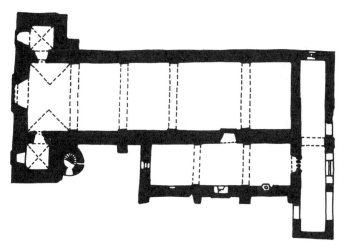

FIGURE 130. *San Jose y San Miguel de Aguayo,*
San Antonio, Tex., plan, 1720–31.

main body of the building is a long, narrow nave flanked on the entrance end by two towers and terminating in the sanctuary (Fig. 130). In these respects it is similar to many of the mission churches of New Mexico. But here the affinity ends. Instead of adobe, it was built throughout of rough tufa (porous limestone) masonry, surfaced with stucco. But more important, the interior space was entirely vaulted (Fig. 131). The first three bays of the nave and the sanctuary were roofed by groined vaults; over the fourth bay was a hemispherical dome sixty feet high which was carried on an octagonal drum. After the mission was secularized in 1794, the church was allowed to fall into ruin, and in the late nineteenth century, the vaults and dome collapsed, but on the basis of records, old photographs, and a few surviving vaults in the mission complex, it was possible to restore the church with reasonable accuracy.

There is no evidence whatever of Indian building methods in this church. Although the Indians provided most of the manual labor, the building is European in both form and structure, and it is certain that the design, supervision, and to a large extent the execution of the vaults must have been done by trained Spanish-American artisans. In terms of interior spatial effects, the dramatic break in the long, horizontal nave created by the soaring volume of the dome is particularly Baroque. There were windows in four sides of the octagonal drum, which brought a greater concentration of light into the vertical domed area than into any other part of the church. This source not only served to bring light to the sanctuary, which had, in addition, its own windows high on each of the side walls, but it also set up an evocative contrast between the lower, shadowy area of the nave's groined vaults and the rising, more brightly illuminated volume of the dome. As we have already seen, this Baroque effect of dark against light was achieved in the more primitive adobe churches of the Rio Grande by the lateral clerestory. At San Jose the vault replaces the primitive wooden roof making possible a vertical extension of the interior space into the dome. Here windows in the drum provide a more Baroque source of secondary illumination.

But this is not all that is Baroque about San Jose. Here, too, for the first time in colonial America, we encounter the fully developed Spanish Baroque church façade (Fig. 129). A rich two-story sculptural portal (c. 1730) is set between flanking towers, which in turn are topped by equally elaborate sculptural belfries. Although only one of the flanking towers at San Jose was ever carried to its full height, the building was obviously designed to have two.[9] As they appear today these towers are random ashlar masonry with dressed corners, but originally they were surfaced with stucco and painted in quatrefoil patterns of alternating red and blue. In the center of these quatrefoils, and placed diagonally between them, are abstract floral motifs of red, blue, and yellow. A fragment of this surface treatment still remains at the base of the southeast tower (Fig. 132). Originally, it covered the entire outside wall of the church.

In opposition to the full three-dimensionality of the sculptured portal, this painted decoration remains flat against the white stucco background,

FIGURE 131. *San Jose y San Miguel de Aguayo,*
San Antonio, Tex., interior, 1720–31.

and from the distance creates the sparkling illusion of a tile surface. The
contrast within the portal, therefore, is not only between sculpture in the
round and its flat painted setting, but also between fully developed
natural forms and abstract geometry. The illusion of tile suggests the
Moorish element in Spanish history, and the vigorous opposition of two
entirely different decorative concepts—found so frequently in the eighteenth-century churches of Mexico—strengthens even further the marked
isolation of the portal motif.

The elaborate sculptured portal was intended to have its counterpart
in the belfries of the flanking towers. The surviving southeast tower has
an open belfry of dark sandstone (Fig. 133) which was obviously supposed
to have been embellished with carved ornament. This decorative work
was never executed, but the intentions are clear since the flat blocks
of stone, which project from the piers, are cut into preliminary curvilinear
profiles.

The portal of San Jose was unique in colonial America, and this is
so primarily because it was entirely sculptural (Fig. 134). It was unlike

FIGURE 132. San Jose y San Miguel de Aguayo,
San Antonio, Tex., detail of wall decoration, 1720–31.

the portals of the hybrid New Mexico churches, which, as we have just seen, were left free of ornament to accommodate the untutored hands of the Pueblo Indians (Fig. 122). It was also unlike the chaste doorways of the eighteenth-century churches in the English colonies, rendered as they were in architectural rather than sculptural terms (Fig. 99). Moreover, the portal of San Jose is a figural design, symbolically conceived and dynamically executed. The use of the human figure in the New Mexico churches was technically impossible; in the colonial churches of the eastern seaboard it was conceptually impossible. The anti-image attitudes of the Reformation, which led during the Cromwellian Revolution to the decimation of the figural sculpture on so many of the English cathedrals, forced English architects to reject the rich sculptural language of the Middle Ages and to think instead in purely architectonic terms. Consequently English churches of the Baroque era, beginning with the Wren London churches in the late seventeenth century, made no use of figural sculpture whatsoever; and if this was true in England itself, it was even more so in the colonies where in many parts radical Separatist views prevailed.

But the portal of San Jose is not only elaborately figural, it is also aggressively anti-architectural, so much so in fact that instead of appearing as an integral part of the building, it seems rather to be in motion before it. In this it is characteristically Spanish and thoroughly Baroque. Although the portal is both central and symmetrical, and is thus related to the axial design of the church itself, the forms are developed almost as sculpture in the round in boldly projecting relief (Fig. 136). Furthermore, the light brown sandstone from which they are carved has innate qualities of softness which deny its solidity, and because of the animation of the carving and the scintillating activity of the sunlight, the forms seem to emerge from the translucent shadows not as stone but as warm, malleable substance capable of movement and growth. Even though the portal is divided horizontally in the center by a heavy and complex entablature, the architectural elements are so fractured, diverted, and transmuted by the swelling three-dimensional rhythms of the figural and foliated ornament that they renounce altogether any identification with structure and become instead an ecstatic choir in which the saints of heaven are joined with the world of nature in a triumphant song of praise.

Because of the inordinate decorative richness of the San Jose portal it is tempting to seek its corollary in the ornate façades of the eighteenth-century churches in Mexico (Fig. 147). But the rich density of the carving and the three-dimensional largeness of the ornament give it a greater plasticity and a sumptuousness that are unequaled in the brittle, sparkling intricacies of the Mexican façades. It therefore seems more Spanish. This becomes even more apparent when we compare the Texas portal to one of the great Spanish works of the period, Pedro de Ribera's portal on the Hospicio de San Fernando (1722) in Madrid (Fig. 135). Here we find not only similar qualities of form but also corresponding decorative devices, such as the vertical oval opening. The carving at San Jose, although inferior to that of the Spanish portal, is of unusually high quality

FIGURE 133. San Jose y San Miguel de Aguayo, San Antonio, Tex., detail of south belfry, 1720–31.

FIGURE 134. San Jose y San Miguel de Aguayo,
San Antonio, Tex. Portal sculpture by Pedro Huizar, c. 1730.

for its frontier environment, and together with the stylistic evidence, strongly suggests that the portal was designed and executed by a Spanish sculptor imported for the purpose. This notion is reinforced by the legend which attributes the work to a young Spaniard, Pedro Huizar, who also carved the equally beautiful baptistry window of San Jose (Fig. 137). The legend also tells us that the two works occupied him for approximately eighteen years and that, rejected by his sweetheart because of his prolonged absence from Spain, he died in Texas of a broken heart.

Pedro Huizar in Texas represents the same type of colonial artist as his contemporary in Maryland, William Buckland. Like Buckland, he was born and trained in Europe, and in his work aspired toward a complete identification with European concepts expressed through European techniques. Like Buckland, too, he was an artist of impressive personal talent and brought to the frontier unique professional qualifications. Yet in terms of European values, he was not an artist of the first rank. Compared with the production of the best eighteenth-century sculptors working in Spain, his San Jose portal is thin, sometimes crude in detail, and

FIGURE 135. *Pedro de Ribera. Hospicio de San Fernando, Madrid, portal, 1722.*

generally lacking in that sumptuous, expansive grandeur which is characteristic of the best Spanish work. The figures, too, have a reverse-curve sweep and elegance, seen especially in St. Joseph to the left of the main door and in the Virgin in Glory above (Fig. 134), which is more reminiscent of late Gothic sculpture than it is of the full-blown Baroque. All of this makes his work outmoded, and touched, as is Buckland's, by that marked provincialism which separates them both from the high style accomplishments in their respective homelands. Like all colonial art, Huizar's is reflective rather than generative, terminal rather than original, seeking both its idiom and its authority in the past.

Although Huizar and Buckland represent the same type of colonial artist, their respective styles are separated by an unbridgeable ideological gulf. Huizar's work at San Jose is the most authentic and moving survival in the colonies of the art of the Catholic Baroque. In its rich abundance, it could hardly be further removed from the calm, delicate classicism of the English middle-class Protestant, Buckland. A comparison between Huizar's portal and Buckland's door on the Hammond-Harwood House in Annapolis speaks for itself (compare Figs. 134 and 111). No more persuasive instrument of communication was available to the Catholic

FIGURE 136. *San Jose y San Miguel de Aguayo,*
San Antonio, Tex. Sculptured door surround by Pedro Huizar, c. 1730. Detail.

FIGURE 137. *San Jose y San Miguel de Aguayo,*
San Antonio, Tex. Sculptured baptistry window by Pedro Huizar, c. 1730.

church than the architecture of the Baroque era, and through the theatrical extravagance of such works as San Jose, the impassioned spiritual forces which carried the Spanish missionary friars into the formidable hardships and dangers of the Southwest were rendered tangible and articulate. The sumptuousness of the Spanish Baroque found justification in the enormous power and wealth of the Catholic Church, its overt sensuousness was sanctified by the mystical materialism of Ignatius Loyola's *Spiritual Exercises*. Though different in form, the architecture of the Atlantic seaboard was an equally powerful expression of the Protestant Reformation. Conservative, chaste, and self-conscious, it was an art of the middle class and of the individual, and sought its confirmation in the detached house and the town hall as well as in the church. The disparate beliefs which separate these two dynamic segments of eighteenth-century society are in some ways more directly revealed in the distilled forms of the colonial artist than they are in the more complex and demanding art of Europe itself.

San Xavier del Bac, Tucson

In the church of St. Francis of Assisi at Ranchos de Taos we discovered an expressive union of the Spanish Baroque with the adobe techniques of the Pueblos; in San Jose, San Antonio, we saw that same Spanish Baroque imposed upon the colonial environment, by a Spanish-born sculptor, with authoritative extravagance. In the grandiose but moving church of San Xavier del Bac, near Tucson, Arizona (Fig. 144), we find neither the bold mutations of Ranchos de Taos nor the flamboyant virtuosities of San Jose. For unlike San Jose, which was in San Antonio, the seat of the Spanish civil government of Texas, San Xavier stood on the northern fringes of the great Sonoran Desert, in a remote and desolate land where a hot dry sky is the roof of the world and a relentless sun its ruler. Even its name, "del Bac," a Spanish adaptation of an Indian place name meaning "where water runs into the ground," proclaims an isolation born of the need for water. Today, even though San Xavier is only nine miles from the tragically commercialized and bloated city of Tucson it is still sufficiently alone to indicate something of its original remoteness. Traveling south from the city toward the upper reaches of the Santa Cruz Valley, the muted yellows and greens of burnt grass and cactus stretch flat to a jagged horizon of transparent violet hills. Against these the mission of San Xavier appears in the distance with exaggerated clarity, a shimmering unreality rendered white and weightless by the cruel splendor of the desert light.

Because it was a child of the desert, there is nothing delicate or refined about San Xavier. Even though it was probably the most aspiring church in the Southwest, there was no Pedro Huizar at Bac to assure its conformity to the Spanish norm. Although the friars who built San Xavier had all been trained in Europe, they were men who had spent their active lives in the mission field. For them the lines of communication with Mexico and Spain were drawn thin by time and distance, and the image of Spanish architecture which they had brought with them, although passionately remembered and revered, was blurred. It was also a quarter of a century out of date. Then, too, like the anonymous craftsmen of Old Deerfield, Massachusetts, the artisans who actually did the work seem to have been men of the frontier. They were trained for their jobs by the friars, and in their brusque hands San Xavier took shape as a remarkable synthesis of Baroque grandeur and the privations of the desert.

Mission San Xavier del Bac was originally founded in 1700 by the courageous Jesuit priest, Eusebio Francisco Kino. It was one of the few Jesuit establishments in the Southwest. The first seventy years of its existence were filled with violence and destruction, and nothing remains of the early building efforts.[10] In 1767, for political reasons, the Jesuits were finally banished from the area, and shortly thereafter their work was taken up by the Franciscans. The present church was begun in 1784, but was not completed until 1797. According to one legend the design was prepared and carried out by two architects, the brothers Gaona, under the general supervision of Franciscan friars. There is no document to sustain this, but recent research proves without doubt that the church was begun by Padre Juan Bautista Velderrain, and was finished after his death (1789 or 1790) by Padre Juan Bautista Llorenz.[11] Most of the structural work seems to have been done by Indian labor, although there must have been skilled masons to lay up the vaults. The sculpture, and most of the painting, too, was certainly the work of Spanish-American artists. There remains the strong possibility that by this time a few of the more talented Indians may have been trained to do some of these more specialized tasks.

Conceptually and technically, San Xavier is European throughout. It is laid out with precise regularity in a cruciform plan (Fig. 138) with a short nave covered by two shallow oval domes oriented with their long dimensions across the church. Each transept, and the apse as well, has a single and similarly oriented oval dome. Above the crossing, however, is a higher circular dome carried on an octagonal drum (Fig. 139). Triangular squinches, flat rather than arched, accommodate the octagon of the drum to the square of the crossing. Both the walls and vaults of the church are made of burned brick covered with hard lime stucco. Above each of the squinches a quatrefoil window is cut into the drum thus bringing light directly to the vertical volume of the dome area. Small rectangular windows with scalloped tops are placed high on the wall on both sides of each bay of the nave, but there are no windows in either transept or in the chancel. Light for these important functional spaces comes indirectly from the windows just described in the drum of the dome.

All these effects of contrasting space and light are typically Baroque and remind one of certain features of San Jose, in San Antonio. But there are a number of important differences here which make San Xavier an even more ambitious church. It has a transept, for example, and instead of the more conventional groined vaults which appear over each bay of the nave at San Jose, San Xavier has the shallow oval domes just

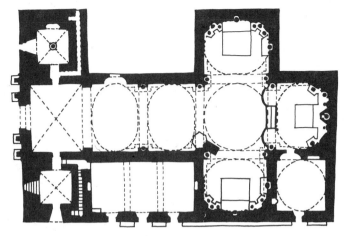

FIGURE 138. *San Xavier del Bac, Tucson, Ariz., plan, 1784–97.*

RE 139. *San Xavier del Bac, Tucson, ., view into crossing dome, 1784–97.*

FIGURE 140. *San Xavier del Bac, Tucson, Ariz., view into oval dome, 1784–97.*

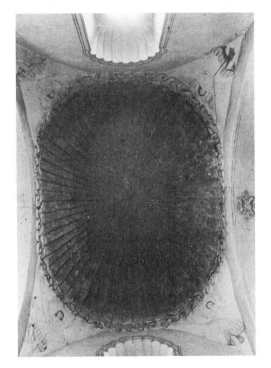

noted (Fig. 140). This latter device, because of the elegant rhythms of its constantly changing curvatures, was favored by many of the Baroque architects of Europe. Close examination reveals, however, that the oval domes at San Xavier are not in fact oval at all. Rather, the end curves are half circles and the long sides are straight. Arranged as they are, they form a rectangular space with circular ends. This overt simplification of an extremely complicated shape had the practical result of simplifying also the shape of the pendentives necessary to support the domes; and it obviated altogether the mathematical difficulties of constructing an elliptical shape. Although this is but one of the many provincialisms at San Xavier, and in a sense sets the tone of the entire church, it is visually effective. Together with the incised radiating lines, which are cut from the center of each dome to create the appearance of depth which is actually not there, the quasi-elliptical shape of the domes brings to the desert church yet another element of Baroque spatial illusionism.

Equally Baroque is the decorative treatment of the interior. There are a few simple sculptural effects, such as the incised ribs in the oval domes, and the curious, unorthodox, heavily molded entablatures at the spring of the arches; otherwise the main walls and vaulted surfaces of the church are perfectly plain. Window openings, however, are painted in crude imitation of molded surrounds, and in the pendentives and in other parts of the dome are figures of saints painted in bold flat patterns of neutral red, green, blue, and yellow. The outlines of these figures are sharp and curvilinear, and related ornamental features have a light, almost Rococo quality of interlocking reverse curves. The drawing of the figures, however, is crude to the point of being childish, and the forms remain flat, no effort whatsoever having been made to develop them in three dimensions.

In contrast to the primitive flatness and simplicity of the wall painting, the walls of the transepts and chancel are covered by a wild proliferation of polychrome sculpture of the most complex and exaggerated kind (Fig. 141). The slight interlocking curves just seen in some of the painted ornament in the vaults here become a riot of twisting interlocking forms which seem to crawl over the area in an agonized effort to exist in spaces many times too small for them. Against the wall behind the high altar, as a climax to this bizarre entanglement, is a fantastic carved and painted reredos. Executed in wood, gesso, paint, and gilt, it is matched in its visual abundance only by the great altar screens of Baroque Mexico, from which it obviously takes its inspiration. A characteristic example is the one at Taxco (Fig. 142). Although the San Xavier reredos is basically architectural, with rusticated columns, entablatures, and arches of varying profiles dividing the space into two levels of three vertical panels, the architectural elements are so fractured and redirected by incutting and appendages, so diversified in surface quality through both intricate carving and a constant interplay of contrasting texture and color, that the whole wall ceases to exist as something substantial and becomes instead a bewildering jungle of unworldly creatures, each vying with the other for its very existence (Fig. 143).

FIGURE 141. San Xavier del Bac,
Tucson, Ariz., reredos, c. 1795.

This sculptural fantasy provides the background for the two principal figures in the design, the Virgin enthroned in the upper level and St. Xavier below (Fig. 141). Under the protection of the Virgin and immediately above the altar St. Xavier stands serenely aloof from the turmoil around him, with sad eyes and a fierce black beard, and splendidly vested in a black alb and gleaming white outer tunic of silk and lace. In his hands he holds a crucifix. The startling visual plausibility of a polychrome sculptured figure arrayed in the actual habits of the Church, so typical of Spanish Baroque practices, creates the effect of reality in a world of total fantasy, which by its very incongruity makes the fantasy all the more unreal.

The exterior of San Xavier is a dramatic contrast of large simplicity and intricate abundance (Fig. 144). The twin-tower scheme with a dome over the crossing brings to the desert the characteristic theme of the Mexican eighteenth-century churches, such as Taxco (Fig. 145). But instead of the sparkling surface treatment found so frequently in the churches to the south, the wall planes of San Xavier are white painted stucco with

FIGURE 142. *Santa Prisca y San Sebastian,*
Taxco, Mexico, reredos, c. 1758.

the only decorative animation provided by a simple balustrade around
the base of each belfry, and a curved and voluted parapet crowning the
main body of the church. Otherwise the forms are large and ponderous,
yet curiously the heavy stucco, because of its whiteness and the penetrating power of the light, is transformed into a buoyant translucent substance which seems almost to hover in the blue and violet medium of the
desert air.

Against and within this world of unbroken whiteness rise the warm
sculptural intricacies of the portal. Two massively scaled identical towers
provide the frame. The upper two stages of these towers are octagonal, and
are set back from the base. Strange flying buttresses spring illogically
from the four square corner piers and terminate against the towers in
enormous flaring scrolls. The left tower is topped by a small dome and
lantern, and there can be no doubt that a similar crown was intended for
the right. Except for their molded cornices and balustrade, however, the
towers are as severely plain as the main body of the church itself.

FIGURE 143. San Xavier del Bac,
Tucson, Ariz., detail of reredos, c. 1795.

In utter contrast to the translucent simplicity of the towers, the portal is richly earth-bound and substantial (Fig. 146). Developed in polychrome as well as relief, it projects and recedes boldly in small increments into and out of space. Unlike the white walls, which reflect the light in all its pervasive luminosity, the portal embraces it, scatters it, denies it, and in the end transforms it with something of itself. The general visual impression is of a spatial and material abundance identical to that of the reredos on the inside (Fig. 141). There is one important difference, however. Where the reredos glitters, the portal absorbs. Instead of gilt it is made of a neutral red-orange brick, elaborately carved, molded, and painted. Forms are larger, therefore, and more slow moving, and surfaces are rougher. Like the reredos, on the other hand, it is basically architectural; it is also divided horizontally and vertically by segmented columns and entablatures, and it culminates at the top in a massive reverse-curve pediment with grotesquely large scrolls. The sculptural ornament, however, is flatter and less convoluted than that of the reredos, and the carving and modeling are very much cruder. The surface animation, in fact, derives less from the modeling than from the painted decoration, which is applied in neutral reds, yellows, and blues to the architectural, floral, and figural elements. Although the surface is vivacious, especially in the full flood of morning light, the carved ornament remains close to the wall and lacks altogether the luxuriant, crisp three-dimensionality of Pedro Huizar's portal on San Jose, San Antonio (Fig. 134).

FIGURE 144. San Xavier del Bac,
Tucson, Ariz., 1784–97.

FIGURE 145. Santa Prisca y San Sebastian,
Taxco, Mexico, 1751–58.

FIGURE 146. San Xavier del Bac,
Tucson, Ariz., portal, 1795.

FIGURE 147. Santa Prisca y San Sebastian,
Taxco, Mexico, portal, c. 1758.

One of the most Baroque aspects of the San Xavier portal is the direct relationship it bears with the reredos behind the altar. Although we have just noted certain qualitative differences made necessary by the differences in materials, the two are similar in design, both in the general shapes and divisions of space as defined by the architectural elements, and in the convulsive nature of the ornament. Conceptually the two are virtually identical, so much so, in fact, that it can be said that the brilliant setting for the high altar is visually anticipated in the façade. In other words, a major theme of symbolic importance is first stated clearly and without accompaniment against the pure white of the façade, and then is repeated behind the altar in richer textures and with a more complex setting. This complex relationship between spatial components seen in time bears a strong affinity with a Baroque fugue, particularly in the way in which the primary theme is introduced alone and without embellishment, only to be repeated later against the contrapuntal harmonies of the secondary themes. Such compositional devices, developed in time as well as space, were characteristic of Baroque design in general, and of the eighteenth-century churches of Mexico in particular. Together with the cruciform plan and vaulted interior they make San Xavier conceptually one of the most advanced churches in colonial America.

In spite of its spatial and schematic sophistications, San Xavier is none-theless an extremely provincial work. This is especially evident when its portal is compared with the portal of Taxco in Mexico (Fig. 147). In the San Xavier portal, and throughout the building, shapes are awkward and detailing is crude. There are also numerous disturbing (and sometimes amusing) unorthodoxies and contradictions. The enormous brackets for example, which connect the freestanding corner piers with the towers, make no structural sense whatsoever, and even though such devices occur in Mexican colonial architecture—for example, on the side of Santa Rosa de Viterbo in Queretaro (Fig. 148)—as used at San Xavier they are particularly clumsy. Moreover, there is no conceivable relationship either in scale or in ornamental intent between these same ponderous brackets and the animated interlace pattern in the pediment of the portal. But most conspicuous of all is the inept, and in some instances primitive, way in which these various details have been handled. Here we encounter conspicuous inadequacies and radical contradictions of style, all of which raise at once the important question of workmanship.

Considered in terms of workmanship, San Xavier reveals several levels of competence, all of which seem related to the degree to which the Indians participated in the work. The highest achievement is found in the structure itself. Here the hand of a master workman or possibly even an architect is everywhere apparent. It is certain that the Indians provided the actual labor, but the building is laid out and built with a precision and care that would only have been possible under the careful direction of men qualified in both the mathematics and the structural techniques of architecture. Altogether, San Xavier is one of the best built churches in the Southwest. In the handling of the ornamental features, however, no such consistent level of accomplishment is apparent. Like the building it-

FIGURE 148. Santa Rosa de Viterbo,
Queretaro, Mexico, 1754.

self, the reredos (Fig. 141) shows qualities of carving and painting which presuppose a direct and skillful response to European intentions and methods. With all its involvements, its design indicates clearly that the artists who made it not only had mastered the architectural, figural, and decorative devices of the Baroque, but also had reasonable command of the complicated techniques necessary to carry them out. It seems altogether improbable that the Indians could have been coached to this level of performance. The quality of the work in the portal (Fig. 146), on the other hand, is much cruder than that in the reredos. Here we encounter a primitivism in the molded and painted ornament which suggests that this work could have been done by the Indians. In fact, some of the carving in the engaged colonnettes has qualities of interlace and geometric stiffness that are even reminiscent of the fascinating decorative sculpture of the pre-colonial Indian cultures of Mexico. In addition, the figural painting in the area of the dome, although clearly European-Christian in content, has a primitive simplicity and flatness which suggest again the high probability of Indian workmanship (Fig. 139).

Despite the signs of Indian participation in the rendering of San Xavier, the church remains essentially European. The style bears no imprint of an Indian imagination, and has none of the nuances of a native craft, as the style of the churches of New Mexico so surely did. It is instead a style in which both the forms and the methods have been imposed upon the Indians by the drive and ambitions of the Spanish friars; and the result is not a mutation of Indian and European, but rather a debasement of the Spanish Baroque by the general lack of comprehension and technical skills on the part of the Indians who did the work. Only in those parts executed by the Spanish-American artists does the church succeed with reasonably authoritative results. In spite of its provincial crudeness, San Xavier is as alien to the great desert in which it stands as the civilization which gave it shape was to the simple Indians upon whom it was imposed. The adobe churches of the upper Rio Grande belong to the desert because they were molded from the earth itself by the hands of the people who inhabited the land. In contrast, San Xavier will remain forever isolated, an awkward foreigner in a primitive land, clinging nostalgically to the last remnants of a faded wardrobe.

The Missions of California

The last mission field to be developed in the Southwest by the Spanish was coastal California from San Diego to San Francisco. Here the first mission was not founded until 1769, and it was almost the end of the century before any architecture of consequence was built. By 1823, twenty-one missions had been established, but the churches were neither as large nor as precocious in style as those of Arizona and Texas, nor do they add anything architecturally to the familiar Mexican idiom. The California Indians, whose culture was less developed than those in the other mission fields, offered little that was original in the way of crafts. In the building of the churches, therefore, those tasks which required higher skills were carried out either by the friars or by artisans imported from Mexico. Even so, the level of craftsmanship was never very high, and nowhere in California is there a portal of the mature stylistic brilliance of Huizar's San Jose, nor is there anything comparable to the primitive dignity of the Indian workmanship at Ranchos de Taos. More remote from the centers of influence, and restrained by a poverty of technical means, the mission churches of California never rose above the level of artisan provincialism, and popular opinion notwithstanding, they exerted no influence whatsoever on later developments in California architecture.

San Carlos Borromeo, Carmel

The most important of the early California mission churches is San Carlos Borromeo in Carmel (1793–97). Founded in 1770 by the indomitable pioneer of the California missions, Father Junipero Serra, it remained for many years the administrative center of the California mission movement, and is thus of great historical importance. The present church (Fig. 149) was built under the direction of Father Serra's successor, Father Fermin de Lasuen, by a master stonemason, Manuel Estevan Ruiz, who was brought to Carmel for that purpose. The building was constructed by the

FIGURE 149. *San Carlos Borromeo,*
Carmel, Calif., 1793–97.

Indians, working under Ruiz's direction, in a soft, ochre-colored, local
sandstone which is easily worked in the quarry but which hardens on ex-
posure to the air. Lime for the mortar was made by burning seashells. Except for the carved decorative features, the stone walls were covered with
a stucco of the same color as the stone.

Two aspects of the Carmel church demand our attention, the façade
and the construction of the nave. In spite of its two towers, the over-all
appearance of the façade is squat and low, and it is conspicuously asymmetrical. The central section is a plain wall set back slightly between the
towers and crowned by a simple semicircular arch, which in turn is topped
by a small reverse-curve parapet. The round-headed door opening is
framed by a molded arch on piers set between Doric pilasters and surmounted by a plain entablature. The relief is very low and the treatment
so flat and austere that it has all the character of the early Renaissance
rather than the Baroque; the motif is one found frequently in Mexico and
may possibly have been derived from a copy book. Immediately above it,
however, is a window of a wholly different character. Shaped as a combined
quatrefoil and star, and cut deeply into the wall in an outward splay, it is
richly sculptural and decidedly Mexican in character. Except for the curious
ovoid shape of the dome on the left tower, it is the only concession to the
Spanish Baroque to be found on the church. The two towers are totally
devoid of sculptural adornment. The one on the left is considerably higher
and twice as wide as the other, and its dome has an octagonal base. This
capricious asymmetry is conspicuously provincial; for Baroque architec-

ture, in spite of its elaborate decorative and spatial preoccupations, was as firmly committed to symmetry as that of the Renaissance. In fact, this unbalanced arrangement, together with the round-arched openings and the weighty simplicity of the walls, gives the church an austere character which marks it for what it is, a Mexican provincial as much Renaissance as it is Baroque.

Structurally, the nave of San Carlos is one of the most unusual on the Pacific coast (Fig. 150). In shape it is long and narrow, and it is roofed by a continuous barrel vault which is parabolic in shape. The inner surface of this vault, which is wood rather than masonry, is carried on a series of parabolic stone arches which in turn spring from quasi-Doric pilasters in the wall. Both the shape and the structural method of the vault are exotic, but the manner in which it is sprung is even more so. The upper third of the wall along its entire length curves inward, thus increasing its thickness by two feet at the top, and making the pilasters seem actually to bend. Nothing could be more anti-structural. The spring of the vault, which is traditionally placed at the top of the entablature, is moved part way down the pier. Thus the pilasters seem to be giving way under the weight of the vault. Although amusing and highly original, it raises havoc with the expected rectilinearity of the classical orders, and creates an uneasy effect, as if there were some instability which would inevitably lead to disintegration and collapse.

The naïve irregularity and bold simplicity of San Carlos were typical of most California mission churches, and of those, only one, San Juan Capistrano (1797–1806), matched the other churches of the Southwest in the magnitude of its conception. One hundred and eighty feet long, with a single bell tower which reached a height of one hundred twenty feet, it was in its day the only cruciform plan church in California and the only one roofed by stone vaults. It was larger than San Xavier del Bac, and may very well have rivaled it in monumentality and ornamental richness. Unfortunately the church was destroyed by an earthquake only six years after its consecration, and not enough of it has survived to justify comparative evaluation with the outstanding churches in the other mission fields. Of those California churches which do survive, San Carlos is the most important.

Santa Barbara Mission

The sources of creative energy which quickened and compounded the rhythms of European life in the seventeenth and eighteenth centuries flooded out to embrace the New World and, in spite of the fierce opposition of the frontier, channeled it toward a similar destiny. The miracle is the degree to which the frontier responded. For it was European ideas and methods which gave shape to American architecture, and even though its outlines were blunted and simplified by the constant abrasion of the ever-deepening frontier, the image itself was never lost. Only in one area in colonial America can it be said that the aboriginal culture determined the form of the architecture, and this was in the adobe churches of the

FIGURE 150. San Carlos Borromeo,
Carmel, Calif., scheme of the vaulted ceiling, 1793–97.

FIGURE 151. Santa Barbara,
Santa Barbara, Calif., 1815–20.

upper Rio Grande. Not only was the influence of Europe pervasive, it was also continuous and as attitudes changed abroad, so did they in the colonial world, although always belatedly and in varying degrees, and constantly transformed by local conditions and available means.

In a manner consistent with this general condition of colonial architecture the last missions of California, which were built in the early nineteenth century, are altogether different stylistically from those of the earlier years. The most impressive of these later missions is the one at Santa Barbara (1815–20). It was not only the largest and most ambitious of the California chain but also one of the latest to be built, and it brings to an appropriate close the story of Spanish-American architecture in the United States (Fig. 151). A significant fact, however, which has not generally been noticed by writers on the subject, is that Santa Barbara is wholly different in style from any of the earlier churches of the Southwest. This can be seen readily in the façade. In contrast to the general vertical emphasis found in the Baroque churches such as San Xavier, the façade of Santa Barbara is broad and absolutely symmetrical. The main block is an unbroken horizontal rectangle of regular ashlar masonry which extends from one side of the building to the other. The corners of this block are sharply cut, and the top is delineated by a simple and rather thin cornice. The symmetrical towers, which rise in two stages above this main mass, are equally severe with a similar stress on the wall plane. On all four sides of each stage of the towers there is a single arched opening, cut cleanly into the mass and unrelieved. Each stage is also crowned by a cornice similar to that on the main block, and the only concession to adornment is found at the corners, which are chamfered rather than square. The domes which crown the towers are given structural emphasis by spurred ribs which rise from the four corners and lend visual support to the modest cupola on top.

Engaged to the main wall between the towers are six Ionic columns arranged in groups of three either side of the simple round-arched opening of the main door. These columns support a full entablature, the architrave of which is continuous with, although separated from, the cornice of the wall; the frieze is decorated with a Greek fret, and above the entablature is a low classical pediment. In order to maintain something approximating their correct proportions, the Ionic columns are raised on pedestals. Above the central door is a simple oculus window with a splayed reveal cut sharply into the wall.

With the possible exception of the curious excrescence which rises above the pediment and supports the central cross, there is absolutely nothing Baroque about this building. The clean geometry of its walls, the evocation of the temple front, the almost total absence of compound shapes, especially those developed in three-dimensional curves, and the horizontal orientation of the façade all create an image which, in terms of formal convention and development, is the direct opposite of such churches as San Xavier del Bac (Fig. 144). In spite of the twin towers, a favorite device of the Baroque era and one which we have come to recognize as the virtual signature of the Spanish-American churches, all of the elements and relationships just described are those which we normally associate with strict theoretical classicism.

How, in this culminating monument in the long tradition of Spanish-American building, can we account for such a dramatic and definitive change in style? A clue is found in the source from which Father Ripoll, the designer of the church, derived his temple front. The specific Ionic order with the Greek fret in the frieze comes from a Spanish edition of the ancient Roman architect and theorist, Vitruvius. The use of this particular source is significant, for it represents a rejection of the liberal classicism of the Renaissance, which formed the basis of the Baroque, and is a revival instead of the architecture of ancient Rome itself. Father Ripoll thus wrote the final chapter in Spanish-American architecture, not in the grandiloquent but weary symbols of the Baroque, but in a wholly different language of form, a mode of building which was already thirty years old on the eastern seaboard and which marks the end of the colonial era and the beginning of modern America.

PART II

Neoclassicism in America

CHAPTER VI

The Background to Neoclassicism in America

> In every architectural order only the column, the entablature and the pediment could form an essential part of its composition. If each of these three parts is suitably placed and suitably formed, nothing else need be added to make the work perfect.
>
> ABBÉ LAUGIER

The Background

Father Ripoll's unabashed use of a Vitruvian temple front for the façade of Santa Barbara Mission Church was not the whim of an eccentric frontier priest. Instead, it was a provincial manifestation of Neoclassicism, a new and vital development in architecture which took place in Europe during the second half of the eighteenth century. The source for this movement was the architecture of the ancient world, and throughout its several and, in some instances, contrasting phases the influence of both Greece and Rome was substantial and direct. But to interpret Neoclassicism in terms of borrowings from the ancient past alone is completely to misunderstand its true character. An enthusiasm for classical architecture, especially that of Rome, was not peculiar to the eighteenth century. In a special sense Roman architecture was the basis of all European architecture from the early fifteenth century in Italy down to the eighteenth century in colonial America. The classical orders, classical structural and decorative methods, and classical spatial concepts—modified, enriched, and expanded—formed the architectural vocabulary not only of the Renaissance but also of even the most extreme phases of the Baroque such as the Spanish colonial architecture in the Southwest. Yet the differences between Neoclassicism and its Renaissance-Baroque predecessors are both considerable and complex; and these differences stem largely from a radical change in attitude toward the ancient world on the part of the architects of the second half of the eighteenth century.

The architects of the fifteenth, sixteenth, and seventeenth centuries, who fashioned from Roman architecture the many variations of the Renaissance style, viewed ancient Rome as the beginning of a long classical tradition of which they themselves were but a later part. To them, this tradition was organic and alive, rooted in the past but at the same time, through growth and renewal, providing a constant source of nourishment for the present. Their own creative efforts therefore bore the same relationship to ancient Rome as that which the branches of a tree bear to its roots.

In contrast to this, the architects of the Neoclassical era saw each segment of the past as a separate entity with its own shape, its own achievements, its own destiny. For them, the architecture of each civilization came increasingly into focus and was different from that of every other civilization, not as branches on the same tree but as *wholly different species of tree*. The Renaissance, for example, understood ancient Greece as primarily an ancestor of Rome; the late eighteenth century, on the other hand, saw it as a civilization complete in itself, with its own special qualities which not only distinguished it from Rome but which in some ways made it superior to Rome. This is essentially the modern critical view of history, and when applied to architecture, as it was in the late eighteenth century, it brought about a wholly new system of values. Once those specific characteristics had been determined through which one style could be identified and distinguished from all other styles, then those same traits became available as means of design; and style, instead of being the product of continuous growth, where one phase of development leads logically into the next, became a matter of objective choice, in which the stream of history was bypassed and specific formal ideas were removed intact from their historical context and applied to problems of the present.[1]

Several developments of the eighteenth century contributed to the formation of this new point of view.[2] The first was the emergence of the science of archaeology. As we have already seen, an interest in the ancient world was one of the major attributes of the Renaissance, and as early as the fifteenth century excavations were being carried out in a search for antique remains. But these first efforts were random, and were motivated more by philosophical and aesthetic, than by historical concerns. During the eighteenth century, however, the search for positive truths gave new and more systematic directions to the curiosity about the past, a trend which received substantial impetus in mid-century from the rediscovery of two ancient Roman towns. In 1738, the first primitive excavations were begun at Herculaneum. Ten years later, work was started at Pompeii, and it was here, in the subsequent years of excavation, that archaeology took shape as a positive science.

Although the excavations at Herculaneum and Pompeii were the first major archaeological undertakings of the eighteenth century, and were subsequently to exert varying degrees of influence in the Neoclassical movement, they were by no means the only efforts of their kind; nor were they in the end the most important. Shortly after 1750 a small group of Englishmen, under the leadership of Robert Wood, arrived in Palmyra to record the Roman ruins that were still extant in that isolated and desolate Syrian city; and in 1757 another expedition, this time under the leadership of Robert Adam, set out for the Dalmatian coast to collect material on the great palace of Diocletian at Spalato. Adam was a talented and ambitious young Englishman, who later, as an architect, was to play a central and creative role in the first phase of English Neoclassicism. His direct experience with the architecture of ancient Rome was to prove a major factor in the development of his style.

All of these efforts in the field resulted in publications which, in their comprehensive coverage of single monuments and in their meticulous attention to detail, were conspicuously different from earlier books on architecture.[3] Moreover, their superb and accurate plates provided authoritative and exciting new visual material on the architecture of ancient Rome. But it was not only Rome which aroused the curiosity of the eighteenth-century architect and theorist. Shortly after 1750 several publications appeared which expressed an enthusiasm for Greece. The earliest of these, the first part of which was published in 1752, was the *Recueil d'antiquités* of the Comte de Caylus. This extensive work was one of the most comprehensive archaeological publications of the period. Although it dealt with the Egyptian as well as the classical world, its primary importance for the Neoclassical movement lay in Caylus's enthusiasm for what he called the noble simplicity of the Greek style. Following Caylus, the Jesuit priest Abbé Laugier published a far more influential work, *Essai sur l'architecture* (1753).[4] Laugier went even further than Caylus in his admiration for Greece by stating quite flatly that "architecture has only middling obligations to the Romans, and . . . owes all that is precious and solid to the Greeks alone." This opinion was a radical departure from the firmly established Renaissance point of view that Rome was the fountainhead of the great classical style.

The growing admiration for ancient Greece was provoked by more than theory. In 1751 the Scottish architect James Stuart, together with Nicholas Revett, left England for Greece to make an actual study of the buildings on the Acropolis in Athens. That same year they announced their intentions to publish *Antiquities of Athens*. When it appeared in 1762 this monumental work brought to European architects for the first time an accurate image of the great Greek style of the fifth century.[5] Finally, these scattered outbursts of enthusiasm for Greece were given a positive historical basis by the writings of one of the most remarkable figures of the period, the great German archaeologist J. J. Winckelmann. His renowned *Geschichte der Kunst des Alterthums,*[6] appearing in 1764, was the first major attempt to develop the history of Greek art and to define the principles upon which it had been based. Greece, of course, had long been revered for her accomplishments in the realm of the mind. Now, through the revelations of the archaeologists, all that had been admired about the ancient Greeks was given visual embodiment in the arts. Greece thus began to be understood as a total civilization rather than as a philosophical phenomenon, and Greek architecture, long recognized as the ancient ancestor of Roman architecture, rose from obscurity and revealed its own special qualities, which in some ways made it superior to that of ancient Rome.

Both the character and quality of Greek architecture posed a serious threat to the established doctrine that Rome was the primary authority in all artistic matters. Coming as it did from the archaeologists and theorists of France, England, and Germany, this challenge met vigorous opposition in Italy. In part the resistance derived from a natural patriotic sympathy. But more than that, the new thesis opened to question the pre-eminence of Rome itself as the foundation of European culture. For it was to Rome that Frenchmen, Englishmen, and Germans had been coming for generations in quest of knowledge about the ancient world, and to throw into doubt the supreme authority of either the modern city or the ancient civilization bordered on heresy. In addition, from about 1725 onward the Italians had been developing their own thesis that the origins of Roman culture were to be found in the Etruscans and not the Greeks.

Leadership of the Italian opposition fell not to an archaeologist or an architect but rather to one of the most flamboyant and imaginative artists of the eighteenth century, the Venetian etcher-engraver G. B. Piranesi. Piranesi's published works comprised several series of magnificent etchings, all containing highly romanticized views of ancient Roman remains. By far the most important of these was his *Della magnificenza ed architettura de' Romani.*[7] It was published in 1761 as a direct and intentional rebuttal to the pro-Greek publications. These vivid etchings, in their extravagant abundance of Roman architectural form, convey with impassioned ferocity the artist's unshakable belief in the supremacy of ancient Rome. Piranesi's many publications did little to stem the rising enthusiasm for Greek architecture, but they did much to bring the whole question into focus. As a result, men were forced to think in more specific and demanding terms about both Greece and Rome and the stylistic distinctions between the two were more sharply defined.

Neoclassicism in architecture was not only an archaeological movement. The austere geometric simplicity of the Greek Doric temple, long viewed as a mark of primitivism, could not be understood in the same terms that had traditionally been applied to Roman architecture. The reasoned design and structural purity of the Greek temple demanded instead new rational and functional attitudes which would take into account the organic nature of the building itself and the spaces it was meant to enclose. As man sought more and more to define the physical world through the demonstrated truths of science—replacing empirical discovery by knowledge gained through experimentation—so, too, he sought meaning in architecture, not in systems of proportions or in ornamental embellishment, but in the fundamental necessities of function and structure.

Although such rational ideas were probably first expressed in the eighteenth century by the Italian theorist Carlo Lodoli, it was in France that they were most persuasively articulated. On the theoretical side, it was again the Abbé Laugier who was the most eloquent spokesman. Laugier was not only among the first to proclaim the priority of Greek over Roman architecture, he also developed a rational doctrine in which he sought to define architecture in terms of true principles. Beauty, he argued, was to be found only in that which was absolutely essential, or, as he expressed it, "one should never put anything in a building for which one cannot give a solid reason."

With respect to structure Laugier was even more emphatic. According to his theory, the column as a supporting element should always be freestanding and rise directly from the platform of the building without an intervening pedestal. He vigorously opposed engaged columns and pilasters, considering them a contradiction to structure. Instead, the pure column, together with the entablature, should be used in order to reveal the true meaning of the structural elements. In the part-to-part relationships within the building, geometry should provide the guiding principles, with variety achieved through the opposition of simple geometric shapes. Although Laugier was not himself an architect, his highly reasoned views were at once attractive to the younger revolutionary architects of the second half of the century, and he became, in a real sense, the intellectual leader of Neoclassicism.[8]

There was yet another aspect of Laugier's theories which gave to the Neoclassical movement a dynamic potential which it might not otherwise have had. Although an ardent champion of Greek over Roman architecture, Laugier at no time advocated a literal imitation of either the Greek or the Roman style. He not only challenged the authority of Vitruvius,[9] he even went so far as to suggest that the Greek orders themselves should be tested to see whether or not they conformed to modern needs. He also offered the possibility that new orders might be more suitable to modern conditions than those of the classical past. This rational point of view, which sought fundamental truths on the one hand and identification with the present on the other, became the incentive for some of the most astounding works of the late eighteenth century.[10]

Both the archaeological and the functional attitudes just described would seem to have been the result of rational thought, but this was not entirely the case. They were also the consequences of powerful romantic tendencies. The attempts to identify and reconstruct the lives and art of people remote in time and space were in themselves irrational acts, involving imagination and feeling as well as pure reason. Moreover, the efforts to equate order in architecture with order in nature, such as Laugier's insistence upon that which is "natural and true, wherein all is reduced to simple rules and executed according to great principles," were in fact attempts to equate the origins of architecture with natural law. Laugier finds fundamental truths in the primitive hut, where one can distinguish those parts of the building "which necessity has introduced" from those which have been added by "caprice." When he rejects preconceptions about proportion and says instead that "only taste and experience can guide the architect" he rejects the absolute in favor of a free choice sympathetic to environment and time. Laugier's ideas were in varying degrees influential upon the architects of the second half of the eighteenth century. To the extent that these men identified themselves with the antique world on the one hand, and with natural law on the other, even the most radical of their schemes reflected something of a romantic attitude.[11]

Neoclassicism in America

In many ways Neoclassicism in America was no more than a provincial extension of Neoclassicism in Europe and it can therefore be defined in the same basic terms. At the same time, the unsettling effects of the Revolution, the subsequent urge toward national cultural identity, and the geographical remoteness from the main centers of architectural activity introduced several factors for which there was no counterpart in Europe. American Neoclassicism, therefore, will be seen to have a number of characteristics which distinguish it at once from its European sources and give it an altogether national character. But in order properly to define and evaluate these we must first review briefly prevailing critical attitudes in America toward the period.

In general, the Neoclassical movement in America has been divided by authorities into two distinct stylistic periods. The first is the post-colonial or, to use the more common and familiar term, the Federal Style. Applied more to define a block of time than a coherent style, the term "Federal Style" has been made to include most American building between approximately 1780 and 1820. Following this in point of time, the second accepted stylistic division is the Greek Revival. More readily definable than the Federal Style, because of its strict adherence to the Greek idiom, the Greek Revival spread to every civilized part of the country in the years between 1820 and the Civil War. It has been recognized by many, in fact, as America's first truly national style. But as in the case of "Federal Style" the term "Greek Revival" has been applied so indiscriminately that all buildings of the period which display the classical orders are automatically swept up under its all-inclusive heading.

Although the Federal Style and the Greek Revival are very different from one another they are deeply rooted in the classical tradition and are therefore coherently related. At the same time there are numerous significant works of the period, all of them equally classical, which do not seem to fit into the pattern of either of these two styles. The work of Thomas Jefferson, for example, has been frequently identified with the Federal Style, even though it is primarily Roman in origin; and in the case of the English-born Benjamin Latrobe there is an even greater divergence of opinion. His work has been placed by some authorities in the Federal Style, by others in the Greek Revival. Actually, it belongs to neither and will be seen rather to represent the first important infusion into American architecture of the more rational attitudes of European Neoclassicism. Because of these and many similar contradictions it is essential that we re-examine the whole question of American Neoclassicism and seek to redefine both its relationships with its European sources and its own peculiar characteristics and achievements.

American architecture of the Neoclassical movement derived from that of Europe in precisely the same way as that of the colonial period had before it. Those affluent and influential individuals on the eastern seaboard who had imposed a thoroughly British pattern of social and cultural values on colonial life continued their pro-British sentiments in spite of the Revolution. Although the war led to dramatic political change, the firmly established British cultural tradition remained in most areas virtually unaffected; in some instances it became even stronger. At the same time, friendship for France, which came as a result of aid received during the war, opened the way to new cultural resources, and by the turn of the century French influence, both directly and indirectly, was to join and mingle with the British. Finally, and most important of all, there were the new archaeological and rational attitudes which belatedly filtered through the gravel beds of residual colonialism to strengthen a growing nationalism and to add those new vital ingredients so necessary to the development of a viable American architecture.

From these European sources four, rather than two, distinct phases of the Neoclassical style were to emerge. We will define them as the Traditional Phase, the Idealistic Phase, the Rational Phase, and the National Phase. In these four diverse but related developments are to be found both the depth and the breadth of the nation's early struggle for cultural identity. Even though all four were motivated by the same family of ideas, each was conspicuously different from the others and together they demonstrate, at the very beginning of this country's existence as an independent nation, one of the basic characteristics of American architecture, its heterogeneity. To be sure, the architecture of the late colonial period was anything but heterogeneous. Except for the architecture of the Southwest, which remained through its history a provincial proliferation of the Catholic Baroque in Spain, that of the British colonies in the years immediately preceding the Revolution had achieved a remarkable homogeneity of style. By 1750 even the highly individual modes of the Dutch and the Swedes had been largely overwhelmed and modified by the pervasive English influence. Although marked regional characteristics are recognizable, the architecture of the eastern seaboard was conceived and executed in a common language of style. Following the war, however, this consistency began to break down. For a variety of reasons, all of them associated with the formation and growth of the new nation, a more complex, expressive, and experimental architecture began to take its place.

American Neoclassicism: The Traditional Phase

The Traditional Phase of American Neoclassicism was both the earliest and the least aggressive. In its stanch conservatism it was, in fact, little more than a provincial transformation of the first phase of English Neoclassicism. At the same time, in its basic characteristics it did not represent a radical break from the architecture of the late colonial era. Fundamental building types were modified only slightly, if at all, and those changes which did occur were primarily refinements in proportion and scale. The greatest innovations appeared in the interior decoration, where new motifs, many of them derived indirectly from ancient classical sources, were used with restrained elegance. It is this delicate and refined mode of design which we will identify as the Federal Style, and it is precisely because it represents a development from, rather than a revolt against, the architecture of the late colonial period that we have termed it the Traditional Phase of American Neoclassicism.

The Federal Style was the creation of an affluent mercantile aristocracy. Concentrated primarily in the coastal communities of New England, the men who made up this segment of American society were both ambitious and competitive, and in their eyes the new nation was still New England with Boston the hub of the universe. They formed, in fact, the hard core of the Federal party. Yet they were also conservative, bound to the mother country by powerful cultural as well as economic ties; recognizing in the architecture of England the reassuring graces of a venerable tradition, they had no desire to depart from it. Sharing their views, and catering to their taste, were New England's two most talented architects, the impeccable Boston classicist Charles Bulfinch (Fig. 198), and his contemporary in Salem, the gentle but matchless wood carver Samuel McIntire (Fig. 160). In the work of these two men the Traditional Phase of American Neoclassicism reached its most expressive heights.

American Neoclassicism: The Idealistic Phase

Quite the opposite of the conservative but exquisite Federal Style was the architecture of Thomas Jefferson.[12] Thoroughly anti-British in his attitude toward architecture, and consciously seeking a mode of building symbolic of the new republic, he discovered what he considered an appropriate idiom in two non-English sources, the Neoclassical architecture of contemporary France, and the architecture of ancient Rome. From these he created an intensely personal style, indeed one so reflective and so highly symbolic that few, if any, of his contemporaries were able to grasp its full significance (Fig. 242). Rational at the same time that it was romantic, it remains one of the most brilliant creative outbursts of the entire Neoclassical movement. In its thoughtful social and political implications it bears a direct relationship to the ideals and aspirations of the new republic, and can therefore be defined as the Idealistic Phase of American Neoclassicism.

In spite of its highly individual character, and precisely because of its expressive symbolism, Jefferson's architecture became in an abstract way the architecture of those radical idealists whose dreams of a free society had formed the theoretical spearhead of the Revolution. Their antagonism toward all things British led them, like Jefferson, to reject tradition and to seek in all walks of life new forms which would be expressive of the political and social ideals for which they had fought. For them the destiny of America lay in the vast potential of the unexplored, and thus, like Jefferson, they sought not only to construct a political state which would assure that destiny, but also, in Jefferson's words, "to bring into action that mass of talents which lies buried in the poverty of every country, for want of the means of development, and thus give activity to a mass mind, which, in proportion to our population shall be the double or treble of what it is in most countries." Such challenging ideals found their expression in Jefferson's own architecture, for it is one of those remarkable turns of history that Jefferson the idealist and statesman was also Jefferson the architect. More than any other man of his day, Jefferson understood the larger functions of architecture in society and used it as a symbol of political and social values. It was he, too, as Secretary of State under Washington, who provided the leadership and the knowledge which ultimately led to the planning and building of the city of Washington; to him and to other idealists like him it was the new nation's capital, and not Boston, that would someday be the hub of the universe.

American Neoclassicism: The Rational Phase

The third phase of American Neoclassicism, which we have designated the Rational Phase, was centered in the architecture of Benjamin Latrobe. Coming to America in the late eighteenth century, Latrobe brought with him two enormously important qualifications which no American architect up to this time could possibly have had, a highly professional attitude toward his work, and the theoretical knowledge and practical skills of an engineer. Both were gained from his early experience in England.[13] Unlike Bulfinch and Jefferson, who came to know architecture through the attitudes and methods of the gentleman-amateur, Latrobe was trained from the beginning as a professional architect. His work, therefore, was conceived and executed at levels of professional competence that no contemporary American was able to match (Fig. 265). His influence was considerable on the younger generation of Americans, especially Robert Mills, and he established once and for all in America the image of the professional architect.

An enormously vitalizing force during the early years of the American republic was the influx of new men from abroad like Latrobe. During the colonial years the majority of the new arrivals had been merchants, sea captains, craftsmen, government officials, off-beat religious groups, and adventurers. Now the promise and excitement offered by the new republic, with its ever widening horizons, attracted an increasing number of individuals with specialized, and in some cases professional, training and skills; and many of them came from countries other than England. Of particular importance to American architecture were the engineers, the mechanics, and the professional architects. Architecture of the colonial period had been limited in design by the knowledge of the gentleman-amateur, and in construction to that which could be accomplished by the carpenter and the bricklayer. With but one known exception, not a single important building of the colonial period was vaulted.[14] These vaulting limitations were to become dramatically clear during the early phases of the building of the United States Capitol in Washington. It was recognized at once that there were no masons available in America who could lay up a masonry vault, nor any native-born engineers with the knowledge and experience necessary to plan and supervise the work. In the face of expanding demands imposed by wider visions, the gentleman-amateur was no longer adequate and the professional moved in to take his place. Latrobe was the first to arrive from abroad and he brought with him both the new concepts of European Neoclassicism and a superior technical competence. Through his work and influence American architecture ceased to be colonial and began its long struggle toward national identity.

American Neoclassicism: The National Phase

The fourth and final phase of American Neoclassicism, which we have called the National Phase, culminated in the Greek Revival (Fig. 310).[15] Like Jefferson's adaptation of the Roman style, it was a revival rather than an evolution, for it reached back over the centuries and lifted intact certain specific characteristics of an ancient style and applied them, both symbolically and practically, to the needs of a rapidly expanding and intensely self-conscious new nation. As in the case of Jefferson, too, the specific features of an ancient style were understood and applied with an authenticity which would not have been possible without the discriminating evidence provided by the new science of archaeology. But whereas Jefferson's use of Roman architecture was both rational and philosophical, and remained the isolated and fiercely personal accomplishment of a singularly versatile individual, the Greek Revival was irrational and sentimental, and flourished at every level of American society. It is because of this that we have defined it as the National Phase. Indeed, in 'the hands of the local carpenter it permeated every corner of the land to blossom into one of the most remarkable flowerings of folk art in Western history.

The broad folk character of the Greek Revival is but one manifestation of an important change which was taking place in American society during the first half of the nineteenth century. This change resulted in part from a fundamental aspect of the democratic system, the endowed right of every individual to judge things for himself. Extended into the realm of taste and patronage this concept was to have far-reaching consequences. With the growing nationalism which became noticeably more acute after the War of 1812, there developed a new cultural self-consciousness in America which found the average citizen expressing an active and critical interest in the arts. During the first part of the nineteenth century this particular characteristic was noticed by one foreign traveler who observed with some amusement that Americans were defensively sensitive to any criticism of their art and were thoroughly convinced that what was being done in their country was superior to that which was being done abroad.[16] During the colonial period standards of taste had been set by the mercantile-planter aristocracy. These standards then spread throughout the frontier society, in the same way that the artistic assumptions of the aristocracy of England had been accepted and imitated by the English middle class. During the first half of the nineteenth century in America, however, the common man became increasingly his own arbiter of taste. Basically uneasy and therefore aggressive in his unfamiliar role, his approach to architecture was both impulsive and romantic, motivated more by sentiment than reason, and developed entirely within the physical limits of traditional materials and methods. The result was the Greek Revival, a style as rich and original in its individual characteristics as the variety of people and regions concerned. Although manifestly derived from the architecture of ancient Greece it was both literary and pictorial in conception, and because it was unencumbered by any technical or formal predispositions it became equally accessible to all levels of society. Nowhere in American history up to this time had a mode of building been so closely identified with the common man, and in its fulfillment of a common need it assumed all the characteristics of a national style.[17]

The Federal Style

We have already identified the Federal Style as the Traditional Phase of American Neoclassicism, and we have also said that it was the earliest and the least aggressive. Rooted as it was in the architecture of the late colonial era, it represented a natural stylistic evolution from that earlier and wholly provincial English mode of building. The three-story town house, the ubiquitous rectangular block-type house with its door in the center of the long side, and the Wren-Gibbs type church continued without interruption. At the same time, however, the Federal Style was a new mode developed on wholly new concepts of proportion and scale and utilizing equally new systems of ornament. In its Englishness it is a thoroughly traditional style, but it also has moments of sparkling originality, and certain traits which can be identified as uniquely American appear for the first time.

The Federal Style was the favored mode of the Federalist aristocracy on the eastern seaboard. After the Revolution, the coastal cities became centers of a lively trade with the far reaches of the world, including India and China. Salem, Massachusetts, is characteristic. With the closing of the port of Boston by the British in 1774, Salem became the temporary capital of Massachusetts. It also achieved pre-eminence as one of the principal trading centers of the entire Atlantic seaboard. Through the rapid expansion of its trading interests it emerged from the war with a large and efficient fleet of swift sailing vessels which were the match of anything on the high seas. These ships and the merchants who guided their destiny brought to Salem, and later to Boston, an accumulation of wealth which had never been known in the colonial era. It was in fact in Salem, in 1799, that the first fortune of one million dollars was recorded in American history.

These powerful and affluent men were the patrons of the Federal Style. Through the complex involvements of international trade they were still in very close contact with England at the same time that they were in competition with it. Although daring and original in their trading exploits, they remained cautious and conservative in the fulfillment of their cultural needs, and English taste and many English social attitudes still shaped their way of life. Because of this the architecture which they commissioned and enjoyed had the same fundamental roots as that of the colonial period. At the same time, it differed from the colonial architecture of the eighteenth century in the same way and to the same degree that English architecture after 1760 was different from that which had preceded it. The character of the Federal Style, therefore, must first be examined in the light of what happened in England between 1760 and 1790.

English Background: The Adam Style

The most creative and original architect in England during these years, and the one who was indirectly to have the greatest influence on the development of the Federal Style, was Robert Adam.[18] We have already encountered Adam as one of the leading archaeologists of the century. But it was not in the realm of archaeology that his full genius was to assert itself. He was above all a powerful and original architect of great poetic sensitivity who, together with his brother James, brought about the most significant stylistic revolution that occurred in English architecture after the Palladian movement of the first years of the century. The Adam Style in England was a complex and highly sophisticated mode of design, and since its influence on American architecture was indirect most of the details of its character and development are of no concern to our story. Certain of its aspects do form the basis of the Federal Style, and these we must examine with some care.

It is important to establish first that the Adam Style, although highly original, did not represent a major break from the English Palladianism which preceded it. Adam's preference, in his arrangement of mass, for the alternation of contrasting but connected units, and for the forward and backward movement of wall planes owes much to the great Palladian, William Kent. Only in an occasional motif of obvious Roman derivation does Adam's Neoclassical enthusiasm reveal itself on the exterior of his buildings. His interiors, however, are another matter; for the Adam Style is above everything else a delicate and imaginative mode of interior decoration, and it is here that Adam's very special and ardent form of Neoclassicism is to be found. It was here, too, that he exerted his greatest influence on American architecture.

Two aspects of Adam's handling of interiors are significant, the rich and varied organization of his spatial volumes (Fig. 155), and the extraordinary grace and elegance of his unique and vivacious ornament (Fig. 152). His attitude toward interior spatial arrangements is indicated in the preface to his famous *Works,* the first volume of which was published in 1773. There he writes that "the parade, the convenience, and social pleasures of life, being better understood, are more strictly attended to in the arrangement and disposition of apartments."[19] This interesting passage not only tells us something of the architect's personal preference for variety, it also expresses one of the basic concerns of Neoclassicism, the disposition of interior space according to need rather than, as the Palladians had done, according to formal principle. On the exterior the components of buildings were still symmetrically disposed, but in the interior the spaces did not always correspond reciprocally around the central axis. Nor did these spaces necessarily correspond in shape. Instead, a number of geomet-

FIGURE 152. *Robert Adam. Derby House,*
Grosvenor Square, London, England, drawing room, 1773–74.

ric forms—the rectangle, the circle, and the oval—were used in a variety
of arrangements, and all were specifically related to the functions they
were intended to perform. This is a basic tenet of Neoclassical doctrine,
first propounded by the Abbé Laugier and later developed with special
ardor by the French.[20] Adam's method was in part derived from his knowledge of French architecture, but in greater part from his careful study of
Diocletian's palace at Spalato, where he discovered the rich spatial com-
plexities achieved in Roman domestic planning.

Adam also found in Roman domestic architecture a joyous and infinitely varied world of interior decoration, delicate in scale and complex
in color. It was a world of architectural forms totally different from the
monumental public buildings of ancient Rome to which the masters of the
Renaissance had primarily directed their attention and on the basis of
which they had constructed many of their various systems and theories.
Above all, Adam discovered that the Romans themselves, in spite of
Vitruvius,[21] had not hesitated to alter proportions and decorative arrangements if it suited their purpose. In the ancient wall paintings, both
in the Etruscan tombs and in the houses at Pompeii and Herculaneum,
he encountered a lavish and felicitous ornamental idiom, delicate and
capricious, and developed with an inexhaustible variety of pictorial and
decorative treatment (Fig. 153). "With regard to the decoration of their
private and bathing apartments," he wrote, "they [the Ancients] were all
delicacy, gaiety, grace and beauty." He noted further that the Romans
proportioned their decorative components according "to the distance from
the eye and the objects from which they were to be compared." Like

FIGURE 153. *Roman wall mosaic, Herculaneum.*

Laugier, who recommended a re-examination of the classical orders that they might be made more appropriate to their present use, Adam varied the accepted theoretical proportions and specific arrangements of the orders that they might be better fitted both to their location and to his own decorative intentions. Inspired by both the system and the motifs of the Romans, he took the classical idiom and fashioned it into a matchless prolific style uniquely his own (Fig. 152).

Adam and the Federal Style

The Federal Style in America varied from the colonial style in precisely the same way that the Adam Style departed from English Palladianism. The Federal Style, like the Adam Style, was an interior style. It employed the same attenuated proportions, it drew upon the same decorative conventions. Yet the American idiom was simpler than the British, more severe, more chaste. House plans were less complex, ornament was thinner, flatter, and even more refined. Instead of the delicate but sparkling color of Adam's most characteristic work (Syon House), the Americans preferred gently tinted grays with pure white.[22] These deviations from the Adam Style are accounted for in part by the more conservative and more provincial taste of both the American patron and the local designer. A strong thread of Puritanism still ran through the fabric of American society, especially in New England. On the other hand, these differences also resulted from the fact that the Adam Style was communicated to America primarily through books (Fig. 152). Already sharpened and made excessively linear by the nature of the engravings used as illustrations, the English Neoclassical motifs were even more finely drawn in the hands of the local designers and craftsmen.

The most effective way to establish the character and variety of the Federal Style, as it blossomed in the cities of the eastern seaboard, is to examine it in its broadest aspects through a selected group of representative works. Our first concern is with the arrangements of interior space. This can best be seen in one of the most monumental houses of the period, Woodlands in Philadelphia, which was built in 1770 but completely remodeled in the years 1788–89. It is the later phase of the house which is characteristic of the Federal Style. In plan (Fig. 154) it would seem to be symmetrical with areas of space corresponding exactly left and right of the central axis. Actually, however, no two of these spaces are the same shape, nor are they similarly proportioned. The hall immediately behind the portico is a prominently rectangular space running across the main axis of the house with its lateral position emphasized by semi-circular ends. Immediately adjacent also on the main axis is a smaller hall, circular in plan, and flanked by two stair wells. One of these is rectangular, the other has a curved end. To the left of the main hall is a rectangular room, to the right

FIGURE 154. *Woodlands,*
Philadelphia, Pa., first-floor plan, 1788–89.

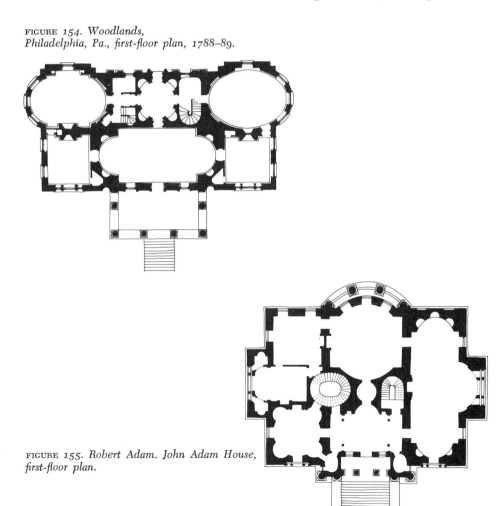

FIGURE 155. *Robert Adam. John Adam House,*
first-floor plan.

FIGURE 156. *Woodlands,*
Philadelphia, Pa., façade, 1788–89.

FIGURE 157. *Robert Adam.*
Design for High Down for John Radcliffe, Esq.

is a square one. The room to the left behind is rectangular with enormous bowed ends, the one to the right is oval. All of this has its counterpart in the interior planning arrangements of Adam and his circle (Fig. 155), and is in direct contrast to the severe formalism of such late colonial houses as Mount Airy (Fig. 73).

On the exterior of the house there is no hint whatever of this internal variety (Fig. 156). Although the symmetrical distribution of the relative spaces is clear enough, there is nothing to indicate the differences in shape, proportion and orientation. The exterior is, in fact, one of the earliest examples in America of the classic Palladian block with free-standing projecting portico. Yet the rich variety of interior space and its anomalous relationship with the exterior mass together with the strictly Palladian character of the façade are the very features which relate the work to Robert Adam (Fig. 157), and they make Woodlands one of the most conservative and clearly English houses of the period. The introduction of complex curved shapes for interior spaces is also characteristic of the Federal Style. Although few of the Federal houses were as monumental as Woodlands, they nonetheless show the same trend toward a variety in plan.

In spite of its fundamentally Palladian character, the exterior of Woodlands also exhibits several features which are characteristic of the Federal Style. The proportions of the freestanding Doric columns, for example, are tall and thin and the modillioned cornice which crowns the house is delicate in scale. Over the central door is an elliptical fanlight. This is one of the most prominent features of the style, and its elegant shape anticipates the oval room on the interior. The Palladian windows to the left and right of the portico are set back slightly in a secondary plane of the wall, which in turn is contained within a wall arch. This is another device frequently found in the work of Adam (Fig. 158), and it became one of the most popular for the Federal architects. Furthermore, the house originally was covered with stucco so that the walls were smooth and flat with the window openings sharply defined. The corners of the building too, constructed without quoins, are precisely cut, and from a side view the walls of the oval rooms are seen to push out in a swelling curve. This contrast of curved and rectilinear surfaces was widely practiced by Federal designers, and its novelty can best be understood by comparing Woodlands with an early Philadelphia house which we have already examined, Mount Pleasant in Fairmount Park (Fig. 84).

Samuel McIntire, Wood Carver

That aspect of Woodlands which is most expressive of the underlying spirit of the Federal Style is the use of the circle and the ellipse. From the Carolinas to Maine, these shapes occur over and over again in room plans, staircases, and window and door openings and they give to the Federal Style some of its special qualities of grace and elegance. But what is true of these larger elements is found in even greater abundance in another facet of the style, its ornament. In fact, it is in this area that the style achieved its most distinctive character, for like the Adam Style from which it derived it was essentially a mode of interior decoration; here, too, the most radical departures from colonial precedents are to be found. Federal Style ornament marks the ultimate refinement of classical taste in American architecture. Supremely rhythmic, wire-fine, and delicately scaled, its attenuated ranks of geometric and natural motifs are drawn in elegant but circumscribed patterns, like the resilient threads of a spiderweb, across the taut surfaces of the spatial volumes. It is chaste, serene, and controlled.

Of all the designers and craftsmen of the period, the one who felt these qualities most deeply and the one whose hands were most capable of giving them life was the Salem wood carver, Samuel McIntire.[23] McIntire

FIGURE 158. *Robert Adam. Society of Arts Building, London, England, detail of entrance.* (*Copyright* Country Life)

brought to his work no special qualities of mind, no insatiable curiosity, no probing imagination. He repeated himself often in his work and seems to have been content wth a limited number of simple motifs which he re-worked and refined and then brought together in a variety of arrangements. But those things which he did combine were adjusted and related with an impeccable sense of rightness and were executed with matchless skill. What McIntire did have above everything else was an exquisite sense of beauty and a deep poetic feeling for the qualities of wood. In his hands the tool had a touch as delicate and as sure as the beak of a hummingbird caressing the heart of a flower. Both in quality and in spirit his decorative work stands at the summit of the Federal Style.

Samuel McIntire learned his trade as a wood carver from his father; he received no higher education; he never traveled; in architecture he was completely self-taught. In the words of one of his contemporaries: "by his own well directed energies he became one of the best of men." In every respect McIntire was a typical American-born architect-builder, differing only in his infinitely greater personal talent from his colonial predecessor Richard Munday.

McIntire spent his life in Salem working for the wealthy and ambitious patrons of that thriving seaport town. One of the masterpieces among the many houses which he built there is the Pingree House, completed in 1805 (Fig. 159), a building remarkable for its combination of austerity

FIGURE 159. *Samuel McIntire. Pingree House,*
Salem, Mass., 1805.

and grace. On the one hand it is simple to the point of being stark, on
the other it is finely tuned in its proportions to a degree of vibrant
resonance that is matched only in the open strings of the violin. Metric sequences and controlled curves are the essence of the design. Beginning
with the overriding rectangle of the façade, it develops in a continuing subdivision of delicately related parts which, compartment by compartment,
descend in a rhythmic diminuendo to the smallest bead in the thinnest
molding of the fireplace mantel.

We can best see these qualities of the Pingree House by focusing our attention on one of its principal decorative components, the fireplace in the front parlor (Fig. 160). As a unit, it is a coherent whole, a symmetrical system of horizontal rectangles—clean, sharp, and exact. The rectangular theme is decisively stated in the hearth opening; in the frieze of the mantel this fundamental shape is reduced in size, varied in proportions, and embellished with different ornamental figures to form three subparts, which, like musical phrases, are then combined to form a complete balanced section. The rhythmic pattern can be stated as A–B–A. The two identical end panels (A) are larger than the central panel (B) and contain delicate foliated chain motifs which not only are elliptical in shape but which also grade from thin proportions at their extremities to heavier in the center (Fig. 161). This rhythmic variation creates the same visual effect as the frieze itself, which grades from the exquisite thinness of the side panels to the greater sculptural richness of the elliptically framed basket of fruit in the central panel.

In a still smaller division of parts the rectangle appears again in the alternating rhythm of the reed and rosette motifs of the architrave; and the whole elegant progression is crowned at the top by the rapid staccato patterns of the reed and dentil moldings of the cornice, motifs which in spite of their tiny size are still made up of basically rectangular shapes. On the ends, the entire composition is brought to a conclusion by the decisive vertical lines of the elegant attenuated engaged columns and their corresponding projecting entablature blocks.

This system of sharply defined self-contained and independent parts, rhythmically joined and related in a coherent decisive whole, so subtly developed by McIntire, is a fundamental condition of Neoclassicism. In its clarity and compartmentation it is diametrically opposed to the freer more flamboyant principles of Baroque design which dominated the interiors of the colonial period. The fireplace motif in the Lee Mansion in Marblehead (Fig. 91 b), for example, which is typical of the late colonial era, is much heavier in scale than the Wentworth-Gardner mantel (Fig. 91 c), and the forms are fuller and more three-dimensional. Instead of delicate foliated chains with each connecting part independent of the next, the richly carved ornament of the Lee mantel is in the form of garlands and volutes with parts interlocked and continuously joined in a proliferous three-dimensional rhythm. The delicately controlled curves of McIntire's work, in contrast, are geometrically exact, and each rhythmic unit is individually determinable from the next; each is also held flat to the surface to which it is joined. Furthermore, the mantel in the Lee Mansion is surmounted by an elaborately carved overmantel, and the whole is unified, both in texture and color, with the sumptuous wood paneling of the entire room. The McIntire mantel is painted a chaste white. This isolates it from the color and texture of the walls which, from the beginning, were covered with wallpaper. But at the same time that the Pingree mantel is independent of the wall, it is also coherently a part of the total interior space in which it is placed; for not only does a similar motif with a similar entablature

FIGURE 160. Samuel McIntire. Pingree House, Salem, Mass., parlor, 1805.

FIGURE 161. Samuel McIntire. Pingree House, Salem, Mass., parlor, mantel detail, 1805.

FIGURE 162. Samuel McIntire. Pingree House,
Salem, Mass., façade, detail of portico, 1805.

frame the broad opening between the front and back parlors, but the exact
replica of the mantel itself is found on the chimney of the back parlor (Fig.
160). The two mantels thus form, with the door, another A–B–A balanced
relationship like that already described in the frieze of the mantel. Thus
the two rooms become identified as one, and a spatial theme which was
originally stated in two dimensions in the mantel is now expanded into a
coherent three-dimensional system.

The same qualities of precisely related and elegantly proportioned spatial
components are found in the brick façade of the Pingree House (Fig. 159).
The primary rectangle of the building is given horizontal emphasis by the
stone stringcourses which divide the wall into three elongated subunits,

FIGURE 163. *West side of Washington Square,*
Salem, Mass.

units which vary in proportion from the widest at the bottom to increasingly narrow dimensions toward the top. The vertical rhythm, therefore, is a graded rhythm, reflecting the similar gradations which we found
in the interior. The gracefully flared stone lintels are set flush with the
wall, which, except for the stringcourses, is otherwise unadorned. Centered
in this simple but elegantly proportioned façade is the exquisite portico
(Fig. 162), sharply isolated from the surface of the brick by its clear-cut
outline yet unified with the whole by the congruence of its cornice with the
first stringcourse. In the delicately proportioned projecting semicircular
portico, which is seen as a changing ellipse as one approaches the house,
and in the elliptical fanlight over the door, we encounter once more those
contrasting controlled curves which McIntire used with such refinement in
his interior decoration.

The chaste simplicity of McIntire's style makes it different from the
extravagant and colorful elegance of the Adam Style in England. In fact,
it is this very quality of reserve which reflects so emphatically the strain
of Calvinistic severity which carried over into nineteenth-century America
as an important and formative inheritance from the colonial years. At
the same time, all that has been described in McIntire's design—the attenuated proportions, the delicate scale, the unity of multiple parts, the
division and subdivision of motif—all these are also characteristic of the

Adam Style, and were acquired by the Salem wood carver primarily through architectural handbooks. Although the style came to him at second hand, it was refined by his own innate artistic sense and by the Puritan taste of his wealthy patronage.

The attitude toward life which found delight in the refined classicism of McIntire and the Federal Style prompted similar gratification in the work of another great classicist of the era, the impeccable string quartets of the Austrian composer Franz Joseph Haydn. Building as they do with meticulous precision from figure to phrase, from phrase to section and from section to movement, each defined and felt with the same clarity, each one ornamented with the same felicitous grace, these neat and elegant designs were the very embodiment of the Neoclassical age and the exact counterpart in sound to the spatial qualities of the Federal Style. The American people, conditioned as they were to a particular concept of form, sensed these qualities in music as well as in art and they responded to the works of Haydn with an enthusiasm comparable to any known abroad. It is no accident of history that the oldest Haydn Society in the world was founded in Boston during the Neoclassical era.

Permeation of the Federal Style

The type of house represented by the Pingree House became a favorite in the New England coastal communities during the first few decades of the nineteenth century. In its basic form it does not represent a radical break from the three-story town houses of the colonial period, such as the Royall House in Medford, Massachusetts, and thus by indirection it continues to assert its ancestry in the London town houses of the early eighteenth century. The changes which did occur were changes in proportions, scale, and ornament. Tuned to the ambitious but conservative taste of an affluent merchant class these elegant Federal houses were built by the score in seaport towns from Rhode Island to Maine, and many of them still exist.[24] Among the most remarkable is the cluster on the west side of Washington Square in Salem (Fig. 163). In Providence, Rhode Island, however, stands one of the most ambitious, the Thomas Poynton Ives House (Fig. 164), completed in 1806, a year after McIntire's masterpiece. This impressive mansion was obviously inspired by the Pingree House. Although taller in proportions and made of a darker brick, it has similar windows and a portico which is almost identical except that it projects farther from the wall and is topped by a delicately scaled balustrade. The compound window above this portico is reminiscent in its narrow side lights of a Palladian window and is surmounted by an elliptical fanlight. Unlike the Palladian motif, in which the crowning arch covers only the central window, the. elliptical stone relieving arch which supports the wall above this window embraces the entire group of three and is tapered, with the outer arch higher in shape than the inner arch. It is keyed by an elegant triple keystone similar to those in the flat arches above the regular windows. Altogether the Ives House is more pretentious than the Pingree House and, lacking McIntire's sure sense of

FIGURE 164. *Thomas Poynton Ives House,*
Providence, R.I., 1806.

FIGURE 165. *Nickels-Sortwell House,*
Wiscasset, Me., 1807–12.

proportions, it is more awkward and provincial. The compound window, for example, is out of scale with the portico and therefore upsets the coherent unity so consummately achieved in McIntire's design.

Even more provincial, yet typical of the variety found from location to location, is the Nickels-Sortwell House in Wiscasset, Maine (Fig. 165), built between 1807 and 1812. Unlike the other two houses, this one is made of wood, as were a great many others of the period, but the siding is laid up in closely fitted matched boards rather than the overlapping clapboards of the colonial houses. The surface is thus smoother and more tautly drawn than would be possible with either brick or clapboard. The house is also more elaborate than the other two and at the same time it is more conservative. The window above the portico, for example, is a traditional Palladian window but above this is a half round double arched window with radiating and oval mullions. This vertical combination of elaborate centrally located windows is flanked by slender Corinthian pilasters. A second pair of similar pilasters separates the vertical ranks of windows left and right of center to enframe a central pavilion which projects slightly from the main wall of the building. Further to accent this pavilion, the first-floor windows left and right of the portico are set back under segmental wall arches, an arrangement characteristic of the Adam Style in England (Fig. 158). Unlike the other two houses, the Nickels-Sortwell House does not have a crowning balustrade but is topped by a very low-pitched hipped roof. Although exceedingly elegant in detail this house, in its extraordinary combination of motifs, is more an encyclopaedia of the Federal Style than a coherent design.

In the farming communities of the New England hinterland the Federal Style house assumed its most traditional form. Instead of the three-story town house, the ubiquitous two-story horizontal block prevailed. In some instances these houses were almost exactly like those of the colonial period: the only perceptible change was a shift toward a more delicate scale and more slender proportions in such things as moldings, door casings, and window mullions. In others, efforts were made to imitate more closely the sophistications of the style of the eastern seaboard. The Sloane House in Williamstown, Massachusetts (Fig. 166), for example, is a basic rectangular clapboard-covered box no different from scores of other houses in the region; it is decorated, however, with an elaborate combination of applied ornament, and this conveyed an air of sophisticated grace both to the house itself and to its frontier setting. It was built in 1801 by General Samuel Sloane, as a wedding present for his son, at a time when the unadorned brick front of West College, the oldest building in Williams College, was the most advanced work of architecture in the area.[25] The elaborate Federal Style ornament, however, which must have made the house seem inordinately grand in the simple frontier environment of 1801, was not local at all. Instead, it was made in a Boston shop, sent by ship to New York, then hauled up the Hudson by river boat to Albany, where it was transferred to ox carts for the trip over the mountain. The house, therefore, is one thing, the ornament another. This is especially evident at the corners of the façade, where the quoins have been combined with

FIGURE 166. *Sloane House,*
Williamstown, Mass., 1801.

corner pilasters which run the full height of the building. Robert Adam
used corner pilasters in England, he also used quoins, but he never used
them together. To the local craftsman in the Berkshire hills, a sumptuous
house without quoins was unthinkable. He therefore used them without
hesitation, thereby rendering the pilasters both redundant and incongruous.
Although graciously elegant in its imported decoration, the Sloane House
is nonetheless charmingly naïve and typical of many houses to be found
throughout the New England hinterland.

Even more traditional and infinitely more characteristic of the Federal
Style as it developed in the hands of the local craftsman is the David Aubin
House, built in Vergennes, Vermont (Fig. 167), in the early years of the
nineteenth century. It is typical of both the era and the region in that it
is made of brick with marble lintels. Although the majority of New
England houses during the first quarter of the century continued to be
made of wood, a considerable number were built in brick. By 1810 all
the houses of Boston were being constructed of brick[26] and, combined
with the chaste ornaments carved in white wood, the material became a
major characteristic of the style. In the outlying regions it also became
common, although never dominant. The Aubin House is a typical and
particularly beautiful example. Handsomely proportioned and unpretentious, it is honestly the work of local hands. Only in the elliptical arched
door do we find any hint of the decorative elaborations of the Federal
Style. And even here the statement is impressively simple. The elliptical
relieving arch is cut from a single piece of Vermont marble and sweeps
boldly across the entire door motif. The pilasters and entablature are
slender in proportions but are otherwise unadorned. The mullions of the
fanlight and side lights are fashioned in a graceful combination of ovoid

FIGURE 167. *David Aubin House,*
Vergennes, Vt., early nineteenth century.

shapes. The Aubin House is a superb example of the conservative but refined taste of rural New England at its best.

Outside of New England, American domestic architecture of the Federal
period assumed a variety of forms, each characteristic of its own region.
Yet all were conceived within the same system of proportions and ornament, and with the same preference for complex shapes both in structure
and in plan. Of these, the most interesting are found in the only important
seaport town of the South—Charleston, South Carolina. Here we encounter not only an affluent patronage whose taste and means sought fulfillment in houses comparable in quality and size to those in New England,
but also a regional house type which developed from conditions peculiar
to Charleston. This is the so-called "single house," a house one room in
depth, oriented with its short end toward the street and with a piazza along
the entire long side (Fig. 168). These features seem to have been imported
from the West Indies and were intended to afford space for outdoor living
and to protect the house from the sun.[27] The type is thus distinctly
regional.

In Charleston houses of the early nineteenth century the piazza often
gave way to more decorative concerns, but the basic form and orientation

FIGURE 168. *Single houses, East Bay Street, Charleston, S.C.*

of the house itself remained essentially unchanged. The Nathaniel Russell House, built before 1809, is typical (Fig. 169). In many ways this is one of the most magnificent and fascinating houses in Charleston. Its main block is a single range of rooms three rooms long and one room deep. Projecting from the center of the garden side is an octagonal bay. The house is three stories high, and the main living spaces are contained on the second and third stories. The main door (Fig. 170) is on the short end facing the street and enters into a spacious first-floor hall, which in turn opens into the main stair hall at the center of the house. Access to the principal rooms on the upper floors is gained from here by means of a spiral staircase (Fig. 171). The spiral staircase, sometimes circular, sometimes oval, in plan, is one of the most ingenious and gracious devices of the Federal Style and came to America from the England of the Brothers Adam. The one in the Russell House is among the loveliest of them all.

Opening from the stair hall on the second floor and breaking into the octagonal projection on the garden side is a spacious oval room which is oriented across the house (Fig. 172). Flanking the entrance door and corresponding exactly to the full-length windows in the octagon are two mullioned mirrors framed, as are the windows, by tall slender pilasters with an extremely elegant entablature that is curved to the shape of the room.

The outside (Fig. 169) of the house is much more sumptuous than any of its New England contemporaries. Not only is it more vertical in its proportions, especially when seen from the entrance side, but the three floors are separated by double stringcourses of glazed brick, and the tall full-length windows of the second floor are set back in recessed wall panels which are topped by circular arches of glazed brick. The tall

FIGURE 169. *Nathaniel Russell House,*
Charleston, S.C., garden façade, before 1809.

FIGURE 170. *Nathaniel Russell House,*
Charleston, S.C., main entrance, before 1809.

windows on the second floor open onto wrought-iron balconies of the most exquisite design, instead of onto a typical porch of the traditional single house. Although the architect of the Russell House is not known, he produced one of the most original houses in America and in every respect a masterpiece of the Federal Style.

In our general discussion of the Federal Style the church remains to be considered. By no means all of the churches built in America during the first quarter of the nineteenth century can be classified with the Federal Style. As we shall see, some of the important ones were not. In New England, however, Congregationalism continued to grow in strength at the same time that it remained fundamentally conservative in taste. Under these conditions some of the rare buildings in the New England church tradition were erected during these years in the Federal Style. Just as in the case of the New England house, the connections with the colonial era remained unbroken, and without exception the important churches of the region continued the Wren-Gibbs type. St. Martin-in-the-Fields still remained the major source of inspiration. A rigidly conservative church which is closely related to St. Martin's is Center Church in New Haven, Connecticut (Fig. 173), designed by the Boston architect Asher Benjamin and built by his young assistant Ithiel Town.[28] It was begun in 1812 and finished in 1814. At first glance Center Church seems to follow St. Martin's very closely. Yet there are several significant differences. The steeple and spire are taller and thinner in proportions; details are more finely scaled. In addition, a central vestibule, which corresponds exactly with the base of the tower, projects out from the main wall beneath the colonnade to be included between the two central columns; in the center of the front wall of this vestibule is a round-headed window set in a large recessed wall arch. In fact, the wall arch, a principal characteristic of the Federal Style, is employed in Center Church for all of the major windows. The church, therefore, in spite of its conspicuous derivation from St. Martin's, is adorned with the proportional and decorative characteristics of the Federal Style.

Numerous churches throughout New England during the first quarter of the nineteenth century were built in brick with white wood trim, but the majority, like the houses, were still built in wood. Lending itself as it did to slender proportions and delicate detail, wood provided the ideal medium for the Federal Style and many of the churches in New England were built in this manner. Of them all, the Congregational Church in Old Lyme, Connecticut (Fig. 174), built by Samuel Belcher in the years 1816–17, is probably the most inspired. Like Center Church in New Haven, it, too, is obviously based on St. Martin's. Something of the severity of the early New England meetinghouse also prevails in the simple and domestically scaled main body of the church. In the graceful Ionic portico, however, and in the soaring steeple and spire, all the possibilities of the Federal Style as rendered in wood have been realized. In general, ornamental features project only slightly and proportions are thin and drawn out. The gracious spirit of Samuel McIntire is summarized at Old Lyme but on a more monumental scale. Here the carpenter and

FIGURE 171. *Nathaniel Russell House,*
Charleston, S.C., spiral staircase, before 1809.

the wood carver joined together to elicit from wood all that its fibrous
resilience would render.

The Congregational Church at Old Lyme represents the highest creative
effort and dedication to craft that the New England builder was capable
of. It established the criteria for countless other New England churches,
large and small, which have left their lovely stamp upon the region.

The First Congregational Church (1806) in Old Bennington, Vermont
(Fig. 175), a charming building situated on a hill above the present city

FIGURE 172. *Nathaniel Russell House, Charleston, S.C., oval room, before 1809.*

of Bennington, is flanked on either side by several handsome houses of the same period. Seen in the reflective gold of autumn's fire, it rises in provincial elegance before a shaded common to form the focal point of one of those ravishing fragments of early nineteenth-century New England which have somehow escaped the intrusion of late nineteenth-century industrial erosion. When compared to the sophisticated and graceful Old Lyme Church, the one in Bennington has a disjointed pattern-book character. Nevertheless, it displays all the proportional and ornamental features of the Federal Style. This is seen especially in the oval lights of the spire and in the tall slender columns which support the belfry.

It does not surprise us that so many small provincial churches like the one in Old Bennington were built in New England during the Federal period. The small towns of rural New England remained strongly traditional well into the nineteenth century, and the sharp accents of attenuated whiteness which were scattered across the countryside by the Federal Style church spires served only to reaffirm the strength of Congregationalism in the region. What does surprise us, however, is the number of similar churches which were built in parts of the country outside of New England, some of them as late as mid-century. As American civilization moved westward, and as settlers from New England made their way into the Western Reserve, they took with them the familiar architectural habits of

FIGURE 173. *Asher Benjamin and Ithiel Town. Center Church, New Haven, Conn., 1812–14.*

FIGURE 174. *Samuel Belcher, Congregational Church, Old Lyme, Conn., 1816–17.*

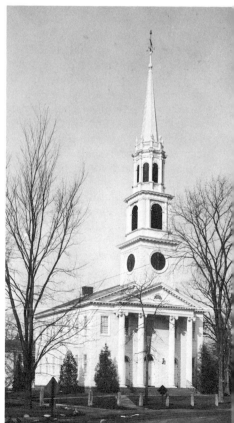

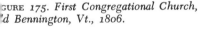

ᴳURE 175. *First Congregational Church,*
d Bennington, Vt., 1806.

FIGURE *176. Lemuel Porter, Congregational Church,*
Tallmadge, Ohio, 1825.

their background, and of all their buildings their churches were the most traditional. The Congregational Church in Tallmadge, Ohio, for example, built in 1825, at a time when the Federal Style was already being challenged in the east by the Greek Revival, is a remote but graceful reflection of early nineteenth-century New England at its best (Fig. 176). Similar in so many ways to the church at Old Lyme, and yet so provincial by comparison, this little gem and others like it brought to the promising new lands of the West the last phase of the great Wren-Gibbs tradition in church architecture. But the greatest creative accomplishments of the Federal Style did not occur in the breadth of its proliferation, although its pervasiveness can surely be measured in these terms. They are to be found rather in the work of a single individual, the Boston architect Charles Bulfinch, and no complete understanding of the Federal Style can be reached without a thorough examination of the man and his buildings.

CHAPTER VII

American Neoclassicism, The Traditional Phase

CHARLES BULFINCH

Boston was the child of my father's and he did pretty much as he pleased with it.
FRANCIS VAUGHAN BULFINCH

When Charles Bulfinch returned to Boston in 1787, after almost two years in Europe, it was still a provincial town, secure in the insular fastness of the Shawmut Peninsula. Mean narrow winding streets crawled in a random interlace around the Town Cove and the docks. There had been no significant new building in the town for almost thirty years and many of the surviving buildings were still medieval in character. There was, to be sure, a scattering of somewhat elegant houses, and there were several simple but handsome churches, all of them built during the first half of the eighteenth century, but for the most part both the mood and the character of the town were still cast in the awkward manner of the colonial years.[1]

Thirty years later, when Bulfinch left to take up his duties as architect to the Capitol in Washington, Boston was stamped with new qualities of dignity and elegance. Throughout the city not only were there clusters of useful and handsome new buildings, but streets had been improved and beautified by planting, park areas had been projected if not actually developed, and in general new levels of taste and sophistication were apparent on every hand. "I am really astonished at the appearance of Wealth magnificence & taste, thro'out the town,"[2] wrote one Bostonian (in 1809) who had not seen the city in over thirty years. All this had been accomplished by Charles Bulfinch.

The transformation which Bulfinch brought about in Boston bears a direct relationship to his total involvement in the life of the town. There is first his identification with the ruling aristocracy. He was born in 1763, only a few years before the Revolution, into a well-to-do and prominent professional family. His father was one of the great physicians of his day; his mother was the daughter of one of the city's richest and most influential merchants. His social credentials, therefore, were unimpeachable. Moreover the Bulfinch family, although stanchly on the side of the Revolution during the war, was Anglican by persuasion, inherently conservative, and it readily identified itself with the Federalist party; and Bulfinch himself, although not an aggressive personality, was motivated by the same ideals and objectives.

Bulfinch also enjoyed the best educational advantages of his day. He graduated from Harvard in 1781 and a few years later, in 1785, he went abroad for the Grand Tour. He was to remain in Europe for almost two years. At the suggestion of Thomas Jefferson he went to Paris, then to southern France and on into Italy, where he visited Florence and Rome. The remainder of his time he spent in England.

The young Bulfinch emerged from this background as a dedicated and imaginative public servant. In 1791, at the age of twenty-seven, he was elected to the Board of Selectmen of the town of Boston and except for four years (1795–99) he served continually until his departure for Washington in 1817; during the last eighteen years he was Chairman of the Board. In 1799 he was also appointed Superintendent of Police, a thankless job which he never relished but which he carried out faithfully primarily because it brought him his only fixed income, six hundred dollars a year.

These official connections, together with his own natural civic minded-ness, brought Bulfinch into intimate contact with every dimension of Boston. Through the affairs of government he became involved in the schools, the hospitals, and the prisons, as well as the commercial and financial life of the town; and he saw all this at decisive levels of association and leadership. Moreover, his firsthand knowledge of the great cities of Europe made clear to him the inordinately provincial character of his native town and moved him to change it. It was in the ful-fillment of this ambition that Bulfinch rose to prominence as an architect, and his work in architecture cannot be understood apart from his civic commitments; for Bulfinch designed government buildings, schools, pris-ons, churches, banks, markets, wharves, warehouses, and theaters, as well as numerous houses.[3] He also planned important parts of the town and spent considerable effort not only in improving but also in beautifying many of its important streets. What he achieved in Boston was as much a part of the town as the countless ships which crowded its wharves, and in spite of Bulfinch's dedicated public service it was as an architect that he was best known and honored by his fellow citizens.

That Bulfinch thought of himself as an architect and that he was so accepted by the men of his time is a thoroughly substantiated fact.[4] But the frequent use of the term "architect," as it appears in the documents, raises the question of what it means when applied to Bulfinch. In our considerations of the Colonial period we discovered two types of "ar-chitect," the architect-builder, whose main occupation was that of house-wright, and who was a designer secondarily as a condition of his trade, and the gentleman-amateur whose principal vocation might be anything from merchant to college professor and who designed buildings as a con-dition of his status as a gentleman. He rarely, if ever, played an active role in construction, however, and he was never paid except in the form of some token gift. William Buckland was characteristic of the first type, Peter Harrison of the second.

Certainly at the beginning of his career Bulfinch's attitude and activity were those of the gentleman-amateur. We know from his own brief autobiographical sketches that his original intention was to study medicine, but his father counseled against this and instead he was placed in the accounting room of the merchant Joseph Barrell. In the unsettled period which followed the war, Mr. Barrell's business was not very flourishing and the young Bulfinch found himself, in his own words, "at leisure to cultivate a taste for architecture, which was encouraged by attending Mr. Barrell's improvement of his estate and on our own dwelling house and the houses of some friends, all of which had become exceedingly dilapidated before the war."[5]

In this early contact with the practical problems of building, Bulfinch's enthusiasm for architecture began, an enthusiasm which he took with him on his trip abroad and which must have opened his eyes to things which the average traveler would never have seen. He tells us that on his return to Boston he "was warmly received by friends, and passed a season of leisure pursuing no business, but giving gratuitous advice in Architecture, and looking forward to an establishment in life." Thus as a young man of leisure he performed as a gentleman-amateur. But this condition of casual commitment was not to last for long. His own talents and a driving desire to improve the town of Boston took him very quickly into planning and building projects which demanded his total creative effort. Then in January 1796, through circumstances quite beyond his control, Bulfinch's personal holdings were liquidated in a declaration of bankruptcy and his activities as a gentleman-amateur came rudely to an end.[6] From this point on, of necessity and by natural inclination, his practice became increasingly professional, and by the turn of the century his career as an architect was firmly established.

Charles Bulfinch brought to his work several qualifications that gave him his professional standing. The first was his use of drawings as a means for developing his ideas. From the period prior to the late 1760's no important drawings survive for any American building,[7] although it is known that Peter Harrison made drawings for King's Chapel, and a painting by Charles Willson Peale shows William Buckland with his drafting instruments and a plan of the Hammond-Harwood House on the table. There must have been others, but the general lack of evidence makes it impossible to determine to what degree and for what purposes earlier architects used drawings. Since 1800, however, more and more drawings have been preserved which provide new insights into the architectural methods. As early as the late 1760's we find Thomas Jefferson using them in a professional way,[8] while in New England from the 1780's onward Samuel McIntire seems also to have relied heavily on them in developing his ideas. Bulfinch was not the first, therefore, to work with drawings. In view of the number of buildings known to have been designed by him, the surviving drawings are disappointingly few. But those that do remain display modest drafting skills and differ from those of Jefferson and McIntire in their use of both perspective and a very modest light and shade (compare Figs. 178 and 181 with Figs. 209 and 210). They have, therefore, a tentative pictorial quality which is unique for their time in America, and which is also indicative of Bulfinch's sensitive response to the spatial qualities of architecture, a response which is especially manifest in his own town planning projects.

Another aspect of Bulfinch's work which sets him apart from the gentleman-amateur is the extent of his participation in the actual construction of his buildings. As early as 1795 we find him in full supervisory capacity over the building of the new Massachusetts State Capitol after his own designs, deeply involved in such problems as estimating the price of constructing, carving, and turning the columns for the façade, including the cost of labor. This degree of technical participation is not the mark of the gentleman-amateur, but rather of the professional. At the same time, his activity differed from that of the craftsman-builder in that he came to the work not as a builder, but as the designer in supervision of construction. Unlike his predecessors, Bulfinch, as his work matured, was not satisfied with selecting an appropriate group of decorative motifs from recognized architectural handbooks and then assembling them into a design. Instead, he came to understand the totality of a building, to know it in terms of materials and structure as well as decoration, to recognize a tangible and fruitful relationship between the building and the purpose for which it was intended. Not until after 1800, in the later work of Thomas Jefferson, did any other American architect, whether craftsman-builder or gentleman-amateur, attain such a comprehensive and responsible level of identification with his work. It is true that some aspects of Bulfinch's work, especially the relationship between him and the builder, still reflected traditional ideas and methods. In some of his most important buildings, for example, he provided only the designs, relying entirely upon the builder to understand and carry out his intentions;[9] and in most instances the amount he was paid for his services was absurdly low. But in quantity and variety as well as quality, and to the remarkable degree that it shows him to be in touch with the pulse of his time, Bulfinch's architecture bears the stamp of the true professional, and it is in this sense that he and not Peter Harrison may be regarded as America's first professional architect.[10]

The Early Works

Bulfinch's career as an architect may be said to have begun with three very different yet stylistically related works, the Federal Street Theatre (Fig. 177), the Tontine, or Franklin, Crescent (Fig. 179), and the new Massachusetts State House (Fig. 183). Of these, the first two were the fruit of the architect's own enterprising spirit. Begun within a few months of one another, both were dramatic innovations, and when completed, they were unparalleled in the America of their day. The third, and slightly later, work was a more conventional commission for a well established type of public building, yet it was proposed for new purposes of state

FIGURE 177. *Charles Bulfinch. Federal Street Theatre,*
Boston, Mass., 1794.

and on a scale which provided a brilliant opportunity for a young man
who had only recently returned from the London of Robert Adam and
William Chambers.

Although the Theatre was the first of the three to be built, Bulfinch
seems to have had all of them in mind at the same time and to have
been working on them simultaneously. Moreover, they seem to have
been related to a deliberate though nebulous attempt on his part to improve
and update the town of Boston. It is in this connection that his trip
abroad assumes particular importance. Bulfinch was only the second
talented American architect to enjoy this experience,[11] and although the
surviving letters home tell us virtually nothing about his activities and
reactions with respect to architecture it is apparent, as evidenced by his
performance in later years, that it was indeed this very subject which
occupied a major share of his time and interest. After the weeks spent
in London, Paris, Florence, and Rome, his home town must have seemed
starkly provincial, and as these early projects make clear, he wasted
no time in initiating his own program for the reshaping of Boston.

The first object of his attention was the State House. Its total in-
adequacy[12] to meet the demands of the new government was a recognized
fact, and as early as November 5, 1787, less than a year after his
return to Boston from Europe, Bulfinch submitted his first plans for a
new state capitol building. But the political wheels moved with reluctance
and it was not until February 16, 1795, that a resolve of the General
Court was approved by the Governor and the architect's plan was accepted. In the meantime, Bulfinch turned his attention to the two other
projects, the Theatre and Tontine Crescent.

The Federal Street Theatre and Tontine Crescent

The Theatre and Tontine Crescent were conceived by Bulfinch as parts
of a coherent architectural scheme. As originally planned, the Crescent

FIGURE *178. Charles Bulfinch. Tontine Crescent,*
Boston, Mass., central pavilion, elevation drawing, c. 1793.

was in fact to have been two crescents of connected houses facing
one another to form an oval park; at the east end of this group was to
be the Theatre. Because of the street arrangement, however, the latter
building was not quite in line with the long axis of the park. Only the
crescent on the south side (its curve is still preserved in the present-day
Franklin Street) and the Theatre were ever built; the crescent on the
north side was replaced by detached houses in a single line, also designed
by Bulfinch. Land for both projects was purchased in 1793; on February
3, 1794, the Theatre was opened to the public,[13] and by that time, too,
work on the south crescent was well advanced. Although neither of these
buildings still survives, we know their appearance with reasonable cer-
tainty. The façade of the Theatre has been accurately preserved on one
side of a medal given to Bulfinch as a token of gratitude by the proprietors of the Theatre (Fig. 177); the Crescent we know in even greater
detail through the architect's drawings (Fig. 178), old photographs (Fig.
180), and a published engraving (Fig. 179).

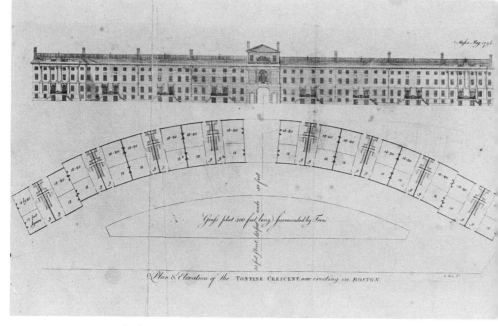

FIGURE 179. *Charles Bulfinch. Tontine Crescent, Boston, Mass., elevation and plan.*

In his design for the Theatre the façade appears as a classical rectangle with a level entablature and engaged Corinthian pilasters carried on a high basement. Projecting prominently from the center of this main block was a pavilion with a colonnade of two pairs of coupled Corinthian columns supporting a classical entablature and pediment. Like the main wall, the order rose from a high basement into which was cut a central arched opening with flanking doors to form the main entrance to the Theatre. In the center under the colonnade, and in the main wall left and right of the projecting pavilion, were Palladian-type windows set in recessed panels beneath wall arches.

This strictly Neoclassical design, so unlike anything else in the Boston of its day, reveals to us the nature of Bulfinch's creative personality in its formative stage. It shows us first the eager young enthusiast, fresh from all the excitements of his experiences abroad, impatiently pouring out his newly acquired knowledge. The building is obviously derivative. The over-all design was taken from a contemporary English architectural book which Bulfinch owned,[14] and the Palladian window motif appears in a little sketch by Bulfinch marked "Crunden's device." As we have already seen, this particular form of window was used frequently by English architects of the late eighteenth century, especially Robert Adam (Fig. 158). It was also employed by Bulfinch in a number of other designs, including Tontine Crescent (Fig. 178) and the State House (Fig. 181), and it ultimately became a distinctive feature of the Federal Style. We have already seen an earlier example in the façade of Woodlands in Philadelphia (Fig. 156).

FIGURE 180. Charles Bulfinch. Tontine Crescent,
Boston, Mass., general view, 1794.

The façade of the Federal Street Theatre was a prologue to the design
of Tontine Crescent. An intentional architectural relationship was established between the two by Bulfinch not only through a uniformity of
materials (both buildings were brick) and scale, but also through the
motif of the projecting portico; for in the center of the Crescent was a
similar pedimented pavilion with pilasters and engaged columns carried
on a high basement as at the Theatre (Fig. 177). The two buildings
are thus drawn into a visual unity. At the same time, however, there
are interesting functional differences. To maintain the continuity of the
long curved brick wall in the Crescent, the order is engaged rather than
freestanding, and the central arched opening in the basement goes through
the entire building, thus providing a secondary access to the Crescent from
the street behind (Fig. 179). Beyond this central pavilion the Crescent
takes on a character quite its own. The graceful curved surfaces of the
main walls stretch left and right, unbroken by any ornamentation (Fig.
180), until they reach the last two house units on either end.[15] These
were made to project slightly and were adorned with pilasters to form
terminating pavilions in the design. All the window openings were cut
sharply into the wall without ornamentation.

Seen in the light of contemporary architecture in England there was
nothing original about Bulfinch's crescent scheme. During his stay in
England he no doubt saw the great crescents, circuses, and squares of
Bath[16] as well as the elegant brick façades of Robert Adam's Adelphi
Terrace and Portman Square in London. Equally important, he was
also familiar with the less pretentious housing units of London such as

Robert Adam's Mansfield Street (Fig. 190). In his frank adaptation of these urban projects he re-established contact with English architecture for the first time following the Revolution, in the same way that the Federalist merchants of Boston were renewing their economic ties with the mother country. It is an interesting fact of history that Jay's Treaty, which reopened trade with the British, was ratified in 1794, the same year that Bulfinch completed Tontine Crescent. Thus the English cultural heritage, so passionately revered by the upper class of Boston's society, was not only reaffirmed, it was also recast in the chaste and elegant forms of the Neoclassical era, and the direct and pervasive influence of England, which had shaped American architecture during the colonial years, remained unbroken.

In spite of, or perhaps because of, its obvious English derivations, Tontine Crescent was a welcome and promising innovation in Boston of the late eighteenth century. Because of both the practical conveniences offered by Bulfinch's plan and the new qualities of style which he introduced, the Crescent was praised and put to immediate use; every one of its sixteen houses was occupied within a year of its completion. It became an island of reasoned dignity in the awkward meanderings of a provincial colonial town. Indeed, from every practical and emotional aspect it was a triumphant success.

It was also a personal disaster for the architect, for it was Bulfinch's involvement in Franklin Crescent that brought about his bankruptcy. The method used to finance the project was questionable,[17] and because of the unfavorable economic conditions in Boston which preceded the ratification of Jay's Treaty the enterprise failed and Bulfinch's financial resources were completely wiped out. Although this brought great hardship upon him and his family, in respect to his career as an architect it was a blessing in disguise. With his worldly assets gone, he was forced to find other means of support. From that point on he was drawn more and more into architecture as his major vocation.

The Massachusetts State House

With the architectural success of the Theatre and the Crescent behind him, and with the prospect of making a living confronting him, Bulfinch gave his entire attention to the State House. Other commissions also began to come his way. In 1795 he even declined to serve on the Board of Selectmen because of his preoccupation with architectural projects, and for three years he seems to have been totally immersed in the affairs of building. Moreover, up to that time the new State House was the most ambitious building ever undertaken in New England, and it provided the young man with the very opportunity he needed. With its completion his reputation as an architect was firmly established, and when it was officially opened in 1798 he marched triumphantly in the procession which made its way from the old State House to the new.

The new State House was the crowning achievement of the architect's early years (Fig. 183). As a design it was conceived in the same basic language of style as the Theatre and the Crescent, and it was equally derivative. The spell of London was still with Bulfinch and because of his lack of experience and his provincial background it was natural that he should yield to its persuasion. Bulfinch was perfectly frank about his dependence upon English sources and even spoke of the design of the State House as being "in the style of a building celebrated all over Europe." He was referring to William Chambers's Somerset House, the new government building in London, the central portion of which was finished in 1786 while he was still there. Chambers was an exact contemporary of Robert Adam, and next to Adam was the most important figure in early English Neoclassicism.[18] But his style was more conservative than Adam's, combining as it did a strong underlying ingredient of English Palladianism, and a considerable French influence, inspired no doubt by a year spent in Paris studying architecture. Somerset House was a proud climax to an immensely successful career, and to the young provincial from Boston it must have seemed wonderful beyond imagination. In any case, its influence on the new State House was substantial. The main colonnaded pavilion of Bulfinch's façade, from arcaded basement to dome, was directly inspired by the central pavilion in the river front of Chambers's design (Fig. 182), and in the lateral wings we encounter once more the familiar Palladian window, set in a recessed wall arch.

In all its major components Bulfinch's design is the product of English Neoclassicism. Yet it is different. It has none of the weight and largeness of Somerset House, nor is it as sculptural. The effect, on the contrary, is light and airy. Bulfinch accomplished this through the use of much more delicate scale, and through more attenuated proportions. His columns are more slender than those at Somerset House, and ornamental details such as moldings are thinner and more finely drawn. This can be seen especially by comparing Bulfinch's elevation for the façade (Fig. 181), where his proportional intentions may be grasped as a whole, with the engraved elevation of Somerset House (Fig. 182).

The Massachusetts State House is, in fact, more Adamesque than its London prototype. At the same time it is more austere and simple, reflecting its provincial origins (Fig. 183). The Boston architect eliminated altogether Chambers's heavy rustication and relied instead upon clean flat walls of brick, discreetly divided by thin white stringcourses. Window and door openings are sharply cut and unadorned in the same way as those which he used at Franklin Crescent. His simplification of the wall surface is particularly effective in the basement arcade. The clean brick piers, carefully spaced to correspond to the coupled and single columns which they carry, assert their function as vertical supports without the interruption of surface ornament. Each of these lines of vertical force is delicately terminated by a thin horizontal course of white, which in turn provides the spring for the rhythmic sequence of the equally unadorned brick arches. Together these arches and their supporting piers form one of the most expressive and lovely structural passages in American architecture.

Even though the sources of Bulfinch's motifs are obvious, the propor-

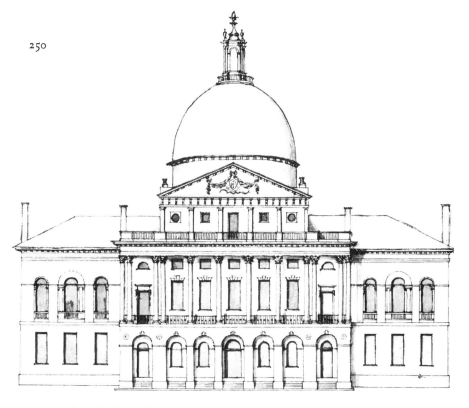

FIGURE 181. Charles Bulfinch. Massachusetts State House, Boston, original elevation drawing, 1795–98.

tions, the scale, and the part-to-part relationships, have all been deeply felt by his responsive artistic personality with its innate sense of formal rightness. Yet there is also something prim and unsubstantial about the building. It is masonry and yet it isn't masonry. Certain of its qualities make it seem as though a long tradition of wood architecture in New England was still seeping through the Neoclassical vocabulary. In both scale and surface quality the dome and its drum are conspicuously wood and therefore rest uneasily atop the brick walls, like a shining bald head emerging from the resplendent elegance of a neatly trimmed red beard. The columns, the crowning entablature, and the balustrade are also of wood, turned and fashioned by the same hands and the same tools that built many of the wood houses of Boston. The fact remains that a tradition of wood architecture was not to be denied, nor was the conservative taste of the town itself. As a product of that environment, Bulfinch performed with judicious restraint within its prescribed limits.

In all probability Bulfinch would have preferred to build the new State House in stone. He had seen the monumental Neoclassical architecture of England with its unbroken walls of stone cut and laid up with the most consummate precision. Tightly joined stonemasonry must have offered those very qualities of flat clean surface and cool neutral color which his discreet Neoclassical taste would have found attractive. This preference is borne out by the fact that he actually painted some of his

FIGURE 182. *William Chambers. Somerset House,
London, England, central pavilion of the river front, 1776–86.*

FIGURE 183. *Charles Bulfinch. Massachusetts State House,
Boston, 1795–98.*

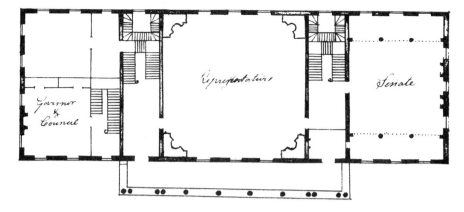

FIGURE 184. *Charles Bulfinch. Massachusetts State House, Boston, plan, 1795–98.*

FIGURE 185. *Charles Bulfinch. Massachusetts State House, Boston, House of Representatives Chamber, 1795–98.*

brick buildings gray to make them look like stone, and when he worked with wood, instead of using the conventional clapboard, he relied upon matched boards tightly drawn together. It is this which gives the drum of the State House dome its taut membranous quality. Moreover, of the later buildings which he was responsible for in Boston, at least a quarter of them were actually in stone.[19] But Boston of the 1790's could not bear the cost of a stone State House and the building was therefore brick. Whether or not Bulfinch originally intended it to be painted is not known, but if he did, the very fact that the white decorative elements rely so conspicuously upon color contrast for their effect suggests that he probably would have painted it either gray or a neutral yellow. Sometime before 1825 the building was painted yellow and so it remained into the twentieth century. There is nothing to indicate that this was Bulfinch's intention, however, and for a quarter of a century it remained red brick. In fact, brick was to become the principal building material in Boston for some time to come, not only because most of Bulfinch's buildings were of brick, but also because of the ordinance passed by the Board of Selectmen in 1803 which required that all buildings more than ten feet high should be either brick or stone.[20] Throughout the Federal period almost all residential architecture of Boston was to be of brick, although many of the civic and commercial buildings were stone.

The plan of the new State House (Fig. 184) is a perfectly straight-forward accommodation of rectangular spaces within a symmetrical rectangular mass. Bulfinch did make some effort to introduce Neoclassical variety in the House of Representatives Chamber (Fig. 185) by cutting off the corners of the square space and thus creating the suggestion of an octagon, but the rest of the rooms are simple rectangles. The House of Representatives Chamber is the largest room in the building and occupies a central position beneath the dome; it is flanked on either side by the main halls and stair wells. The interior space occupied by the room itself is articulated on the exterior of the building by the pedimented central block which rises above the portico. The hall and stair wells are expressed by the paired coupled columns in the portico and at the ground level by the wider spacing of the end arches in the basement arcade.

It is on the interior of the State House that the Adam influence is most in evidence. This is seen especially in the ceiling of the old House of Representatives Chamber (now the Senate Chamber) (Fig. 186). The entire room is covered by a plaster ceiling suspended from wooden trusses and shaped in the form of a segmental, or saucer, dome. Visual support is gained by four depressed segmental pendentives which rise from the octagonal corners. These shallow segmented shapes, which contrast with the high semicircular vaults of the Wren churches, were favorite devices of Robert Adam (Fig. 152) and the other English Neoclassicists.[21] So too was the sharply linear compartmented ornament which Bulfinch employed throughout the interior of the State House. In the center of the dome just described, for example, is a series of concentric circles made up of delicate plaster ornament, and radial patterns which alternately contrast with the plain surfaces. Within these bands each individual motif is decisively separated from the next. In typical Neoclassical manner, each decorative feature, down to the tiniest ornamental device, is made to relate to or join its neighbor, but is never permitted to overlap. The outer circular band of the central ornament is scalloped and contains the large elliptical curves of a garland and swag motif; between the scallops flat unadorned ribs radiate to the rim of the dome.

FIGURE 186. *Charles Bulfinch. Massachusetts State House,*
Boston, House of Representatives Chamber, ceiling, 1795–98.

FIGURE 187. *Robert Adam. Ceiling design.*

Between these ribs and just above the rim is a series of round soffits containing finely scaled decorative wheels not unlike the larger wheel at the center. The effect again is of a regular spacing of tangential compartments which are totally independent at the same time that they are joined together in a continuous concentric rhythm.

The compartmentation, the elegant curved shapes, and the delicate scale of Bulfinch's ceiling are all Adamesque (compare Fig. 187), yet there are other qualities which are not. The ornament is simpler, flatter, and more sharply geometric than that of Adam, and much more emphasis is placed upon plain surfaces. The flat, unornamented ribs, for example, would never be found in Adam's work. These differences can be explained in part by the limitations of craftmanship in Boston at this time— but only in part, for not only is Bulfinch's ornament simpler than Adam's, there is also less of it and here we are confronted with a matter of taste. Lingering in the Boston temperament was a survival of Puritan austerity, and Bulfinch's chaste and severe style reflects to some degree this peculiar characteristic of both his environment and his own natural inclinations.

The new Massachusetts State House was at once acclaimed as a masterpiece, not only by the proud citizens of Boston but by visitors as well. And so it was. Except for Thomas Jefferson's Virginia State Capitol,[22] built a decade earlier, no other public building in America could match it, and together with the Theatre and Franklin Crescent it established Bulfinch as New England's leading architect. Commissions began

FIGURE 188. *Charles Bulfinch. Colonnade Row, Boston, Mass., 1811.*

FIGURE 189. Houses at 13, 15, and 17 Chestnut Street, Boston, Mass.

coming to him from every hand and his work embraced all dimensions of the public and private life of the town. Moreover, his work was immediately influential, and the character of the Federal Style as it developed in New England and elsewhere in America owes much to Charles Bulfinch.

Town Planner and Domestic Architect

Most of the commissions that Bulfinch undertook were conventional ones for houses, civic buildings, and churches. Others for commercial buildings, warehouses, stores, hospitals, and prisons were more unusual and drew him into a wider range of the town's life.[23] All his designs were cast in the language of the Federal Style, but as he matured he became less eclectic and more austere, with less concern for ornamentation and a greater feeling for pure geometric form. Morever, his interest in city planning, already

FIGURE 190. *Robert Adam. Mansfield Street, London, England. (Copyright* Country Life)

manifest at Franklin Crescent, led him into a number of similar projects, all of which proved to be of enormous importance in the formation of the character of the town. Before the State House was even completed he became involved with the Mt. Vernon proprietors, a group of wealthy Bostonians, in the development of the land adjacent to the Capitol as an exclusive residential area. The Tontine Crescent had been a series of attached houses; this time he thought in the more luxurious terms of single units with space around them grouped around an open garden square, reminiscent of the proprietory squares of London.[24] Although for reasons of economy his initial plan was not accepted, the approved scheme did call for the detached houses to be set back thirty feet from the street. The second house which Bulfinch designed for Harrison Gray Otis on Mt. Vernon Street (Fig. 191) was one of those built under this limitation and is distinguished even today from the other houses around it by the modest strip of lawn which separates it from the sidewalk.

FIGURE 191. *Charles Bulfinch. Second Harrison Gray Otis House, Boston, Mass., 1800.*

Bulfinch also saw the possibilities of the Common as a park area, and in 1804 he laid out a row of eight attached houses on Park Street which faced the Common toward the Charles River to the west. Seven years later he was commissioned to design his famous Colonnade Row (Fig. 188), a similar range of attached houses, this time of nineteen units.[25] It was located on the south side of the Common. With Beacon Hill and the State House to the north, and Park Street to the east, it formed a frame of elegant new buildings and changed the whole character of the Common from a country pasture to a city park. Bulfinch further enhanced the area by laying out walks and planting trees in the Common. The effect of this moved a contemporary writer to describe it as "one of the finest scenes in the world."

Virtually nothing remains today of either Colonnade Row or the Park Street group,[26] but on Beacon Hill, from the State House to Louisburg Square, are several streets of proud elegant houses, all of them directly inspired by these earlier projects. Built shoulder to shoulder, with their doors opening directly from the sidewalk, these neat brick façades circumscribe a world that is more Bulfinchian than Bulfinch himself (Fig. 189). The flavor is that of late eighteenth-century London (Fig. 190), somewhat more prim perhaps and more lightly scaled, but the London of Adam nevertheless, with flat brick walls broken only by crisply cut window openings and arched or colonnaded doorways. This idiom, which Bulfinch introduced to Boston in the Tontine Crescent, Park Street, and

Colonnade Row, was to flower on Beacon Hill into a neighborhood of remarkable charm and homogeneity. Even after 1825, when the Federal doorways were made to mingle with many designed in the Greek Style, the underlying character of the houses remained unchanged. As the century progressed, and the sonorous tones of an aggressive romanticism began to demand an audience, Beacon Hill remained aloof. In a rising tide of abundance, it became an island of restrained classicism, serene and secure in the strength of its Bulfinchian heritage. So it exists today—one of the most complete survivals of an era in the whole of American architecture.

The Harrison Gray Otis Houses

In the midst of these attached houses, Bulfinch's second Otis House (1800) stands in aristocratic isolation, with space on either side and in front of it, the only remnant of the scheme which he originally proposed for Mt. Vernon Street. The architect designed three houses for Harrison Gray Otis, and the second one in this remarkable trilogy is eloquently expressive both of Otis's ambitions and of Bulfinch's continued efforts to cater to his patron's taste.[27] Otis was one of the architect's most enthusiastic supporters and the relationship between the two was very close.[28] As one of the most powerful figures in the Boston of his day, and as a recognized leader in the Federalist party, Otis enjoyed a position of immense social prominence. It was a role, moreover, which he thoroughly enjoyed and for which he was eminently qualified. Intelligent, articulate, and possessed of wide cultural interests, he lived with a zest for fine things, and over the years in his several Bulfinch houses he entertained many of the most distinguished personalities of the day. The architect was not as aggressive socially as his ebullient patron but he shared his refined taste and understood exactly what he wanted. Because of this the Harrison Gray Otis mansions have become the architectural embodiment of the Federal era in New England.

The second Otis House (Fig. 191) is probably the best known and the most widely praised of the three. It was also the most important outgrowth of Bulfinch's plan for urbanizing Beacon Hill and is the climax of the architect's early work. Yet it is a restless design. To be sure, it reflects readily enough its English origins. By setting the full-length windows on the ground floor in segmental wall arches, and by topping them with a light stringcourse, the architect created the effect of a basement story which carries two lighter ranges of windows above. This was a standard formula for the fashionable town houses of London and Bath. In addition, the slender flat pilasters, which contrast in color with the wall, are strongly reminiscent of Adam's treatment of the end pavilions in his Adelphi Terrace. With all this the building has qualities that are un-English, and certain aspects of the design are unresolved. Bulfinch's pilasters, for example, are more austere than Adam's, lacking altogether the ornamental elegance so characteristic of the Englishman's work. Moreover, the entablatures which crown the pilasters are not carried across the entire façade, a curiously unclassical treatment which breaks the continuity of the eaves. This places an overemphasis at the top of each bay, particularly as each relates to the thin molded stringcourse upon which the pilasters rest. Instead of two classical pavilions supported on a substantial base, the effect is of two inverted open rectangles uneasily balanced on a thin white line. More than that, these same entablatures, by pressing down upon the top windows, cut the lintel stones in half and create the disturbing impression that the entablature and windows are competing with one another for adequate space in which to exist.

Such awkward passages betray Bulfinch's provincial background, which persistently asserted itself in spite of his native talent. But the native talent was there nevertheless, and if we strip away the pilaster frames (added, one is tempted to conclude, as a concession to the owner's social prominence), we encounter a very different kind of building. What remains is a system of clean geometric walls with sharply cut openings, each sensitively proportioned and rhythmically graded from bottom to top; and in this system structural means and materials are used without pretense. Reflecting its Yankee background, the house is austere and without emotion, yet it is poignantly resonant, and beneath the surface clutter of traditional elements one senses the gentle stirrings of new directions.

Unfortunately little remains of the original interior of the second Otis House. In fact, the only one of Bulfinch's domestic interiors to survive in anything like its original form is the one in the first Harrison Gray Otis House (1795–96). On the basis of this and fragments of evidence provided by early photographs, it seems apparent that both the quality and the character of the interior decoration in Bulfinch's houses varied considerably. In contrast to the coherent interiors of McIntire, which bear the unmistakable stamp of his genius, those of Bulfinch appear to be the work of several hands not all of which were equally skilled. The only logical conclusion that can be drawn from this evidence is that Bulfinch relied almost entirely on individual craftsmen to carry out this part of the work for him. It is not necessary to conclude from this that Bulfinch was uninterested in this aspect of his buildings, nor does it follow that the ornament because it was designed by another artist would be inappropriate to the building for which it was intended. It means only that Bulfinch, as an architect, was more concerned with the larger problems of planning, spatial arrangements, and construction. He viewed the detailing as the work for specialists. It is known that by the turn of the century numerous plaster workers as well as wood carvers were practicing their trade in Boston, and it seems clear that Bulfinch relied upon such craftsmen to carry out his intentions. For his more demanding commissions he unquestionably chose his men carefully and worked closely with them; in some of his monumental works, such as the State House, he may even have been active in designing the decorative elements. But no drawings or documents survive to sustain these assumptions, and the fact remains that the deep personal involvement with

FIGURE 192. *Charles Bulfinch. First Harrison Gray Otis House,
Boston, Mass., dining room mantel, 1795–96.*

detailing, so conspicuous in the work of the craftsman McIntire (an involvement supported by numerous surviving drawings) simply did not
occur in the case of Bulfinch.

The character of the ornament in the first Otis House bears this out.
The most important single unit in the scheme is the well known mantel
in the dining room (Fig. 192). As a design it has many of the characteristics seen in the Pingree House in Salem (Fig. 161): attenuated
proportions, compartmentation, and elegant detail. It does not have the
same sparkling quality, however, nor does it display the same sureness
of execution. The figures in the central panel reveal uncertain, general-
ized modeling with none of the crispness of McIntire's work. Moreover,
the various decorative elements have a stereotyped character, which
contributes to uniformity but drastically inhibits originality and freshness.
That the mantel was done by a Boston craftsman is further indicated
by the fact that the central figural panel appears in identical form
in another house in the Boston area which was not designed by Bulfinch.[29]
Both panels were probably made from the same mold. Nevertheless,
the mantel is a typical ornamental feature of the Federal Style and is
absolutely appropriate to the house itself. The delicate green background
against which the white carved and molded figures stand out in delicate
relief is a characteristic touch that betrays its English sources. The use
of cool neutral tones as a foil for the lacelike white or gilded ornament
is typical of Adam's interiors.[30]

FIGURE 193. *Charles Bulfinch. Third Harrison Gray Otis House, Boston, Mass., façade, 1806.*

Bulfinch's domestic style reached maturity in the third house which he designed for Harrison Gray Otis (Fig. 193). It was finished in 1806 and is on Beacon Street immediately facing the Common. In this superb building all ornamental pretense is stripped away, and the brick wall, which we were forced to discover behind the pilasters of the second Otis House, is here permitted to speak for itself. In actual measurement the façade forms a simple rectangle only slightly wider than it is high. As seen from the street, however, it gives the appearance of being tall in proportion. Bulfinch has created this impression through subtle and expressive means. By spacing the windows more closely vertically than horizontally he has drawn them into five rising tiers. Then he has accelerated this vertical movement by varying the shapes of the windows at the different floor levels. Those in the basement are conventional classical rectangles. On the second—in this case, the principal—floor, however, they are full-length and triple-hung so that in proportion they are very tall and narrow. Those on the third floor are shorter by one sash but still tall; at the top they are conventional rectangles again, identical to those in the basement. The result is a swelling graded sequence from small to large to medium to small which tapers off toward the top. This is the primary rhythm of the façade. But a second rhythm is also found in the vertical spacing of the windows. The closest together are those in the basement and on the second floor, those farthest apart are on the second and third floors. The medium spacing is between the third and fourth floors. Together these two changing sequences form an interlocking gradation both in size and interval which not only increases the sense of verticality but does so with the same qualities of rhythmic grace that are experienced in the controlled curvatures of an oval.

The exquisite subtlety of Bulfinch's façade becomes vividly apparent when we compare it to the awkward spacing and shapes of the windows in the later house (to the right in Fig. 193) built immediately adjacent to it on Beacon Street. But it is also apparent in a comparison with his own second Harrison Gray Otis House (191). Instead of the encumbering pilastered bays which we saw in the earlier house, the ornamental enrichment of the Beacon Street house is discrete and strictly functional. Thin

FIGURE 194. *Charles Bulfinch. Third Harrison Gray Otis House, Boston, Mass., detail of second-floor window, 1806.*

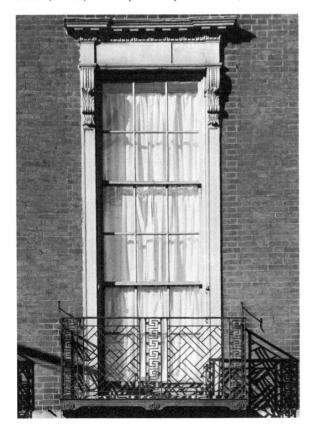

flat pilasters and bracketed entablatures frame the tall windows on the principal story (Fig. 194); gracing their feet are delicate iron balconies with Chinese fretwork.[31] Similar iron balconies were common to English town houses of the Neoclassical era and were used frequently by Bulfinch. This decorative emphasis on the second-floor windows, combined with their length, indicates that the principal rooms in the house are on this floor. In contrast, all the other windows are not only smaller but are cleanly cut, held close to the wall, and their lintel stones are set flush with the brick surface. On the upper two floors the only decorative touch is provided by the elegantly tapered and modestly carved keystones which project slightly from the wall and stress again the general vertical orientation of the façade.

The primary aspects of Bulfinch's third Otis House which distinguish it from the other two are its supremely beautiful attenuated proportions and its soaring vertical elegance. Attenuated proportions and verticality have been the basic ingredients of most elegant buildings throughout the history of Western architecture. The Ionic order (Fig. 4), for example, is more elegant than the Doric (Fig. 1) primarily because it is more thinly proportioned and more vertical, and the Gothic cathedrals (Fig. 2) achieve their lofty grace because their proportions are drawn to a maximum of attenuation in a soaring vertical thrust. In the third Otis House these qualities are carried to a supreme level of refinement.

A natural sensitivity for proportions is apparent in all Bulfinch's earlier work but it was frequently inhibited by his amateur eclectic methods. All too often his admiration for the specifics of English architecture intruded upon his own sensibilities. In the third Harrison Gray Otis House, however, the British ancestry, so conspicuous in the second Otis House, has been sublimated by an original and exquisitely subtle design. The refined adjustments of shape and interval, and the elegant rhythmic sequences, were achieved by the architect through an extraordinary economy of means, and it is precisely because of this that the ultimate experience of the house is primarily an experience of proportions. The shape and location of the windows *are* the design. Bulfinch's proportional system was, to be sure, derived from that of Robert Adam, but the third Otis House also displays qualities and relationships which are uniquely his own.

The second distinguishing aspect of the third Otis House, its vertical orientation, is a direct consequence of its proportional system; and it is this same vertical orientation, rhythmic and controlled, which gives the house its extraordinary buoyancy and grace. Bulfinch was struggling to achieve something of this quality in the second Otis House, but he was still too enchanted by the classical precept of a basement story supporting a colonade to make it possible.[32] Even though in the earlier house he carried a continuous wall plane from top to bottom, and articulated the basement with the thinnest possible line, that line is nevertheless an unbroken horizontal, and together with the superb but assertive rhythm of the segmental wall arches it creates the effect of a strong horizontal base carrying an equally horizontal superstructure. So much is this so that in

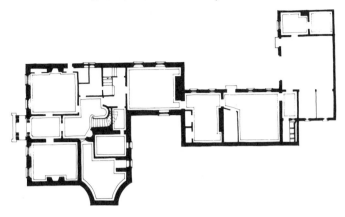

FIGURE 195. Charles Bulfinch. Third Harrison Gray Otis House, Boston, Mass., plan of ground floor, 1806.

spite of the pilastered bays one can read the windows in horizontal as well as vertical sequences. The result is a tension of unresolved forces. In the façade of the third Otis House, on the other hand, there is not a single continuous horizontal to interrupt the vertical flow. As though in response to the long slim reach of the house, as it is pressed to the rear by the narrow confines of its city lot (Fig. 195), Bulfinch's elegant façade stretches easily and gracefully upward, a cool urbane aristocrat in a world of conformity.

The unique qualities of the third Otis House are even more apparent when it is compared with the façade of McIntire's Pingree House in Salem (Fig. 159). We have described this latter building as an accomplished example of the Federal Style, and so it is. But when it is compared to Bulfinch's highly original scheme, its conservatism is immediately apparent. The strong lines of the horizontal stringcourses leave no doubt as to its traditional horizontal orientation, and the windows, although sensitively spaced, have the classical proportions of earlier houses. In spite of its clarity and simplicity the Pingree House, as a fundamental house type, is no more than an enlargement and refinement, through changes in scale and proportion, of the ubiquitous horizontal block of the late colonial years. In the mature work of the Boston architect, however, natural talent transformed tradition; and the incipient originality so evident in his early work is released in the third Otis House in one of the first creative outbursts by a native architect in American history.

The concern for vertical thrust which marks the façade of the third Otis House also directs the internal spatial design. The plan shows it to be arranged asymmetrically behind the symmetrical façade, and extending in considerable depth from the street (Fig. 195). A long off-center attached wing containing servants' quarters joins the kitchen ell with a carriage house behind. This forms a service court to the west; on the other side, the mass of the house breaks back and forth in its stretch

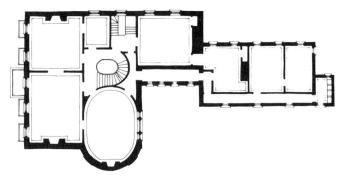

FIGURE 196. *Charles Bulfinch. Third Harrison Gray Otis House, Boston, Mass., plan of principal floor, 1806.*

in depth to form a smaller court opening into the garden. The most interesting feature of this east side was the semicircular bay which originally projected from the main block of the house into the garden (Fig. 196). Sometime in the nineteenth century, however, a tall narrow house was built adjoining the east wall of the Otis House with the west wall of the Sears House above, thus making it part of a continuous row of houses up Beacon Street. This new building incorporated the curved bay into its own structure; although the elegant shape is no longer visible from the outside, the oval room still remains on the inside. In spite of its symmetrical front, therefore, the original house was asymmetrical, designed this way to meet both the complex needs of the family and the peculiar fall of the land.

The main entrance with its projecting portico is the central issue of the façade and provides the fulcrum for its symmetrical balance. The door opens into a small vestibule, on either side of which are identical rooms (Fig. 195); the one to the right served as Mr. Otis's office, the one to the left as his library. Like the façade therefore, this part of the plan is symmetrical, and the main door together with the vestibule suggests the beginning of a strong central axis. But once we leave the vestibule and move into the stair hall itself this promise of a classically balanced scheme comes abruptly to an end.[33] For the stair hall is off center, and from this point back and upward the spatial components are placed asymmetrically around an oval spiral staircase that rises through the full height of the house; and neither this staircase nor any other major component of the design aligns itself with the central axis of the plan. The axis, in fact, is not horizontal at all but vertical, rising through the center of the spiral staircase. On each floor level the rooms are arranged around this axis, not symmetrically like the spokes of a wheel but informally, either singly or in varied suites, according to the function they are intended to perform.

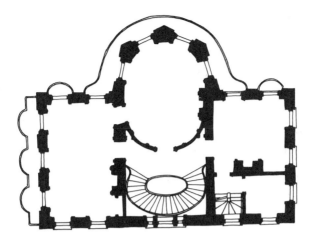

FIGURE 197. Nathaniel Russell House,
Charleston, S.C., plan of principal floor, before 1809.

The asymmetrical cluster of rooms on the second floor (Fig. 196) forms
the main entertainment suite of the house: an oval drawing room, a
rectangular drawing room, and the dining room. Together with the hall,
service stairs, and pantry they comprise an almost square rectangle which
is extended, however, by the projection of the curved bay on the east
side, and by the kitchen ell on the north. Beyond the kitchen, but set
in from its west wall and intruding into the garden, is the service wing,
which extends deeply into the property and together with the kitchen
transforms the squarish rectangle of the main house into a deep narrow
building with its short side to the street. Except for the lateral projection
of the oval bay, the house could be a single unit of a row house, conceding
the limitations of a narrow frontage, and gaining space by a radical extension in depth. Variations on this staggered off-center scheme are also
found in the upper two floors. Through the vertical axis of the stairs,
however, the asymmetrical plan of each floor is unified with the others,
at the same time that a positive directional relationship is established with
the vertical orientation of the façade.

Bulfinch's flexible and imaginative plan, organized as it is for convenience rather than according to formal principle, can perhaps be better appreciated by comparing it with the much more conservative design of the
Russell House in Charleston, South Carolina (Fig. 197). The plan of the
Russell House is a conventional rectangle with a semicircular bay projecting from the center of its long side. Like those in the third Otis House,
its stairs run through the entire height of the building. They are placed
firmly on the main axis, however, and join with the oval drawing room
as part of a dominating central core which serves as the fulcrum for the
rest of the design. As a concession to the traditional "single house" of

Charleston,[34] the Russell House is oriented with its short side to the street; the plan, however, is typical of the Neoclassical era, with its main axis emphatically drawn through the center of the short dimension of the building. We would expect, therefore, that the main entrance would be centered on this axis (see Fig. 155). But it is not. Because of the unconventional orientation of the house, the main entrance is cut into the short end which faces the street (Fig. 170). In this way the conflicting demands of tradition and necessity are resolved by the accommodation of a conventional scheme to a regional condition.

The third Otis House on the other hand was not designed by Bulfinch to accommodate one thing to another, but rather to meet certain conditions squarely and to meet them in his own architectural terms. Although the Otis House, like the Russell House, is strongly rooted in English Neoclassicism, it is nevertheless thoughtfully planned and sensitively composed by an architect whose own sense of design made it possible for him to transcend tradition. The Otis House is not a conventional plan turned short end to the street, it is an intelligent response to the problems of an urban dwelling set in the restrictions of a city site. The façade is not the end of the house masquerading as the front, it is the gracious proclamation of the elegant spaces contained within. To be sure, its serene symmetry gives not the slightest hint of the variety of internal spatial arrangements. But in this seeming contradiction we encounter not so much a peculiarity of Bulfinch as a fundamental dichotomy of the Neoclassical movement itself: its protagonists were obsessed with classical principle at the same time that they sought functional solutions to practical problems. Even though each of these points of view was in itself rationally derived, there were times when in terms of formal relationships each was in mortal conflict with the other. The result was a dilemma which was never completely resolved by even the greatest Neoclassical architects. It was a dilemma moreover which could not be resolved until the classical principles of symmetry and axis gave way, under the pressures of the Romantic movement,[35] to the principles of asymmetry and occult balance in all phases of design. Bulfinch's failure, therefore, to unite the façade and interior spaces in a common asymmetrical scheme was a failure of his time rather than of his own talent, and what is remarkable is the degree of unity he was able to achieve in spite of the contradictions within his Neoclassical convictions. He designed the third Otis House for a particular man in a particular setting to make possible a particular way of life, and because of the vitality and refinement with which he met these conditions it is one of the most expressive and beautiful houses in America.

An American Masterpiece: The Lancaster Meetinghouse

The third Harrison Gray Otis House was the last great house which Bulfinch designed in Boston. It was also the climax of his career as a domestic architect, and in both its practical ingenuity and its refined elegance it stands as a supreme embodiment of Federalist Boston. But Boston was not the whole of New England, even though its citizens may have thought so, nor were the mansions of its wealthy merchants necessarily expressive of the total Yankee temperament. We have already seen that at the turn of the century the small towns of the back country retained much of the character of the earlier New England communities. Except for a small cluster of tiny textile mills and their associated towns, which were scattered along the Blackstone Valley in Rhode Island, the New England hinterland remained firmly agrarian and Congregational. The meeting-house at the head of the common was still the center of the community, and the town meeting was the forum for its political life. In fact, it was at just such a town meeting in Lancaster, Massachusetts, on May 1, 1815, that plans were begun for a new meetinghouse in that town, and Charles Bulfinch was commissioned to design it. It is interesting that the greatest single work of the architect's career and one of the masterpieces of nineteenth-century American architecture was a meetinghouse, since of all the building types developed in early New England it was the most expressive of the Puritan mind.

The surviving accounts of the planning of the Lancaster Meetinghouse tell us how little the relationship between the church and the town had changed since colonial times. Town and church were not separated in Massachusetts until 1830. The issue of a new meetinghouse was thus initiated by the town and not by the congregation of the church. Moreoover, it was the selectmen of the town who were authorized to receive the deed for the land upon which it was to be placed. With respect to the planning of the building, committees were appointed from the town at large to study problems and recommend appropriate courses of action. These recommendations were in turn thoroughly discussed and voted upon at town meeting. The question of which way the new building should face, for example, aroused heated discussion and in the end was so controversial that it was necessary to bring in an outside committee to arbitrate the matter.[36] Altogether, the records present a picture of hard-nosed Yankees hammering out in open debate every aspect of the new building; and over it all hovers the figure of the minister, the Reverend Nathaniel Thayer, whose imagination was certainly a major factor in launching the venture, and whose powers of persuasion were absolutely essential to its peaceful conclusion.

It was probably also the Reverend Thayer who brought Bulfinch into the picture.[37] The architect had already designed five churches in Boston, including the Church of the Holy Cross, the first Catholic church in that city.[38] It was located in Franklin Street immediately adjacent to the Tontine Crescent and was consecrated as a parish church in 1803. The first resident priest in Boston was the Reverend John Thayer, a converted Congregational minister and a kinsman of the Reverend Nathaniel Thayer who in 1793 became a minister to the town of Lancaster. Father Thayer was no longer the parish priest at the time the new Catholic church was built but the association with Bulfinch had already been established, and when the time came to find an architect for the Lancaster Meetinghouse there seems to have been no question in the mind of his brother as to who should be its designer. Bulfinch's reputation was such by this time that in all probability he would have received the commission even if there had been no prior personal association. Moreover, of the three members of the building committee one was a local carpenter and builder, another a local cabinetmaker; and all three men had at one time been members of the General Court in Boston and would thus have been thoroughly familiar with Bulfinch's new State House.[39] With all this in his favor it was inevitable that Bulfinch should receive the commission.

The cornerstone for the Lancaster Meetinghouse was laid on July 9, 1816 with an impressive ceremony which included a full procession and a moving address by the Reverend Thayer.[40] One hundred and fifty-one working days later the building was completed. It was dedicated on January 1, 1817. The rapidity with which the work was accomplished would have been an extraordinary feat in any age, especially in view of the high level of craftsmanship it displays. All this implies a well coordinated effort and raises the interesting question of the relationship between Bulfinch and the local workmen.

The extraordinarily high quality of the building and the short time required to bring it to completion tempt one to conclude that Bulfinch played a continuing and active role throughout its construction. But this was not the case. Although it is certain that Bulfinch designed the building, there is no evidence whatever that he ever came to Lancaster during its construction.[41] It seems reasonably certain that the man who did supervise the work was at least known to Bulfinch. Thomas Hersey, the master builder, was a carpenter who ran a shop on Essex Street in Boston at the very time when Bulfinch was working on the new State House and on his other Beacon Hill projects. Because of his fine reputation Hersey must certainly have been known to the architect and may even have worked for him. In any case, sometime after 1813 the master carpenter moved to Harvard, a neighboring town to Lancaster, and in 1816 he appears in charge of the building of the new Lancaster Meetinghouse. As must have been the case in a number of Bulfinch's buildings, therefore, we find the actual construction being supervised by a skilled, sympathetic craftsman who through natural inclination as well as professional competence was fully capable of carrying out the architect's intentions. This, of course, was a long-established procedure in New England, and those instances when Bulfinch did keep in close touch with construction were exceptions to the traditional practices of the building trade.

We have already said that one of the things which distinguished Bulfinch from the earlier gentlemen-amateurs such as Peter Harrison was his identification with the actual construction of his buildings. But if this was not the case at Lancaster how then can we say that Bulfinch in this instance performed any differently from Harrison? The answer is, of course, that we cannot, yet there is an enormous difference between the two men. First, Bulfinch was far more deeply involved with the totality of architecture than Harrison. For Bulfinch it was a vocation, not an avocation. He actually participated in the construction of some of his most important

FIGURE 198. Charles Bulfinch. Lancaster Meetinghouse,
Lancaster, Mass., 1816–17.

commissions, and because of his extensive practice as an architect he was
in much closer touch than Harrison with all the problems of building.
More than that, his knowledge of contemporary building practices made
his designing more sensitive to both the potentials and the limitations of
available materials and techniques. In the end our deepest concern is for
Bulfinch's ideas at the conceptual level which he provided in the form
of drawings, and here there is no comparison between him and Harrison.
The Rhode Island architect remained a confirmed eclectic, wedded to
his books throughout his career; Bulfinch designed with flexibility and
grace in a manner uniquely his own.

The role that Bulfinch played in the Lancaster Meetinghouse was not
unlike that of a composer in respect to the performance of his music by
a symphony orchestra. Bulfinch provided the score. Thomas Hersey, as
the conductor, was the interpreter of that score, and only someone like

Hersey who understood what Bulfinch was searching for could render his design in wholly sympathetic terms. The orchestra in this case consisted of the several corps of craftsmen, all highly skilled and themselves artists, fully capable of rendering the most subtle passages of the composition. Once they had learned the score these men could have carried it out even though neither Bulfinch nor Hersey was there to provide direction, in the same way that a great orchestra would continue to play without dropping a beat if for some reason the conductor suddenly disappeared from the podium.

Turning now to the building itself, we note first that there is nothing unusual about the plan. It is the traditional New England type of meetinghouse with an almost square auditorium, a vestibule and an open freestanding portico (Fig. 198). The formula is familiar, one we have seen in such early nineteenth century examples as the church in Old Lyme, Connecticut (Fig. 174). But within this basic theme Bulfinch's variations are subtle and expressive. Much was gained, for example, through the use of brick. This eliminated at once the tight thin surface quality of wooden siding and made possible a bolder and more substantial statement in large and simple planes. Cubes and cylinders, squares, triangles and circles, these are the components of the design, described by unadorned walls intersecting at decisive edges and enlivened on their surfaces by the alternating rhythmic pattern of the Flemish bond brickwork.

Rising from the plan, each internal volume of the building presents its own geometric form. The first is the auditorium which is contained in a horizontal rectangular mass topped by a pitched roof. The whole space is readable behind clean walls with no part advancing or receding. Except for the Doric cornice which graces the eaves this main part of the building is devoid of any ornamentation whatsoever.

Up to this point there is no fundamental difference between the Lancaster Meetinghouse and the Congregational Church in Old Lyme. In each the main body is a simple rectangle with a pitched roof, similar to hundreds of meetinghouses throughout New England. But here the similarity ends, for the vestibule, which in the Old Lyme Church is incorporated along with the auditorium in a single templelike block, is conceived by Bulfinch at Lancaster as an entirely independent spatial volume. Adjoining the auditorium at its front end and extending above it almost to the ridge line is a clean vertical block which houses not only the vestibule but also, as expressed by its vertical orientation, the rising components of the stairs. Unlike the auditorium block with its pitched roof, this mass terminates in a flat top and is dressed by a modillioned cornice, more finely scaled than the heavier Doric cornice on the main body of the building. The vestibule block is not as wide across the front as that which houses the auditorium (49 feet instead of 67 feet), so that altogether it appears as an attached yet wholly separate spatial unit, vertical rather than horizontal in its orientation and cleanly defined by its own system of flat wall planes. It is here, in this decisive visual separation of the main functional components that we encounter Bulfinch the architect.

Since the traditional meetinghouse did not make this distinction it was necessary that he do it in his own terms.

Once Bulfinch had introduced the counter movement of the vestibule it was essential that he resolve its vertical thrust. Here again he rejected traditional solutions. In most colonnaded churches of the period, following the example of St. Martin-in-the-Fields (Fig. 92), the tower and spire rose directly from the roof at the front of the main body of the church. But this arrangement produced too many unresolved tensions for Bulfinch's increasingly rational approach. He therefore visualized the firm but vertical mass of the vestibule as a logical and organic support for the cupola complex. Rising in the same plane as the front and back walls of the vestibule therefore are the corresponding front and back walls of the tower, which is square in plan and half again as wide as it is high. Above this is the pure cylinder of the cupola, crowned by a dome and surrounded in its lower stage by twelve attenuated Ionic columns with full entablature. Except for the Ionic columns, the only ornamentation of this splendid motif is a simple garland of drapery which embellishes the deep cylindrical drum upon which the dome rests. To effect a visual transition from the horizontal of the façade to the vertical of the tower and cupola, elegant wooden brackets, adorned with splayed fan patterns, almost fill the angles between the top of the vestibule block and the tower.

In the portico Bulfinch has again defied tradition. Structurally it is supported by four wide but thin brick piers which are only two brick lengths thick through their entire height; carried on these piers is a series of five brick arches, three across the front and one on either end. The arches themselves (Fig. 199) are only a single brick deep and spring directly from the piers without any transitional element whatsoever. Seen from their inner surfaces, therefore, each seems to be no more than a simple continuity of the end plane of the pier upon which it rests, while from the front and from within the portico (Fig. 200) each reveals itself, with subtle elegance, as a single curving course of bricks which have been laid on edge to form the voussoirs. The result is a structural sequence of extraordinary vitality and grace. Nowhere in American architecture has brick been used with greater expressiveness and refinement.

Between the arches, in response to the monumental demands of the basically classical scheme, Bulfinch has achieved an alternating rhythm by using slender Doric pilasters which project no more than the thickness of one brick and are painted white. These pilasters carry a wooden Doric entablature and pediment, also painted white. Except for this engaged order however, the arches are absolutely clean, and because of the width of the brick piers they create the unusual effect of a single wall plane into which round-headed openings have been cut rather than a series of posts carrying brick arches. This is an important visual distinction which can best be appreciated by comparing the inside of the porch at Lancaster with that of the Massachusetts State House in Boston (Figs. 200, 201). Then the daring thinness and wall-like flatness of the Lancaster

FIGURE 199. *Charles Bulfinch. Lancaster Meetinghouse,
Lancaster, Mass., portico arch, 1816–17.*

piers immediately become apparent. It is true that the State House piers
carry far greater weight and were of necessity thicker. Nevertheless, the
soaring piers and arches at Lancaster are a remarkable structural tour de
force, carrying over into the portico the same sense of planar enclosure
that dominates the vestibule and auditorium blocks. The building is a
composition of rectangular blocks, a cylinder, and a sphere, each assigned
to its own purpose. Ornament is permitted to intrude into this world of
geometry only to the extent that it either participates in structure or
clarifies the overriding system of proportional and functional relationships.
The pilasters, for example, are of brick and are bonded into the wall[42]
so that they reinforce the piers at their centers. They also visually
strengthen the centralized focus so essential to the classical symmetry of
the façade at the same time that they sharply define the limits of the
portico as the foremost element in the design. In contrast, the cornice,
which continues uninterrupted around the entire building, unifies into a
coherent whole the three major geometric components, the auditorium,
the vestibule, and the portico.

The immense expressiveness of Bulfinch's design for the Lancaster
Meetinghouse is summarized in the relationship between the inside and
the outside of the building; for there are no important spatial volumes
on the interior which are not articulated in an equivalent mass on the
exterior. The auditorium is contained within the main horizontal block,
the vestibule in the attached vertical block, which is continued by and
culminates in the tower and cupola. These two masses, although clearly
separate, are nevertheless given continuity by the wall planes and by
the embracing cornice. The cornice also defines the vertical limits of the

FIGURE 200. *Charles Bulfinch. Lancaster Meetinghouse, Lancaster, Mass., portico, 1816–17.*

auditorium block, but the walls of the vestibule pass through and behind it to assert their upward thrust toward the tower and cupola. At the same time, the secondary divisions of space within the auditorium, created by the balconies, and the corresponding two-story division in the vestibule defined by the stair landings, reveal themselves on the exterior by the two horizontal ranges of classically proportioned windows. Through these various means the two major masses of the building, which perform separate but related functions, are visually joined.

The third major block, the portico, embraces a different kind of space (Fig. 198). Instead of the two story division of the auditorium and vestibule, it contains a vertically continuous volume of semi-interior space, and is therefore more sharply separated from the others by the precise enframement of the engaged Doric order. But once again the wall-like character of the piers relates them to the walls of the rest of the church, and final unity is realized through the all-embracing line of the cornice. Altogether, because of his rational handling of relationships, and because

FIGURE 201. *Charles Bulfinch. Massachusetts State House,*
Boston, inside of portico, 1795–98.

of his highly developed sense of classical order, Bulfinch has been able
to achieve a remarkable unity of functionally separable parts in a manner
comparable in its simplicity and coherence to the finest designs of European Neoclassicism. Yet he has done so wholly within the idiom of his
New England tradition.

After the reasoned and expressive design of the building itself the
treatment of the interior of the auditorium comes as a disappointment
(Fig. 202). Perhaps this is because so little of its adornment is by Bulfinch or even dates from his time.[43] The decoration of the walls and
ceilings, for example, is much later work, and even though it is cast in
the language of the Federal Style it lacks altogether the austerity, delicacy, and flatness so characteristic of the best work of that period. The
severe Doric columns, however, and the balconies with their finely scaled
balustrades are original, and in their delicate linearity and lack of bold
projection they create an atmosphere of cool refinement which is quietly
antagonistic to the latent exuberance of the three-dimensional plaster

FIGURE 202. *Charles Bulfinch. Lancaster Meetinghouse, Lancaster, Mass., interior toward pulpit, 1816–17.*

ornament of the ceiling. There is a slightly aggressive bulbous character in this ornament, and in the moldings of the ceiling and the walls, which hints at a frustrated taste for abundance, a taste reluctantly held in check by the imposed simplicity of the original Bulfinch style.

The auditorium is also uninteresting because it has none of the bold innovative character of the exterior design. As in all the New England meetinghouses of the period it is a broad spacious room, well lit by ample windows, with a balcony on three sides and the organ and choir loft in the center of the rear balcony. The unsupported sweep of the flat plaster ceiling was made possible by the traditional technique of suspension from the roof trusses above. Bulfinch adds nothing, therefore, either structurally or visually which was not already a familiar part of the New England meetinghouse. In fact, the only aspect of the Lancaster auditorium which differs radically from the original concept of the meetinghouse is the re-affirmation of the longitudinal axis by placing the pulpit in the center of the short side. We remember that in their early meetinghouses the colonials rejected the longitudinal orientation of the Anglican Church by placing the pulpit in the center of the long side; and we have seen further that this practice continued in many instances well into the eighteenth century, even after the introduction of the Wren-Gibbs type of church. In the churches of the Neoclassical era, however, the concern for axial planning and absolute symmetry, stimulated by the widespread and in some instances impassioned acceptance of classical principles of design, overcame the earlier religious bias and re-established the pulpit as both the visual climax and religious focus of the church interior. In this regard the only difference between the Congregational and Anglican churches of the period rests in the fact that in the Congregational meetinghouse it was the pulpit and not the altar which occupied this central axial position.

As the focus for the service in the Lancaster Meetinghouse, the pulpit is the most splendid architectural feature of the interior (Fig. 203).[44] It is a high expansive platform, carried on six elongated Ionic columns and enclosed by a paneled parapet. The latter breaks out on each side at right angles from the wall, then moves inward and forward in reverse-curve panels to form a central projecting unit which contains the lectern. Above each of the supporting Ionic columns, and continuing their strong vertical thrust, are six engaged Corinthian columns of rather short proportions. Both these and the lower Ionic columns carry their appropriate entablatures. Behind the pulpit, and rising well above it, is a round-arched opening framed by a full-height Corinthian tabernacle. The arched opening, which was once a window, is now screened by a heavy drapery and provides access to the pulpit. Entrance to the pulpit was originally gained through small doors in its lower structure.[45]

Both in scale and proportion the pulpit is a logical extension of the refined Doric order of the balconies into the more elaborate Ionic and Corinthian modes. It seems certain that together they were part of the original fabric. In all probability the columns and other ornamental details were produced by the same craftsman, or at least by the same workshop. The tabernacle, on the other hand, is totally unrelated in scale to any other part of the interior and one wonders whether it might have been added later.

In contrast to the sparkling decorative climax of the pulpit, the stairs in the vestibule are austerely simple (compare Figs. 203 and 204). Yet they are every bit as elegant as the pulpit, perhaps even more so. We have already said that elegance is not restricted to rich and delicate ornamentation but is found equally in certain qualities of proportion and movement; and in this respect the stairs in the Lancaster Meetinghouse are as refined and expressive as any other part of the building. They are also strictly functional. Three doors give entrance to the vestibule from the porch, a tall one on the central axis, and a smaller one on either side. From immediately inside each of the flanking doors a pair of stairs ascends toward the far wall of the vestibule, and then winds left and right to a common landing in the center. From here they join in a single broad flight which breaks back in the opposite direction to arrive on the second floor level. Square, thinly proportioned newel posts, topped by simple turned knobs, carry similarly simple handrails. In surface and color both the knobs and the rails display the warm signs of use and are magnificently scaled and shaped to the human hand. The area between the rails and the stairs, instead of carrying a balustrade, is filled with strip panels running from newel post to newel post and set off from both the rail

FIGURE 203. *Charles Bulfinch. Lancaster Meetinghouse,*
Lancaster, Mass., pulpit, 1816–17.

and the baseboard by a thin delicately scaled molding. The stairs are thus
boxed in, presenting a bold system of unadorned planes, as severe and
definitive in their geometric purity as the clean brick walls of the exterior.
Yet they are graciously buoyant, lightened by the thinness of their parts,
and held easily aloft by the rhythmic progression of the ascending planes.
The purity of the design is breath-taking. There is no question as to
either function or structural principle. But most evocative of all is the
animated pattern of angular shapes which builds as the various elements
intersect and pass one another in their controlled ascending flight. Pure
white in parts, modulated to delicate grays by the changing light in
others, and sharply divided by the dark lines of the rails and newel
posts, the flat taut planes climb, separate, and reunite with all the finely

FIGURE 204. Charles Bulfinch. Lancaster Meetinghouse,
Lancaster, Mass., stairs, 1816–17.

tuned resonance of a Mondrian, and in the end combine in one of the
most gratifying spatial experiences in the whole of American architecture.
Here all the grand geometric promise of the exterior is quietly reduced to
human scale and rendered tender and poetic by the most exquisite of
means.

It would be wrong to assume that Bulfinch arrived at his expressive
mature style without outside influences. By the turn of the century, the

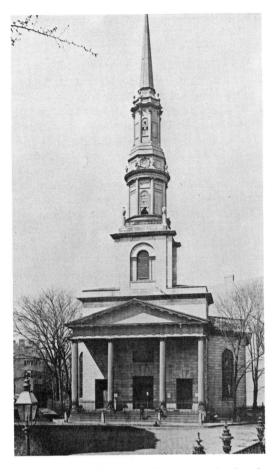

FIGURE 205. *Charles Bulfinch. New South Church, Boston, Mass., façade, 1814.*

early Neoclassicism of Adam and Chambers in England, which had inspired the young Bostonian in his early years, had given way to the more muscular and rational work of such men as George Dance, Jr., and John Soane;[46] and it seems impossible that Bulfinch, whose enthusiasm for English architecture continued throughout his life, would have been unaware of current English trends. Even more important, in 1796 a young Englishman, Benjamin Latrobe, arrived in Virginia, fresh from the European milieu, to begin his career as one of America's leading architects.[47] By 1812, the main fabric of his Baltimore Cathedral, probably the most provocative and influential building of its day, was substantially completed (Fig. 261). There is no reason to believe that Bulfinch saw this building before he started work on the designs for the Lancaster Meetinghouse, but he must surely have known about it. In fact, something of the new rational ideology which it proclaimed was already appearing in scattered works in various parts of the country, and Bulfinch's mature buildings show a similar radical distillation of form and a similar absence of ornamental embellishment.

We have seen something of this new rational spirit in Bulfinch's design for the façade of the third Harrison Gray Otis House, but it appears in an even more severe form in his New South Church, which was built in Boston in 1814 (Fig. 205). This building was in every way a prelude to the Lancaster Meetinghouse. Here, as in the Baltimore Cathedral, the walls were stone rather than brick, and the ceiling, although unlike the vaults of the Cathedral, was still wood and plaster suspended from a wooden truss. The stonemasonry gave Bulfinch's building a largeness and monumentality which was further emphasized by the geometric simplicity of the walls. The octagonal plan, with its variety of geometric shapes, was a particularly Neoclassical feature, and was aggressively contemporary in relation to the traditional four-square plan of Lancaster. On the other hand, just as at Lancaster (Fig. 198) the mass containing the vestibule was made to project well above both the portico and the main auditorium blocks. The steeple and the spire, however, were conspicuously in the Gibbsian tradition, and the portico was the conventional classical type with four widely spread attenuated Doric columns. The main massing of the building, however, was broadly geometric and in its weight and substance represented a marked departure from the boxlike character of the traditional churches of New England.

The use of brick at Lancaster was a compromise between wood and stone which made it possible for Bulfinch to achieve the geometric breadth of the New South Church without sacrificing all the graces of his own building tradition. Stone was rarely used in New England during the colonial era and with a few important exceptions did not appear in Boston until after 1800, when it was introduced by Bulfinch in a number of his monumental works. By 1800, on the other hand, brick was almost ubiquitous in Boston. There were several reasons for this. First there was the ordinance requiring brick. Then there were the practical difficulties of quarrying and handling stone. This, combined with the general lack of skilled stonemasons,[48] made it a more expensive and difficult medium than brick. But equally important were the differences in the visual character of the two. It is hard to imagine unadorned stone walls, regardless of how tightly they are laid up, evoking qualities of delicacy and grace. The effect rather is heavy, monumental, large. As we shall see, it is precisely because of this that the important stone buildings to appear in the United States after 1800 were generally associated either with the drive toward monumentality which was stimulated by the building of the new national capitol in Washington, or with the rational phase of Neoclassicism as it was introduced into this country by Benjamin Latrobe. The Federal Style, on the contrary, was not a monumental style. Based as it was on the Adam style, it was a mode of elegant interiors and graceful façades, and of the masonry techniques only brick provided these qualities. In a brick wall the contrast in color between the mortar of the joints and the bricks themselves sets in motion a rhythmic but extremely delicate interlocking pattern which not only animates the surface but also establishes at once that ingredient essential to all architectural experience, scale. A stone wall, even when finely dressed, is large, heavy, aloof; a brick wall vivacious, intimate, touchable. Brick enlivens a wall in the same way that a flock of small birds brings to life the still blue vault of the sky; and brick can also be exquisitely elegant. For the refined taste of the men of Boston, therefore, brick was a natural medium and it is partly because of this that the Lancaster Meetinghouse, in spite of its pure, magnificent geometry, retained all the vivacious loveliness of the Federal Style.

Bulfinch's search for the monumental in the New South Church was not without its contradictions. The rational juxtaposition of clean geometric shapes which he achieved with the auditorium and the vestibule was a large and simple statement which challenged tradition and sought new solutions to the long-established form of the New England church. The portico, however, could hardly have been more conventional. With its four widely spread, thinly proportioned columns, it was as light as the church behind it was heavy and thus bore no tangible relationship with it either in scale or character. The spire, too, even though it was elegantly proportioned in the best Federal manner, was no more than a reworking of the established New England formula, graceful and beautiful in its own right, but still firmly rooted in the Wren-Gibbs tradition. Here, too, the delicate scale was in conflict with the weight and substance of the stonemasonry below.

Bulfinch resolved all this at Lancaster through decisive and imaginative innovations. First, he did away with the flimsy open colonnade and gave positive geometric identity to the portico by introducing in its place the arched brick wall. There is no question in this church that the portico is a containing block and not an open porch. Further, he substituted pilasters for columns, making them slightly heavier in proportion and holding them flat to the wall so that they did not destroy its surface continuity. In the spire his transformations were equally drastic. Here he changed the base from a vertical to a horizontal mass and eliminated the upper stages altogether, putting in their place a simple dome carried on an equally simple cylindrical drum. In this way the residual soaring Gothicism of the New South Church spire, which had been carried over deliberately by Wren in his London churches and continued as a powerful traditional element in the churches of colonial America, was totally eliminated by Bulfinch in favor of a positive geometric system, more rational than emotional in its visual appeal, and thoroughly rooted in the reasoned order of classical design. It is as pure as the classical portico upon which it rests.

Of all the components of the Lancaster spire, only the circular colonnade of the first stage seems directly related to the spire of New South Church, but even here immensely significant changes were made. In the earlier church this part of the spire had eight engaged columns, each coinciding with an intersection of its octagonal core. At Lancaster there are twelve columns, thus quickening the interval between solid and void and generally increasing the cylindrical effect. Moreover, these columns are freestanding, and the core of the belfry behind them, which is cylindrical rather than octagonal, passes vertically through the circular entablature to form the drum of the dome above. Thus the columns, which in the New South Church were attached, at Lancaster stand free to form an independent geometric unit, a semitransparent cylinder behind which the cylindrical heart is visible, and through which it passes like the sections of a telescope, to support the sphere of the dome. The stress shifts, therefore, from the surface animation of applied ornament to the fundamental relationships between one spatial component and another, so that the cupola and the portico, both in character and scale, are made to unite with the rest of the building in one coherent geometric scheme; and the wonder of it is that Bulfinch, through discreet adjustments of the internal proportions, was able to achieve these qualities of largeness without sacrificing even a small part of the poetic refinement so characteristic of all his work.

We will probably never know all the factors that moved Bulfinch toward such a drastic distillation of form. Certainly, he had a natural genius for architecture, which led him more and more to think in fundamental rather than ornamental terms. But equally important must have been his keen awareness of the new attitudes of the rational Neoclassicists. The kinship between his later work and Latrobe's Baltimore Cathedral is too obvious to ignore; in certain instances the similarities are remarkable. Bulfinch's belfry at Lancaster with its arched openings and cylindrical core is notably like the belfries which Latrobe designed for the Cathedral (Figs. 206, 207). There is no reason to assume, of course, that Bulfinch saw the Latrobe belfries. Indeed, unless he had access to Latrobe's drawings, he could not have seen them for they were not completed until the 1860's. Rather, Bulfinch and Latrobe arrived at similar conclusions because they were thinking along similar lines, and there can be no doubt that Bulfinch not only knew about the more radical developments in the Neoclassical movement, but in his own quiet New England way was also deeply involved with them.

The Lancaster Meetinghouse reveals Bulfinch as a leading figure in American Neoclassicism and qualifies him as one of the most creative architects of his time. In this superb building he refined to its utmost the very style which he helped to create. But in the process his own conditioned taste for the elegant was cleansed and strengthened by the purifying forces of reason to produce an architecture which was rational, beautiful, and workable in a way especially suited to its time and place. In the readily accessible logic of its geometry it was an architecture poignantly expressive of both the Puritan primness and the earth-bound pragmatism of the New England temperament. Although Bulfinch accomplished all this entirely within the structural and aesthetic framework of his English tradition, his remoteness from the European mainstreams of activity made it inevitable that his work would be marked by a certain provincialism. Boston was not London, and even though he had experienced the latter firsthand, he still had to work within the technical and intellectual limitations of his own environment. But his keen sensitivity to the life around him, and his complete identification with the affairs

FIGURE 206. *Charles Bulfinch. Lancaster Meetinghouse, Lancaster, Mass., cupola, 1816–17.*

FIGURE 207. *Benjamin Latrobe. Baltimore Cathedral, cupola.*

of the new nation, gave to his provincialism a very special character, and for the first time in the development of the English-oriented architecture of New England the term "American," as defining a quality decidedly un-English, becomes meaningful.

Bulfinch arrived at this position through a continuing evolution, fired by the power of his own genius and directed by his unique sensitivity to the mood and quality of his time. He did so, moreover, entirely within the architectural idiom of English Neoclassicism. His older contemporary Thomas Jefferson, who, like Bulfinch, was the most important native-born architect of his generation, achieved similar ends but through wholly different means and for wholly different reasons. Jefferson's particular form of Americanism was not only a generation earlier than that of Bulfinch[49] but it was also deliberately anti-British. Where Bulfinch's probing of the American character was passive and empathetic that of the great statesman was militant and aggressively objective. To Jefferson cultural independence was as imperative to the health of the young America as political and economic independence. How he accomplished his objective through the medium of architecture is one of the most compelling episodes in America's search for cultural identity.

CHAPTER VIII

American Neoclassicism, The Idealistic Phase

THOMAS JEFFERSON

Architecture is my delight . . .
But it is an enthusiasm of which I am not ashamed, as its
object is to improve the taste of my countrymen, to increase
their reputation, to reconcile them to the rest of the world,
and procure them its praise.

THOMAS JEFFERSON

Thomas Jefferson, like Leonardo da Vinci, was a Jack-of-all-trades and master of them all. Gifted with one of the most extraordinary minds of his time, he left few facets of life unexplored, and the diversity and scope of his accomplishments were prodigious. Seen in their broadest aspects, Jefferson's achievements were humanistic and egalitarian; his methods were those of a disciplined lawyer and a shrewd politician. He was an idealist and perfectionist, whose aspirations found their most substantial embodiment in the institution of American democracy, and for this institution he assumed the full responsibilities of citizenship. But citizenship to Jefferson not only required participation in the political system, it was also a way of life, and for him architecture was both an expressive and a functional means toward the fulfillment of his ideals. For he was not only a politician, statesman, lawyer, scholar, author, educator, farmer, archaeologist, and musician, he was also an architect of immense creative power. His role in the evolution of American architecture was as decisive as his role in the formation of American democracy; and the two are inseparable.

A precise evaluation of Jefferson as an architect is made difficult by the dual nature of his involvement. The first impression is of a gifted amateur who performed wholly within the expected patterns of the traditional eighteenth-century gentleman-amateur. At the same time, his wide experience and knowledge as a classicist and his firm adherence to ancient Rome as the ultimate architectural authority placed him in the vanguard of the Neoclassical movement. But Jefferson's contribution to American architecture cannot be understood in terms of Neoclassicism alone. As one of the pivotal idealists of the Revolution and as one of the creative figures in the formation of the new republic, Jefferson spoke for an aspiring America. His architecture, therefore, takes on its full meaning only when viewed as both instrument and symbol of his social and political purpose. Jefferson became the first American leader to think in terms of cultural as well as political independence and to him this independence could nowhere be better expressed than in architecture. He was the first American architect consciously to reject the English tradition and to seek instead an architecture appropriate to the new nation.

Jefferson's interest in architecture must have begun during his student years at the College of William and Mary. When he arrived in Williamsburg in the spring of 1760, he was a confident but provincial frontiersman who would seemingly have brought with him little formal knowledge of architecture. Yet nine years later he was engaged in designing an elaborate house, his own Monticello. Furthermore, he was developing his ideas in a systematic manner through a series of skillfully executed preliminary drawings. These included plans, elevations, and a topographical map of the site. What happened during these nine years to turn Jefferson toward architecture with such professional purpose?

The first awareness must have come through personal contact with enlightened men of his time. At William and Mary, Jefferson showed himself at once to be more mature than the average student, and his astonishing precociousness was soon to attract the attention of Dr. William Small, a Scotsman, who was professor of mathematics at the College. Dr. Small, in Jefferson's words, was "a man profound in most of the useful branches of science, with a happy talent of communication, correct and gentlemanly manners, and an enlarged and liberal mind." From his conversations with Dr. Small the young man received his "first views of the expansion of science and of the system of things in which we are placed."[1] Through Dr. Small, Jefferson came to know two other distinguished colonials, Lieutenant Governor Fauquier, an able, well connected and widely traveled sophisticate, and George Wythe, the finest Greek and Latin scholar in the Colony. Wythe was also a lawyer and from him Jefferson received his classical and legal training. It was the young man's good fortune to be taken into intimate association with these three gentlemen, and from their frequent and prolonged conversations he gained fresh insights into his ever-widening world of cultural interests. Like all cultivated gentlemen of the late eighteenth century, Jefferson's older companions would have had at least a theoretical knowledge of architecture; in fact George Wythe was the son-in-law of Richard Taliaferro, who as a gentleman-amateur seems to have been involved with the architecture of the Virginia tidewater. Wythe and Taliaferro lived in the same house in Williamsburg and because of Jefferson's frequent visits to the Wythe house there can be little doubt that he came to know Taliaferro well.

Equally important for the probing young Jefferson were the books on architecture which were available to him in Williamsburg. There were a few in the College library, but of special significance were those in the library of William Byrd at Westover. This remarkable collection was not only the largest in the colonies but it was only a few miles from Williamsburg and contained twenty-six architectural works, among them Andrea Palladio's *Four Books of Architecture*. There were also several volumes on the monuments of ancient Rome.[2]

Between the pages of these books Jefferson discovered a new world of architecture. He found what he considered to be the elements of architecture—the classical orders—drawn, described, and praised by one of the great architectural theorists of the Renaissance. In the vivid, precisely delineated engravings unfamiliar types of buildings were revealed to him, some ancient, some modern, all rendered at a scale and in a manner which threw into the disparaging light of provincialism the buildings of his own colonial Virginia. But above all he came to realize that architecture was a discipline. He found himself confronted by an orderly world governed by laws and principles, a world of tangible, measurable, repeatable relationships. All this had an immediate appeal to his alert and methodical nature. Moreover, that he should have discovered all of this in books carried with it a special authority for Jefferson. From the very beginning of his career as a student he regarded books as the most precious heritage of mankind, and he never ceased to rely on them in his search for truth.[3] It was not only the provincial condition of his architectural environment, therefore, that turned Jefferson to books, it was also a deep, abiding conviction that books were the repository of all knowledge and wisdom, and throughout his lifetime his architecture was to have its roots in books. But books like foundations are earth-bound whereas buildings like trees rise to the sky, and although Jefferson's early work was largely derived from books, his later efforts, as his creative powers increased, became more and more a confrontation with the building itself; and in his mature years books became useful tools rather than absolute authorities.

Once Jefferson's enthusiasm for architecture had been aroused he seems to have put his newly acquired knowledge to practical use. Unfortunately, we know virtually nothing of his architectural activity between his arrival at Williamsburg as a student and his early work at Monticello, which he seems to have begun in the late 1760's. In 1770 his ancestral home, Shadwell, burned to the ground, destroying all his private papers.[4] If his career had ended at this point we would have only fragments of direct evidence to indicate that he was even curious about architecture, let alone that he designed any buildings. Yet from that date onward his involvement in architecture, despite many other demands, was virtually continuous, and was of a highly professional nature. It was supported at almost every point by a host of documents ranging from letters, personal papers, published works, and official records, to his original drawings, of which more than five hundred still survive.[5] Moreover, the sureness of his approach to the early planning of Monticello makes it unthinkable that this work, one of the most demanding involvements of his career, should not have been preceded by experience of some kind both in the problems of designing and in the resolution of those problems through drawings. From every point of view, there must have been earlier architectural experience and there must have been numerous related documents. That there are only a few, and that after 1770 they should suddenly be numerous, seems certainly to bear out that the early ones were all consumed in the flames of Shadwell. There may have been earlier designs than Monticello and plausible attempts have been made to identify some of these,[6] but in the absence of documents such identifications remain a matter of scholarly conjecture.

There is one important document, however, which throws considerable light on Jefferson's attitude toward architecture as it was formed during the early years. In a remarkable and well known passage in his *Notes On Virginia* published in 1782, Jefferson makes some highly critical and revealing comments about the architecture of Williamsburg, and because it tells us so much the passage is worth quoting in its entirety:

The only public buildings worthy of mention are the Capitol, the Palace, the College, and the Hospital for Lunatics, all of them in Williamsburg, heretofore the seat of our government. The Capitol is a light and airy structure, with a portico in front of two orders, the lower of which, being Doric, is tolerably just in its proportions and ornaments, save only that the intercolonnations are too large. The upper is Ionic, much too small for that on which it is mounted, its ornaments not proper to the order, nor proportioned within themselves. It is crowned with a pediment, which is too high for its span. Yet, on the whole, it is the most pleasing piece of architecture we have. The Palace is not handsome without, but it is spacious and commodious within, is prettily situated, and with the grounds annexed to it, is capable of being made an elegant seat. The College and Hospital are rude, mis-shapen piles, which, but that they have roofs, would be taken for brick-kilns. There are no other public buildings but churches and court-houses, in which no attempts are made at elegance. Indeed, it would not be easy to execute such an attempt, as a workman could scarcely be found here capable of drawing an order. The genius of architecture seems to have shed its maledictions over this land. Buildings are often erected, by individuals, of considerable expense. To give these symmetry and taste, would not increase their cost. It would only change the arrangement of the materials, the form and combination of the members. This would often cost less than the burthen of barbarous ornaments with which these buildings are sometimes charged. But the first principles of the art are unknown, and there exists scarcely a model among us sufficiently chaste to give an idea of them. Architecture being one of the fine arts, and as such within the department of a professor of the college, according to the new arrangement, perhaps a spark may fall on some young subjects of natural taste, kindle up their genius, and produce a reformation in this elegant and useful art.

The most obvious fact to be gleaned from this criticism is that Jefferson had a sharply focused classical taste based on strict principles. He complains that there are no examples of architecture in Virginia "sufficiently chaste" to demonstrate these principles. When he speaks of "the burthen of barbarous ornaments" he is referring to the sculptural richness of the Wren-Baroque style as he knew it in the early eighteenth-century mansions of tidewater Virginia. The river front door at Westover is typical (Fig. 36). Its swan's-neck pediment and elaborate Corinthian order are the epitome of the restrained exuberance of English-Baroque taste; in contrast, the strict classical bias from which Jefferson's criticism proceeds can be illustrated by comparing the Westover door with the garden door from his own house at Monticello (Fig. 208). In his design the austerity of the unbroken classical pediment and the simple architrave surround could hardly be more different either in spirit or in fact.

Classical taste in architecture was epitomized for Jefferson by the classical orders. This is conveyed especially in his analysis of the Capitol building, which he describes entirely in terms of the orders.[7] The things which he stresses are the shape, placement, and proportions of parts, and the appropriateness of the ornament. In other words, his evaluation assumes its authority from a preconceived proportional and decorative system, on the basis of which the building can and must be judged. To be sure, he does speak of materials but only in terms of their arrangement, and stress is placed, as he put it, on "the form and combination of the members."

The classical principles of proportion and decoration which guided Jefferson in his criticism were largely those set forth by Palladio. As we have seen, the works of Palladio were among the first books on architecture which he saw, and the Italian's systematic and determinate arguments had a natural appeal to Jefferson's disciplined and orderly mind. Here was something which, like a well-founded legal system, one could count on, and although his attitude toward Palladio changed as he gained experience in architecture, he never ceased to maintain a close kinship with the venerable theorist. He also found in Palladio a sustaining authority for his own eclectic methods. Jefferson remained both an eclectic and a classicist throughout his career and this would seem to reduce him to a position of mediocre conformity in the broad spectrum of American architecture of his time; for so was every other American architect an eclectic and a classicist. But there was nothing mediocre about Jefferson or his architecture. A keen practical bent, an innate sense of refinement, and a virile probing imagination gave to Jefferson's impeccable classicism qualities of originality which had never been seen before in American architecture.

Jefferson's impatience with the architecture of Williamsburg was not only a matter of taste. As a result of the anguished years of the Revolution he carried over into all his thinking a strong anti-British sentiment. This was not only reflected in what he had to say about the architecture of Williamsburg, which in the eighteenth century was in many ways the most distinguished and sophisticated architecture of the entire eastern seaboard, it is even more explicitly expressed in an interesting letter to his friend

FIGURE 208. *Thomas Jefferson. Monticello, Charlottesville, Va., garden door, c. 1805.*

John Page. Writing from Paris in the spring of 1786, shortly after his return from a two-month trip in England, Jefferson said that "English architecture is in the most wretched stile I ever saw, not meaning to except America where it is bad, nor even Virginia where it is worse than in any other part of America, which I have seen." Although Jefferson might not have admitted it, his architectural judgment was clearly tinged by his political opinions, and it was in part this attitude which motivated him in his search for an architectural idiom which would be non-English and at the same time expressive of American democracy. It is this idealism, too, which separates his architecture so decisively from other American work of the period.

There is yet another and even more important aspect of the Jefferson documents which tends to set him apart from his contemporaries. This is the quantity and character of his architectural drawings.[8] Jefferson's skill as a draftsman and the way in which he used drawings to develop his ideas were unique in the America of his day. His drawings are entirely schematic, drawn in simple outline, without any pictorial suggestion what-

ever, but they are done with infinite precision, and for technical competence alone they were unmatched by those of any other American architect
or builder of the eighteenth century. Carefully preserved by Jefferson
himself, they remain for us a remarkable and illuminating document of
the great man's activity as an architect. It seems plausible to assume
that Jefferson learned drawing and the basic techniques of space description from his father, who was a surveyor. But wherever he may have
acquired his skill, it provided him the power to visualize and cope with
problems of space relationships in a way that would not otherwise have
been possible, and it gave to the gentleman-amateur both the mark and
the means of the professional.

The Early Monticello

Jefferson's career as an architect effectively begins with the planning and
building of Monticello. Although interrupted by long periods of absence,
this activity occupied Jefferson for over thirty years, and the house as it
finally took shape in 1809 was substantially different from his original
designs of 1769. In a real sense, Monticello was the experimental laboratory in which Jefferson first put his ideas and theories to the test. During
the early phase of the house he appears as an aggressive amateur,
pedantically sure of himself in some respects, yet groping in others and
touching only the surfaces of things as they were revealed to him through
his books. But when the building was finished he emerged with the relaxed
self-confidence of a high professional, fully in command of his medium
and profoundly aware of both the practical and the emotional demands
of architecture. Monticello also was Jefferson's home, thought out and
planned in every inch of its space to meet the practical and social needs
of himself and his family, and because of this it yields many and varied
insights into the complex and baffling personality of Jefferson the man.

Very early in the planning of Monticello, Jefferson's aggressive individuality asserts itself in his decision to locate the building on the top
of a mountain. This alone makes it unique among plantation houses of
its day for the great mansions of the eighteenth century were without
exception located in the lowlands, generally along the banks of a river.
Jefferson's dramatic location is not only intensely romantic but it shows
him to be—as were many of the ancient Romans whose works he had
read with such pleasure—deeply sensitive to the relationship between a
house and its natural setting. His attachment to his beloved mountain
seems to have begun during his childhood, and as early as the 1760's,
during his student years at William and Mary, his first ideas about building a house on that site must have crystallized. By 1768 he was leveling
the hilltop and having fruit trees planted; two years later concrete plans
for the house were already well developed. The first structure completed
was a small one-room brick cottage which was planned from the beginning
as the southeast pavilion in the over-all scheme (Fig. 228). On February 20,
1771, Jefferson wrote to James Ogilvie: "I have lately removed to the
mountain from whence this is dated. . . . I have here but one room,

which like the coblers, serves me for parlor, for kitchen and hall. I may add, for bedchamber and study too. . . . I have hopes, however, of getting more elbow room this summer."

Before March 1771 both the form of the main house and its relationship with its dependencies had been established. The plan (Fig. 209) of the building itself Jefferson derived from a plate in Morris's *Select Architecture*, one of the earliest architectural books owned by him.[9] The façade (Fig. 210) on the other hand, came from Palladio (compare Fig. 72). In order to accommodate the Palladian façade to Morris's plan certain modifications were necessary, and Jefferson's adaptation of Palladio was therefore not literal. But the source is obvious, nevertheless. Because of his piecemeal methods the design has an awkward, disparate character with little coherent relationship between the busy superposed portico and the rather austere depressed wings on either side. For the young Jefferson, however, Palladio provided the stamp of authority, and in the spring of 1771 work was begun. By 1782 much of the interior seems to have been finished although the portico was apparently completed only to the top of the lower order. At this point construction ceased altogether because of Jefferson's prolonged absence on the affairs of state.

Work was not resumed at Monticello until 1796. At that time, however, we find much of the original house being dismantled for a complete remodeling. What the new house was to look like can be seen in a drawing made later by the young American architect Robert Mills (Fig. 211), who seems to have been at Monticello as an assistant to Jefferson shortly after the turn of the century. This new scheme is so radically different from the original that to understand it we must leave Monticello briefly and follow Jefferson through some of his experiences during the intervening years.

Jefferson in France: the Virginia State Capitol

Early in August of 1784 Jefferson arrived in Paris to replace Benjamin Franklin as Minister to the Court of France. He was to remain abroad for a period of approximately five years. During this time a wholly new world of architecture opened up to him. For the inexperienced enthusiast, coming as he did from the provincial background of colonial architecture in America, the grandeur of Paris must have been overwhelming. With the possible exception of Rome, the French capital was unmatched by any other European city and Jefferson arrived there at a time when some of the most impressive buildings of the Neoclassical movement had either just been completed or were under construction. These were years of excitement in French architecture, quite apart from Jefferson's responsiveness, and the American was quickly caught up in the dynamic new spirit.

Jefferson's experience was not limited to the architecture of Paris alone. Shortly after his arrival in France he established a close working relationship with the French Neoclassicist C. L. A. Clérisseau, a distinguished

FIGURE 209. *Thomas Jefferson. Monticello,
Charlottesville, Va., drawing of first plan, before 1772.*

FIGURE 210. *Thomas Jefferson. Monticello,
Charlottesville, Va., drawing for first façade, 1771–72.*

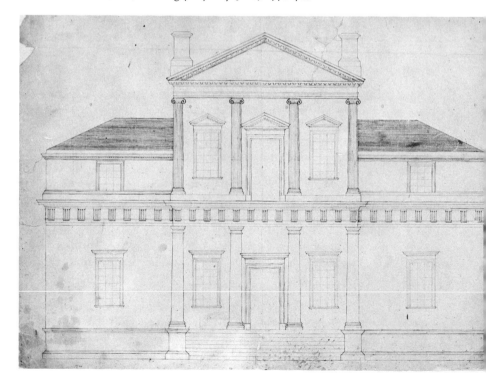

member of the French Academy at Rome and the author of *Monuments de Nîmes*. This book, which was one of the leading publications of the Neoclassical movement in France, was acquired at once by Jefferson for his library. Jefferson visited southern France, where for the first time he saw actual surviving examples of the architecture of ancient Rome. Foremost among these was the famous Maison Carrée in Nîmes (Fig. 5), a superbly preserved Roman Republican temple which had been restored by Louis XV. This was the first and only important Roman temple which Jefferson saw, and the immediate effect was to intensify his already ardent classical enthusiasm. All that he had read about and admired in the civilization of ancient Rome was confirmed for him in this building. How the experience aroused him is best expressed in the often quoted passage from a letter to the Comtesse de Tessé. "Here I am, Madame," he wrote, "gazing whole hours at the Maison Carrée, like a lover at his mistress."

Jefferson's discovery of the Maison Carrée was quickly to bear fruit in the first of his public buildings, the Virginia State Capitol (Fig. 212).[10] As early as October 1776, Jefferson took the initiative in proposing that the capital of Virginia be removed from Williamsburg to Richmond. This would not only eliminate the last vestiges of British colonial rule, but it would also put the capital city in the center of the state where it would be more accessible to the western regions. This was legally accomplished in 1780, and Jefferson immediately submitted to the House of Delegates a bill which provided for appropriate government buildings.

A remarkable feature of Jefferson's proposal is that it specified a separate building for each of the major departments of the government, one for the legislative, one for the judicial, and one for the executive. If the provisions of this bill had been carried out it would have made the

FIGURE 211. *Thomas Jefferson. Monticello, Charlottesville, Va., drawing by Robert Mills of final façade, c. 1803.*

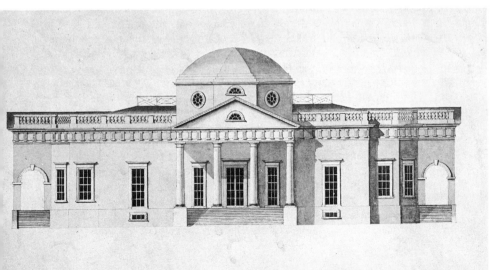

FIGURE 212. *Thomas Jefferson. Virginia State Capitol, Richmond, Va., 1785–89.*

Virginia government buildings unique in their day. They would have given visual expression to the major functions of the new government and they would have done so in monumental terms, making the complex comparable to many of the great city squares of Europe. But this was not to be. Shortly after Jefferson departed for France the Virginia Legislature modified the original bill, reducing the number of buildings from three to one, and shortly thereafter the Directors of Public Buildings wrote to Jefferson, asking him to "consult an able Architect on a plan fit for a Capitol." Jefferson did more than this, he prepared the designs himself. He took for his model the Maison Carrée, which he described in a letter to Madison as "one of the most beautiful, if not the most beautiful and precious morsel of architecture left us by antiquity . . . it is very simple, but is noble beyond expression, and would have done honor to any country. . . ." He further explained his choice by stating: "You see I am an enthusiast in the subject of the arts. But it is an enthusiasm of which I am not ashamed, as its object is to improve the taste of my countrymen, to increase their reputation, to reconcile to them the respect of the world, and procure them its praise." Here we have an early expression of Jefferson's idealistic understanding of one function of architecture in society.

To assist him in carrying out his scheme Jefferson employed Clérisseau as a consultant and the two worked closely on the project. Yet in spite of the Frenchman's greater experience, the conception and all major aspects of the design seem clearly to have been Jefferson's. In adapting the Roman temple to the needs of the Virginia state government, Jefferson simplified the building by changing the order from Corinthian to Ionic, and on Clérisseau's advice he reduced the depth of the porch from three to two columns. He also eliminated the pilasters from the side walls and introduced windows instead at the first and second floor levels. Beyond this he maintained as closely as possible the general form and proportions of the Roman temple. The design, which he began in 1785, was communicated to the Virginia officials through drawings and through a plaster model which Jefferson had made with the help of Clérisseau. The building was not completed until 1789.

As a practical solution to the problems of housing the state government, Jefferson's design leaves much to be desired. Indeed, had his original scheme calling for three buildings been carried out, many of the difficulties which he encountered never would have arisen. Forced to work with one building, and fiercely determined to use the temple form, he created innumerable problems with respect to the interior spatial arrangements which could not all be happily solved. As a building related to its time, however, Jefferson's design is an innovation. In its Romanism it met squarely his sharp aversion to the architecture of colonial America, and in so doing became the first American public building to reject altogether the English tradition. It thus stands as the first positive step toward American cultural independence. In a similar sense, the conscious choice of an ancient temple for his model, with all its symbolic overtones, was an act of free will on Jefferson's part. Thus through its stylistic independence, the building becomes expressive of a fundamental Jeffersonian principle, freedom of choice. Architecturally, the Virginia State Capitol not only was the first application of the pure classical temple form in American architecture,[11] but also anticipated by twenty years Napoleon's similar evocation of classical authority in a building which is now the great church of the Madeleine in Paris. In this single effort Jefferson was transformed from the meagre provincial Palladian of his early years to an ardent leader in the most advanced architectural movement of his day.

One important consequence of Jefferson's discovery of the architecture of ancient Rome was the change which it brought about in his attitude toward Palladio. His books were among the first acquired by Jefferson and in the early years, as we have seen at Monticello, Palladio stood as a definitive authority to whom Jefferson paid loyal homage. Here the Italian was the teacher, the young American the avid listener. During his years in France, however, Jefferson discovered that ancient Rome was the true fountainhead of Palladio's inspiration, and once he became aware of this, Palladio shifted from his role of teacher to that of fellow Romanist. Palladio's relationship with Jefferson became very much like that of Clérisseau, whose work the American admired, whose opinion he respected, and whose ideas he frequently accepted but toward whom he reserved the right of critical appraisal. One might say that after his experience in France, Jefferson and Palladio entered into a conversation with each other as two professionals, and the subject of their conversation was the architecture of ancient Rome. Jefferson continued to rely on Palladio but just as he always read classical literature in the original language, so too he now viewed Palladio as a translation useful as a reference, but not a substitute for the buildings themselves.[12] If Jefferson had had the opportunity to visit the ancient Roman monuments with *I quattro libri* in hand he would, as Inigo Jones had done before him, have checked all the measurements for himself.

Another important discovery made by Jefferson while he was in France was the domestic architecture of Paris. With the shift in the patterns of social behavior during the eighteenth century away from the pomp of the court at Versailles toward the more intimate conversations of the Parisian soirée, a wholly new concept of the town house developed. With the problems of Monticello still very much in his mind Jefferson was intensely curious about these houses and was constantly alert for ideas which might be useful to him. Because he was intensely practical he seems to have been particularly attracted to the rational nature of French planning. "All the new and good houses," he wrote, "are of a single story that is of the height of 16. or 18f. generally, and the whole of it given to rooms of entertainment; but in the parts where there are bedrooms they have two tiers of them of from 8. to 10f. high each, with a small private staircase. By these means great staircases are avoided, which are expensive and occupy a space which would make a good room in every story."

One of the French town houses in particular attracted his attention. In the letter to the Comtesse de Tessé just quoted, he went on to say that "while in Paris I was violently smitten with the Hôtel de Salm and used to go to the Tuileries almost daily to look at it." This imposing house (Fig. 213), which was finished just two years after Jefferson's arrival in Paris, was not only brilliantly planned to meet the requirements of the new social order, but was also carried out in the best Roman style of French Neoclassicism. It thus combined for Jefferson those two ingredients which he instinctively sought but never achieved in his first naïve adaptation of Palladio at Monticello, the convenience of rational planning and the gracious dignity of the Roman style.

The Later Monticello

Monticello (Fig. 214), as it finally took shape during the second building campaign (1793–1809), clearly reflects Jefferson's years in France. The low horizontal appearance of a single story, interlocked in the center by the spherical mass of the dome, is strongly reminiscent of the river front of the Hôtel de Salm. Jefferson achieved this effect by eliminating the original second-floor portico with its thin widely spaced columns, and by introducing instead the simple geometry of a low octagonal dome and its supporting drum. The general lowering of the profile which results is stressed by the addition of arcaded porches beyond each octagonal end bay and is aided by the depressed attic story. The continuous balustrade also emphasizes the horizontal and joins with the entablature to unify the many parts of the extended mass. Together with the volume of the dome,

FIGURE 213. *Hôtel de Salm,*
Paris, river façade, 1782–86.

FIGURE 214. *Thomas Jefferson. Monticello,*
Charlottesville, Va., garden façade, 1793–1809.

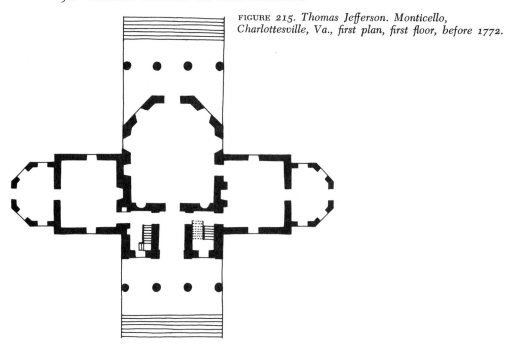

FIGURE 215. *Thomas Jefferson. Monticello, Charlottesville, Va., first plan, first floor, before 1772.*

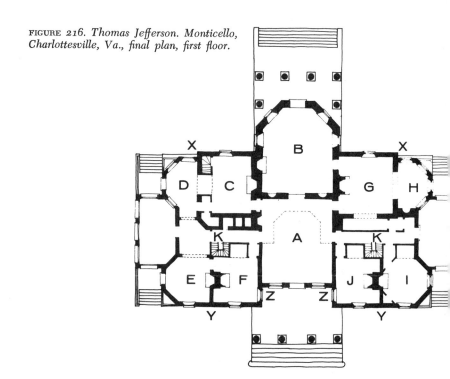

FIGURE 216. *Thomas Jefferson. Monticello, Charlottesville, Va., final plan, first floor.*

it also gives the building greater monumentality. The over-all effect is more coherent and broader than the earlier scheme at the same time that it is very much more complex.

Equally decisive changes were made in the plan. The earlier plan (Fig. 215) shows on the first floor a central room with an octagonal side which projects as a bay beneath a four-columned portico. Adjoining this room on its inner side is a small entrance hall with flanking stairs. It, too, is fronted by a portico. These central spaces, from portico to portico, constitute a continuous block and delineate the primary axis of the building. Flanking this block on either side are identical square rooms which in turn are extended by octagonal bays. Taken together these lateral rooms create a secondary cross axis. No plan of the second floor survives, but the elevation makes it certain that the arrangement was probably similar to that on the first. The elevation also suggests that the height of the first-floor rooms must have been equivalent to the full height of the lower order of the portico.

Altogether, there is nothing remarkable about this plan. In its absolute symmetry and its lateral extension of sharply defined compartments it is a typical Palladian-type concept which, as we have already seen, Jefferson derived from a book source. In his revised plan (Fig. 216), begun after his return from France, Jefferson retained both the main room with its octagonal end and portico, and the flanking rooms with their octagonal bays. The meagre entrance hall and stairs, he eliminated altogether. Then by extending the outer walls of the old hall to more than twice their original length he created a new entrance hall (Fig. 216: A), spacious in area and placed with its long dimension coinciding with the primary axis of the building. Like the adjoining central room, the hall terminates in a portico. On either side of this hall, but projecting slightly beyond it so as to form a recessed porch beneath the portico (Fig. 216: Z), Jefferson put a second pair of balancing rooms with attached bays (Fig. 216: E and F; J and I). Access to these new rooms and to all but one of the original flanking rooms was by narrow lateral passageways which opened from either side of the main hall; narrow stairs off each of these passageways (Fig. 216: K) provided access to the second floor. The whole house was thus deepened by more than twice its original area and the plan made much more complex.

The changes in Jefferson's new arrangement are more subtle than is immediately apparent. At first glance he seems to have done no more than duplicate the original rooms, but careful examination reveals that this is not so. First, there is a bold separation of spaces according to public and private functions. The major public rooms, or what Jefferson would have called the "rooms of entertainment," are the hall and the parlor (Fig. 216: A and B).[13] In height they both go through the full vertical dimension of the building, to a level which corresponds on the inside to the top of the main entablature on the outside of the house. Each room is entered from without by a door located on the central axis of the building. They are thus visually accented, spatially unified, and clearly differentiated from the other rooms in both size and orientation.

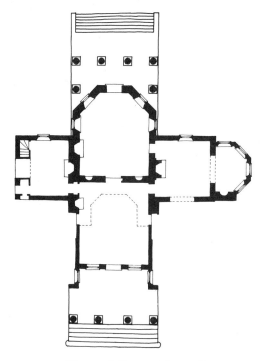

FIGURE 217. *Thomas Jefferson. Monticello, Charlottesville, Va., final plan, first floor, central core rooms.*

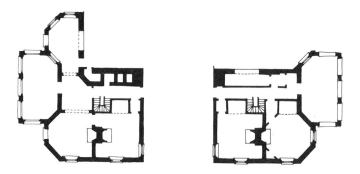

FIGURE 218. *Thomas Jefferson. Monticello, Charlottesville, Va., final plan, first floor, wing rooms.*

Together with their porticos they form a unified spatial volume which is visually and functionally circumscribed as the primary core of the building.

Closely related to this sharply defined axial core are the two original lateral rooms (Fig. 216: C and G), the dining room to the right, and Jefferson's bedroom to the left. Functionally, these rooms are next in importance to the hall and the parlor, and together with the tearoom (Fig. 216: H) are the same height. They are thereby joined to the main space as the arms of a coherent cross-shaped internal volume (Fig. 217).

Further to express this spatial grouping the plan reveals that the abutting wall of each of the octagonal bays is held back slightly from the main wall of the garden façade (Fig. 216: X) so that the outer corner in each case is emphasized and the lateral limits of the cross-shaped spatial volume are clearly defined. On the other side of the house (Fig. 216: Y), where a different grouping of interior space was intended, the wall of the façade is continuous with the wall of each octagonal bay. Circulation between the lateral rooms and the central core is also functionally controlled. Because of its semipublic nature the dining room (Fig. 216: G) opens into both the drawing room and the hall; for greater privacy Jefferson's bedroom (Fig. 216: C) is reached primarily from the hall.

All the other rooms on the first floor—Jefferson's cabinet, book room, and the south square room (Fig. 218), and the square and octagonal bedrooms on the northeast side—are only slightly more than half as high as the core rooms; and above them, yet still contained within the same building height as the central core, is a series of second-story rooms (Fig. 219) identical in their general layout to those upon which they rest. In Jefferson's time these upper rooms were all used as additional bedrooms. This two-story arrangement itself was obviously inspired by the "two tiers" of rooms observed by Jefferson in the new town houses of Paris, so too were the narrow stairs (Fig. 216: K) which gave access to the second floor. On the second floor, the rooms are connected by passageways identical to those on the first floor. These two-story components interlock the main central core at the same time that they are spatially separated by the full two-story height of the hall (Fig. 219). They are connected at the second-floor level, however, by a balcony across the inner end of the hall which not only gives access from side to side, but which also articulates in the hall the difference in the vertical division of space between the full height central core and the two-story flanking units.

Although Jefferson's over-all scheme seems locked in symmetry (the exterior of the house is absolutely symmetrical) the fact is that no two of the internal spaces are exactly alike. All the rooms to the left of the main hall make up Jefferson's private quarters. The three most important —his bedroom, cabinet, and book room—are virtually one continuous space (Fig. 216: C, D, and E). Not only does the bedroom open into the cabinet through a conventional door, but in addition a large section of the wall between the two rooms is open to accommodate Jefferson's bed (Fig. 223). As a result there is a definite visual continuity between the bedroom and the cabinet. The cabinet in turn flows without interruption into the book room to form the library suite. The fourth room in the group, the south square room, is more isolated than the others and is closed off by conventional doors only, which open from the library on one side and from the lateral passageway on the other. There is no door into the main hall, thus assuring privacy from that quarter. A window, however, looks out onto the recessed porch under the main entrance portico.

The rooms on the other side of the hall correspond in their placement to those just discussed, but their character is quite different (Fig. 218).

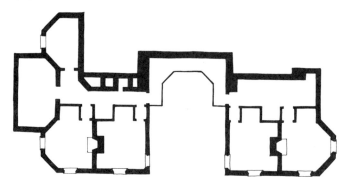

FIGURE 219. *Thomas Jefferson. Monticello, Charlottesville, Va., final plan, second floor.*

The dining room, for example, not only opens through doorways into both the hall and the parlor, but on the other side has a wide arched opening into the octagonal tearoom beyond (Fig. 216: G and H). Thus the two rooms intended for dining are permitted to flow together as one continuous space. To emphasize this functional spatial unity, the tearoom is cut off completely from all adjoining spaces except the dining room. The result is a marked separation between the unified semipublic dining area and the two guest bedrooms on the other side of the lateral passage (Fig. 216: I and J), a separation which contrasts with the spatial continuity we have just observed in Jefferson's private quarters. But this is not all. As if to emphasize the isolation of the two guest bedrooms even further, they are different in shape. One is rectangular, the other octagonal, and they were known by Jefferson as the "north square room" and the "north octagonal room." To assure their complete privacy each can be entered only by a single door from the lateral passage.

The variety within unity, the purposeful grouping of rooms, the functional continuity or isolation of spatial components, all these thoughtful adjustments and relationships make the new Monticello a living organism which contrasts dramatically with the sterile symmetry of his first design. Based as his first plan is on the immutable absolutes of Palladian theory, it leaves little room for the necessities of function. Not that Jefferson in the later Monticello was no longer concerned with formal absolutes. Running through all of his work are the principles of classical design. At Monticello his general scheme is symmetrical, he adheres strictly to axial arrangements, and his handling of all classical elements is impeccably correct in proportion and detail. But once his eyes had been opened to the supreme flexibility and logic of French rational planning he never again saw architecture as only a matter of applied theory derived from books. Through personal association as well as natural sensitivity Jefferson understood better than any other American architect of his day precisely what the French were trying to accomplish, and during those years of absence from Monticello it must have been with frustration and impatience that he waited for the opportunity to return.

The discriminating and practical spatial organization which Jefferson achieved in the plan of Monticello is clearly revealed on the exterior of the building. We have already noted the greater coherence which resulted from Jefferson's radical changes to his original design. Coming back now to the exterior, but keeping the plan in mind, we discover a number of fascinating relationships between the two. The main approach to the house is from the northeast with the entrance through the east portico into the entrance hall. We remember from our analysis of the plan that the lateral rooms on either side project slightly beyond the hall to form a recessed porch under the portico (Fig. 216: Z). Viewing this from the outside (Fig. 220), we see that in response to this internal arrangement, the outer wall of the hall is set back from the main wall of the house. This creates under the portico a spatial volume which actually penetrates the main mass of the building. This not only results in a greater sense of enclosure beneath the portico, but together with the three tall round-headed glass doors, it tends to dissolve the wall at the critical point and to draw one into the house. In contrast, the flat brick walls on either side stretch left and right in a continuous plane, without indentation or projection, until they break on a diagonal toward the flanking porches. The widely spaced windows add rhythmic vertical accents but do not break the continuity of the wall plane.

FIGURE 220. *Thomas Jefferson. Monticello, Charlottesville, Va., main façade, detail, 1793–1809.*

The windows on the main façade are important from yet another point of view. We know from the plan that the rooms on this side of the house are arranged in two-story blocks on either side of the tall central hall. The contrast which is established is between the high separating space of the hall articulated on the exterior by the recessed porch and projecting portico, and the two-story blocks of the lateral rooms articulated by the windows. The windows, like the rooms they illuminate, are also arranged in tiers. There is a conventional classically proportioned window on the first floor, and above that, forming a continuous vertical panel, a square attic-type window. The actual location of the second floor itself is revealed in these panels by the entablature which crowns the top of each of the first-floor windows.

Jefferson's spatial handling of the garden façade is just the opposite (Fig. 221). Unlike the cave-like recessed porch of the main façade, the central octagonal room on the garden side projects boldly, and its portico is two columns deep rather than one. This tends to accentuate the outward thrust of the central core. But this vigorous movement is contained by a counter movement. Rising above the central parlor, and cutting through the templelike mass of the portico, is the dome. This bold geometric motif adds a discrete vertical accent to this side of the house, and thereby becomes the culminating motif in the entire design. But its profile is low and it is partially screened behind the combined horizontals of the entablature and balustrade so that its ultimate effect is to enhance rather than counteract the long extended mass of the house. At the same time, however, the outward and upward thrust created by the combined dome and portico is just the reverse of the inward penetrating movement of the portico and recessed porch on the other façade. What Jefferson has created here is a spatial inversion, a juxtaposition of contrasting thrusts which is not only fascinating in itself but which also expresses, from yet another point of view, the functional separation, on the interior, of the public from the private rooms.

There is yet another important difference between the two façades. Our analysis of the plan revealed that the two rooms flanking the drawing room and hall, that is, the dining room and Jefferson's bedroom, are the same height as the two larger rooms and thus form a unified spatial core in the shape of a cross (Fig. 217). It is the head and arms of this cross that are seen from the garden.

Jefferson gives outward affirmation of this internal condition in two ways. First, on this side of the house, as already observed in the plan (Fig. 216: X), the octagonal bays are set back from the main wall of the house at that point on the outside which corresponds exactly with the inner walls of the lateral rooms (Fig. 221). This defines the corners and creates a slightly projecting pavilion which expresses on the exterior the exact limits of these rooms. Second, all the windows in the octagonal projection, and the single windows left and right in the lateral rooms, are the full-length, triple-hung type set at floor level, rather than the conventional classically proportioned windows in the lateral bays or the long paneled double windows on the other side of the house (compare Fig. 220). Since they are set at floor level there is a considerable area of plain wall between their tops and the bottom of the main entablature. The effect is to isolate them in large areas of wall. This, together with their tall proportions, clearly articulates the full height of the rooms behind. The fact that they are set at floor level also identifies and strengthens the base of the entire geometric system of the garden façade.

All these sensitive and expressive relationships in design make Monticello the most imaginative house of its day and one of the most provocative in the whole history of American architecture. To be sure, it can be shown that Jefferson took many of his ideas from books, but this does no more than shed light on his methods and identify him with the general and accepted practices of his time. In spite of the fact that his training and resources were those of an amateur, he was able to perform with all the insight and boldness of a high professional; and it is in precisely this role that he finally emerges at Monticello. But Monticello was not only consummately designed, it was also highly personal and it is here that we encounter some of the more delightful facets of Jefferson's genius.

We discover, for example, his impeccable classical taste. Even though many of the decorative components of the house came from various classical or Palladian sources (which Jefferson identifies for us) they are brought together at Monticello, through refined adjustments in scale, into a coherent whole. There is nothing that does not seem to belong; in this house, as in all great architecture, a discriminating eye has scrutinized everything down to the smallest detail. The highly functional stairs, for example (Fig. 222) though deliberately located in an inconspicuous but efficient place, are nevertheless designed with infinite care. Their balus-

FIGURE 222. *Thomas Jefferson. Monticello, Charlottesville, Va., stairs, 1793–1809.*

trades, although simple, are as finely scaled and graciously shaped as the most authoritative classical ornament in the house, and they are many times more original.

Then there are the gadgets. There is the weathervane on the ceiling of the entrance porch which can be read without going out into the weather; and on the wall beneath it is the face of a clock so that Jefferson could record the time of his meteorological observations (Fig. 220). Directly inside is the clock itself with a second face in the hall and with its weights recording the day of the week as they descend the wall. The location of Jefferson's bed is equally ingenious (Fig. 223). With his knowledge of meteorology Jefferson was aware that air moves more quickly through a narrow passage, so his bed is placed in an opening between the bedroom and study. If there was any air stirring on hot summer nights it would be bound to pass over his bed. In wintertime, to shut out the cold drafts, he had Venetian blind curtains which could be dropped to enclose the bed. At the entrance to the drawing room are double doors which are mechanically connected in such a way that when one is opened the other opens automatically. On the side of the fireplace in the dining

FIGURE 223. *Thomas Jefferson. Monticello,*
Charlottesville, Va., Jefferson's bedroom, 1793–1809.

room (Fig. 224) is a small dumb-waiter for transporting wine from the
cellar.

The humanized aspects of Monticello are inexhaustible. Each room is
not only planned differently from all the others to serve some specific
purpose but each also has its special visual quality. The drawing room
(Fig. 225) is cool and exquisitely chaste, a thoroughly appropriate setting
for the many formal social occasions and musical events which we know
were held there. The dining room is totally different (Fig. 226). Within
the limits of its classical idiom it is heavier, richer, and more sensuous.
Jefferson's library suite is sunlit and intimate. And overall there is a fine
sense of human scale. Although Monticello is monumental in many of its
aspects, it is also intimate and livable. The rooms are small and are
conceived in every aspect for human habitation.

Everywhere at Monticello are the signs of Jefferson's insatiable curiosity, and if this is so today how much more so it must have been
when Jefferson lived there. The great hall, for example (Fig. 227), where
formal receptions were held, was also a museum for the many-sided
Jefferson himself. George Ticknor, who visited Monticello in 1815, describes it in fascinating detail.

> You enter, by a glass folding door, into a hall which reminds you
> of Fielding's "Man of the Mountain," by the strange furniture of its
> walls. On one side hang the head and horns of an elk, a deer and
> a buffalo; another is covered with curiosities which Lewis and Clark
> found in their wild and perilous expedition. On the third, among
> many other striking matters, was the head of a mammoth, or, as
> Cuvier calls it, a mastodon, containing the only *os frontis,* Mr.

FIGURE 224. *Thomas Jefferson. Monticello,*
Charlottesville, Va., dining room mantel, 1793–1809.

Jefferson tells me, that has yet been found. On the fourth side, in
odd union with a fine painting of the Repentance of St. Peter, is an
Indian map on leather, of the southern waters of the Missouri, and
an Indian representation of a bloody battle, handed down in their
traditions.[14]

This room reveals not only the gracious host but also the scientific in-
vestigator, the man seeking documented truths in the vast cosmos of
nature.

Monticello was a productive farm, and here we encounter another of
Jefferson's diversified interests. His ideal of the agrarian state centered
around the farm as an independent economic and social unit; and in the
realization of this ideal ancient Rome came to play a fundamental and

fruitful role. As one of the distinguished classicists of his day, Jefferson not only drew heavily on Rome in architectural and legal matters but in his reading on Roman farming methods he also derived many useful ideas about agriculture. Even more important, in the writings of Varo and Pliny the Younger, he discovered both the practical and aesthetic amenities of the Roman villa. In these loosely ordered and highly individual dwellings, situated as they were in rural settings, Jefferson recognized certain deep-rooted affinities with his own concept of living. His image of the Roman villa was an idyllic one. Here the life of the farmer could be carried out in a sweeping sunlit landscape against the background of a classical architectural setting, and it all seemed to fit exactly his life on the Virginia plantation.[15] Perhaps this image was most vividly expressed for him in a poem which he copied from Horace several years before he even began his first plans for Monticello:

Happy is he who far from business,
like the first race of man,
can till inherited lands with his teams,
free from all payment of interest.

He who avoids the market and
the proud thresholds of mighty citizens . . .

He may recline now under an old tree
and again on the soft meadow,
while the waters fall down from the steep banks,
birds lament in the woods,
and the springs with murmuring veins,
suggest soft sleep.

Jefferson went on to copy much of the rest of the poem which deals with life on a Roman farm, and the similarity between what Horace describes and what must have transpired on a Virginia plantation is obvious. That Jefferson clearly had this in mind when he copied the poem is further emphasized by the fact that those parts which he did not copy are precisely the ones which bear no direct relationship with the Virginia plantation.[16] It is perfectly clear from a substantial body of evidence that Jefferson intended to incorporate into Monticello many of the practical and visual qualities of the Roman villa.

There is first its widespread but coordinated plan. In our discussion of Monticello thus far we have concerned ourselves with the main house alone. The house, however, is but a part of a larger complex of utility buildings and dependencies, most of which are hidden below ground level. These are arranged in the form of an open U with the house at the center of the closed side (Fig. 209). Terminating the end of each arm of the U is a small brick pavilion (Fig. 228). Villa plans of this kind are to be found in the works of Palladio, and in view of Jefferson's sources at the time he first conceived Monticello it is almost certain that he took the basic plan from Palladio. On the other hand, the Roman villa was

FIGURE 225. *Thomas Jefferson. Monticello, Charlottesville, Va., drawing room, 1793–1809.*

the source for Palladio himself, and numerous aspects of Jefferson's scheme indicate that he, too, had the Roman villa in mind. The small brick pavilions at the end of the service wings, for example, are not unlike the outbuildings described by Pliny in both his Tuscan and Laurentine villas. In the Roman villa these remote apartments, separated from the mansion, were given over to solitude and quiet work; at Monticello they served as Jefferson's law office and the estate office. Another interesting feature which derives from the Roman villa is the below-grade passageways which connect the service wings with the main house (Fig. 229). Called *crypto-porticus* by Pliny, such a feature was typical of most Roman villas, and the underground passages at Monticello, which have small high windows along one wall, are remarkably similar to those described by Pliny in his Laurentine villa. Hadrian's Villa at Tivoli (Fig. 230) had a similar arrangement and it is altogether possible that Jefferson was familiar with this from published engravings.

The most exhilarating feature of Monticello, and the one which identifies it with the Roman villa is its location on the top of a mountain. Almost all the great Roman villas, such as Pliny's Tuscan villa in the foothills

FIGURE 226. Thomas Jefferson. Monticello,
Charlottesville, Va., dining room and tearoom, 1793–1809.

FIGURE 227. Thomas Jefferson. Monticello,
Charlottesville, Va., entrance hall, 1793–1809.

of the Apennines and Hadrian's Villa near Tivoli, were situated on high ground with panoramic views. Even the name Monticello, which means little mountain, implies this intent on Jefferson's part. The view from Monticello, across the lawn and through the ancient trees to the Blue Ridge Mountains beyond, is one of the most commanding in America and is described by Jefferson with moving eloquence in a famous letter to the beautiful Maria Cosway. In an impassioned effort to persuade her to visit him in America he wrote:

. . . The falling Spring, the Cascade of Niagara, the passage of the Potomac through the Blue Mountains, the Natural Bridge; it is worth a voyage across the Atlantic to see these objects; . . . . And our own dear Monticello; where has nature spread so rich a mantle under the eye? mountains, forests, rocks, rivers. With what majesty do we there ride above the storms! How sublime to look down into the workhouse of nature, to see her clouds, hail, snow, rain, thunder, all fabricated at our feet! and the glorious sun, when rising as if out of a distant water, just gilding the tops of the mountains, and giving life to all nature![17]

Such subjective responsiveness to the vastness and wonder of nature is not only similar to the sensuous delight with which the ancient Romans viewed the world around them, but it also identifies Jefferson with the nature-romanticism of his own country. Only a few years after his death Emerson and Thoreau would begin to weave the threads of man and nature into an elaborate philosophical fabric, and the first indigenous school of American landscape painting would be born in the north. At the same time, the intelligence and sensitivity with which Jefferson combined his highly rational house with a capricious natural setting show him to be equally a product of the rational-romantic attitudes of eighteenth-century Europe. Because of its connotations Jefferson despised English architecture, but as a man of free will he expressed open admiration for the English informal gardens. And one cannot contemplate Monticello without remarking its kinship with the formal country houses of eighteenth-century England and the ingenious way they are set in the contrived meanderings of their picturesque gardens.

As it stands today Monticello is one of the most civilized houses ever built. It is disarmingly simple at the same time that it is intricate; it is practical at the same time that it is easy, flowing, and gracious; it is dignified and yet is filled with charming informality. In all aspects of its attractiveness it reflects the uninhibited outpouring of a sensitive and dynamic intelligence, and it owes its success to the astonishing identification of the house with the man who designed it. Because Jefferson was his own architect he was able to confront each problem at intimate levels of practical and emotional involvement which would never have been possible in the normal relationship between architect and client. Monticello, therefore, is intensely personal, so personal, in fact, that it would be difficult for another to live in it. In addition, it is an exalted embodiment

FIGURE 228. *Thomas Jefferson. Monticello,*
Charlottesville, Va., southwest dependency and servants' quarters, 1768–1809.

FIGURE 229. *Thomas Jefferson. Monticello,*
Charlottesville, Va., underground passage, 1768–1809.

FIGURE 230. Hadrian's Villa, Tivoli, crypto-porticus, 117–138.

of Jefferson's concept of the agrarian state. Through his practical but imaginative planning he was able to achieve an easy and happy union between the amenities of gracious living and the necessities of a working, self-contained economic unit. Jefferson would have wished that his whole beloved America could be transformed into a macrocosm of his microcosm. Unfortunately for him, in those very years when Monticello was functioning most effectively in the realization of his vision of life, a youthful aggressive industrialism was already firmly implanted on the banks of the Merrimack River in Lowell, Massachusetts; and during the 1860's the agrarian ideals toward which Jefferson had struggled throughout his life were shattered altogether. Monticello became obsolete at the moment of Jefferson's death, for the house and the master were one, and when he left it he took with him the very reason for its existence.

The University of Virginia

Jefferson's other great undertaking in architecture, the University of Virginia, was more far-reaching in its accomplishments, for it sprang from the heart of his vision of society. Throughout his career this great man clung to the idea of education as a fundamental prerequisite for responsible citizenship, and he never missed an opportunity to foster this idea. As early as 1779, only three years after the Declaration of Independence, a "Bill for the More General Diffusion of Knowledge," written by Jefferson, was introduced into the Virginia Legislature. Although it was never passed, it provided a graded system of secular education which, in Jefferson's own words, would ". . . give to every citizen the information he needs for the transaction of daily business . . . and, in general, to observe with intelligence and faithfulness all social relations under which he shall be placed." This was the primary level. The secondary and university levels were planned that those "whom nature hath endowed with genius and virtue should be called to that charge without regard to wealth, birth or other accidental condition or circumstance," and should be rendered "by liberal education worthy to receive, and able to guard the sacred deposit of the rights and liberties of their fellow citizens." What Jefferson envisaged was an aristocracy of the mind. The opportunity to achieve an education was available to all citizens, but only those who proved themselves capable would advance to the higher levels.

At the top of this educational pyramid, as the crowning achievement in Jefferson's career, was the University of Virginia. Unparalleled in its day, this institution still stands as one of the most enlightened and visionary conceptions in the history of Western man. At the center was a revolutionary concept of education. The curriculum, which was designed by Jefferson, challenged many established educational practices. Because of its sectarian complications theology was not included as a course of study; science, agriculture, and modern languages were given a status equal with the classics. All academic matters were established under a system of democratic self-government by the faculty, and discipline, at least in the beginning, was a matter of student honor. Far from being religiously oriented, the University, Jefferson said at the time, "will be based on the illimitable freedom of the human mind . . . for here we are not afraid to follow the truth wherever it may lead or to tolerate any error so long as reason is left free to combat it."

The radical nature of the educational process proposed by Jefferson required an equally radical environment in which to flourish. This, too, he provided, for he not only conceived and planned the academic structure of the University, he also designed the architecture which was to house its various functions. In deriving his plan Jefferson showed himself to be keenly aware of the many-sided nature of his project. At one moment he reveals himself as a shrewd positivist seeking convenient accommodations for a multitude of practical problems, and then synthesizing them in a coherent workable scheme. The next, he appears as an urbane humanist seeking sympathetic surroundings in which human beings may be drawn together in civilized discourse with one another. And above all, is the persistent idealist, evoking expressive images and symbols appropriate to the new order of society that he had struggled so hard to achieve. All of this is communicated at the University with such inexhaustible freshness and vitality as to make it one of the most modern works in the history of American architecture.

The idea for a university seems always to have been in Jefferson's mind. As early as 1803 he was thinking in terms of a specific proposition to the Virginia Legislature for the establishment of a true university, and during the following decade there are many indications that his plans were already taking shape. But not until 1817, after years of involved negotiations, was his dream finally realized. A bill passed by the Legislature in 1816 established a Central College and Jefferson proceeded at once with the selection of an appropriate location. From the beginning his practical sense asserted itself. "What we are seeking," he wrote, "is an eligible site for the College, high, dry, open, furnished with good water, and nothing in its vicinity which would threaten the health of the students." Two hundred acres west of Charlottesville were chosen, in the very shadow of his beloved Monticello, and on October 6, 1817, the cornerstone was laid.

In planning the architecture of the new university Jefferson could have drawn on the experience at the already established colleges of America. By the 1750's, Harvard, Yale, and the College of New Jersey (Princeton) were flourishing institutions and as the century progressed they were joined by several others. In Williamsburg the College of William and Mary, Jefferson's own alma mater, continued as the major institution of higher learning in the South. Architecturally, all these had one thing in common; they began as single all-purpose buildings, and became compounds of several buildings only after their needs and resources made expansion essential and possible. When new buildings were added they were sometimes arranged, as at Harvard (Fig. 231), in quasi-formal groups; and the Wren Building at William and Mary actually occupied a position of axial prominence at one end of the Duke of Gloucester

FIGURE 231. *Harvard College, 1726.*

Street vis-a-vis the colonial Capitol at the other end. It thus functioned as a terminal monument in a large formal town plan. But these were exceptional; in general, the various American colleges grew in a random fashion without any long-range coherent scheme. With each new building they simply expanded, spreading across fields or clinging to hillsides in the abandoned freedom of irregular and in some instances indiscriminate growth. Out of this came the campus, that loose but spacious grouping of buildings which is so characteristic of the older colleges of America. By Jefferson's time the campus was an established concept in the layout of American educational institutions.

Jefferson was also familiar with the collegiate architecture of England. Here the arrangement was different. Dating back well into the Middle Ages, and taking their form from the cloisters of the medieval monastery, the colleges of Oxford and Cambridge were built as enclosed although not always regular quadrangles. A chapel formed the nucleus of each and served as a reminder that up to that time education in England had traditionally been a function of the church and not the state.

Neither the American campus nor the English quadrangle in itself offered meaningful solutions to what Jefferson sought to achieve. As a man of the Enlightenment he would have found the English quadrangle incompatible with his own ideas in almost every respect. The prominence of religion as a motivating force in the intellectual life, symbolized by the looming presence of the chapel, the rejection of the world of reality in the confinement of the cloister, the residual aura of medieval mysticism implicit in the irregular plans and the tangle of Gothic tracery, all these would have been offensive to his humanistic ideals and his meticulous sense of order.

For quite different reasons the American campus was equally unsuitable for his purposes. First, American collegiate architecture remained stanchly in the English-oriented form and styles of the colonial and Federal eras. This in itself would have made them abhorrent to his highly developed Roman taste. But even more important, Jefferson saw the existing colleges as disorderly and inefficient, and incapable of providing the controlled environment that to him was so essential to the rational pursuit of knowledge. His feelings in this respect were clearly stated when he scornfully referred to such an institution as a "large and common den of noise." For his university Jefferson proposed instead what he called an "academical village," a unified coherent design, efficiently disposed, aesthetically and symbolically expressive, and scaled to human habitation. (Fig. 232). His scheme is described in detail in a letter which he wrote to the architect Benjamin Latrobe.

. . . We propose to lay off a square or rather 3. sides of a square about 7–or 800 ft. wide, leaving it open at one end to be extended indefinitely. On the closed end, and on the two sides we propose to arrange separate pavilions for each professor and his school. Each Pavilion is to have a schoolroom below, and 2. rooms for the Professor

FIGURE 232. *Thomas Jefferson. University of Virginia, Charlottesville, as it appeared after 1853.*

above; and between pavilion and pavilion a range of Dormitories for the students, one story high, giving to each a room 10 f. wide and 14. f. deep, the Pavilions about 36. f. wide in front, and 24. f. in depth. . . .

The whole of the pavilions and dormitories to be united by a colonnade in front, of the height of the lower story of the pavilions and about 8 f. wide under which they may go dry from school to school.

This was the concept, and as completed Jefferson's proposed open square forms the core of the scheme. It is best seen in a nineteenth-century print[18] and in Jefferson's own drawing for the plan (Figs. 232; 233). Two rows of dormitories, connected by colonnades face one another across an expansive lawn. Beginning at the north end of each row, and spaced at *regularly increasing intervals* are the ten pavilions for the professors. They rise above the colonnades, five on each side, and face each other exactly across the lawn. Added to Jefferson's early idea of the open square, however, are several important elements. In the center of the north, or closed, side Jefferson placed a large rotunda with a projecting portico; this contained the library, lecture room, and other common facilities, including a gymnasium and the first planetarium in the United States (Fig. 234). The idea for this building was suggested to Jefferson by Latrobe and it establishes the all-important central axis from which the rest of the design generates. Also added to the proposed scheme are two parallel ranges of dormitories, one behind each of the inner rows. They are separated from the inner ranges by gardens, which in turn are enclosed by serpentine walls (Fig. 235); the rows of dormitory rooms are connected with one another along their outer fronts by arcades rather than the colonnades which connect the rooms facing the central lawn

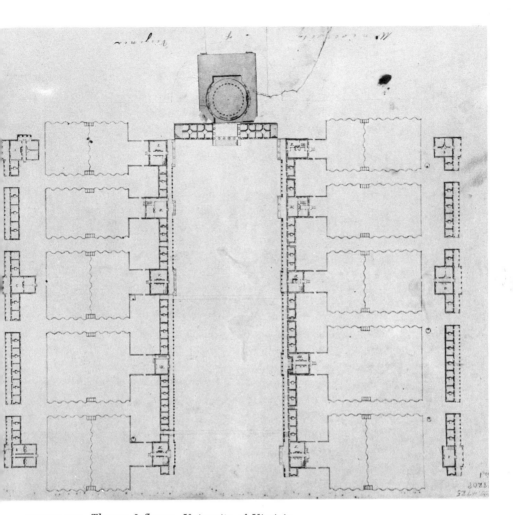

FIGURE 233. Thomas Jefferson. University of Virginia, Charlottesville, plan, before 1822.

(Fig. 236). Also contained in the outer ranges are six more pavilions (Fig. 237), called "hotels" by Jefferson and intended for dining rooms. There are three on each side and they are spaced directly behind the first, middle, and last pavilions on the lawn.

In spite of the fact that Jefferson's plan basically rejects both the American campus and the English quadrangle, it incorporates with exquisite subtlety an enormously important aspect of each. The American campus is spacious and open. It reaches out with delight toward the sky and land to participate in, rather than close out, the world of reality. To be sure, Jefferson replaces its looseness with a controlled and meaningful order, but the living quarters at the university on both the central lawn (Fig. 239) and the ranges (Fig. 236) face outward not inward and are accessible only from their open side. At the same time, Jefferson recognized that in the life of the mind there is a need at times for seclusion. Thus behind the dormitories and pavilions are lovely walled gardens. The en-

FIGURE 234. Thomas Jefferson. University of Virginia, Charlottesville, Lawn and Rotunda, 1817–26.

FIGURE 235. Thomas Jefferson. University of Virginia, Charlottesville, serpentine walls, 1817–26.

FIGURE 236. *Thomas Jefferson. University of Virginia, Charlottesville, West Range, 1817–22.*

FIGURE 237. *Thomas Jefferson. University of Virginia, Charlottesville, garden and refectory, 1822.*

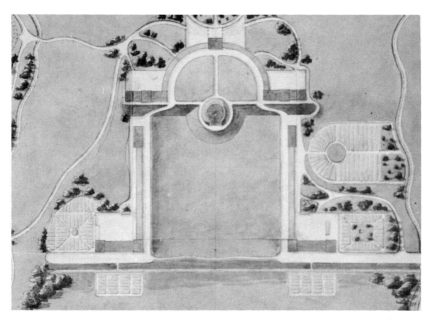

FIGURE 238. *J. J. Ramée. Plan for Union College,
Schenectady, N.Y., 1812.*

closing walls are not as high as those of an English quadrangle and visual
communication with the world beyond is never completely lost. But the
sense of seclusion is there nevertheless and something of the quiet of the
cloister is achieved. Finally, as in the English quadrangle, one building
in Jefferson's university rises in dominance over all the others to serve as
a symbolic center for the whole. This building is the library, not a chapel,
and thus stresses the intellectual rather than the spiritual focus of the institution.

Jefferson's revolutionary scheme was not without an important counterpart in American architecture. Union College in Schenectady, New York,
designed by the French architect Jean Jacques Ramée (1764–1842),
was planned in 1812 and construction was begun the following year, four
years before Jefferson started building the University (Fig. 238). Like
Jefferson's, Ramée's scheme was U-shaped. It also had a rotunda in the
center, although it was not attached to the main range of buildings. Because of these similarities and because of the earlier date we must consider Ramée's design first as a possible source for Jefferson.

Ramée was a French *émigré* who came to the United States in 1811
and for five years practiced architecture in New York, Philadelphia, and
Baltimore. He was commissioned to design the new grounds and buildings
for Union in 1812. Because of Jefferson's interest in architecture and his
concern with the University of Virginia it is unthinkable that he did not
know of Ramée's presence in this country, or that he was unaware of the
Frenchman's activity at Union. Moreover, there is no doubt that Union
was the first comprehensive plan for an educational institution in America
to be carried into effect. Its relationship to the University of Virginia,
therefore, is extremely important.

We are first impressed by the similarities in the basic schemes, particularly in Ramée's use of an open rectangle with a rotunda as the central motif (compare Figs. 233 and 238). But his dormitory buildings are four stories high, thus taking on something of the character of the traditional American dormitory and lacking altogether the intimacy and breadth of Jefferson's one-story scheme. Moreover, Ramée does not make use of the individual pavilions, the connecting colonnades, or the enclosed gardens with their refectories. Finally, because of limited funds only a part of the total scheme was completed in the original building campaign, and later in the century drastic changes were made so that Ramée's intentions were never fully realized. But quite apart from all this there is documentary evidence to prove that Jefferson's idea was already well formulated several years before Ramée even came to this country. A letter from Jefferson to L. W. Tazewell, written on January 5, 1805, establishes that Jefferson was already thinking of "an academical village[19];" and by 1810, in a letter from Jefferson to the trustees of East Tennessee College, the scheme is described in terms almost identical to those used in the letter from Jefferson to Latrobe which was just quoted above.

The truth is that the University of Virginia and Union College represent separate developments from a common source, rather than a relationship in which one derives from the other.[20] The open colonnaded rectangle was a popular scheme among the French Neoclassicists of the late eighteenth and early nineteenth centuries, especially in some of the grandiose projects submitted for the Prix de Rome competitions.[21] Jefferson, as well as Ramée, was familiar with the French trends of his time, and it is clear that the impact of France on the University was every bit as strong as it was at Monticello.

It has also been suggested that Jefferson's monumental colonnaded scheme bore a direct relationship in his mind with the great fora of ancient Rome. In view of Jefferson's classical enthusiasm this is a plausible suggestion. But the life envisaged by Jefferson for the University was not the life of the Roman forum. His objective was to create an intimate community in which professor and student could meet and exchange ideas in a civilized and sympathetic environment, and to this end both France and Rome would make significant contributions.

In spite of its firm roots in Neoclassical and ancient architecture Jefferson's plan was practical, humanistic, and intensely personal. Remembering the close association he enjoyed with Dr. Small at William and Mary, he arranged the University so that as far as possible students were housed in the rooms adjacent to the pavilion occupied by the professor with whom they were doing their major studies; at the same time, they were free to eat in any one of the six dining rooms, although no more than fifty students were allowed in any one dining room at a given time. Thus the various spatial units were divided and positioned in such a way as to provide close communication between instructor and student, centered around the individual pavilions. Jefferson also made possible a wide interschool social and intellectual life through the dining arrangements; and all of this was contained within the spacious shaded lawns and intimate gardens to afford what Jefferson called, "that quiet retirement so friendly to study."

Jefferson's success in achieving this objective needs no special architectural expertise to be felt and understood. It requires only a visit to the University. Whether it be in the saturated heat of midsummer, with the seductive smell of warm boxwood on every hand, or in the sharp air of fall, when the leafless trees are etched against a clear sky, the quiet matchless beauty of Jefferson's architecture is there, dignified in its simple but intensely individual classicism, hospitable in its refined scale, sparkling in its visual animation. There is the spacious sweep of the lawn, framed by the colonnade and crowned by the rotunda (Fig. 234); behind is the intimate enclosure of the gardens, enlivened by the sweeping serpentine wall (Fig. 235). This ingenious device is one of the more typical Jeffersonian touches. It is pragmatic in that its curvature made it possible to build it one brick thick rather than with the two required to bond a straight wall; it is capricious and elegant in its undulating rhythm. Not only does it break the severe classical lines of the architecture but within its protective seclusion the visual delights are endless, the contemplative mood complete. Indeed, the image of life which we encounter here is precisely that which Jefferson had already established for himself at Monticello, and rather than the Roman forum, with its official grandeur it was the Roman villa with its open plan, its intimate scale, and its unified but widely separated parts, which provided the model.[22]

Jefferson's plan also bears a direct relationship to the academic organization of the University. Under his radical new curriculum the subjects to be taught were divided into ten separate schools, and because usefulness in everyday life was an important criterion for evaluating a course, the curriculum was heavily weighted toward science. Jefferson's source for this concept of curriculum structure has never been firmly established, and it is altogether possible that it was his own idea. On the other hand, it may have been one of the many inspirations which he derived from his years spent in France. For the University of Paris, with which he must have been thoroughly familiar, was organized along similar lines.

This thoroughly modern curriculum is boldly expressed in the actual design of the University itself. From the general view and plan (Fig. 233), it is apparent that the two rows of pavilions oppose one another exactly in their positions around the central axis, yet no two of them are alike (Fig. 239). This was not mere caprice on Jefferson's part, nor does it indicate an indifference toward the demands of architectural symmetry. Rather, the contrasting styles of the individual pavilions reflect the diverse personalities and disciplines represented by the individual professors. There were ten schools and there are ten pavilions (Fig. 232). Each professor, symbolized by the architectural individuality of his own pavilion, stands decisively separated from the others; around him are grouped the students with whom he works. At the same time, through the unifying forces of the over-all symmetrical arrangement, and through the continuous

rhythm of the colonnade, the many contrasting individual units are brought together in a single cohesive whole.

This diversity among the pavilions had yet another and more immediately practical meaning for Jefferson. Actually, each displays a different style of architecture based on a well-known example from the past. The whole was intended as a kind of encyclopedia of architecture for the benefit of the architectural students. Pavilion I, for example, has a Roman Doric order taken from the Baths of Diocletian as illustrated in a book owned by Jefferson (Figs. 240, 241). Pavilion II has an Ionic order from the Temple of Fortuna Virilis in Rome, taken from the same book. The Rotunda (Fig. 242), conspicuously, is based on the Pantheon in Rome. "Now what we wish," Jefferson explains, "is that these pavilions, as they show themselves above the dormitories, shall be models of taste and good architecture, and of a variety of appearance, no two alike so as to serve as specimens for the architectural lecturer."[23] A unique way to create in America a collection of authoritative models of the kind for which Jefferson himself had yearned through most of his life.

Because of his keen awareness of the symbolic function of architecture, it is significant that Jefferson did not include a single English model. Instead, he provided a selection of Roman and Palladian orders; and so that they might be authentic models he has been meticulous in his rendering of proportion and detail. It is this which gives to the main lawn at the University a pervasive archaeological flavor, and in spite of Jefferson's

FIGURE 240. *Thomas Jefferson. University of Virginia, Charlottesville, Pavilion I, entablature, 1822.*

FIGURE 241. *Doric order from the Baths of Diocle*

expressed purpose, much criticism of his design centers around this point. Even his friend and architectural consultant, Benjamin Latrobe, was caustic about his bookishness. In a letter discussing Jefferson's revisions of the plans for the proposed new president's mansion (now the White House) he says: "I am sorry that I am cramped in this design by his (Jefferson's) prejudice in favor of the old French books, out of which he fishes everything . . . But it is a small sacrifice to my personal attachment to him to humor him."[24]

Latrobe, of course, was speaking as a high professional, and he identified Jefferson quite rightly with the amateur methods which were then common to the American architectural practice. But what he missed altogether was that Jefferson's deliberate adaptations, which seemed so doctrinaire, were also surprisingly free. Even though the Rotunda is a half-size replica of the ancient Pantheon, with the proportions of the order rendered with infinite care, Jefferson felt free to make significant changes.[25] To accommodate the classical building to the character of the rest of the campus he reduced the colonnade from eight to six columns, thus giving a greater vertical effect to the façade. But most significant is the change he made in the relationship between the portico and the main drum of the building. In the Pantheon itself the entablature of the portico stops where it abuts the drum of the building, thus making a marked separation between the two spatial elements. Further, the stringcourses which surround the drum of the Pantheon bear no relationship with the portico. In Jefferson's design the full entablature of the portico is carried entirely around the building, thus unifying the whole and providing an effective base for the drum of the dome. Jefferson has also broken the main walls of the building by windows at both floor levels. Such radical changes in the fundamental character of the ancient model were surely motivated by the designer's own instinctive sense of formal relationships, and show him to be perfectly willing to change the classical prototype wherever it was either practically or aesthetically necessary.

Even more remarkable in its originality is Jefferson's design for Pavilion IX (Fig. 243). Although by his own account the two Ionic columns which stand in antis before the main entrance were taken from the temple of Fortuna Virilis, the pavilion otherwise bears no relationship with the other nine and cannot be shown to derive from any ancient source known to Jefferson. It is in fact a wholly different kind of building. The main block is a simple horizontal rectangle, slightly favoring the square in proportions, and is flanked by two low balancing wings. In the center of this block is a large semicircular niche which serves as a recessed porch for the main door; crowning this niche is a half-round vault. The arch of this vault springs from the entablature line of the long connecting colonnade where it joins to and passes in front of the building. At the opening to the niche, contained in the plane of the wall and running from the floor to the roof of the colonnade, are the two Ionic columns (Fig. 245). As we approach from the lawn, the half-round vault is seen to rise above the colonnade; the niche with its fronting Ionic columns is behind it (Fig. 243). The half-round opening of the half-dome is framed

FIGURE 242. *Thomas Jefferson. University of Virginia, Charlottesville, Rotunda, 1823–27.*

by a simple entablature set flush with the wall. To either side of the niche and at both floor levels are full-length triple-hung windows. These, too, have simple, finely scaled surrounds which are set close to the wall. Consistent with the simplicity and purity of all these effects, the crowning entablature on the main block of the house is narrow, delicately scaled, and except for its thin cornice, is virtually without projection from the plane of the wall. The effect is of unbroken planes constructing simple geometric elements without sculptural embellishment of any kind. Moreover, all this is in absolute contrast to the other nine pavilions, where Jefferson's efforts to render the orders with authentic detail, led inevitably to a considerable sculptural richness, especially in the more elaborate Corinthian order of Pavilion III (Fig. 239).

The sharp stylistic separation of Pavilion IX from the others on the lawn clearly indicates Jefferson's intention to present a different idea, and in this respect the most revealing comparison that can be made is not with classical models, but with a work by one of the most radical contemporary French Neoclassicists, Claude-Nicolas Ledoux. The major motif of Pavilion IX, a block with low wings and a domed-niche door opening, is remarkably similar to Ledoux's Hôtel Guimard, which was erected in 1770 (Fig. 244).[26] In view of Jefferson's interest in recent

Parisian town houses, this would surely have been one which would have attracted his attention. Moreover, we know from his writing that he admired Ledoux's Gates of Paris, in which the Frenchman's notable distillation of form to pure geometric shapes is conspicuously displayed (Fig. 246). Jefferson's express concern for what he called "cubic" and "spherical" architecture shows that he was very much aware of the tendency of the French Neoclassical architects to think in terms of the basic geometry of architecture. Pavilion IX, with its geometric simplicity and its play upon "cubic" and "spherical" shapes, is a daring recognition of this point of view (compare Figs. 245 and 246). Pavilion IX brought to the University of Virginia at least one example of a thoroughly contemporary attitude, an attitude which Jefferson understood and enthusiastically endorsed and one which, in Pavilion IX, he carried out with a special flair of his own.

In the subtle and complex design of Monticello, Jefferson shifted from an architecture of surface to one of mass. This asserts itself again at the University of Virginia, not only in Pavilion IX but also in a special and heretofore unnoticed relationship between all of the pavilions. Not only do they differ from one another in the classical order which each displays but they also vary in orientation, shape, and size. Of these variations those in shape are the most interesting (Fig. 239). Of the nine, only Pavilions I, II, and IV are of the simple temple type, that is, with the end columns of the order continuous with the side planes of the wall; even so, they differ from one another in size and orientation. Pavilions II and X have colossal orders extending through the full height of the building, but the width of their projecting porticoes is less than the full width of the pavilion itself so that the effect is of an attached porch rather than a fully developed temple. Pavilion VI has no order at all, and presents itself as a simple rectangular block parallel to the line of dormitories. Pavilion VIII has a Corinthian order *in antis* before a recessed porch, Pavilion V shows a colossal order without a pediment, and Pavilion VII has a superposed order on an arcade. Finally, Pavilion IX is a simple mass penetrated by a cylinder and a sphere.

Jefferson's play on variety in the pavilions was far more than a demonstration of classical erudition. It was motivated by the same sense of rightness—appropriate to function—which we have seen at Monticello. Like Monticello, the University is alive precisely because it is organically rather than formally conceived. By introducing meaningful tensions, Jefferson avoided the sterility of the absolute. In fact, in his search for the vital not even the over-riding concept of symmetry was free from his will. Few people have ever noticed that the parallel rows of dormitories on the east side of the lawn are almost twenty feet farther apart than the corresponding rows on the west side (Fig. 233). Why? Because the slope of the land on the east side was such that Jefferson had to go farther downhill to find a level spot on which to build the east range. He could easily have leveled the land and maintained his formal symmetry. But he chose instead to let the buildings follow the gentle rise and fall of the terrain; for not only does the east side decline more sharply than the west, but where the main lawn slopes downhill from north to south, the west range slopes in the opposite direction, from south to north.

All this we would expect from a man as uninhibited in his search for truth as Jefferson. It reveals him as a man of free will, as ready to question the authority of classical principles as he was to admit an interest in, and to make use of the English informal garden. Jefferson's brilliant scheme of variety ruled by apparent symmetry reveals to us the practical educator seeking to give order and cohesiveness to the diverse requirements of a university. It also reveals the humanist and poet concerned with the goodness of life. But at yet another level, it shows us the social and political idealist giving tangible expression, in monumental architectural terms, to his fundamental principles of human rights as set forth in the Declaration of Independence. In the architectural complex of the University (Figs. 232, 233) the dignity of the individual is symbolically sustained and protected by the unity and power of government. For just as each pavilion rises above the colonnade as an independent volume, and yet remains an irrevocable part of an architectural whole, so, to Jefferson, each citizen, and each state, maintains its individual rights even though it is an inseparable part of the Federal union. No more eloquent expression of the fundamental nature of American democracy was to be produced in Jefferson's time.

Jefferson's architecture was far too complex and sophisticated to be understood by his fellow Americans. In fact, his influence on subsequent American architecture was one of principle rather than style. He was the first to introduce into this country the concept of revivalism, an attitude toward architecture which was to dominate the major part of the nineteenth century. But in the wave of nationalism, which swept America after the War of 1812, Jefferson's highly reflective and personal style,

FIGURE 243. *Thomas Jefferson. University of Virginia, Charlottesville, Pavilion IX, 1821.*

FIGURE 244. C. N. Ledoux. Hôtel Guimard,
Paris, 1770.

FIGURE 245. Thomas Jefferson. University of Virginia,
Charlottesville, Pavilion IX, entrance, 1821.

FIGURE 246. C. N. Ledoux, Paris Gate, 1748–89.

with all its vitality and wonder, was overshadowed by the indiscriminate excesses of the Greek Revival,[27] and all the promise of both Monticello and the University ended with his death. An objective evaluation of his architecture also reveals that Latrobe's professional reservations were not without foundation. As an amateur, Jefferson's command of structure was limited and his experimental attitudes frequently caused him trouble. Moreover, a discerning eye will quickly discover numerous awkward and unresolved passages in his designing. But all this is beside the point. Part of the charm of Jefferson's architecture stems from its provincialism —from the use of red brick and white painted stucco or wood, for example, instead of stone—and in many ways it makes his work more suitable to its environment.

Monticello and the University of Virginia are not *by* Jefferson, they *are* Jefferson, in Virginia, during the first quarter of the nineteenth century.[28] Passionately conceived, and built under the persistent and demanding supervision of the master himself, both works reflect a degree and intensity of personal involvement which could not be surpassed by any other architect of the time, including Latrobe. Each design was born of a rationally perceived and urgent necessity; each fulfilled that necessity with simplicity and delight. Monticello and the University of Virginia are among the most modern architectural conceptions of all time and as such they stand on the threshold of a new and living tradition in American architecture; for the first time the weary cliches of the English colonial styles were rejected in favor of a belief in the present. Jefferson's plans for both works were motivated by an unshakable faith in the rightness of his time and place, a faith which has been the mark of all great creative men through all generations of time. Indeed, it was this same faith which formed the basis of his whole way of life. "No society can make a perpetual constitution," he wrote, "or a perpetual law. The earth belongs to the living generation." So do Monticello and the University of Virginia.

CHAPTER IX

American Neoclassicism, The Rational Phase

BENJAMIN LATROBE AND ROBERT MILLS

*Nothing can be allowed in good architecture for the intro-
duction of which a good reason cannot be assigned.*
SIR JOHN SOANE

Bulfinch's Yankee classicism and Jefferson's idealistic Franco-Romanism
are as different as they could possibly be and still remain within the context of early nineteenth-century American architecture. They derive from
different Neoclassical sources, are based on different proportional and
ornamental systems, and contrast in practical arrangement as well as in
poetic intent. Moreover, to a far greater degree than we have yet encountered, the styles of Bulfinch and Jefferson are intensely personal,
each presenting special qualities which are the architects' own. Here the
differences are sophisticated and difficult; sometimes they are impossible
to define. But they are differences nevertheless, differences which take
us into that realm of experience and understanding which Summerson
has called the "mystery of style."[1] The work of both men shows qualities
of originality which in its day set it apart from the pattern-book conformity
of the colonial years and brought American architecture to levels of individual creativity never before achieved.

If the styles of Bulfinch and Jefferson differ, they also have much in
common; for Bulfinch and Jefferson were American-born architects working in the American environment. As we have already seen, there were
major environmental distinctions between New England and the South
which obviously contributed much to the shaping of each man's style.
At the same time, the firmly established methods and attitudes of the
colonial years survived in subtle ways well into the first half of the
nineteenth century. These too had a strong influence upon both Bulfinch
and Jefferson and tended to unify their respective styles.

To be specific, there was the colonial sense of scale. Nowhere in
colonial America, either in the plantations of the South or in the cities
and towns of the North, were there buildings which could match in size

and monumentality the major architecture of Europe. Even the foremost government buildings, such as Independence Hall in Philadelphia, were diminutive in size and domestic in scale. In fact, the image which they presented was hardly distinguishable from many of the middling houses of England. It is true that smallness in itself is a consequence of measure, and need not necessarily affect scale. Numerous small buildings have been built which are gigantic in scale. But scale, like water, seeks its own level, and smallness as a pervasive architectural characteristic will of necessity lead to smallness of scale. In colonial America this is precisely what happened. A consistent scale appropriate to size developed throughout the colonies and became one of the factors which gave colonial architecture its remarkable homogeneity. It also set it apart from the monumental buildings of the homeland and contributed much to its low style, provincial character. Neither the architecture of Bulfinch nor that of Jefferson ever broke completely from this environmental condition.

Bulfinch and Jefferson also shared a common structural heritage. Without exception, the colonial buildings of America were either wood-frame or wood-frame-and-masonry construction. By 1800, throughout the South and in the cities of the North, the most common masonry material was brick, and even though the first years of the nineteenth century saw a considerable increase in the use of stone, masonry vaulting was virtually unknown and brick walls with a wood-frame interior still remained the popular structural method. Moreover, both the size of the bricks and the actual techniques of bricklaying imposed a uniform quality upon American building and together with the wooden frame contributed to the smallness of both size and scale.

Most of Bulfinch's finest buildings and all of Jefferson's were conceived and executed with brick walls and wood-frame interiors. Both architects recognized the monumentality of stone, and might even have preferred to work in that material had the technical means been available. But neither had the knowledge and experience necessary for structural innovation and they therefore relied upon traditional methods. In their work, however, both showed special sensitivity to the peculiar qualities of brick, and used the material toward their own poetic ends.

Bulfinch and Jefferson were alike in yet another important respect; each came to architecture as a gentleman-amateur. Neither received formal training in the office of a professional architect, neither was qualified as an engineer. They relied heavily on books, at least in the early phases of their respective developments. On the other hand, both enjoyed a significant advantage over earlier native-born architects in that they were privileged to spend considerable time abroad and were thus able to see American architecture in the light of larger European developments. There can be no question that for each in his own way this experience brought deeper insights into the nature of architecture and resulted in a more sophisticated approach to the problems of planning and design. Yet a lack of professional expertise, especially in the realm of structure, together with the economic and technical limitations of the American environment, kept them from escaping completely the narrow world of the gentleman-amateur.

Latrobe in England

When Henry Benjamin Latrobe arrived in America from England in mid-March of 1796, he was a very different kind of architect. He came to this country as a fully qualified professional, with training as an engineer as well as an architect; he had already spent approximately three years in the office of a London architect and had experienced several moderately productive years in a practice of his own. His attitudes and expectations, therefore, were anything but those of a gentleman-amateur, and because he was the first of his profession to appear on the American scene the opportunities which opened up for him were great indeed. The new country needed Latrobe, although it was not altogether ready for some of his innovations. Nevertheless, his role was absolutely central in the development of American architecture, and before his career ended, the major links with the colonial past had been broken and American architecture was self-consciously reaching toward a national mode of expression.

Latrobe was born in a small Yorkshire village in 1764.² His father was a prominent Moravian minister; his mother came from one of the Moravian settlements in Pennsylvania. In 1776, at the age of twelve, he was sent to study in Germany and he remained there for eight years. When he returned to London in 1784 he was a promising European sophisticate, fluent in several languages, actively involved in publishing and writing, an expert on the clarinet, and a political radical. Talented and articulate, this mercurial young man fitted easily into the intellectual society of London. Here, through family connections he enjoyed the privilege of intimate association with such prominent figures as Dr. Johnson, and with firm social contacts to open the way his success seemed assured.

Exactly when the young Latrobe decided upon architecture as a career is not known, although it seems to have been about 1783, shortly before he left Germany. In any case, after his return to London, and a brief period of employment as a clerk in the Stamp Office, the evidence suggests that he probably worked for two or three years with the famous engineer John Smeaton, who, like Dr. Johnson, was a friend of the family. Then in 1787 he entered the office of the London architect A. P. Cockerell. In this position he is known to have worked on the new Admiralty Building in Whitehall, then under commission to Cockerell. Early in 1790 he married Lydia Sellon, the daughter of the famous clergyman William Sellon, and shortly afterward, in 1791, he left Cockerell to set up practice on his own. It cannot be said that the young architect was overwhelmed by work but occasional small assignments did come his way. Between 1791 and 1793 he received two substantial commissions for houses, Hammerwood Lodge (Fig. 252) and Ashdown House (Fig. 250), both of which are still standing. These houses give us a definite idea of his style as it first emerged.

Sir John Soane

Hammerwood and Ashdown represent a phase of Neoclassicism which we have not encountered before, and in order to understand Latrobe's accomplishments in these two buildings we must turn once more to the larger issue of English architecture and examine the second phase of English Neoclassicism, particularly as it is found in the work of Sir John Soane. We recall that the first phase was dominated by Robert Adam, whose fresh ideas about planning and interior decoration were based on the new archaeological knowledge of the ancient world, especially as it was found in the recently discovered Roman and Etruscan wall paintings. In spite of its brilliance, Adam's style was restrained, with numerous traditional elements, and appealed to the conservative taste in English society.

The work of the new generation of Neoclassicists was far more radical. It forsook altogether the refined elegance of Adam for a bold muscular system of simple massing and unbroken walls. Ornament was either stripped away altogether or held flat within the plane of the wall, and brand new decorative features were introduced. Along with a re-examination of the function of the orders, advances in engineering led to refinements in vaulting which made possible exciting and imaginative new concepts of interior space. As in the case of Adam, ancient Rome was a constant source of inspiration for the new generation of Neoclassicists, but unlike Adam the proponents of the new "plain style" also drew heavily on Greece. They saw in Greek architecture qualities of rational beauty and structural logic which bore a direct relationship to their own objectives. Their approach was not so much that of the archaeologist as that of the architect. Their concern, therefore, was not for such things as correct proportions and the application of the orders, but rather for the organic nature of a building, the arrangement of its interior space as it relates to use, and the eternal and fundamental dialogue between structure and form.

Behind this rational attitude lay the writings of the Abbé Laugier. As we have seen, not only was Laugier one of the first to proclaim the pre-eminence of Greek over Roman architecture, but, even more important, he analyzed architecture from a purely rational point of view, stating that all buildings had their origins in the primitive hut, that columns should never be used for any other purpose than support, that architecture was basically an art of geometry, and that nothing should be put on a building for which there was not a substantial reason. Laugier's writings were known to all second-generation English Neoclassicists, and his influence on their thinking and their work is of consummate importance.

Of all the later English Neoclassicists the pre-eminent one and the most original was Sir John Soane.[3] In 1806 Soane was appointed to a professional chair at the Royal Academy and beginning in 1809 he lectured there on architecture. He thus became an influential spokesman for

Neoclassicism and much of what he had to say closely paralleled the ideas of Laugier. Like Laugier, he urged a return to the "great Primitive Principle on which the Architecture of the Ancients rests," to the principles "founded on the immutable laws of Nature and Truth," and even to "the primitive model of the Greeks." He also said 'that everything in Architecture is to be accounted for' and 'nothing can be allowed in good Architecture for the introduction of which a good reason cannot be assigned.' "[4]

Soane's reliance on Laugier is obvious enough and need not be argued further. But Soane was an architect whereas Laugier was not, and it is in the former's buildings, therefore, rather than in his written or spoken word that his rational ideas achieved their fullest expression. An appropriate example is the Gateway and Lodges at Tyringham, finished in 1794 (Fig. 247). This remarkable little building, so modest in purpose yet so bold in conception, is one of the important early monuments in the· rational phase of English Neoclassicism. Not only is it expressive of the functionalism and structural logic of Laugier, but in its austere geometry it reflects also the work of the radical French Neoclassicist Claude-Nicolas Ledoux. In every way it is the embodiment of the new age.

The general appearance of the building seems strictly classical; in its symmetry of alternating parts it may even be said to be Palladian. But in its bold primitive simplicity it is neither classical nor Palladian. The fulcrum of the design is the gateway itself, a massive rectangular block penetrated only by a segmental arch which passes through its entire width. Balancing left and right of this are the two lodges. These are identical rectangular blocks, lower in profile than the central block, and joined to it by short, slightly recessed units. Each is crowned by an ornamental frieze which overhangs very slightly the main wall plane and is separated from it by a three-stage delicately profiled Ionic architrave. Together they create a horizontal element which passes across the central block and terminates at the arched opening. At this point the frieze functions as the impost for the segmental arch. Furthermore, by continuing across the entire design it also serves to unify the five major blocks into a coherent whole.

Although much of what we have just observed is faithful to classical procedure, certain aspects of the design are nonclassical. There is no cornice above the frieze, for example, so that in spite of the architrave below it, it does not form a full classical entablature; and there are no classical pediments to destroy the cubical simplicity of the individual blocks. The only direct quotation from the classical past is the Greek Doric columns which flank the single windows in each of the lateral lodges. But these columns are held back within the recessed window bays so that they do not project beyond the wall, and they are unfluted. They thus remain firmly within the limiting planes of the geometry. Moreover, the architrave does not carry across the window bays so that the columns, instead of making contact with the architrave, as they would in a classical order, abut directly against the frieze. Seen this way the frieze immediately becomes ambivalent, for where it combines with the

FIGURE 247. John Soane. Gateway and Lodges, Tyringham, Buckinghamshire, England, 1794.

FIGURE 248. John Soane. Bank of England, Stock Office, London, England, 1792–93.

Ionic architrave it functions as an Ionic frieze, but over the windows where it joins the Doric columns it functions as a perfectly authentic Doric architrave. In terms of classical precedence, therefore, we are faced with a contradiction which helps to give the design its extraordinary dynamic quality.

Except for the recessed window bays with their columns, and the Ionic architrave, the only other violations of the plane of the wall are the single semi-domed niches in each of the connecting blocks, a delicate two-stage flat architrave which outlines the segmental vault of the main gate, and an equally delicate recessed flat molding which crowns the main central block. All of these are held close to or within the plane of the wall, however, and serve primarily to give sculptural density to the design. The columns and niches articulate the weight of the masonry, the architrave and crowning molding give the building its scale.

Soane's style, as seen in the general massing of the Tyringham Gateway and Lodges, is an art of geometry contained within the limits of its defining planes, a style of stark primitive force in which vertical meets horizontal in bold confrontation. Equally aggressive is his imaginative development of interior space. One of the most brilliant examples is the Stock Office in the Bank of England. This room (Fig. 248) is a large cross-shaped space with the great central area crowned by segmental pendentives carrying a twelve-sided glazed lantern. The two lateral bays are shallow rectangular spaces covered by wide segmental barrel vaults; the deeper longitudinal bays have segmental groin vaults. Light passes into the latter through clerestory windows, formed by the open ends of the lateral groins. The pilasters, introduced for rhythmic emphasis, are held within or slightly behind the plane of the wall, and are defined both by moldings and incised lines so delicate as to be almost imperceptible. For variation in texture the spherical triangles of the pendentives are scored with horizontal lines. Visual stress is placed on the supporting piers by slightly projecting pilasters whose rectangular strip fluting is incised rather than projecting. These pilasters connect directly, without intervening capitals, with a delicate fretted stringcourse which goes around the entire room. Thus the walls and pilasters, with their sharply defined right angles, are basically classical in their immobility, and are more Greek than Roman in spirit. But Soane's thin flat surfaces and finely drawn decoration lack the sculptural density of the classical orders. In fact, it is the plane as it circumscribes the space and articulates the structure which is the essence of his design.

Perhaps the most exciting aspect of Soane's design is the superb articulation of the vaults (Fig. 249). The ends of the cross vaults, on which the pendentives rest, are defined on their inner surfaces by slightly projecting panels which spring from the pilasters. The main rib structure of the vaulting system is thus visually expressed. The triangles of the pendentives, on the other hand, which are exerting continuous symmetrical thrusts throughout their spherical fabric, remain inviolate, their sharply cut edges sweeping rhythmically downward to four needlelike points, each delicately making contact with the corner of one of the four piers. At this junction

FIGURE 249. John Soane. Bank of England, Stock Office,
London, England, detail, 1792–93.

we encounter Soane's style in its most subtle form, for the corner pilaster
panels, instead of abutting one another to make a common corner, are
held back slightly so that their edges join to form a re-entrant angle. It is
this recessed angle, therefore, and not a projecting corner, which receives
the point of the spherical triangle and contains it as though it were growing from the pier, rather than resting upon it. As a result, the vaults seem to
be springing upward rather than pressing downward. Consistent with this
expressive demonstration of structure is the fact that the only sculptured
ornament in the entire room is found in the single medallions which ac-

FIGURE 250. *Benjamin Latrobe. Ashdown House,*
Berkshire, England, 1793.

cent the center of each of the pendentive triangles, and in similar smaller
rosettes which subdivide the long rib panels of the cross vaults. Except for
these, the sweeping planes of the vaults remain continuous and the general effect is of a structural integument as thin and light as an eggshell.

Ashdown and Hammerwood

The work of John Soane formed the creative core of the new architecture
which Latrobe found, either recently completed or in progress, when
he returned to London from Germany in 1784. As a young beginner
he was in no position to receive monumental commissions such as the
Bank of England, and he thus never had the opportunity to cope with
sophisticated spatial problems of the kind which confronted Soane. But
that he knew the Bank of England and was aware of Soane's work at
Tyringham is certain, and the influence of Soane would be felt strongly
in Latrobe's work in America. The two houses which he designed in
England, Hammerwood Lodge and Ashdown House, show qualities that
relate them directly both to the primitivism of Soane and to the growing
enthusiasm for the architecture of ancient Greece, which was common to
all the later Neoclassicists.

At Ashdown (Fig. 250), the simpler and more coherent of the two,
one's first impression is of a single horizontal rectangular mass with an
attached semicylindrical porch.[5] Actually the building is made up of two
strong vertical blocks, separated by a less assertive vertical block and joined
by the embracing sweep of the cylindrical porch. The balancing end masses
rise through a full attic story and are topped by a depressed hipped roof.
There is no traditional cornice to separate the walls from the roof planes,
so the effect, as in Soane's Tyringham Gateway, is of pure geometric units.
The central block is somewhat narrower than those on the ends and is

FIGURE 251. *Benjamin Latrobe. Ashdown House, Berkshire, England, portico, 1793.*

set back slightly in two stages. Thus the central unit in the design, which in Palladian language should be a dominating projecting element, is negative and receding, an effect which is further enhanced by the fact that it is crowned only by a parapet and is thus lower than the end units. Overlapping this recessed central section, and projecting boldly from the planes of the end units, is the cylindrical shape of the colonnaded porch (Fig. 251). The porch, the unadorned frieze, and the cornice (there is no

FIGURE 252. *Benjamin Latrobe. Hammerwood Lodge, Sussex, England, side portico, 1792.*

architrave so it is not a full entablature) which separates the attic from the second story, unify the three major masses of the building into a cohesive whole.

The first-floor windows in the façade are full-length and set in recessed wall arches. The other windows are cleanly cut into the wall without any surround. The only ornament to appear on the building, in fact, is the elegant Ionic capitals which derive from those on the Erechtheum in Athens. The supporting columns, however, are unfluted and there is no relief sculpture in the frieze. In this way, even the quotation from ancient Greece becomes conspicuously primitive and more basically geometric than the Greeks themselves would have made it.

Latrobe's earlier house (1792), Hammerwood, is less direct than Ashdown and adds nothing to our knowledge of the architect's early style that is not better illustrated in the later house. There is one feature of Hammerwood, however, which tends further to illustrate the importance of pure geometric elements in the work of the rational Neoclassicists. The over-all design is more ambitious than that at Ashdown, with balancing colonnaded pavilions connected to the main house block by wings with arched openings on the first floor. This arrangement is a straightforward Palladian scheme found in any number of earlier English houses. The Doric porticoes which articulate the pavilions, however, are most unusual (Fig. 252). Like the porch of Ashdown, they are Greek, but they are Doric rather than Ionic, and moreover they are an extremely primitive form of the Doric style, showing the wide flaring capitals and exaggerated taper in the columns which are characteristic of the early Greek colonial temples such as those at Paestum and Sicily. But just as at Ashdown, the columns are not fluted (except for a short piece between the necking and the echinus), and the characteristic architrave and frieze of the Greek Doric order, with its metope and triglyph motif, has been eliminated and replaced by a single unadorned slab. This deliberate distillation of the classical motifs to basic geometrics is strongly reminiscent of Soane's primitivism and is even more assertive here than at Ashdown. It should also be said that the use of pure Greek motifs as early as 1792–93 is itself remarkable and anticipates Latrobe's fondness for the Greek style as he introduced it into American architecture.

Latrobe in America: the Early Works

The geometric simplicity of Hammerwood and Ashdown identifies Latrobe with the most radical phase of the Neoclassical movement, and as designs these buildings reveal him as one of the promising young men of his day. In addition, there is also evidence which attests his skills as an engineer. In 1793 and 1794 he submitted proposals for the rerouting of the Chelmsford Canal. Although neither was ever carried out the surviving drawings leave no doubt of his ability. But with these works Latrobe's professional career in England came to an end. The uncertainties occasioned by the French Revolution, and the subsequent declaration of war against France in 1793, reduced building activity in England virtually to nothing. Further, Latrobe's liberal tendencies, which led him to champion the radical cause, probably closed the door on a number of possible commissions. The decisive blow came, however, with the death of his young wife, Lydia, late in 1793.

Latrobe seems to have been an intense and sensitive young man, desperately in need of affection, and Lydia had provided this for him in abundance. She also took an active interest in his work, often going with him on his inspection trips to his various jobs. The companionship between them was so close, and Latrobe's emotional dependence on his wife so extreme, that with her death the first phase of his life came pathetically to an end. Primarily as an escape from his grief, but also because his mother had come from Pennsylvania, the young man began to look toward America. Here, surely, he could make a new life in a promising new land, based on the social and political ideals which he so fervently embraced, and offering professional opportunities which a man of his qualifications had yet to exploit. With his inherited lands in Pennsylvania as security, he set sail late in November 1795, and arrived in Norfolk, Virginia, in mid-March the following year.

Opportunities to put his knowledge and experience to work opened up almost at once for Latrobe. Even though at the time of his arrival he was an unknown figure, his personal charm and wide cultural attainments made him attractive to the intellectual aristocracy of Virginia and we find him moving quickly and easily among an ever-widening circle of intellectual and interested friends. Ultimately these were to include even such national figures as Washington and Jefferson. Almost at once, too, his professional advice was sought in the construction of the Dismal Swamp Canal, and as a result of this association he was sent to survey the Appomattox River with the view of improving it as a navigable waterway. Soon thereafter we find him in Richmond, where he designed several houses, most of which were never built; he also proposed designs for a church and a theatre, and he was commissioned to design the new State Penitentiary (Fig. 253).

In every way the penitentiary assignment was the most important work that Latrobe received during his first years in Virginia. As a problem it was particularly suited to his ideals and experience. His liberal and humane attitudes made him at once sympathetic to Jefferson's long-expressed ideas on penal reform; moreover, his experiences in architecture in London provided exactly the qualifications needed for the commission. As he later expressed it in a letter to his pupil Robert Mills, there was no one in Virginia who "could have the same means of information as myself, for independently of my general professional character I had been surveyor of the police in the districts of London, & had not only erected the buildings belonging to that branch of the government of the metropolis but necessarily acquired a knowledge of all that others had done in the erection & improvement of the prisons."[6] In spite of his qualifications this commission was not to be easy. It introduced Latrobe into the vagaries and frustrations of government contracts; it also brought him into a direct confrontation with the stubborn, entrenched, and outmoded attitudes toward building which prevailed in a provincial society. Both were to plague him throughout his professional career.

The plan of the prison contained numerous features which show Latrobe's unusual concern for both the practical and humane problems which confronted him. The cell block was arranged in the form of a semicircle, three stories high and a single cell in depth. Each cell was vaulted and opened onto a cantilevered balcony on the inside of the semicircle. The open end of the semicircle was closed by a wall, forming a court. In the center of this wall was the keeper's house. Situated as it was on the radii of the semicircle, it offered an equal view into each cell, thus providing maximum visual supervision from a single point. Entrance and exit to the cell blocks was controlled by carefully placed access stairways.

On the humane side, a primitive water closet was included in each cell, and dormitory-type cells for small groups of reformed prisoners provided better opportunities for social intercourse. Special provisions were also made for ventilating both the court and the cell block. Beyond the straight wall of the semicircular court were two rectangular courts formed by straight-sided building units which contained a women's prison as well as separate infirmaries for men and women. On the outer wall of this complex, and on the axial center of the entire design, were the guard house and entrance gate.

The first floor of the penitentiary was built of random ashlar masonry, with brick in the upper stories (Fig. 253). In its outward appearance it had all the geometric simplicity of Latrobe's English style. A cylindrical mass and several rectangular ones made up the design, each clearly articulated from the other. Unbroken wall planes were pierced by sharply cut window openings, some of them arched, others set in shallow wall arches. To form the entrance gate (Fig. 254), an enormous stone arch

FIGURE 253. *Benjamin Latrobe. State Penitentiary, Richmond, Va., 1797–98.*

without molded embellishment of any kind sprang from the foundation line in a bold lateral sweep. The effect was of awesome strength, expressive both of the specific function of the building and of an architectural ideal, and comparable in simplicity and directness to the most radical projects of Ledoux in France. The powerful entrance arch was matched in English building only by the magnificent wall arches which Soane designed—fifteen years later—for the stables of the Chelsea Hospital in London (Fig. 255). In American architecture, it was not to have a counterpart until the massive arches of H. H. Richardson appeared in the late 1870's.

The Bank of Pennsylvania

The penitentiary was the last work of Latrobe in Virginia, and even before it was commissioned in 1797 he was beginning to look toward Philadelphia as the most promising and logical place for him to be. Philadelphia was at the time the national capital. It was also the largest city in America and, in spite of Boston's opinion to the contrary, was probably the cultural center of the new nation. As an urbanite, familiar with London society, Latrobe would have found more to stimulate his intellectual interests in Philadelphia than in the plantation society of the South. Moreover, he was drawn to Philadelphia by family ties. His mother's family was still well known in Pennsylvania, and it was there that his

FIGURE 254. *Benjamin Latrobe. State Penitentiary, Richmond, Va., entrance gate, 1797–98. Water color drawing.*

FIGURE 255. *John Soane. Stables, Royal Hospital, Chelsea, England, 1814.*

inherited lands were located. In the spring of 1798, therefore, we find the young architect in Philadelphia, primarily to study its famous vaulted prison. But he also hoped to receive the commission for a new Quaker school (which never materialized), and he carried with him a letter of introduction to Samuel L. Fox, president of the Bank of Pennsylvania. This proved to be an extremely productive contact. Fox told Latrobe of the Bank's plans for a new building and the architect immediately submitted sketches. After returning to Richmond he learned from his new friend that his design had been accepted and in December of that year he moved to Philadelphia.

The Bank of Pennsylvania (Fig. 256) has universally been called the first monument of the Greek Revival in America. In one sense this is correct. The building carried the first Greek order to appear in American architecture, and its simple stone walls were reminiscent of the pure geometry of the Greek Prostyle temple. In other ways, however, the building was not really Greek at all. It was a podium-type temple with the steps contained at both ends by walls. This was Roman. Moreover the building was vaulted throughout, with a large circular dome as its principal interior space. This, too, was Roman. The truth is, the building was neither pure Greek nor pure Roman, but rather Neoclassical; and it was Neoclassical not only because of its synthesis of the ancient classical styles, but because of its rationalism. There was a coherent relationship here between space and structure, the interior spaces were arranged to satisfy a particular function, and the exterior massing reflected that arrangement in the purest geometric terms. The Bank of Pennsylvania was a superb embodiment of Laugier's teachings, and as such was the first example on American soil of the rational phase of European Neoclassicism. Even though it was built in Philadelphia by Philadelphia craftsmen, there was not the slightest hint of American concepts of

FIGURE 256. *Benjamin Latrobe. Bank of Pennsylvania, Philadelphia, Pa., 1799–1801. Water color.*

scale and massing, nor was it built by the traditional masonry and wood-frame method. Instead, it was monumental in scale and was vaulted throughout. It was, in fact, the first building in America in which vaults were used as an integral part of a total architectural scheme.[7]

The Bank of Pennsylvania was a simple temple-type building with a colonnade on each end, one facing the street, the other facing a garden. Entrance was gained from the street end through a barrel-vaulted vestibule with offices on either side (Figs. 257 and 258a). The main banking room was the large circular space extending the full height of the building. It was crowned by a segmental dome carrying a glazed cupola through which light entered the room. The entrance vestibule opened into this room; at the other end of the building was a large stockholders' room, which could be entered from either the banking room or from the garden portico. Above the street entrance on the second floor (Figs. 257 and 258b), and accessible only by a secluded winding stairway, were the bank vaults; over the stockholders' room, and also accessible by winding stairways, were additional offices and the directors' room.

The plan was a straightforward solution with related rooms functionally grouped, and with the spatial focus of the building in the domed banking room at the center. This dramatic soaring space was conceptually and structurally unlike anything ever before built in America. Contained within a cubical mass, it rose as a pure cylinder, approximately forty-five feet in diameter, to the dynamic flare of the segmental dome, thirty-five feet above the floor. Beyond this dome, through the twelve-foot

FIGURE 257. *Benjamin Latrobe. Bank of Pennsylvania, Philadelphia, Pa., longitudinal section, 1798. Water color drawing.*

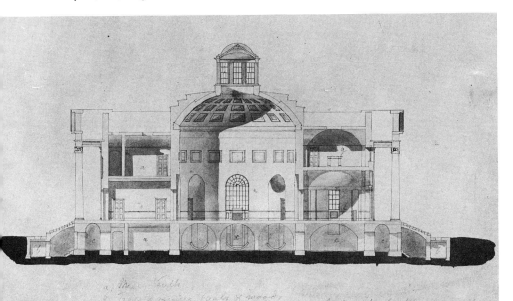

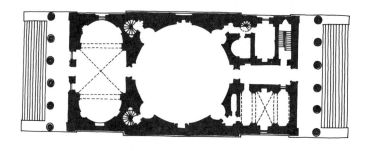

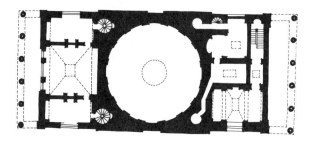

FIGURE 258. *Benjamin Latrobe. Bank of Pennsylvania, Philadelphia, Pa., 1799–1801. (a) First-floor plan, above. (b) Second-floor plan, below.*

opening of the oculus, rose the second cylindrical form of the glazed cupola.

At the main floor level the clean walls of the cylindrical banking room were sharply cut by eight arched openings. On the longitudinal axis were the doorways into the entrance vestibule and stockholders' room, on the lateral axis were two round-headed windows. The diagonal axes terminated in four curved niches which gave onto stairways and other service rooms. Apparently none of these openings had enframing moldings of any kind. The sheer curve of the wall above was given rhythmic variety by a horizontal sequence of rectangular panels which repeated and doubled the rhythm of the arched openings below. These panels were recessed, however, so that they did not break the continuity of the wall surface, and were defined by very thin moldings. Above the panels, serving both as a crown to the room and as an impost for the dome, was an extremely flat partial entablature (it had no architrave). The only ornamental treatment of the dome was the recessed coffering which preserved the surface of the vault, manifest in the intervening ribs, as a continuous spherical plane. The effect was of a pure monumental geometry, wholly unencumbered by either the diminutive scale or the conventional ornamental devices of the colonial tradition.

The refined simplicity of the Bank interior was further enriched by a superb and appropriate use of color. The architect described it in a fascinating letter to his patron, Samuel Fox.[8] He stated that the plaster surfaces of the walls and the dome were to be done in a scheme of pale neutral yellow, blue, and white. The openings, recessed panels, and coffers were to be delicately outlined in white. The only strong color accent was to be in the frieze immediately below the dome, which was to display a dark russet-colored Greek fret against a background of pure white. On the other hand, those structural elements which were made of marble, such as the impost from which the dome was sprung, were left unpainted. The effect must have been light and airy and breath-takingly beautiful. At the same time the continuous planes of the geometric system were left intact.

Both the logic and the geometric purity of Latrobe's interior design were expressed in the exterior massing of the building (Fig. 256). The central mass appeared on the outside as a pure cube crowned by the depressed sphere of the dome and the cupola. Projecting symmetrically from either side of this cube and set back slightly from it were the blocks of the two-story utility and office spaces. Both of these terminated in identical Ionic pedimented porticoes. The roofs of these end blocks were pitched and abutted the central cube, which in turn rose to a height equivalent to the ridge line, and had a flat roof. An entablature common to both porticoes extended completely around the building and unified the three main masses; at the same time it articulated the spring level of the vault on the inside of the central cube.

The walls of the building were clean, dressed masonry and were unadorned, except that each block was pierced by round-arched windows. These windows were all the same height, and were all cut flush with the wall without ornamental surround. In one respect, however, they differed significantly. The window which opened into the central dome space was a full-height window, undivided by any major horizontal bars, indicating that the space within went to the full height of the building. Those on the end blocks were cut by a horizontal recessed lintel which was just below the spring of the arch and corresponded with the second-floor level of the interior space. This made it clear to the observer that the interiors of the end blocks were two-story spaces. This distinction was further emphasized by the fact that the square-headed windows, which opened into the first-floor rooms, were divided into a wide central light and two narrow side lights, in contrast to the unbroken expanse of glass in the central windows. The thin vertical bars which effect this division also provided a more intimate scale, appropriate to the smaller rooms in the two-story sections.

Latrobe left no doubt in the exterior massing of the building as to functional distribution of the interior space. The interior arrangement was simple and its expression on the exterior was correspondingly simple; and it was lucid. The great central room, with its continuous vertical space, was decisively separated from the end blocks and stood as a geometric unit complete in itself. At the same time, it was visually part of the whole. But its dominating position at the center of the design nullified at once any idea that Latrobe was thinking only in terms of the Greek temple form. A Greek temple is a single horizontal block with a pitched roof which by its very simplicity reveals nothing of its inner parts. The Bank of Pennsylvania, on the other hand, was a symmetrical composition of opposing blocks, each rationally projecting the image of its own inwardness for all to see.

We cannot fully appreciate the supreme logic of Latrobe's design unless we carry our examination one step further and consider his structural methods as they relate to form; for the Bank of Pennsylvania was not only the first building in America in which vaulting was used to cover a large public space, it was also the first in which vaulting was exploited by the architect as an integral, determining factor in the evolution of his design. In a real sense, no earlier American architect, whether gentleman-amateur or architect-builder, was in a position to approach his designing from this point of view. Before Latrobe arrived in America, structure was understood entirely in long-established, traditional terms, and served primarily the practical necessities of enclosing the building. Men like Bulfinch and Jefferson did develop personal sensitivities to the traditional materials and methods, and they frequently used them in a particularly personal and expressive way. But there is no evidence that any of them were ever concerned with basic philosophical considerations in which structure was examined as a determining factor in the aesthetic as well as the practical character of a building. At that moment in the Neoclassical movement, however, when men began to question the validity of applying the column for pure decorative reasons, when they urged instead that it never be used for any other purpose than support, at that moment structure became an active, indeed an essential factor in the creative process. No building could be conceived apart from structural necessity.

Latrobe was the first American architect to bring to his work both the theoretical and practical knowledge essential to such an approach. He not only thoroughly understood the science of vaulting, but he had seen at first hand Soane's daring and imaginative use of vaults in the Bank of England. Moreover, as a young architect in England, he had identified himself with the radical ideas of his time and for him to have conceived the Bank of Pennsylvania in terms of a wood frame and suspended plaster ceiling—both common to the prevailing American practice—would have been unthinkable, even though the same spatial effects could have been achieved. It was essential to use vaulting for fire and security reasons, if for nothing else. But in Latrobe's eyes those qualities of strength and permanence potential to masonry must also be expressed in the visual character of the building itself. This he accomplished in the unbroken walls, sharply cut openings, and heavy scale. At the same time it was necessary that the dynamics of the vaults be expressed. To achieve this the architect crowned the great banking room with a daring segmental vault of brick almost forty-five feet in diameter, which he articulated and revealed in depth through simple coffering, and keyed at the top with a marble ring twelve feet in diameter. The latter formed the oculus which opened into the glazed cupola above. The enormous thrust of this depressed vault was received at the spring by a marble impost, and was contained by two iron bands which encircled the impost. From without, the flat curve of the vault asserted itself in a stepped curved profile rising only slightly above the central cube, thus articulating the cylindrical spherical space within. At the same time, the stark simplicity of the cube communicated the sense of weight necessary to contain the potentially destructive pressure of the vault within. These qualities, which distinguished the Bank of Pennsylvania from other American buildings at the turn of the century, can best be visualized when we compare Latrobe's design with Bulfinch's State House in Boston (Fig. 183), which was completed at almost the same time. In Latrobe's design the depressed sphere which pushes above the supporting mass is a positive outward imprint of the negative space within. It appears as though the spaces of the banking hall were capable of exerting pressure against the structural elements thus causing them to shape themselves in response. The dome emerges from the mass, therefore, as an integral part of the fabric. In contrast, Bulfinch's dome sits awkwardly and lightly on the brick building, conspicuously made of wood, and without any apparent textural or structural continuity with its supporting mass. Unlike the Latrobe dome, it was conceived as a decorative and symbolic adjunct, rather than as a coherent part of a structural system.

Even the character of the architects' drawings emphasizes this contrast (Fig. 181, 184). Bulfinch's elevation and plan are barren schematics which give only the fundamental shape and dimensional aspects of the building. Read together they record three-dimensional relationships, but only by cross reference. Even the New Englander's primitive light and shade in the elevation do little to communicate the illusion of three dimensions. Latrobe's perspective and section (Figs. 256, 257), on the contrary, are conspicuously the work of a highly trained and skillful hand, and are rendered in a convincing full light and shade which help to clarify the basic structural system as it develops and encloses the space. More than that, the whole character of the building, as a dialogue between mass and interior space, is also brought into vivid visual reality. In the architect's perspective drawing, the building is set in a plausible pictorial environment so that it comes alive as an experience in scale as well as in plane and dimension; moreover, the architectural setting which Latrobe shows, provides a superb demonstration of the fundamental differences between Latrobe's rational, monumental, and highly professional design and the traditional, small-scale, and provincial character of the earlier American buildings which flank it.

One other important aspect of the Bank of Pennsylvania needs to be considered. In its highly rational, geometric character, and in many of the spatial devices employed by Latrobe, such as the segmental dome with a wide oculus supporting an open cupola, the building is strongly reminiscent of the work of Soane, particularly as Latrobe knew it in the Bank of England. There can be no doubt about either the young architect's indebtedness to Soane or his complete identification with the most advanced ideas of the contemporary Neoclassical movement abroad. In its provincial American environment, the Bank of Pennsylvania was a radical alien which challenged the status quo at a number of significant points. But there is one aspect of the design which cannot be readily related to Latrobe's European background, and that is its classical temple form.

We have already discussed this question and pointed out that Latrobe's design was, in fact, much more than the simple application of the temple form. The fact remains, however, that in spite of its domed middle section the general form of the classical temple is conspicuously in evidence; nor is there any doubt that Latrobe intended it to be so. What inspired him to use it?

Except for a few small garden pavilions built in England during the eighteenth century, there was nothing in English architecture to serve as a prototype for Latrobe's design. Nor was there anything in France. Indeed, as we have seen, the first building in the Western world to evoke the pure classical 'temple type was Jefferson's State Capitol in Richmond (Fig. 212), begun just a year after Latrobe returned to London to take up his training as an engineer and architect. It was not completely finished until after the Englishman arrived in Richmond in 1796. Latrobe therefore knew the building well and must have been impressed by its classical purity, for it would seem that it was this building, not a European model, which inspired his use of the same basic form a few years later. He may have sensed the appropriateness of the classical temple as a symbol of the new nation, he may even have discussed it with Jefferson, whom he met for the first time in Fredericksburg shortly before his departure from Richmond for Philadelphia. In any case, the similarity between the two buildings is too close to be ignored, and it seems apparent that Latrobe was alert to the current attitudes of his new environment and was deliberately designing in a way that would better fulfill the expectations of his American patronage.

The fact that both Latrobe's and Jefferson's buildings were based on the classical temple is of immense historical importance, for it links the two men early in their architectural careers. Architecturally, however, what each man did with the temple was worlds apart from the other. Jefferson saw it as an end in itself, as a noble and monumental symbol of the democratic form of government. For him it had no direct connection with the English architectural tradition which he wanted to reject but took its authority instead from the great classical ideals of republican Rome. Ruled by this concept of the temple, Jefferson made no attempt to manipulate its form to accommodate the functions of state government. Instead, he simply worked the government into the temple. His only outward concession to the interior spatial arrangements was to break the wall with two horizontal rows of windows arranged between the pilasters. But because these windows are domestic in scale and are framed by classical ornament, they tend to minimize the large geometry of the wall and to belie the monumentality of the great Ionic portico. Although Jefferson was never to work in such naïvely eclectic terms again, his first major effort remains more idealistically than rationally conceived, and tends to emphasize the provincial attitudes which marked his beginnings as an architect. We do not need to re-examine the Bank of Pennsylvania to reaffirm the wide differences of architectural temperament that separated the two men. Latrobe's rational solution made of the temple something uniquely his own and brought to the American scene new professional attitudes and standards which Jefferson himself was quick to recognize.

The Philadelphia Waterworks

Considered in the American context, much of Latrobe's success in the Bank of Pennsylvania was due to his knowledge of engineering, and his capacity to plan in terms of masonry vaults. The real test of his engineering skills, however, came in another important project only a few weeks after his arrival in Philadelphia. During his trip to this city in the spring of 1798, Latrobe had already become aware of the serious problem involving the municipal water supply. The water came entirely from wells, and in the crowded sections these were being contaminated by seepage from cesspools and privies. To alleviate this situation the city fathers were working on a scheme to bring water to the city from the Schuylkill River by means of a four-mile aqueduct, but major engineering obstacles were delaying the idea. With characteristic enthusiasm and speed Latrobe plunged into the problem and came up with a counterproposal. It was described in a report dated December 29, 1798. His idea was to take the water from the Schuylkill directly where it passed through the city. Then, by a system of steam pumps and a short aqueduct, he would carry the water to a storage tank in the center of the city, from which it could then be distributed by gravity.

Latrobe's proposal forced him at once into the center of a raging controversy and brought devastating attacks upon him and his integrity. Nevertheless, he was commissioned to carry out the project, and on January 26, 1801, less than two years after the first brick was laid, the water began to flow from the city hydrants. Latrobe was widely acclaimed for this accomplishment and the waterworks established for him a national reputation as an engineer. But the project also included an important work of architecture which, together with the Bank of Pennsylvania, also helped to strengthen his growing reputation as an architect. This was the pumping station which he erected in Fairmount Park as the central point in the entire water system (Fig. 259). It contained the second of the two major pumps which raised the water to a tank at the top of the building. From there it was fed by gravity throughout the city. The building also contained the offices of the waterworks.

The design of the Center Square Pump House was as interesting as that of the Bank of Pennsylvania. It was planned with the same accommodation to purpose and was executed in the same language of stark geometric forms. The core of this design was a cylindrical mass which rose through the whole height of the building. Contained within its walls at the top was the water tank. The whole was crowned by a depressed dome. At the bottom was a square structure which housed the pumping machinery and the offices of the waterworks. Visually, this lower section also served as a kind of pedestal which embraced and supported the cylindrical water tower. The composition of masses therefore

FIGURE 259. Benjamin Latrobe. Philadelphia Water Works,
Philadelphia, Pa., 1801. Detail from painting by John Krimmel,
Fourth of July in Centre Square, c. 1810–12.

was a bold piling of geometric shapes, from a cube to a cylinder to a
hemisphere.

Entrance to the building was gained through a recessed porch cut
sharply into one side of the cube and divided in the front by two Greek
Doric columns set *in antis*. The entablature related to these columns was
carried entirely around the building but its projecting moldings were kept
flat to the wall, and like the Greek Doric order which Latrobe used at
Hammerwood, the frieze was a simple flat band totally devoid of the
characteristic triglyph and metope decorative treatment. In its austere
simplicity the device is not unlike Soane's use of the Doric order in
the Tyringham gateway (Fig. 247). The windows on the ground floor
were round-headed and set in recessed wall arches without molded surround; those in the water tower were square-headed but also without decoration and cleanly cut into the wall. Above these windows, at the level
of the water tank itself, was a series of recessed horizontal rectangular
panels, one above each of the windows, which gave outward expression
to the area of the tank within; at the same time it repeated the rhythmic
pattern of the windows in the upper level of the design. An oculus in the
dome served as the opening for the flues of the boiler. The solution was
practical, and was carried out in a pure primitive geometry without
ornamental conceits, in a manner wholly consistent with rational Neo-

FIGURE 260. C.-N. Ledoux.
Paris, Barrière de la Villette, 1784–89.

classical doctrine. In this respect, too, the little building shows an interesting connection with the most radical of all the Neoclassicists, Claude-Nicolas Ledoux. Latrobe had been to Paris and was familiar with the Frenchman's famous city gates. The combination of forms which he used in the Waterworks, a cylinder emerging from a cube, may very well have been inspired by Ledoux's Barrière de la Villette (Fig. 260), in which the same basic forms are joined with a similar primitive boldness.

The monumentality, the strength, and the articulate simplicity of the Bank of Pennsylvania and the Philadelphia Waterworks made them unique among American buildings and posed a serious challenge to prevailing attitudes and practices. At its most subtle level this challenge was conceptual, opposing as it did the conventional pattern-book methods of the colonial era, and demanding instead a direct confrontation between architect and builder in all questions of planning, structure, and form. Bulfinch and Jefferson were already moving in this direction, and Latrobe's commanding performance must have stimulated them. But the entrenched attitudes of the average American builder-designer would be harder to change. It would be some years before pervasive changes could take place, and when they did occur they would move in a direction quite different from Latrobe's. Latrobe's influence would not be felt as much in the broad spectrum of American building as in the institution of a new kind of architect, the trained professional.

What Latrobe was quick to recognize in the practice of architecture in America was the prevalence of the two types we have already defined, the gentleman-amateur and the builder-designer.[9] The idea of a professional architect who prepared the designs, supervised construction, and was paid for his services by his patron was unheard of in America, and neither the patron nor the builder was ready to accept the idea. But fierce resistance came from the builders who assumed as part of their responsibility the function of designer, and who stood in absolute authority over all questions of construction. They were perfectly willing to accept the gentleman-amateur, who gave them the barest outline of a design and then left them on their own. But the professional architect, who came to them not only with the design but also with detailed working drawings, specifications, and the authority to supervise their work, was an intruder. As Latrobe was immediately to discover, the American builders would have no part of this. The greatest opposition came from the Philadelphia Carpenters Company, whose entrenched authority had imposed on the buildings of the area standards so outmoded that they did not even concede to the most conservative ideas already introduced by the Federal Style. Although this particular group was probably the most powerful and adamant in the country, it typifies the kind of antagonism which Latrobe was to encounter throughout his career. The professional architect was a radical idea in the provincial milieu of America, but it was absolutely essential to the healthy growth of a national architecture, and Latrobe's courageous perseverance was a major factor in the establishment of a truly creative profession.

The Baltimore Cathedral

Although the Bank of Pennsylvania and the Philadelphia Waterworks brought Latrobe national recognition as an architect and engineer, the years following their completion did not bring him the further commissions he might have hoped for. Philadelphia itself produced nothing for him. Outside of the city he received two important engineering assignments and a few minor architectural commissions, but on the whole the period was a disturbing one in which moments of triumph were often darkened by subsequent defeat. Immensely important in sustaining him through these years was his second marriage. On May 2, 1800, he was married to Mary Elizabeth Hazlehurst, the daughter of a prominent and well-to-do Philadelphia family. Unlike his first in-laws, the Hazlehursts thoroughly approved of the marriage. This not only gave the young people the assurance of constant and affectionate support but gave the architect important social and professional connections. Most important, Mary proved to be the exact counterpart of the sensitive and impulsive artist. Tender, patient, and understanding, she provided Latrobe with the kind of serenity and stability that his more volatile nature demanded. She ran an impeccable household, was socially witty and gracious, and had the intellectual stamina and curiosity to keep up with her husband's wide-ranging enthusiasms and interests. And when things went wrong, as they frequently did (like most imaginative people, Latrobe was a terrible businessman), she was on hand to reason and comfort. On the darker side, because of his impulsive and gullible nature, Latrobe was in almost constant financial difficulty. Moreover in Philadelphia he was incessantly beleaguered by the Federalists because of his liberal views. Even his French name was in some instances held against him. During these same years, however, two opportunities occurred which were to provide a challenge commensurate with his professional capabilities and were to establish him without question as the nation's leading architect.

The first of these was his appointment in March 1803, as Surveyor of the Public Buildings of the United States.[10] This began an involvement with the buildings of the city of Washington which was to occupy much of his time for the next fifteen years. But since most of his work in the national capital was concerned with undoing and completing works already started by other people, Latrobe's creative power as an architect was never permitted completely to assert itself. The second opportunity was the Baltimore Cathedral. Here he was offered the challenge of the first monumental Roman Catholic cathedral in America. He received the commission in 1804.

The Diocese of the United States had been planning a new cathedral for some time when a scheme proposed by Dr. William Thornton, the architect of the United States Capitol, came indirectly into Latrobe's hands for an opinion. As a qualified professional he saw the glaring inadequacies of Thornton's amateur solution and he pointed them out in a letter to Bishop John Carroll. As an alternative he offered to design the building himself free of charge. It does not seem to have taken any urging on the architect's part to convince the Bishop to accept the offer. As one of the enlightened churchmen of his day, Carroll saw immediately that he was associated with a professional with precisely the qualifications essential to the success of his project, and subsequently a productive and rewarding relationship developed between the two. This proved to be of great importance for Latrobe in his work on the Cathedral since almost at once he began to encounter difficulties. A decisive incident occurred early in the construction when he discovered that during his absence changes had been made in the building without his permission. He saw this quite rightly as a violation of his authority as the architect and offered his resignation. But Bishop Carroll intervened and in spite of a delicate internal situation was able to assure Latrobe that he would be recognized as the final authority in all matters related to design and construction. The architect thus found that his position in relation to his patron and to the builders was closer to that of the professional architect than any other American practitioner had ever achieved.[11]

If Bishop Carroll proved to be an enlightened patron, Latrobe was also a responsive architect. Because of his own youthful involvement, through family and personal ties with a religious community, he seems to have been particularly sensitive to the many and complex aspects of Catholicism which directly affected the form of the Cathedral. This manifested itself at once in the remarkable nature of his original proposal. Thoroughly aware of the venerable architectural tradition of the Catholic Church, especially as found in the great cathedrals of England, *he gave his patron a choice of styles.* Of the two designs he prepared, one was Gothic and the other Roman; and for traditional reasons he urged the Gothic as the first choice, even though he hinted that as an architect his own preference might be the Roman.[12]

The choice which Latrobe presented was essentially a choice between a traditional and a modern point of view. The Bishop and his trustees showed their own progressive spirit by choosing the modern. This decision must have pleased Latrobe. With the knowledge of Soane's Bank of England still fresh in his mind, he must surely have recognized the greater spatial flexibility of the spherical technique over rib-vaulting. The traditional associations which would inevitably be lost by rejecting the Gothic style would be more than compensated for by the dramatic possibilities of the segmental vault and the dome. But it is even more significant that Latrobe offered a choice at all. By committing himself to either the Gothic or the Roman he professed himself capable of performing them both with equal ease. In offering the choice, too, he displayed his awareness of current trends in England, where even a man like James Wyatt was designing in both the Neoclassical and Gothic modes. Even more important, he introduced into America the eclectic attitude, which saw style not as something derived from, but rather as something appropriate to, a particular condition. It was a point of view in which style received its authority from the approbation of the past and was deemed potentially functional as it related to the present. Jefferson, of course, showed a similar point of view in his objective adaptation of Roman architecture at the University of Virginia. But Jefferson never offered a choice, and in his unswerving loyalty to ancient Rome he emerges as a revivalist rather than as an eclectic. To be sure, Latrobe was also at heart an ardent Neoclassicist and the overwhelming majority of his buildings were designed in the Neoclassical mode. On the other hand, he did not hesitate to become an eclectic if a change in style seemed

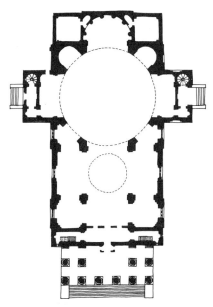

FIGURE 262. *Benjamin Latrobe. Baltimore Cathedral, Baltimore, Md., plan as originally built, 1804–c. 1818.*

FIGURE 263. *Benjamin Latrobe. Baltimore Cathedral, Baltimore, Md., plan as it is today.*

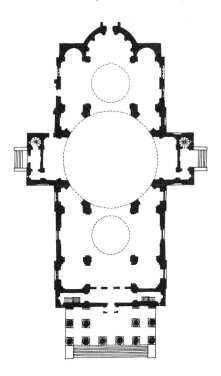

appropriate, as it did in the case of the Baltimore Cathedral, and, in offering the Bishop a choice he opened the door to a flood of eclecticism which was to inundate American building during the nineteenth century. But the fact remains that the authorities of the diocese chose the Roman design and Latrobe was thus afforded the opportunity to perform at his creative best. As a result the Baltimore Cathedral (Fig. 261) was the first church in America to break completely with the Wren-Gibbs type, and the first major church since the Bruton Parish Church in Williamsburg to be designed and built on the cruciform plan.

A glance at the plan (Fig. 262) suggests that Latrobe's solution is a straightforward use of the traditional cruciform arrangement, with nave and side aisles, crossing, transepts, and choir.[13] But it is much more than that. At the heart of the design is a juxtaposition of geometric spatial units similar in principle to that of the Bank of Pennsylvania. The central space at the crossing is a cylinder topped by a segmental dome; the main mass in which this is contained is a cube. On the longitudinal axis, and projecting in both directions from this central cube, are secondary rectilinear masses with low pitched roofs. So far the basic geometric system is similar to the earlier design. Probing more deeply, however, we find ourselves in a far more complex world of geometry than the relatively simple bank building.

Latrobe's scheme was developed over two years of modification and change, some of which was motivated by his own sense of design, some in a lively dialogue between himself and his patron. Throughout this period the architect seems to have had a relatively free hand, with the only serious obstacles to his thinking being those imposed by cost. These were to affect the design in a number of ways but the most serious was the size of the building. He originally planned a deep choir with a vaulted bay separating the apse from the central dome space, but the bay had to be eliminated, thus shortening the church and depriving it of the spatial symmetry which the architect had originally intended (Fig. 262). Latrobe's original intentions were ultimately realized, however, when in 1890 the choir was extended to include a domed bay and thus make it symmetrical with the nave (Fig. 263). The church as it stands today, therefore, is closer to Latrobe's original intentions than the one which was completed and dedicated in 1821. Because of this our analysis of the church will be based upon the existing building.

The plan is a traditional Latin cross generating from the large central domed area, a scheme which Latrobe evolved only after numerous modifications. The most important change was in the size and character of the crossing. In one of his more advanced schemes the architect showed a dome on pendentives at this point, the diameter of which would encompass the nave only. In the end, however, this space was completely redesigned with dramatic results. The diameter of the dome was increased from forty to approximately sixty-five feet so that its circumference stretched across almost the full width of the building to include the area of the side aisles as well as the nave (Figs. 262, 264). The pendentives were eliminated and the dome was placed atop a pure cylindrical drum. This changed the

FIGURE 264. *Benjamin Latrobe. Baltimore Cathedral, Baltimore, Md., 1804–c. 1818. Latrobe's section.*

area in such a way that a crossing through which the nave and transepts passed became a dominating concentric space from which the nave, transepts, and choir radiated; and the crossing, instead of being a static point of intersection, became a dynamic area quite different from the rest of the church and, because of its lofty spaciousness, far better suited to the functions of an auditorium. The secondary spaces of the nave and choir, although square in plan, are topped by segmental pendentive domes so that they are immediately related in shape to the main rotunda. The choir terminates in an apse crowned by a segmental half dome. The nave ends in a rectangular bay covered by a segmental barrel vault, sprung from side to side across the nave, so that it opens easily into the curved spaces beyond. Similar barrel-vaulted rectangular bays form the aisles, but they are sprung parallel to the main axis of the church so that they too present their curved openings to the inner spaces of the design. Each of the three major spatial units therefore—the choir, the crossing, and the nave—becomes a coherent volume with a domed center and reciprocally corresponding arms. Yet each is an integral part of the other, so that the total spatial organization of the church is seen to be an interlocking, on the longitudinal axis, of three concentric domed units, the large one in the center and the two corresponding smaller ones at the head and the foot, all contained within the major rectangular mass of the building. The arms of the cross are formed by the transept bays which oppose one another on the lateral axis of the rotunda and project beyond the main body of the church as two rectangular wings.

This is the over-all scheme, a complex system of interrelated vaults which takes the general configuration of the cross at the same time that it builds to a spatial climax in the great rotunda beneath the central dome. Latrobe's integration of structure and geometry is brilliant. The structural core of the building is the great cylindrical drum which supports the central

FIGURE 265. *Benjamin Latrobe. Baltimore Cathedral, Baltimore, Md., view into central rotunda, 1804–c. 1818.*

dome (Figs. 265, 266). At the floor level this drum is cut by four square openings approximately thirty feet across, each of which is topped by a segmental arch with an extremely flat profile (Fig. 265). The arches on the long axis open into choir and apse, those on the lateral axis into the transepts. The remaining lower sections of the cylindrical wall are further cut, this time on a line diagonal to the main axis of the building, by four other square openings, half the size of the larger ones and this time

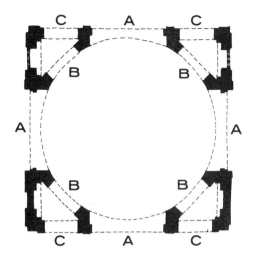

FIGURE 266. *Benjamin Latrobe. Baltimore Cathedral,
Baltimore, Md., plan of central rotunda area, 1804–c. 1818.*

crowned by full half-circle arches. The result is eight massive piers with
segmental inner surfaces and clustered in four groups of two, each group
arranged at a forty-five degree angle with respect to the main axis of the
building (Fig. 266).

At this point we encounter one of the most provocative aspects of
Latrobe's design. Although the inner surface of each pier, as an extension
of the cylindrical wall, is curved, the outer or back sides are flat (Fig.
266: A). Moreover, if we strike lines from pier to pier on the back side we
find that in plan we have constructed an octagon. Extending this observation through the entire vertical stretch of the mass itself, we find that
Latrobe has contained the cylindrical rotunda within the structural elements of an octagon. The spatial variety which results from this play
upon geometric relationships can best be seen by comparing the inner and
outer edges of the arched openings in the cylindrical drum. Those on the
inner or cylindrical side curve in both the vertical and horizontal plane;
those on the outer or octagonal side curve in the vertical plane only.
The inner surface of these arches is therefore wider at the spring than
it is at the crown (Figs. 265 and 266: A).

But this is not all. The forty-five degree angle of the four grouped
piers, as they relate to the outer wall of the building, create a small
triangular space which Latrobe has then enclosed by another wall connecting the aisle pier with the outer wall of the building (Fig. 266: C).
These walls are pierced by arched openings identical to those in the rotunda wall itself, thus permitting a continuous flow of space through the
pier, into the aisle beyond. At the same time, these same walls define the
four corners of the great central mass of the building, which turns out to
be a square. Thus the geometric units which make up the core of the

FIGURE 267. *Benjamin Latrobe. Baltimore Cathedral, Baltimore, Md., view into choir vault, 1804–c. 1818.*

FIGURE 268. *Benjamin Latrobe. Baltimore Cathedral, Baltimore, Md., flank view of central domed area, 1804–c. 1818.*

design consist of a cylinder within an octagon within a square. The segmental dome which tops the whole springs directly from the cylindrical wall of the rotunda itself thereby obviating the need for transitional pendentives from either the octagon or the square (Fig. 265). The lofty volumetric sequence of cylinder to sphere is thus maintained, while in the lower reaches of the rotunda, space is permitted to flow through and join with the more complicated geometry of the subsidiary spaces beyond.

The abutting vaults of the choir and nave are pure segmental pendentive domes, (Fig. 267) profiled on the same curve as the large arched openings from the rotunda, and delicately sprung from the aisle piers. In a manner remarkably similar to the vaults in Soane's Stock Office (compare Figs. 248 and 249), the sharp points of the pendentive triangles are saddled securely in the angles formed by the intersection of the lateral and longitudinal ribs of the supporting arches. An almost imperceptible molding outlines the entire vault area including pendentives; a similar molding circumscribes the saucer dome itself. Otherwise the continuous spherical surface runs from pendentive point to pendentive point without a projecting interruption. The rectangular aisle and transept bays, which flank all the domed spaces, have segmental barrel vaults for ceilings, again profiled on the same segmental curve as the main arches in the rotunda. These vaults are sprung longitudinally down the church, their crowns tangential to the base of the saucer domes which they join and support. In all the vaults throughout the church, there is no three-dimensional embellishment to interrupt the continuity of their curving surfaces. Even the sunken coffers, circular in the domes and square in the barrel vaults, remain isolated rhythmic accents with all enframing moldings and three-dimensional rosettes held back from the structural surface so that the sheer curved planes remain inviolate.

It is obvious from Latrobe's drawing (Fig. 264) that in order further to preserve the geometric purity of his various spatial components he planned a completely architectonic use of color, not unlike that which he called for in the Bank of Pennsylvania. There have been several over-abundant painted embellishments of the interior since Latrobe's time, but fortunately the most recent redecoration seems very close to the architect's intentions. Except for the pictorial panels in the center of the domes, color has been used to articulate structure and to preserve the simplicity of surface which Latrobe so conspicuously had in mind. As it stands today the Baltimore Cathedral has one of the most original and beautiful church interiors in America.

Here, as in the Bank of Pennsylvania, Latrobe's intricate interior spatial system is clearly expressed on the exterior of the building (Fig. 261). The cross shape is recognized at once. So, too, is the dome rising above the crossing. Infinitely more subtle and rewarding, however, are the many refined adjustments that the architect has made to articulate the more complicated aspects of the inner design. Primary stress is placed upon the crossing as the epicenter of both the structural and spatial dynamics. The limits of the cube which contains the rotunda are revealed on the outside by a slight projection in the lateral wall (Fig. 268). Above this rises the octagon, and farther up, the dome. All this proclaims the fundamental geometric system of cylinder within octagon within cube. Equally discriminating adjustments have been made in the octagonal mass as it rises above the crossing. The four primary planes of the octagon, which correspond to the nave and choir on the longitudinal axis and to the transepts on the cross axis, are made to project slightly farther from the drum than the secondary or diagonal planes. They are also slightly longer. Thus the alternating rhythm of the major and minor arched openings in the rotunda wall asserts itself in the outer image of the building.

Progressing toward the front of the church from the central block (Figs. 261, 269), the wall runs smoothly until it reaches the base of the tower, where it encounters another slight projection. This continuous stretch of wall corresponds exactly on the inside to the domed section of the nave, and to its related barrel-vaulted aisle bays. The second projecting section of wall, which forms the visual base for the tower, also defines the first barrel vaulted bay of the nave. From here the wall breaks back to its original plane and proceeds forward a short distance before it turns the corner to receive the colossal freestanding portico. Behind this narrow strip of wall is the entrance vestibule, or narthex, which provides a transition from the area beneath the portico to the vast and continuous worship space beyond.

Another expressive variation is found in the three major windows along the side of the building. They are all the same size and are round-headed, and all occupy central positions with respect to a major spatial division on the inside (Figs. 261, 262). The wall arches, however, in which these windows are set are not the same size. The one in the center, which relates to the domed section of the nave, is larger than the other two which open into smaller internal units, the first bay of the nave on the one hand and the small triangular space at the corner of the central octagon on the other. Each of these spaces is therefore shown to be secondary to the larger and more dynamic domed nave; all three are subordinate to the simple largeness of the round-arched entrance to the transept (Fig. 268), which in its primitive unadorned power foreshadows the climactic space of the rotunda behind.

The structural daring and rational purity of Latrobe's design may be traced to his Neoclassical antecedents in England. The bold juxtaposition of light segmental vaults, both barrel and spherical, are conspicuously reminiscent of Soane's Bank of England. So, too, is Latrobe's respect for the continuity of plane surfaces. It is also obvious that it was the engineering skill which he acquired in England that made his American achievement possible. Yet these are matters of fundamental character rather than specific detail, for the truth is that there was no church in England comparable to the Baltimore Cathedral, thus none which could have served as a specific model. It is possible that its cross-shaped plan, simple walls, and colossal freestanding portico were suggested to Latrobe by the Panthéon in Paris, one of the earliest Neoclassical buildings in France, and one which was nearing completion when the Englishman was in Paris in

FIGURE 269. *Benjamin Latrobe. Baltimore Cathedral, Baltimore, Md., flank view toward portico, 1804–c. 1818.*

the early 1780's. Yet the hall-like interior makes the American church manifestly different from the Panthéon, as do the twin towers on the façade. This latter feature is one of the most interesting aspects of Latrobe's design. The geometric simplicity, depressed dome, and temple front are straightforward Neoclassical features. The twin towers, however, are not (Figs. 207, 261). The Wren-Gibbs tradition, which established the form of the American church up to the time of the Baltimore Cathedral, called for a single tower only. This was true even when the tower was used in conjunction with a colossal portico, as it was at St. Martin-in-the-Fields in London and at St. Michael's, Charleston (Fig. 96).

Perhaps the concept of a tower springing from the center of a pitched roof would have been incompatible with Latrobe's Neoclassical taste. Perhaps at the urging of his patron he was recalling something of the monumental grandeur of the twin tower façades of the Catholic-Baroque in Europe. Whatever his motivation the Cathedral was absolutely unique among the Anglo-American buildings of the eastern seaboard. In fact, the only other example of twin towers combined with a temple front is the

Santa Barbara Mission Church in California (Fig. 151), which we have already studied as an intrusion of Neoclassicism into the Spanish-Baroque stronghold of the Southwest. This church was begun ten years after the Baltimore Cathedral, and there is no known connection between the two, yet both arrived at similar solutions. What this points up is the nature of Latrobe's problem, and his particular sensitivity to it. The Baltimore Cathedral was a church for Catholic worship and as such would find nothing in the Wren-Gibbs type which would satisfy its many and quite specific needs. To provide for them the architect had to turn in an absolutely different direction. He had to lay up his walls on the solid foundation stones of the great Catholic tradition in church architecture. The degree to which he was able to do this, and still cast his image in the bold rational geometry of his own Neoclassical taste, makes the Baltimore Cathedral one of the most extraordinary moments in American architecture. For Latrobe was not only a consummate engineer whose command of the science of vaulting made him unique in his American environment, he was also a sensitive artist with the insights to express and gratify human aspirations and human needs in forms of the most practical and exquisite beauty.

In one sense it can be said that the Baltimore Cathedral was not an American building at all. Its vaulted construction and pure spatial organization were the very epitome of English Neoclassicism, its stanchly Catholic form was an affront to the severe Protestantism of the puritanized Wren-Gibbs church. But America of 1800 was a different country than America of the colonial years. After the drastic political upheaval which came with the American Revolution we encounter a growing nationalism and general broadening of the spectrum of American society. From this point on, the country could no longer exist as an idealistic microcosm on the remote shores of a colonial land. It had to face the hard facts of independence, to assume the responsibilities which went along with it, and to perform in new areas of activity where there was no established tradition, no line of descent upon which to build. To fill the inevitable vacuums specialists came from all walks of life and from many nations, bringing with them new skills and fresh attitudes to challenge colonial traditions, to generate new ideas, and to point new directions. The land absorbed them into its multicolored fabric to establish at the very beginning of its independent history the heterogeneous character of its creative community. For by the very nature of its geography the United States could not populate itself, and its ultimate growth and expansion westward would not have been possible without a continuing flow of humanity from Europe. Latrobe was only one figure in this never-ending migration and was therefore as much a part of American building as Peter Harrison and William Buckland had been before him, as John Roebling and Leopold Eidlitz were to be later in the nineteenth century, and as Walter Gropius and Mies van der Rohe are today. The Baltimore Cathedral could not have been built outside of this country and because of its innovations it remains one of the most important and original buildings in American history.

Robert Mills

Latrobe was not the only architect to come to America from abroad. We have learned in our chapter on Thomas Jefferson that in 1812 the French architect J. J. Ramée was in this country working on the designs of Union College, and in the next chapter we shall encounter two other Frenchmen, Major Pierre Charles L'Enfant and Stephen Hallet, both in connection with the designing of the national Capitol in Washington. Also in Washington was the Irishman James Hoban, who won the competition for the President's House (the present White House), and in 1805 another Frenchman, Maximilian Godefroy, came to St. Mary's College, Baltimore, as the first professor of architecture in the United States. Godefroy was later to collaborate with Latrobe on the Baltimore Exchange. J. F. Mangin, also from France, participated in the design of the new city hall in New York; and besides Latrobe there were two other English architects at work, George Hadfield in Washington and William Jay in Savannah, Georgia.[14] All these men brought a lively infusion of European ideas to the American scene which helped to break the provincialism of the colonial years. They also did much to strengthen the image of the professional architect.

All this activity, together with the increasing demand for monumental building, encouraged a number of young Americans to enter the field of architecture. They did so, however, not in the traditional manner of the gentleman-amateur or builder, but as trained, motivated professionals whose skills and creativity were given wholly to the designing and construction of buildings. All of them were born after the Revolution and therefore had no direct knowledge of the colonial years; all, too, began their careers in the very years when an aggressive nationalism was seeking expression in almost every phase of American life. In general, they will be the subject of our next chapter. But one of these young Americans, Robert Mills, because of the unique nature of his style, must be considered in this chapter as the central native-born figure in the rational phase of American Neoclassicism.

Mills was born in Charleston, South Carolina on August 12, 1781.[15] His father came from Scotland, his mother from Charleston. As a young man he had the advantage of a classical education at Charleston College, from which he was graduated at the age of twenty. This was followed by a brief period with Hoban, who practiced briefly in Charleston. When the Irishman went to Washington in 1800 the young Mills seems to have followed him there and worked for him as a draftsman. Almost at once, however, he met Thomas Jefferson and in 1801 or 1802 he was at Monticello where he helped the great man in his work on that building. Then in 1804, armed with letters of introduction from Jefferson and Hoban to a number of American architects (including Charles Bulfinch) he traveled to several cities on the eastern seaboard. The object of this trip, perhaps the first of its kind ever undertaken in America, was to study

American architecture. Upon his return he entered the office of Latrobe, apparently at the suggestion of Thomas Jefferson, where he received his final professional training in both architecture and engineering. He was to remain with Latrobe for five years and was thus to become, in his own words, "the first native American who directed his studies to architecture as a profession"[16] in the United States.

Mills total commitment to the profession of architecture is borne out by the excellence of his work. Because of his training with Latrobe, he developed engineering skills which no other native-born architect could equal at the time. He was not, of course, America's first architect. Thomas Jefferson and Charles Bulfinch performed as true professionals, even though their backgrounds and training were those of the amateur. But Mills was certainly the first American to decide from the beginning on architecture as a career, and all his education and training were directed toward this end. In this respect his years with Latrobe were decisive, for here he gained a professional experience which he could not have received anywhere else in America. It was this, together with his total involvement in architecture, that distinguished Mills from his American born predecessors. Bulfinch was as much selectman and police commissioner as he was architect (although it was in architecture that he performed best) and Jefferson was many times more the statesman, politician, and humanist. Neither was an engineer. Mills devoted his life to buildings and engineering, and his work is based on a thorough understanding of the fundamental relationships between structure and form.

Mills also received from Latrobe a thorough indoctrination into the meaning and potentials of rational Neoclassical doctrine. The simplicity and primitive directness of the Neoclassical style were conspicuously attractive to the young man's spartan taste; its structural purity appealed to his keen practical sense. Here was a mode of building devoid of pretense and based upon nature for its order. "Utility and economy," he wrote in his autobiographical notes, "will be found to have entered into most of the studies of the author, and little sacrificed to display; at the same time his endeavors were to produce as much harmony and beauty of arrangement as practicable. The principle assumed and acted upon was that beauty is founded upon order and that convenience and utility were constituent parts."[17] On another occasion he said that the proportions of the ancient orders "are founded upon nature," and that "we have the same principles and materials to work upon that the Ancients had, and we should adapt these materials to the habits and customs of our people as they did to theirs."[18] Further, in a thoroughly practical response to the function of a column, he adds that "a Column, never appears to possess that degree of Solidity, that Composure when placed upon a Pedestal, which it does on the pavement, or level of the Floor."[19]

Here in the blunt, provincial vernacular of a youthful American is a clear affirmation of Laugier's rational theories. Mills places similar stress upon essentials, upon structural logic, and upon the origin of all architecture in natural law. At the same time he adds to this doctrine an ardent national flavor. Like Laugier, he prefers the Greek style over the Roman because of its greater simplicity, and in his own American way he also sees it as appropriate to the ideals of the new nation. "It was fortunate," he wrote "that this style was so early introduced into our country, both on the ground of economy and correct taste, as it exactly suited the character of our political institutions and pecuniary means." Moreover "our artists, therefore, should never forget the original models of their country, neither the customs nor manners of their people, when they execute works of art either for their government or for their fellow citizens." Finally, there was the practical necessity of considering each building as related to a particular situation in the present. Mills made it a practice "never to consult books" when designing a building. Instead, "his considerations were . . . first, the object of the building; second, the means appropriate for its construction; third, the situation it was to occupy; these served as guides in forming the outline of his plans."[20]

Mills's stress upon practical concerns was natural in a society still in confrontation with the frontier. Similarly, the identification of architecture with the laws of nature had a familiar ring to a man whose native legends were filled with ancestors who had actually built primitive huts in the wilderness. Thus Mills not only spoke in abstract theoretical terms, he also spoke as a native American (which Latrobe did not), to a fertile and ready land in which the ideas he so vigorously expressed had ample opportunity for realization. His architecture was among the first native fruits of that land. It is stark and bold, sometimes even awkward, always muscular and direct. In many ways it is a more natural expression of Neoclassical primitivism than many of the sophisticated works of the English. One has the feeling that the Abbé Laugier would have found the ultimate embodiment of his ideals in the uninhibited architecture of Robert Mills.

Precisely when Mills left Latrobe and established himself on his own is not exactly clear, but it seems that one of his first important independent commissions was for the Sansom Street Baptist Church in Philadelphia. This was in 1808; the building was finished in 1809. It was followed in 1813, by the Octagon Unitarian Church,[21] also in Philadelphia. During the same period, in Richmond, Virginia, Mills won the competition for the Monumental Church, a building intended to be a memorial on the site where seventy-one persons had lost their lives in a disastrous theatre fire. It was built in 1812. These three buildings, all finished within four years of one another, mark the beginning of Mills's career and reveal him as a thoroughly independent architect working with self-assurance in a manner quite his own.

The boldness and simplicity of Mills's style, as seen in his three early churches, impress us at once. All were conceived in a language of pure geometry which was obviously inspired by Latrobe's rational attitudes. More than that, all three were rotunda type buildings, having a central domed space. Like the Baltimore Cathedral, which Mills would have known intimately from his association with Latrobe, they represented a radical departure from the traditional Wren-Gibbs type church of the colonial years. Latrobe's break with tradition was motivated by the demands of the Catholic liturgy. Mills's departure, too, which in its pure rotunda form was even more radical than Latrobe's, was a similar effort to examine the whole question of church design as it related to the changing character of American religious institutions and practices. His achievement, therefore, as it is preserved to us in the Monumental Church in Richmond, can only be understood in the light of developments in the American religious community.

The religious character of the colonies during the early years was dominated by the Puritans in New England and the Anglicans in Virginia. But at the same time other religious groups were attracted to the new land and in spite of determined resistance both in New England and the South, were able to establish themselves at various points along the Atlantic seaboard. The Baptists in Rhode Island and New Jersey, the Quakers in New Jersey and Pennsylvania, the Dutch Reformed in New York, the Swedish Lutherans in Delaware, the Catholics in Maryland, all formed the vanguard of an increasingly complex melange of denominations which was to become the ultimate pattern in the United States. Before the Revolution these groups remained small and isolated. This was true even in Rhode Island and Maryland, where the principles of religious freedom were first established in America. But after the war, with religious freedom guaranteed by the Constitution, the minority denominations grew in strength and numbers, and by 1800 they were making their own impressions upon American culture. It was in this very proliferation of religious doctrine, now assured by law, that the Catholic Church in America received its first bishop in the figure of John Carroll, and that Benjamin Latrobe was called upon to build the Baltimore Cathedral; it was in this broadening religious environment, too, that Robert Mills was commissioned to build his three churches.

That all three of Mills's churches were designed around a rotunda space has obvious Neoclassical connotations. First used in Western civilization by the ancient Romans, the rotunda was adopted by all classically oriented cultures, and in the late eighteenth century became one of the most important spatial devices of the Neoclassicists of Europe. Once introduced into this country by Latrobe in his Bank of Pennsylvania, it proved to be particularly suitable to the American scene. Its geometric purity appealed to the ordered taste of a pragmatic society, its spacious interior reach was awesome and introduced elements of monumental scale that had never been possible in the colonial styles. For Robert Mills, however, the rotunda form had still another appeal. Sensitive as he was to the functional obligations of architecture, and self-consciously aware of the need for an architectural idiom that would speak for his own generation of men, the young architect saw in the radical shape of the rotunda a practical solution to some of the special requirements of contemporary American religion. Foremost among these was the increasing demand for eloquent preaching. This was true not only of some of the minority denominations such as the Baptists, who by 1800 were becoming a major force in American life, but also of the more conservative groups. Even the American

Catholics, whose highly formalized service centered in the Mass, insisted upon priests who could preach.

The importance of the minister as the purveyor of God's word had long been an established fact in the Congregational services and had been expressed in the early New England meetinghouses by the shift in emphasis from the altar to the pulpit. Yet in the more personal terms of a confrontation between the minister and his congregation, neither the pulpit on the side nor the old box pews offered much in the way of rapport. As in all oratory, the critical question was the relationship between the performer and his audience, and even in the later Wren-Gibbs type church in America, where the pulpit was placed at the end rather than on the side, there were significant numbers of the congregation who were left at a disadvantage as far as seeing and hearing were concerned. By making the main body of the church either round or octagonal, however, Mills was able to arrange his seating on a radial plan, with narrower groupings toward the pulpit and increasingly wider ones toward the rear. This placed the speaker at or near the convergence of radial lines of sight, thus giving each viewer an equal advantage. In the Sansom Street Church in Philadelphia, Mills faced an even more specialized situation. Here the sacrament of baptism required a large open baptistry in which the ritual of immersion could be performed. He placed this at the very center of the church—much like the stage in a theatre-in-the-round—and arranged the seats in straight lines around an open square. In this way everyone in the congregation was able to face the baptistry.

The Monumental Church

The rotunda type of church, which offered a dramatic and central presentation of either the individual preacher or a specialized ritual in the service, became known as the auditorium type church and seems first to have been used in America by Robert Mills. Unfortunately, his two Philadelphia churches have long since disappeared, but the Monumental Church in Richmond, Virginia, still survives in reasonably good condition (Fig. 270). Except for a later addition to the rear and one side, and some minor alterations in the auditorium itself, the basic character of the church, both inside and out, remains relatively unchanged. It will therefore serve admirably as an example both of Mills's style and of his remarkable capacity for functional planning.

The main body of the building is a masonry octagon topped by a plaster segmental dome suspended from a wooden truss. In the center of the dome is a broad circular oculus opening into a short glazed lantern. Projecting from and embracing one whole side of the octagon, is a pedimented porch (Fig. 271). This special feature is square in plan, and in its center, placed on a pedestal, is a funerary urn that symbolically represents the ashes of the fire victims (Fig. 272). Thus what seems to be the front entrance portico to the building is in fact the principal memorial space. Its appearance is appropriately monumental. A drastically distilled Greek

FIGURE 270. *Robert Mills. Monumental Church,*
Richmond, Va., 1812.

Doric frieze is carried directly upon massive corner piers; set *in antis,* and
coupled with the piers on all three sides of the porch, are simplified Doric
columns with widely flaring Archaic echinus blocks. The columns are held
close to the piers so that the inward interval between them is wide and
forms a spacious opening on all three sides of the porch.

Topping the whole is an austere pediment stripped of all projecting
elements except a flattened cornice. This cornice is more lightly scaled
and differently profiled than the deeper cornice of the entablature below.
Moreover, Mills has inserted a low parapet between the entablature and
the pediment in a quite unclassical manner. Since this prevents the raking
cornice from making contact with the horizontal cornice, the pedimental
triangle is never closed. Also unorthodox is the fact that the frieze has no
triglyph-metope motif, and the columns are unfluted except for a narrow
band at the top, immediately under the capital, and another at the base.
The effect is an abstraction of the Doric order which emphasizes its
geometric purity rather than its sculptural richness.

Mills's willingness to re-examine the elements of classical architecture
shows him to have been an ardent disciple of Neoclassical doctrine. At
the same time, the boldness of his alterations reveals him as an uninhibited individual determined to give new meaning to old forms, and to
relate those forms to the life of his own time. As his master Latrobe had
done before him, Mills combined the geometric and structural logic of

FIGURE 271. *Robert Mills. Monumental Church,*
Richmond, Va., porch, 1812.

FIGURE 272. *Robert Mills. Monumental Church,*
Richmond, Va., inside porch, 1812.

FIGURE 273. *Treasury of the Athenians, Delphi, Greece, c. 490 B.C.*

Greek architecture with the spatial daring of the Romans, but he did this with qualities of breadth and vigor which are uniquely his own.

This can readily be seen in the geometric system of the memorial porch which we have just described. Although it is seemingly composed of the major elements of the Doric style, particularly as exemplified in the smaller Greek buildings such as the Treasury of the Athenians at Delphi (Fig. 273), Mills's design is, in fact, something quite different. It is simpler at the same time that it is more dynamic. Its simplicity derives on the one hand from its stripped down character, on the other from the continuity of the wall planes. The main frontal plane, established by the outer faces of the corner piers, carries through the full height and breadth of the porch. In other words, the outer faces of the entire entablature, the parapet, and the pediment, are in the same plane as the piers, and the moldings which define the entablature project from that plane. This emphatically reduces the sculptural variety of the original Greek form and glorifies instead the severe geometry of a simple cube with a pitched-plane top and triangular front.

Yet the whole is dynamic. This quality derives primarily from Mills's subtle variation of the Greek structural system. In the Treasury of the Athenians the support function is distributed equally between the two columns and the two piers which form the ends of the side walls. In Mills's porch (Fig. 271), however, the primary support is provided by the piers, with the columns playing a subordinate role. By holding the columns closer to the piers than to one another they seem to be working with, rather than independently of, the piers. By articulating the piers through the entire height of the façade their structural integument is seen to extend past the entablature to the raised pediment above. Mills's method of developing this effect is particularly expressive. He sets back very slightly the entire plane of the columns and their related entablature, and then continues this secondary plane past the cornice to the base of the triangle which forms the pediment. This creates a shallow horizontal recessed panel immediately above the cornice which carries into the area of the parapet the visual limits of the opening below; it also reduces the apparent amount of superstructure being supported by the columns. At the same time, because the plane of the piers is continuous with the plane of the pediment, it seems as though the entire structure of the pediment is being borne by the piers.

Through Mills's highly original manipulation of the Doric forms we are drawn into a structural dialogue in which differing amounts of weight are carried by differing means, a dialogue which is further animated by the varied size and spacing of the supporting members (they are all equal in the Greek building). The resulting rhythmic pattern of pier to column to open space is given its final stress in the frieze. Here, instead of using the traditional triglyph-metope motif of the Greek Doric order, Mills has stripped the frieze to a bare plane, which he has then adorned with two pairs of lachrymatories, vases used by the Romans for containing tears, whose overt function is to serve as symbols of grief. But these vertical accents are so placed as to coincide with the central axis of each supporting member, thus aiding the articulation of the entire structural system. Besides the lachrymatories and moldings, the only other violation of the wall plane is the slightly projecting horizontal panel placed on the outer face of each pier at the level of the fluting in the columns. This breaks the monotony of the piers and carries through, at a critical visual point in the structure, a secondary horizontal stress.

So far we have treated the porch of the Monumental Church as though it were a separate building, and in one important sense it is. The plan, as we have seen, is a square, centered around the memorial urn. As an architectural unit, therefore, it is as complete and self-contained as a small Greek temple. Moreover, it is stonemasonry, while the main rotunda of the church, is brick covered with stucco. Even the character of the moldings used on the rotunda is different. It seems clear, therefore, that Mills saw his problem as two-fold. The commission was for a memorial church. But a church, as an active house of worship for the living, would seem too dynamic to provide the qualities of detachment and repose essential to a memorial for the dead. And so the two were conceived separately but joined in fact, independent but related spaces in a dynamic fulfillment of an unusually complex program.

The dual purpose of the Monumental Church manifests itself first in the fact that the memorial porch does not function as the main entrance to the church. Although a central door on the inner wall of the porch enters directly into the auditorium, there is no intervening vestibule, nor is there vertical access to the balcony at this point. With this door open, however, the memorial and worship spaces can be made continuous; moreover, the altar and the memorial urn then face one another as terminal points on the main axis of the building. But Mills did not make the central door the main entrance. Instead he provided primary access to the church through two side doors (Fig. 270), one in each flank of the octagon. On each side he placed a short projecting wing (the one on the right has been incorporated into an extensive later addition), and together they formed opposing vestibules to the main body of the church; within each vestibule was a stairway to the balcony level. The actual entrance in each case was a tall arched opening, which was fronted on the outside by a Greek Doric freestanding portico without pediment. The two columns in the porticoes were similar to those on the porch, but the entablature was deeper, and had a two-part architrave; these moldings, too, had slightly more complicated profiles.

In appearance the octagonal main building is somewhat simpler than the porch. The painted stucco walls are blander than the variegated stone surfaces of the porch, and therefore seem even flatter. The stringcourses, which carry into the main building itself the horizontal lines of the porch entablature, are without moldings of any kind and are held close to the wall. The upper and larger of these courses also has an expressive function in that it indicates on the outside of the building the top level of the balcony within. A similar pair of stringcourses, more closely spaced, form the bottom defining elements in a second unadorned entablature which crowns the main body of the building. Three-part windows (the stained glass is later), with narrow vertical side lights and a wider center light, are cut crisply into the diagonal planes of the octagon; the ones at the lower level are vertical in their proportions, those at the balcony level are slightly horizontal. Over each window is a flat stone lintel which projects only slightly from the wall and is shaped in silhouette like a depressed pediment with acroteria at the ends. Curiously, in a typical Millsian defiance of classical authority, the base line of the pediment over each center light breaks upward in a slightly triangular shape in lines which are parallel to the raking top of the pediment. The vertical dividing window bars are flat rectangular strips, rather light in scale, and are topped by simple blocks with circles cut into them; similar blocks act as brackets under the acroteria.

The only break in the taut surface of the wall is found in the sides of the vestibule wings where two-stage recessed panels move inward to articulate the density of the masonry. But they are totally unadorned and tend primarily to reaffirm the precise flat limits of the principal planes. The effect is solid and muscular, with all essentials stripped away and only the bare bones of the geometry to define the spaces.

The interior of the auditorium is as straightforward as the exterior (Fig. 274). The altar area (the painting is much later) is the dramatic

FIGURE 274. *Robert Mills. Monumental Church,
Richmond, Va., interior, 1812.*

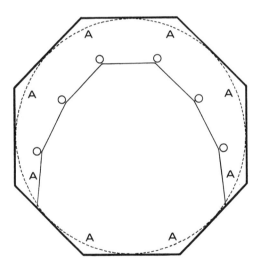

FIGURE 275. *Robert Mills. Monumental Church,
Richmond, Va., schematic diagram showing configuration of balcony
and position of dome.*

center of attention, slightly recessed between a screen of flanking piers
and Greek Ionic columns. The spacing and general configuration of this
enframing motif, with the columns held close to the piers, are identical to
the arrangement of the columns and piers which enclose the ceremonial
space of the porch. Yet the order of the porch is Doric, that flanking

the altar Ionic. This emphasizes the contrasting character of the two major spaces; the elegant and vivacious Ionic order is appropriate to the worship space, the severe Doric to the memorial space. Yet by making the columns perform an identical enframing function Mills also provided a positive architectural relationship between the two spaces, thus binding them together as a conceptual whole.

The seating arrangement in the auditorium is designed to take the best advantage of the visual focus provided by the columns. Closed pews run parallel to the plane of the altar wall. As the octagon widens, these pews get longer, and then as the octagon closes toward the rear, they get shorter again. Access to the pews is gained through one central and two side aisles, which run parallel to the main axis of the building.

Except for the improved sight lines, gained from the octagonal shape of the building, there is nothing unusual about Mills's arrangement on the main floor. The seating in the balcony, on the other hand, shows the architect at his ingenious best. Faced in this instance with the need for maintaining sight lines downward as well as toward the altar, he established a curving front to the balcony by making it a seven-sided figure, semielliptical in plan (Fig. 275).[22] Because of its generally wider angles, this graded shape more nearly approaches a curve than the octagon, at the same time that it provides straight line segments which facilitate construction. Mills fitted this figure into the octagon by centering it on the main axis of the auditorium, with its open end toward the altar. Thus placed, the end segments of the balcony are made to abut those diagonal walls of the octagon which are left and right of the altar. From here the long graded curves sweep backward to close the ellipse at the rear of the auditorium. The floor of the balcony is set on a series of planes inclined toward the front, one for each segment of the curve. The entire structure is then supported by six slender Doric columns strategically placed immediately behind the points of intersection of the seven straight line facets of the balcony front (Fig. 274). These columns, moreover, are set on pedestals so that they show their full profile above the main-floor pews. The upper pews are placed parallel to the frontal planes of the balcony and are thus constantly facing the altar.

The principle of curved seating here employed by Mills was not his own invention. It can be found in its earliest and most logical form in the theatres of the ancient Greeks and it has occurred in countless theatres of the Western world ever since. A particularly relevant example is Christopher Wren's Sheldonian Theatre in Oxford, built during the late seventeenth century. But it was unknown in America until it was introduced by Mills in his auditorium churches.

One final difficult problem for Mills was the handling of the circular segmental dome which covers the auditorium. The outer limits of the base of the dome he established as a circle tangent to the inner planes of the octagon as shown by the dotted line in Figure 275. This meant that in each of the eight corners there would be a triangle of space, straight on two sides and curved on the base, which had somehow to be

FIGURE 276. *Robert Mills. Monumental Church,*
Richmond, Va., ceiling detail, 1812.

accommodated into the structure. If Mills had been vaulting, the solution
would have been simple; these triangular areas would have been filled by
pendentives. But his ceiling, although shaped like a segmental dome,
was in fact plaster suspended from a wood truss. It was not, therefore, an
integral part of the masonry structure but rather sat, like a great inverted
saucer, on top of the masonry walls. It exerted only a minimum of
lateral thrust, all of which was contained by the outer tension members
of the truss itself. If Mills had wished to achieve the visual effects of
Neoclassical vaulting he could very easily have constructed wood and
plaster pendentives to fill the open triangles. But he did not. With
extraordinary candor he simply carried the rim of the dome across each
of the corner triangles, forming small pieces of horizontal ceiling (Fig.
276). It thus became obvious at once that his ceiling was indeed a
plaster ceiling, held in shape by the wooden truss, and resting lightly on
the eight walls of the octagon.

By using the suspended ceiling with such directness Mills gave new
meaning to a long-established structural method, a method which had its
roots in the colonial years, and was as much a part of the American
church building tradition as the four-square meetinghouse. There certainly must have been a temptation to imitate in wood and plaster
Latrobe's daring vaults in the Baltimore Cathedral, which Mills certainly
knew well. Fortunately he resisted this, and by working imaginatively
within the limits of his own building tradition, he showed himself to be
particularly sensitive to the qualities of his environment. At the same
time, he consciously sought to put his own stamp on that environment
and here he was equally direct, for nothing could have been more ex-

pressive of the broad common strength of the new nation than the primitivism of Neoclassical forms and the stark sometimes awkward way, with which Mills used them. His aspiration to be, as he put it, "altogether American in his views,"[23] led him to understand each commission from the broadest possible base. It also inspired him toward qualities of simplicity, ruggedness, and strength which were far more expressive of the emerging American culture than Bulfinch's refined interpretation of the traditional Federal Style, or even than Jefferson's intellectual idealism. For the new America was as much of the earth as it had been in the colonial years, and mingled with the refined threads of European culture, so revered by intellectuals like Jefferson, were the sharp and persistent strands of homespun. The frontier had always been a major force in American life, and the result was an inevitable roughness of character. All this Robert Mills understood and proudly proclaimed, not in words, but in the breadth and vigor of his style.

Mills's achievement in the Monumental Church was manifold. First there is his decisive break with the colonial past. In terms of building type, his design was a total departure from the traditional Wren-Gibbs formula, which was still the dominating mode in American church architecture, even in the years when he was working in Richmond. In terms of style, his innovations were equally radical. The rotunda shape of the church, the highly individual paraphrasing of the Greek forms, the bold primitivism, all were as far removed from the prevailing Federal taste as Latrobe's Baltimore Cathedral. Mills's success lies also in the highly functional character of his building, in the imaginative and practical way in which he resolved an unusual and challenging problem. His design is both subtle and ingenious, an eloquent acclamation of his pragmatic opinion "that convenience and utility were constituent parts" of beauty. Mills's consciousness that practical essentials were the root of good designing was as uncolonial as his preference for the Greek style.

Structurally, Mills's accomplishment is found in the straightforward honesty with which he used his materials. There was no more pretense in the way he handled brick, stone, timber, and plaster than there was in his rejection of all superficial ornament. The young architect arrived at his highly original spatial effects with absolutely traditional means. There is nothing in the structural means of the Monumental Church for which there were not adequate antecedents in earlier American architecture. But Mills's probing curiosity would not permit him to accept without question the conventional building methods, and in his search for more flexible and durable structural techniques he became increasingly involved in the very problem which his Monumental Church was built to memorialize, death and loss by fire.

The Fireproof Building

The widespread prevalence in America of wood as a building material posed the constant menace of fire, and from the very beginning American builders were in search of better means of controlling it. We have already seen in our chapter on Charles Bulfinch that in 1803 the Board of Selectmen of Boston passed an ordinance which stipulated that all buildings over ten feet in height had to be made of brick. But even such laws as this were limited in effect, for as long as wood was used for interior framing the masonry walls contributed little toward reducing the number of fires. In England, during these same years, experiments were being carried out with the use of metal as a means of fireproof construction. This was particularly true in industrial and commercial building.[24] The primitive nature of the American metal fabricating industry, however, precluded experimentation with any such bold new ideas in this country, and it was not until Latrobe introduced his sophisticated techniques of vaulting that means were opened for the Americans to think in terms of fireproof construction. The first to take up this challenge was Latrobe in an addition to the old Treasury Building in Washington which he designed in 1805. The first building conceived from the beginning in terms of fireproof construction was Robert Mills's Record Office, built in Charleston, South Carolina between 1822 and 1827.

Early in 1820, after a short period in Baltimore, Mills moved to Charleston with his young family. He made the move after "receiving the appointment of Engineer and Architect of the State, and a commission seat on the Board of Commissioners of Public Works."[25] In this capacity, in 1822, he was commissioned to design a fireproof record office for the state. This is one of the most innovative buildings of the first half of the nineteenth century and because of its unique construction it has come to be known as the "Fireproof Building" (Fig. 277). The site chosen, on the public square in Charleston, was at the intersection of Meeting and Chambers streets, only a block from St. Michael's Church. One side of the building opens onto Chambers Street, the other onto a small park; on the other corner of the park is the City Hall. Work was begun quickly and by the end of the year the building was well advanced. It remains today virtually in its original form and now serves as the headquarters of the South Carolina Historical Society.

The demands posed by the Fireproof Building commission were very much simpler than those Mills had encountered in the Monumental Church. They called for office and record-storage spaces, planned in an efficient and secure manner. Mills's solution to this highly practical problem is correspondingly straightforward. The building is a two-story rectangular block set on a high basement. In the center of each of the long sides, one on Chambers Street and the other on the park, is a colossal Greek Doric portico with four columns and a pediment. Each of these porticoes is carried on a stone arcade which is a continuation of the basement.

The main massing of the building is as uncomplicated and dignified as the earlier eighteenth century rectangular block houses of colonial America, and it is stanchly Neoclassical in its plainness and its Greek-inspired motifs. The excitement of the building, however, is not to be found in any of this for in spite of its outward simplicity, the building is one in which function and structural necessity, not style and tradition,

FIGURE 277. *Robert Mills. Fireproof Building,*
Charleston, S.C., 1822.

have been the major determinants of the form. From its very conception Mills's governing objective was to make the building fireproof. At that time the only way to accomplish this was to build entirely in masonry, and this is precisely what the architect did. Moreover, the internal arrangement was the order of the structure itself. His basic module was the single groin-vaulted bay (Fig. 279). This unit he repeated end to end to form two in-line clusters of three bays each. In each cluster the end bays are identical, the middle bay slightly longer (Fig. 278, A-B-A). These clusters he extended across each end of the building; in the center he placed a somewhat different but related grouping. Here the end bays are barrel-vaulted rather than groined (Fig. 278 C) and the central bay is the open stairwell. This center group is not as wide as the end clusters and is separated from them by two narrow barrel-vaulted corridors (Fig. 278 D). Thus joined, the alternating groined and barrel-vaulted spaces form the plan and structural system of the basement and first floor, and the plan of the second. The ceilings of the second floor, however, are not vaulted but are flat plaster suspended from the wood roof trusses.

Structurally, the system was simple and logical; on the first two floors each vaulted unit served as buttressing for each adjacent unit; vertically, the internal walls on each floor provided support for the walls above. Functionally, Mills arrived at a system of neat useful cells, eight on each floor, all with outside walls, and all opening conveniently off one of the two barrel-vaulted corridors (Fig. 280). The ninth, or central structural bay, which was the only one without an outside wall, was left open from the basement to a skylighted roof, and contained the staircase (Fig. 281). This area was accessible to each corridor through an arched opening,

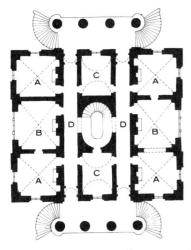

FIGURE 278. *Robert Mills. Fireproof Building, Charleston, S.C., plan of first floor, 1822.*

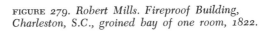

FIGURE 279. *Robert Mills. Fireproof Building, Charleston, S.C., groined bay of one room, 1822.*

FIGURE 280. *Robert Mills. Fireproof Building,*
Charleston, S.C., barrel-vaulted corridor, 1822.

providing vertical circulation by means of the stairs; it also served as a horizontal passageway from one corridor to the other (Fig. 282). Entrance to any part of the building could thus be conveniently achieved from any one of the four outside doors which gave access to the two corridors. These doors opened onto the porches under the two porticoes.

The convenience of Mills's plan was matched by both its strength and security. No timber was used except for the ceilings of the third floor and the roof structure. Walls, vaults and partitions were of brick covered with stucco, the wooden roof was sheathed with copper and all window frames, sashes and shutters were iron. The stairs and their landings were stone, cantilevered from the masonry walls, and the handrailing and balusters were iron. In every way that he could, the architect eliminated combustible materials in order to make his building as fireproof as possible. At the same time, he produced a quality and kind of construction that was unmatched by any other building in America, except for the works of Latrobe. To be sure, his technique of vaulting was not his own invention, nor was it new to his time. It had, in fact, been used by generations of European architects and was as deeply rooted in the classical building traditions as the orders themselves. But Mills's particular application of the vault both for fire prevention and to create cellular

FIGURE 281. *Robert Mills. Fireproof Building, Charleston, S.C., view up into stair well, 1822.*

FIGURE 282. *Robert Mills. Fireproof Building, Charleston, S.C., staircase, 1822.*

spaces based on a structural module was unique in America in his day, and it anticipates by more than half a century the development of similar cellular space through the modules of the steel frame.

Mills's highly reasoned design is easily read in the exterior appearance of the building (Fig. 277). The central unit of interior space, including the two corridors, asserts itself by seeming to press outward on each long side in the two Doric porticoes. Left and right, the side units extend as flanking wings, their three-part internal structure etched incisively in the walls by a variety of means. In a manner reminiscent of Latrobe's handling of Ashdown, Mills articulates the center bay by setting its wall back slightly from the principal plane of the façade. Thus he makes it less aggressive than the two corner units, which thereby assume the positive role of projecting end bays. Unfortunately, the vertical drain-pipes that now occupy each recessed corner give undue visual stress to what is otherwise a very subtle change in depth of plane. The break backward is, in fact, so extremely slight that it does not interrupt the continuity of the end wall, but serves rather as a discreet articulation of the structural division of space within. Moreover, in spite of its recessed position, Mills distinguishes the central unit both visually and expressively as the dominating motif of the end wall. He does this through his development of the fenestration. The windows of the end bays are square in the basement, round-headed and set in wall arches on the first floor, rectilinear on the second floor. In the central bay, on the other hand, he introduces a three-part window with side lights narrower than the center light. He holds this entire motif back from the plane of the wall, and carries its tripartite vertical division from the basement through the first and second floors. Then by terminating the entire motif in a broad circular arch on the second floor, he creates the impression that the openings which appear on all three floors are in fact a single continuous strip-window, broken only at the first- and second-floor levels by horizontal spandrel panels. The sense of vertical continuity thus established relates in part to the even stronger verticality of the porticoes, and provides the visual fulcrum of the symmetrical end wall; at the same time it indirectly expresses the vertical continuity of the stair well in the center, which also rises through the entire height of the building.

All this was developed by Mills with the greatest economy of means. His style, in fact, is so austere that one widely accepted opinion describes it as "sometimes over-heavy, sometimes crude and almost stodgy in detail."[26] There is some justification for this point of view. To see it in this light alone, however, is to miss the whole spirit of Rational Neo-classicism. Primitivism is fundamental to this style, even in the work of its most accomplished practitioners, and Mills was conspicuouly one of the most ardent. Yet with all his stark primitivism, Mills was also capable of extremely refined architectural form. Although the major masses and structural elements are kept in the broadest geometric terms, certain components may be treated with extraordinary delicacy, in provocative contrasts with the bolder forms, much in the same way that the solo flute might be presented over the sustained intonation of the lower strings. Mills delights in the smaller moldings, which frequently are extremely delicate in scale. In functional details, too, he tends toward lightness, and even the basic shapes themselves are simple and without embellishment. There is nothing "stodgy" about the simple fillet molding which marks the base of the frieze in the Fireproof Building, nor about the iron balustrade which graces its stairway (Fig. 282). Indeed, the latter is one of the more elegant stair motifs of the period, and owes its effectiveness to Mills's innate concern for contrast between large structure and intimate detail. The handrail is scaled to the human hand, the balusters are thin and attenuated; and all this is set against the unadorned starkness of the curving wall and the vaults. This aspect of Mills's style foreshadows in spirit the muscular concrete architecture of the twentieth century, particularly in the work of Eero Saarinen, in which enormous bold surfaces of concrete are brought into human scale through such utilitarian details as balustrades.

There is another common attitude toward Mills's work which must be considered. Because of his preference for the Greek style, his work has been called Greek Revival. Again, this is reasonable, for Mills's work derives much, in both fact and spirit, from the architecture of ancient Greece. But just as in the case of Latrobe's works, the structural and spatial characteristics of Mills's buildings are Roman in origin and not Greek. The truth is, Mills was a Rational Neoclassicist rather than a Greek Revivalist and, as we shall see in our next chapter, there is a considerable difference between the two. His work is bold, direct, and totally without affectation. It makes no concession to the earlier American building tradition, which in Mills's day was in evidence on every hand in Charleston; it borrows nothing from the past that has not been subjected to a searching re-examination. In both the Monumental Church and the Fireproof Building the Greek Doric order has been so drastically distilled that it can no longer be said to imitate its Greek prototype. The columns are for the most part unfluted, the frieze is bare of ornament, the pediment is raised on a parapet and left open at the bottom. The entire Doric order thus becomes stark and primitive in a way that is as un-Greek as the arches over the windows and the door. It thus has its own particular simplicity and strength. Yet the shadowy image of ancient Greece was important to Mills, for it functioned for him as a symbol of the democratic society which he so ardently embraced. There can be no doubt of Mills's admiration for Greek architecture but there can also be no doubt of his determination to make it expressive of the practical concerns of his own time. To call it Greek Revival, therefore, is to see no more than the surface of a style which reveals its true self only when examined from the inside out.

In Mills's compelling awareness of the need for a truly national architecture, the Greek bore the same relationship to his work as the Roman did to Jefferson's. Yet there is also a fundamental difference. Jefferson belonged to the generation of the Revolution, and for him Roman architecture not only served as an expressive symbol of the new republic, it was also non-British. For Mills, however, the question of

British or non-British was unimportant. In fact, Mills's stanchly rational form of Neoclassicism came to him through Latrobe, who was himself an Englishman. His concern was architecture, not politics, and although his preference for Greek architecture was as ardently expressed as was Jefferson's for the Roman, it was not as militant. Nor was it as narrow. He was involved in a greater variety of commissions than Jefferson and he was thus in more direct contact with the full spectrum of American society. Moreover, his knowledge of engineering gave him insights into building which Jefferson never could have had. All this made Mills's point of view more positive and practical than Jefferson's and more profoundly expressive of the popular nationalism which followed the War of 1812.

The Fireproof Building in Charleston was the climax of Mills's early career. It showed him to be a master of his profession, with a practical yet refined sense of architectural form, and a supreme command of structure. After its success, it became increasingly obvious to him that South Carolina did not offer sufficiently demanding opportunities for his talents, and in 1830 he returned to Washington, this time to stay. Here he became involved at once in the larger architectural activities of the new nation. In order to understand his mature work, therefore, we must first examine briefly the context in which it would be performed, the planning and building of the city of Washington.

CHAPTER X

American Neoclassicism, The National Phase

THE GREEK REVIVAL

> *It (Washington) is sometimes called the City of Magnificent Distances, but it might with greater propriety be termed the City of Magnificent Intentions; for it is only on taking a bird's-eye view of it from the top of the Capitol, that one can at all comprehend the vast designs of its projector, an aspiring Frenchman. Spacious avenues, that begin in nothing, and lead nowhere; streets, mile-long, that only want houses, roads and inhabitants; public buildings that need but a public to be complete; and ornaments of great thoroughfares, which only lack great thoroughfares to ornament.*
>
> CHARLES DICKENS

Planning of the City of Washington

Dickens's well known description of the city of Washington was written in 1842, the year in which Robert Mills's Treasury Building was completed. As a cultured English liberal, Dickens was appalled by the crudeness of what he saw in Washington, and as a romantic he found only ugliness in the rawboned freshness of the emerging cityscape. The disorder which offended him was not the disorder of nature and of time, it was the clutter of man. Moreover, everything was new. There was not enough moss on the bricks for his taste. To Mills, on the other hand, all these qualities, however distasteful to the eye, were symptoms of action. Beneath the crudeness was the surging vitality, the promise which Mills sensed so deeply and strove so passionately to fulfill. Mills's bold style was nourished in the challenge of things undone. For him Washington was indeed a "City of Magnificent Intentions," a dream slowly taking shape on the rolling Maryland countryside.

When Mills arrived in Washington in 1830 there were two major government buildings complete, the Capitol and the President's House. In addition, there were four office buildings, simply designed in a conservative Neoclassical style, which were occupied by the several departments of the executive branch of the government. Otherwise the city offered only a handful of elegant houses scattered among straggling rows of shanties, boardinghouses, and hotels. There were also a few churches. The rest was muddy dirt tracks and unkempt open fields. But the United States by its very nature was a nation of new towns and cities carved from the wilderness; and Mills, one of its most articulate citizens, saw nothing incongruous about the splendid new government buildings rising from the uncultivated fields and forests. Before he was to complete his work for the government he would add to official Washington three imposing structures, the Patent Office, the Treasury Building, and the Post Office Building. In addition, he would give to the city its finest tribute to a national hero, the soaring obelisk of the Washington Monument.

The grand vision which Dickens never understood and which Mills helped to create was first formed immediately after the Revolution and was an essential by-product of independence. The need for a federal city was obvious and plans were begun at once to establish one. The first question which faced authorities was where it should be located. Rivalry developed quickly between several of the states each of which wanted the capital city for its own, and it was not until 1790, after years of political maneuvering, that the problem was resolved. Through President Washington's patient leadership the decision was finally made not to locate the capital in any existing city, but rather to build a new city, planned from the beginning as the nation's capital. To this end, Washington appointed a commission of three men. The site finally chosen was an area of ten square miles. Two thirds of this tract was on the Maryland side of the Potomac River at its confluence with the Anacostia. The other third was in Virginia, but this was not included in the ultimate plan, and in 1846 was retroceded to Virginia. Included in the tract was the thriving little port town of Georgetown. Across the river in Virginia was the newer but equally active port community of Alexandria, and not far away to the south was Washington's beloved Mount Vernon. Once a federal city had been established by law and the site selected, the next step was to plan the city. In 1791 Washington appointed a French engineer, Pierre Charles L'Enfant to design the new capital.

Unlike any of the other great capitals of the world of its time, Washington was remarkable in that it existed on paper as a plan before it was ever built (Fig. 283). This made possible the development of spatial concepts almost without limitation and L'Enfant took full advantage of the freedom offered.[1] He based his scheme on the broad radiating avenues of the typical Baroque city plan. As a Frenchman he was thoroughly familiar with Versailles and this magnificent Baroque scheme seems to have been a major source for him. But as an engineer he was also aware of other Baroque city plans, and to freshen his memory he wrote to Jefferson asking for any useful information which the latter might have. Jefferson obliged by sending L'Enfant the plans of twelve European cities.[2]

Working in the triangle between the Potomac and Anacostia rivers, L'Enfant established two focal points, one on the east side centered in

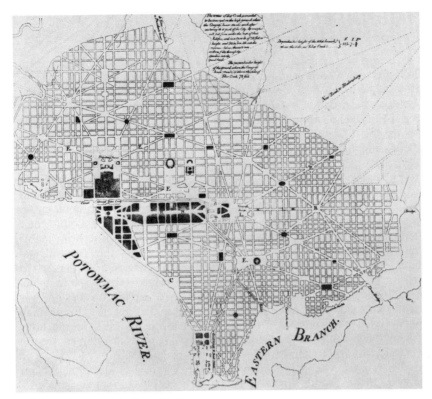

the Capitol Building, the other to the northwest centered in the President's House.[3] Major avenues radiated from these points, one of which (now Pennsylvania Avenue) was common to both and thus provided a dramatic visual connection between the two buildings. Extending due west from the Capitol, in L'Enfant's plan was a wide mall stretching all the way to the Potomac River. Intersecting this at right angles, and extending from the President's House, was another wide park. The point of intersection of these two vistas was later to become the site of Mills's Washington Monument. On this interlocking system of sweeping avenues and parks L'Enfant superimposed the rigid control of a right-angle grid. The city thus offered superb opportunity for the dramatic display of significant architectural monuments at the same time that it provided convenience of circulation.

Unfortunately L'Enfant's temperament brought him into almost immediate conflict with the Commission and in 1792 he was relieved of his responsibilities. He departed in indignation but left his drawings behind, so that his assistant, a surveyor by the name of Andrew Ellicott, was able to carry the scheme forward essentially in the form proposed by L'Enfant.

Although L'Enfant's commission included the design of the government buildings, his dismissal raised anew the question of an architect. Who was to design the buildings, and how was he to be chosen? Once again it was Jefferson, who hovered constantly in the background of all government architectural activity, who provided the answer. With his eye on the democratic process, he suggested that a competition be held, and on March 14, 1792 an announcement was published which solicited designs for both the Capitol and the President's House. The results of this competition constitute one of the most remarkable stories in American history, a story of naïve assumptions, of intrigue and jealousy, which is far too complex to be told here.[4] As the designs began to come in, however, one significant fact became immediately evident: there were no native-born architects in the United States qualified to carry out either building. Hampered by their provincial sense of scale, and by their limited building methods, the American designers were totally incapable of responding, either conceptually or technically, to the monumental requirements imposed by L'Enfant's grandiose scheme. Consequently the award for the President's House went to the trained Irish-born architect James Hoban; but in the competition for the Capitol no design was thought to be suitable, although the one submitted by the Frenchman Stephen Hallet was considered by the judges to be the best. In the hope that something could be salvaged, therefore, Hallet was retained by the Commission to try to improve his original scheme.

At this point a young physician from the Virgin Islands, Dr. William Thornton, wrote to the officials, asking if he could submit designs. Although the competition had officially closed they replied that they would be very glad to receive his plan for the Capitol. Thornton was a typical gentleman-amateur, with no professional qualifications whatsoever, except that he had previously won a competition for a library in Philadelphia. He describes the method which he used: "I got some books and worked a few days, then gave a plan in the ancient Ionic order which carried the day."[5] Nevertheless, the design which he submitted for the Capitol pleased both the President and Jefferson and in the end he was awarded the prize. Hallet in turn was retained to evaluate Thornton's plan and, under Hoban, to supervise construction. This was a serious mistake. Hallet, from his professional position, was incensed that he should be placed in a subordinate role to Thornton, and did everything he could to change the amateur's scheme in favor of his own. As a member of the District Commission he was in an ideal position to harass all the architects who had anything to do with his plan. In many ways the situation became a contest between jealousy and stubbornness which produced nothing but chaos and impeded progress. In the end Hallet was dismissed. But during the time he worked with Thornton he seems to have made some changes in his rival's design, and since Thornton's original competition drawing has been lost, it is difficult from this distant point in time to know exactly how much Hallet was able to accomplish.

In the larger picture of American architecture, the question of precise authorship is relatively unimportant. Regardless of who was responsible for the designs for the Capitol and the President's House, both were uninspired, bookish performances, as oldfashioned and traditional as the

FIGURE 284. *James Hoban. Design for the President's House, Washington, D.C., original drawing, 1792.*

FIGURE 285. *James Gibbs. Design for a house.*

eighteenth-century houses that lined the streets of Philadelphia, Baltimore, and Boston. The President's House (Fig. 284), for example, was a typical mid-eighteenth century English mansion such as those so generously illustrated by James Gibbs (Fig. 285). The Capitol (Fig. 286), particularly after Hallet's modifications, was less overtly derived but it was nevertheless filled with the clichés of an older style. In view of the state of architectural affairs in this country, this is not surprising. The full impact of Neoclassicism was yet to be felt in America. Bulfinch was only just beginning his career in Boston and Latrobe had still to arrive. Only Jefferson's Capitol in Richmond dared to proclaim the bolder theories of the new doctrine.

By 1814 the main structure of the President's House was virtually completed by Hoban in very much the form in which he originally planned it, although the interior was still unfinished. The Capitol, however, was a more complex building and from the beginning progress was very much slower. Moreover, it was to undergo extensive enlargement and modifica-

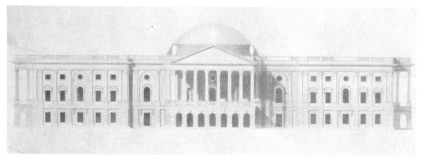

FIGURE 286. *William Thornton. Design for the National Capitol, Washington, D.C., water color drawing, 1794.*

tion up to the present time, and as it exists today it is the work of many men all motivated by different demands. It thus becomes irrelevant to attempt an evaluation of it as a coherent design. From the point of view of our story it is sufficient to recognize the building as the first conscious effort of the Federal Government to provide an appropriate architectural symbol for the new republic. It is ironic, therefore, that it should have been conceived in such stanchly conservative British terms, and so stubbornly carried out by a man whose taste and methods in architecture were still rooted in the British past. For with the dismissal of Hallet, Thornton became firmly entrenched, and not even Latrobe, who took over in Washington in 1803 as Surveyor of the Public Buildings, was able to effect any major changes in Thornton's design.

In his new post, which had previously been held by Hoban, Latrobe was theoretically in complete control of the construction of all government buildings. But Thornton was still in Washington, and even though he no longer enjoyed the leverage of his position as a Commissioner (the Commission was abolished in 1802), he still remained as head of the Patent Office, and up to the time of the War of 1812 he persisted as a constant and irritating force in the building of the Capitol. Latrobe brought to his new office professional skill and knowledge which Thornton could not possibly match and without which the work would never have been accomplished. But Thornton was stubborn and this, together with the frustrations of working for the government, made it impossible for Latrobe to do that which he thought best. He was to learn much about the need for compromise in a democratic society and in many instances he was forced to settle for second best.

In 1814 the British burned the Capitol along with the President's House and in the rebuilding which followed Latrobe enjoyed a greater freedom of action. Although he was forced by Presidential decision to follow Thornton's exterior design, on the interior he was able to redesign both the north and south wings, and to bring both these parts of the building virtually to completion before he left office in 1817. He also submitted a scheme for the entire building, including the central block, which he covered with a low dome of the type which he had already used in both the Bank of Pennsylvania and the Baltimore Cathedral. This monumental proposal, with certain significant modifications, formed the basis of the final building as completed by Charles Bulfinch, who succeeded

him in office (Fig. 287). Except for Bulfinch's dome, which was much higher than the one he planned,[6] Latrobe was able to impose something of his own artistic and practical vision upon the building, and thus elevate it from the depths of mediocrity to levels of quality, both in appearance and convenience, that were more appropriate to its exalted role as the first Capitol of the nation.[7]

Latrobe's touch is particularly evident in many of the individual parts. A characteristic example is the ground floor vestibule of the Senate wing (Fig. 288). The smooth rhythmic surfaces of the canopy vault and the delicate scale of the moldings are rational Neoclassical elements of the purest kind, and we are reminded at once of the architect's similar spatial effects in the Baltimore Cathedral. To these qualities has been added an interesting personal element. Supporting the vault just described, and positioned at the tapered point of the pendentive triangles, are capitals of a most unusual and imaginative design (Fig. 289 a). In place of the acanthus leaf motif of the traditional ancient capital, the architect has used an American motif, the ear of corn; for the fluting of the column he has used the stalk. A similar evocation of a native natural form is found in the small rotunda of the old Senate wing. Here he used the tobacco leaf (Fig. 289 b). We remember that the Abbé Laugier urged modernization of the ancient orders (poetic license which would never have occurred to the pedestrian Thornton) and so in one sense Latrobe performed here as a dedicated Neoclassicist. At the same time, he sought to make his forms directly expressive of the American environment. It is indicative of the literal-mindedness of the American Congress that they found more to applaud in these simple details than in the architect's impressive achievements in the building itself.

As well as rebuilding and completing parts of the Capitol, Latrobe did other works for the government. It was he, for example who designed the colonnaded portico which now graces the front of the President's House (Fig. 290)—a proposal later carried out by Hoban himself. Latrobe thus added to the building the qualities of monumentality which were so lacking in Hoban's original scheme. But equally important was the fireproof addition to the old Treasury Building which he planned and executed in the years 1805–6. The Treasury Department had already suffered one serious fire and was eager to find a building method which would help eliminate this ever present danger. Latrobe met this problem by vaulting his addition throughout, a solution which proved to be correct, for in a later fire, his was the only part of the building not destroyed. Robert Mills was working for Latrobe at the time this building was in

FIGURE 288. *Benjamin Latrobe. United States Capitol, Washington, D.C., ground floor vestibule, Senate wing, 1815–17.*

FIGURE 289. *Benjamin Latrobe. United States Capitol,
Washington, D.C. (a) Corn capital. (b) Tobacco capital.*

FIGURE 290. *Benjamin Latrobe. President's House,
Washington, D.C., portico, 1807.*

progress and it is highly probable that it influenced the younger man in
the designing of his own fireproof building in Charleston seventeen years
later. It was also to have a direct bearing on his still later design for
the new Treasury Building.

Robert Mills in Washington: the Treasury Building

When Robert Mills came to Washington in 1830, he was first employed as a draftsman in the Land Office. In this position he seems also to have served as an architectural adviser to the Secretary of the Treasury, and in 1833 he was asked to write a report on yet another disastrous fire in the Treasury Building.[8] In the document which he submitted he emphasized that Latrobe's fireproof wing had not burned, a fact which he attributed to the vaulted construction. At the same time, with an eye to the future, he prepared his first plans for a new Treasury Building. Because of a controversy between the President and the House Committee on Public Buildings and Grounds, however, no action was taken until three years later. Then on July 5, 1836, orders came from President Jackson, requesting Mills to appear the next morning at 10:00, and to bring his plans.[9] At their meeting Jackson appointed Mills to a position which the architect himself later called "Architect of Public Buildings." This made him an independent officer of the government, responsible directly to the President. A few days earlier, an act of Congress authorized a new Treasury Building and provided $100,000 for construction; in addition it contained provisions for a new Patent Office.[10] Three years later Mills was commissioned to design a new Post Office. Within a very short time, therefore, he found himself completely involved in the design and construction of the three most important government buildings since the completion of the Capitol and the President's House.

Of the three, the Treasury Building was the most important and the most controversial in Mills's career. As it survives today it is also the best one in which to study his style and his method. Although the building was later considerably enlarged, and a number of minor modifications have been made to the interior, the original T-shaped building, designed and built by Mills, is virtually intact. It is located on Fifteenth Street, facing east, between the converging lines of Pennsylvania and New York avenues. This location has been a source of violent controversy ever since the building was originally conceived. Because of his respect for L'Enfant's plan, Mills proposed to site the building fifty feet back from Fifteenth Street, and in a position that would not obstruct the vista from the Capitol to the President's House. Disagreement on this point ensued, however, and the issue was finally decided by President Jackson himself, who directed that it should be built immediately on Fifteenth Street. This was to hamper Mills in the development of his main entrance, and it also placed the building in such a way that when the south wing was added in the 1850's, it interrupted the view down Pennsylvania Avenue. Although Mills has been criticized for this, he was in no way responsible for the location of the building.[11]

The basic problems which confronted Mills in planning the Treasury Building were identical to those he had had to cope with in the Fireproof Building in Charleston. They were: to provide efficiently arranged office

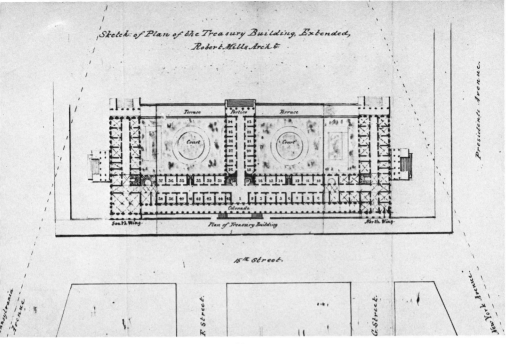

FIGURE 291. *Robert Mills. Treasury Building,*
Washington, D.C., plan, 1836–42. Original drawing made by Mills 1847–53.

spaces, and to make the building fireproof. His solution was essentially
the same as that employed in his earlier building (Fig. 291). He developed opposing ranges of office cells, separated from one another by
long internal corridors. Each office cell is contained within a groin-vaulted
bay (Fig. 292); the corridors are barrel-vaulted (Fig. 293). There is thus
a characteristic Millsian relationship between the structure and the spatial
arrangement. The magnitude of the Treasury Building, however, far exceeded anything Mills had ever confronted before. But the flexibility of
his structural system made it possible for him to meet the requirements
easily. He had only to repeat his structural module to achieve as many
spaces as necessary.

Mills's plan for the Treasury Building was simplicity itself (Fig. 291).
Working with a central stair well as the core, he extended the balancing
corridors left and right, to form a long continuous means of access through
the entire length of the building. On either side of the center stairs and
on each side of the corridor he provided six rooms, for a total of twelve
in each lateral wing, or a total of twenty-four for the entire length of
the building. These he further subdivided into blocks of three by means
of two cross corridors, each of which gave access to a secondary stairs.

Behind the stair well at right angles to the main block, he extended a
wing with four rooms and a water closet on either side of the corridor.
As first built, therefore, the over-all plan was a short T with the main
entrance and vertical circulation at the crossing, with horizontal circu-

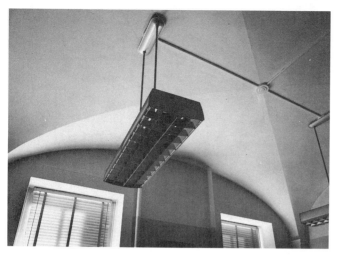

FIGURE 292. *Robert Mills. Treasury Building,*
Washington, D.C., office, groin vaults, 1836–42.

FIGURE 293. *Robert Mills. Treasury Building,*
Washington, D.C., corridor, 1836–42.

lation left, right, and straight ahead from this point, and with secondary vertical circulation in the center of each side of the line crossing the T. As described by Mills in 1847, it was a building "extending 336 feet with a depth in the center . . . including the colonnade in front and portico in the rear . . . of 190 feet. Each floor contains forty-nine apartments, or in the three stories above the basement, 135 rooms. (Note: this building when completed . . . by the extension of wings . . . will have a facade of nearly 500 feet with its porticoes)."[12] It is clear from this, and from the plan which was published with his description, that the rear wing terminated in a portico, and that Mills intended the building to have north and south wings, each with a central portico. This would have made the final plan an E rather than a T (Fig. 291). Along with its superb colonnade on Fifteenth Street, therefore, it would also have had monumental porticoes facing on Pennsylvania and New York avenues. It is essentially in this form that the building was later completed by the Treasury Department.[13]

If the straightforward nature of Mills's plan made it eminently efficient, its strength and security were assured by the architect's supremely integrated structural system. Because the building is vaulted throughout, it is dynamic. As in Gothic architecture, force is opposed by counterforce in a self-contained logical system, thus each part is responding to the pressure of the adjacent parts and is essential to the structural whole. Except for the Baltimore Cathedral, no other building in America at the time was conceived and executed with such an overriding integration of structure and form. Thrusts are exerted and contained from bay to bay and from vault to outer wall in a poised coherent sequence. Moreover, each structural unit is also a practical unit, with each segment of working space contained by either a barrel or a groin vault.

The heart of Mills's system was the continuous barrel vaults of the corridors which ran the entire length and depth of the building in both the main block and the central wing (Fig. 293). The lateral thrusts generated by these vaults were contained by the counterthrusts of the groined vaults which lined them on either side (Fig. 292). The action of the groined vaults, on the other hand, was more complex. Converging like branches to the trunk of a tree, all the thrusts were carried down the diagonal lines of the groins themselves to the corners of each bay, where they were met by the reciprocal groins of the adjoining bay. On the outside of the building, both the thrust and the vertical pressure were carried and buttressed by the walls.[14]

The actual construction of the building was not without its problems for Mills. The first of these was the selection of the materials to be used. Since he would be vaulting throughout, it was his intention to lay up all the walls with granite. On this point, however, he was frustrated by Congress. In 1791 the Government had purchased a quarry on an island at the confluence of the Potomac River and the Acquia Creek. This location was not far from Washington and the stone from the quarry, which was called Acquia stone, could be transported to the city by water. The advantages of this were obvious. But Acquia stone was also easily worked and had, in fact, already been used in the construction of both the Capitol and the President's House. In Mills's opinion, the Acquia stone was too soft to serve his structural intentions, but for economic reasons he was forced to use it. The architect makes this clear in a letter to Congress, dated February 1838: ". . . there is no question in the choice between the freestone and the granite, or the marble. When the subject was under consideration with the President, I respectfully urged the adoption of granite, but the decision by act of Congress had to be based on the least costly of the cut stone material, and the freestone was the selection."[15] Serious problems with the maintenance of the building, later proved Mills's judgment to have been correct.[16]

The vaults throughout the building were laid up in brick, and here Mills's difficulties were not with the quality of the material but with the almost total lack of masons who were qualified to turn the groin vaults. He was therefore forced to train them. At first it took up to seven days to accomplish a single bay, but later, after training, this time was cut in half. In constructing the vaults the architect used the recently developed hydraulic cement, which produced a far greater cohesion of material than did the traditional lime mortar. It was also much less susceptible to settling under compression. As Mills himself put it, the hydraulic cement made the vaults "like one mass of masonry relieving the lateral and increasing the perpendicular press of the arches."[17] This made possible a high degree of stability in the building as a whole, but it was also an important factor in the architect's calculation of the thickness of the walls. To bear the loads he imposed upon them, recognized standards called for walls three feet six inches thick. But Mills's walls are only two feet three inches, thus reducing considerably both the amount of materials and the cost. At the same time several square feet of interior space were gained in each room.

The simple logic of Mills's structural system is clearly expressed in his handling of the details. The basic shapes of the interior spaces are the shapes of the structure itself. Throughout the entire building, the ceilings are formed by the sweeping curves of the vaults. Those in the corridors are semi-cylindrical planes (Fig. 293), in the office spaces they are curved triangular planes with a slightly elliptical configuration (Fig. 292). Where these planes intersect they form sharply defined edges. There is no molded or incised ornament whatsoever to destroy the pure geometry of the system.

In the corridors, the spring of the barrel vault is articulated by a partial entablature made up of a frieze and cornice, but without an architrave (Fig. 294). The cornice is a stripped-down bundle of the simplest possible classical profiles and is not permitted to project very far from the wall. The top of this cornice is placed precisely at the spring of the vault. The frieze, in typical Millsian fashion, is a pure flat surface. The architect has kept it in the same plane as the wall itself, and has defined its bottom limit by a narrow rectilinear channel. This appears as a finely scaled fillet molding, but because it is recesssed rather than projecting it does not break the continuity of the wall. In this same spirit, all the

FIGURE 294. Robert Mills. Treasury Building,
Washington, D.C., corridor intersection, 1836–42.

door and window surrounds are unmolded flat planes, rather broad in
proportions, but held so close to the wall as to be almost imperceptible.

The small cross corridors, which once gave access to the secondary
stairs, have barrel vaults which cross the main corridor at the mid-points
left and right of the main stair well. They are the same height and width
as the barrel vault of the main corridor and thus form symmetrical groins
at the point of intersection. These areas have since been closed off to
make additional rooms, so that the spatial accent which they once provided has been destroyed, but Mills's method of handling the secondary
intersections is still apparent in the walls of the main corridor (Fig. 294).
Left and right of the arched opening itself (now walled up) he articulates
each end of what were once the cross-corridor walls by means of a broad
pilaster which projects only slightly. This creates a second level of plane
which passes into the partial entablature, thus forming a kind of capital.
It then continues up into the curved plane of the main barrel vault. To
accent the actual crossing, Mills outlines the groins with a finely scaled
ovolo molding. This is his only concession to sculptural effect on the entire
surface of the vaults. The groin section is thereby set apart from the

FIGURE 295. *Robert Mills. Treasury Building, Washington, D.C., stairs, 1836–42.*

barrel vault as a contrasting structural bay and as such it becomes a visual point of rest in the stretching sweep of the corridor.

Both functionally and aesthetically the dramatic center of the design is the main stairway (Fig. 295). Here the confined directional space of the long corridor suddenly opens up through five structural bays to move in a clean right-angled break rearward into the corridor of the back wing. On either side of the intersection of the corridors, the space flows upward and downward through the full height of the building. In creating this effect Mills does not alter his structural system. The barrel-vaulted profile

FIGURE 296. *Robert Mills. Treasury Building, Washington, D.C., view up stairs, 1836–42.*

of the main corridor continues unbroken from one end of the building to the other; at the center, the barrel vault of the back wing cuts into it to form a pivotal groin. Horizontal circulation thus remains unimpeded.

To open the corridors to the stair well Mills introduces five additional open groins, two on either side of the center in the main corridor and one in the back corridor. These he supports on the stair well side with four Greek Doric columns, one at the corner of each structural bay. It is from the capitals of these columns that the sequence of groins springs. The columns are heavily proportioned and are unfluted except for a short piece immediately below the necking; the echinus cushions are rather widely flaring. By virtue of these columns the central space is freed of containing walls and opens up for two bays on either side of the center into the unencumbered vertical shafts of the stair wells (Fig. 296).

The stairs ascend from the side of the main corridor, through the extreme left and right bays, in graceful compound curves to the back wall of the wells. From here they continue toward one another in straight runs to the next floor level, emerging in the open groined bay of the back corridor. The stairs themselves are cantilevered from the wall, and each one overlaps slightly the one immediately below. By means of a corbeling effect, part of the stress is thereby communicated from one step to another downward through the whole flight to the crown of the vaults of the corridor below. The stairs thus seem to rise without visible inner support in a sweeping upward ascent; and seen from below, the bottom of each step curves upward from front to back. The visual effect is not unlike the rhythmic undulations of the fluting on a Doric column (Fig. 296).

The treads overhang the stairs slightly and are turned by an echinus molding which in turn is supported by a delicate fillet and a small gracefully curving cove. Reaffirming the rhythm step to step, and binding the entire stairway system into a coherent whole, are the opposing spirals of the wooden handrail. Starting at the very bottom, it ascends without interruption to the top, now turning, now straight, in one continuous line. The rail iself is carried on extremely slender round metal balusters, spaced evenly and rather closely in a sequence of three per tread. Each baluster is encircled slightly above its center by a half-round molding. This adds a secondary spiraling line, this time broken, which echoes in light staccato accents the primary sweeping rhythm of the handrail itself.

From the functional point of view the height and placement of the handrail is precisely right for a person of average size, its shape and texture are molded to the human hand. This, together with the delicate scale of the balusters, establishes an immediate rapport with the men and women who use the building. In contrast to this harmonious relationship, a descent of the stairs is less secure. The hypnotic downward attraction of the rapidly converging spiral is an awesome experience for even the most seasoned mountain climber. To reassure the more timid souls it regrettably became necessary to add the appalling brass handrail which now despoils the top of the wooden one, and shatters the simple grace of Mills's original design.

The interior of the Treasury Building represents Robert Mills at his finest. It is clean and strong, but it is also dynamically graceful and has been accomplished without a single conceit through the simplest possible means. Its origins in the architect's earlier work are obvious enough, but in this, his first major commission for the federal government, the roughness has been smoothed away while the vitality remains and Mills reaches new heights of refined control. It contains those qualities which are the mark of all great rational architecture, and in his own way Mills must be regarded as among the earliest precursors in America of the great contemporary purists such as Philip Johnson. In fact, as a native-born architect, inspired by a European-born master, he stands in the same relationship with Latrobe as Johnson does with Mies van der Rohe. At the same time, because of his command of vaulting, he stood dramatically apart from his own building tradition.

Nowhere is this more apparent than in a comparison between his stairway in the Treasury Building and Charles Bulfinch's in the Lancaster Meetinghouse (Fig. 204). At first glance the two are seen to have much in common. Both are developed in austere geometric terms with an absolute economy of means, both are superbly scaled to man, both have qualities of refined elegance. But Bulfinch's design is dominated by the thin flat planes and straight lines of post-and-lintel construction, and although his stairs spring lightly upward, they do so through the sharp joints of intersecting panels. The movement is angular, stiff, and prim. Mills's design, however, is dynamic. It moves easily and smoothly through the curved lines and planes of the vaults. Moreover, the architect's bold articu-

FIGURE 297. *Robert Mills. Treasury Building, Washington, D.C., colonnade, 1836–42.*

lation of the masonry construction gives it qualities of weight and muscularity which are totally lacking in Bulfinch's judicious thin walls and panels. The New Englander was conspicuously inspired in this mature work by the Rational Neoclassical movement, but in the end he was never able to forsake altogether either his own tradition or his own Puritan taste. Mills, on the other hand, both in theory and in practice, was moving toward wider horizons with aggressive self-confidence, and in a manner wholly in line with the main streams of action in his own time. In spite of Bulfinch's obvious concessions to some of the more radical aspects of Neoclassical doctrine the difference between his work and that of Mills is essentially the difference between the traditional and rational phases of American Neoclassicism.

In some ways the exterior of the Treasury Building was a more complicated problem for Mills than the interior. His natural sensitivities as a designer would have inclined him toward severe treatment which we have already encountered in the Monumental Church and in the Fireproof Building. But Washington was not Richmond or Charleston. As a planned city it was a scheme of the most grandiose proportions, demanding commensurately grandiose embellishments. More than that, it was the capital of a new nation with all that this implied in terms of monumentality, dignity, and appropriate symbolic references. Mills's plain style was sharply in tune with the everyday working world of America, but for the buildings of the national capital, which would be generally viewed as the high style image of the nation at large, it must have seemed to him to be unduly severe. At least his design for the façade of the Treasury Building would seem to indicate that this was so.

The main block of his building presented a continuous front on 15th Street, from Pennsylvania Avenue almost to G Street. Because the building had been located immediately on 15th Street it was impossible for Mills efficiently to develop a monumental approach. He therefore did precisely what the site suggested. He extended across the entire façade a colossal Greek Ionic colonnade three hundred and thirty-six feet long (Fig. 297); on a high basement, there were thirty giant columns, each three stories in height, which carried a continuous Ionic entablature. Crowning the whole was a balustrade, and there was no central pediment to break its continuity. As Mills pointed out, "the effect of a continuous colonnade . . . is both grand and imposing; and its utility justifies its introduction."[18]

To solve the problem of the approach to the building, Mills introduced two straight flights of lateral steps which ascended from left and right of the center. These he masked behind a simple block entrance which gave immediately onto the sidewalk. Entrance could be gained either through doors on the street level into the basement, or up the flanking steps to the main floor and into the principal entrance foyer. Mills's reasons for doing this are revealing; "there is still room enough on the 15th Street front, for the ascent of the steps, without encroaching upon the foot-ways. The principal entrances to the buildings being intended on the south and north, the entrance from 15th Street becomes subordinate. It was to avoid the appearance of steps on this front, (which was advisable for the effect of the colonnade,) that the disposition of the side steps was introduced."[19] As first built there were no ends to the colonnade, but the north and south wings planned by Mills would not only have provided main entrances through imposing pedimented porticoes, but they would also have projected toward 15th Street as pavilions, and would thus have served (and do now so serve) as enframing motifs for the colonnade (Fig. 297).

Mills's continuous colonnade for the 15th Street front of the Treasury Building served to unify the practical and symbolic functions of the building. The long extended block of offices which it screened was a type of building that had never been used before in America. It was a starkly utilitarian building with a sequence of identical working cells on either side of a continuous corridor. It is precisely the concept which is still used for office buildings except that the orientation today is now vertical rather than horizontal. The rhythmic recurrence of identical cells along the horizontal stretch of the building was as regular as the groined bays which shaped them. The central stair wells, which interrupted the offices on the back side of the building, were articulated by the rear wing and its pedimented portico. On the 15th Street side, however, the line of groined bays was continuous, and the unbroken rhythm of the columns was a superb affirmation of this functional and structural condition.

The colonnade was also symbolically appropriate to a federal office building in the grandiloquent scheme of the city itself. The great colonnades fronting both the Capitol and the President's House had established a high classical idiom which met with the unqualified approbation of knowledgeable people both in this country and abroad. It would never have occurred to Mills, who was a stanch Neoclassicist, to have questioned the rightness of this point of view. A classical colonnade was the noblest possible symbol of the lofty concept of federal government. What is significant, however, and altogether indicative of his own enlightened view of classicism, is that he chose the Greek Ionic order. The Doric order might have seemed too severe for the graceful embellishment of the emerging city; it was better reserved for the more practical regions of the working spaces within. At the same time, the Corinthian order of the Capitol Building was too ornate for Mills's personal taste.[20] The Greek Ionic order, elegant and poised on the one hand, yet structurally pure on the other, was a happy concession both to the classical shape of the city, and to the practical realities of the working arm of the government. It was altogether a stroke of inspired genius which brought to the national city the most coherent and expressive work of architecture yet designed by a native American. The Treasury Building is still a magnificent monument which, in a city of grand pretensions, is poignantly conspicuous for its simplicity and utter honesty.

Yet in 1838, in one of the most bizarre procedures ever perpetrated by any American legislative body, a report was introduced into the House of Representatives which recommended the demolition of the half-finished Treasury Building and the use of its materials in the proposed Post Office Building. This fantastic proposal came as the climax to an accumulation of congressional criticism against Mills and the Treasury Building. In one sense it was criticism of the same kind that had plagued Latrobe through his years of government service, and which seems inevitable in the American form of government, where every member of Congress, by virtue of his position of authority, automatically becomes an expert in all phases of human endeavor. In the case of the Treasury Building, however, the opposition was particularly intense, motivated by political maneuvering, ambition, and jealousy. It was led by the chairman of the House Committee on Public Buildings and Grounds, a militant congressman from Massachusetts by the name of Levi Lincoln. To give professional support to his conspicuous bias, Lincoln, with the consent of President Van Buren, employed a promising young Philadelphia architect, Thomas U. Walter, to study the Treasury Building and submit a report. Walter had obviously been well briefed, for his report, which was included as part of the House Report, sustained all the major points of criticism raised by Lincoln.[21] The most important issues were the site, the interior arrangements, the appearance (Walter objected to the uninterrupted colonnade), and the construction. None of Walter's objections was justified, but of the four it was the construction which drew his most damning criticism. With smug self-assurance he reported that Mills's "plan of arching can never be executed with safety to the building. The arches in the lower story would probably stand, provided that the centres are kept under them until the walls receive the superincumbent weight of the structure; but the fate of the upper arches, if executed upon the same plan is certain."[22]

On the basis of Walter's report, a bill to demolish the Treasury Building was introduced into the House by Lincoln and subsequently defended by him in a long and dreary speech which would seem to have assured the end of Mills's building.[23] Two months later, however, when the bill was again up for consideration, Mills had a defender. In a lively attack upon Lincoln's dour polemics Representative Keim of Pennsylvania uncovered a devastating inconsistency in Walter's report. Addressing himself to the architect's predictions concerning the vaults, he pointed out that "if ever the climax of hypothesis was indulged in, this is it. Not satisfied with anticipating evils, they unhesitatingly, and without qualification, predict: 'that the fate of the building is certain.' The building itself, however, exhibits a palpable contradiction of the assertion of Mr. Walter. . . . Now let any member of this house for himself, visit the premises . . . and he will find the very centres 'struck' in both stories, and the naked truth developed, that . . . the walls stand firm and unmoved, without showing either settlement or crack, notwithstanding they are open to very severe weather at all points."[24]

It would seem that Walter, with appalling cynicism, had not even inspected the building. In view of his growing reputation as an engineer this seems incredible, but his willingness to support Levi Lincoln may have borne fruit in the end, for in 1851 he was appointed Architect to the Capitol. Mills's own report to the Committee, made in rebuttal to Walter's, is a clear and persuasive document, and with the help of Keim's speech the bill to demolish his great work was defeated, but by the fantastically narrow margin of only three votes. The final count was ninety-four to ninety-one.

Representative Keim not only understood the practical aspects of Mills's achievement, but he also recognized that its simplicity and strength were eloquently expressive of the emerging new nation. Mills was very much aware of his responsibilities as an architect and strove constantly to make his work relevant to his time, his country, and its institutions. Keim sensed this quality deeply and concluded his defense of Mills with a remarkable reflection on the nature of American architecture. "Some effort should be made on our part," he said, "to be inventors, instead of followers of any system. If science is progressive, so should the polite arts keep pace with them, and American architecture become a new school, in which might predominate as a characteristic feature, the principles of economy, simplicity, and convenience. . . .

"Instead of making this the counterfeit imitation of 'The Eternal City,' would it not be conducive to our better interest if the same simplicity were preserved which the spirit of our constitution inculcates . . . ours is a primitive, not a secondary, Government, . . . having a common interest, and pledged in a common defence of civil and religious rights. Amongst us the gaudy trappings of royalty find no throne to embellish; our only sceptre is the law, and our only sovereign is the people's will. Since, then, it is congenial with all our habits, let us compare our government to a plain, unadorned column, whose base is the people; the shaft the constitution; and the capital the laws.

"Utility is emphatically the American order, and look where you may, it will be found to be consonant with the feelings, as it is compatible with American taste."[25]

Ralph Waldo Emerson had already said essentially the same thing a year earlier in his *American Scholar,* an essay which is generally regarded as America's cultural declaration of independence. But a year earlier than that the Treasury Building, which Keim recognized as so thoroughly American, had been started. Moreover, it was preceded in Mills's own work by two equally revolutionary buildings, the Fireproof Building in Charleston, South Carolina, and the Monumental Church in Richmond, Virginia; and behind them all lay the work of Jefferson, which was as fierce in its rejection of British domination as the Declaration of Independence itself. The truth is that America's cultural independence was not achieved first in literature, but in architecture, and the Treasury Building, far from being a beginning, represents a well advanced condition of precisely the kind of national awareness that Emerson so eloquently urged on his fellow Americans.

The Greek Revival: The Permeation of the Rational Doctrine

Together with Latrobe's Baltimore Cathedral, Mills's Treasury Building was the most accomplished work of the rational phase of American Neoclassicism. It was also the most rationally conceived building yet designed by an American-born architect. It was efficiently planned within a particular American context, and it was boldly executed with extraordinary qualities of geometric simplicity and revealed structure. Its sheer muscularity alone brought to Washington a freshness and vitality which were more in tune with the aggressive national temperament than was the tired dignity of the President's House and the Capitol.

If because of its simplicity, strength, and honesty the Treasury Building was theoretically Neoclassical, it was also aesthetically so, for no matter how much we might wish to stress the rational and practical aspects of Mills's style, the fact remains that he had an ardent enthusiasm for Greek architecture, and that in the end he regarded it as the perfect style for expressing the ideals of American democracy. Nor was Mills alone in this point of view. In the 1830's, when he first took up his duties in Washington, the Greek style was already becoming the dominant mode of building in the United States. By the time he left office in 1851, it had permeated from the high style through the low style to the folk level of American architecture, and geographically had extended to every corner of the land. Adopted by the common man as well as the professional, it became the first style in American history to be consciously understood and embraced as a truly national mode of building.

There were several reasons for this. The first was the strength of the Neoclassical movement itself. Being primitive and practical, it was readily acceptable to a vigorous and rapidly expanding nation. Indeed, it could not have found a more sympathetic environment in which to flourish. Then, too, the Greek Style was attractive to Americans because of its obvious symbolic relevance. In addition it had all the familiar paraphernalia of classicism, which meant that its adoption did not signify an unmanageable break with the respected classicism of the colonial years. In many instances, the only thing necessary to foster the new spirit was to substitute Greek for colonial details.

The enthusiasm for Greek architecture was also inspired by the powerful influence of classical studies, which had long been a part of the American educational system. The kind of training which Jefferson received at William and Mary was typical. In response to the archaeological and intellectual developments of the late eighteenth century, it was heavily weighted on the side of the classics. The excavations of Winckelmann at Troy, the writings of Goethe, the powerful classical sentiment that permeated French culture at the time of the Revolution (and was glorified in the paintings of Jacques Louis David), all these were symptoms of the broadening knowledge of the ancient world. Reflecting these developments in Europe, America established the study of the classics as a foundation stone of liberal education.

After the Revolution, with the formation of the American democratic system, a sense of kinship with the democracy of ancient Greece began to take shape in the American consciousness. By 1800, this would manifest itself in fascinating ways. Consider the names of some of the towns in central and western New York State which, after the opening of the Erie Canal in 1827, became important centers of activity during the years of the Western expansion. Here there are no Exeters, Hamptons, Hudsons, or Rhinebecks, but rather Troy, Ithaca, Utica, Syracuse, as though in the favored stronghold of the American frontier the democracy of ancient Greece could somehow be made to live again. Stirred by the Greek war for independence, a pro-Greece sentiment swept over most of the settled parts of the country like a gathering wave. Perhaps no other single event of the decade had a more profound effect upon American culture. Already caught up in their own search for national identity, the Americans saw in the Greek war the exact counterpart of their own struggle against the British. Whereas Lord Byron was moved as an individual to plead for the Greeks through poetry (and in the end sacrifice his own life to the cause), the Americans, by building throughout the country in the Greek manner, were able as an entire people to identify with the Greeks. From government building to church, house, warehouse, and store—even to privy, the Greek temple and the Greek orders became the outward manifestation of the inward sentiment. Never before in their history had the American people sought more deliberately a viable symbol of their cultural independence.

Into this ferment came an eager and youthful architectural profession, a new generation of men infected by the spirit of their age and motivated by architectural standards that had been unknown to their predecessors. Although their individual styles, and even their methods, would vary, they were all thoroughly schooled in Neoclassical doctrine. They were easily persuaded therefore that in the architecture of ancient Greece were all the essential ingredients of a new and expressive American style. Greek architecture was simple, logical, and dignified. Moreover, it was recognized by all knowledgeable men as the supreme visual embodiment of the oldest democracy on earth; its relevance to their own aspirations needed no exposition. They built joyously and creatively in the Greek style.

At the top of this profession stood the great innovators, Latrobe and Mills. Close behind them, but pressing hard for the advantage, was a group of newcomers, some of them of Mills's generation, some still younger, all talented, all totally committed, all qualified in varying degrees as engineers as well as designers. There was the brilliant but erratic genius in Philadelphia, William Strickland, who was only slightly younger than Mills, and who like Mills had worked in the office of Latrobe.[26] Also from Philadelphia and coming from Strickland's office was Thomas U. Walter, the presumptuous young architect who was brought to Washington by Levi Lincoln to report on Mills's Treasury Building. In Boston was the plodding but productive Alexander Parris. He worked for a time as an executive for Bulfinch in the building of the Massachusetts General Hospital, and later turned out to be one of the most accomplished architects and engineers of his day.

Perhaps most important of all was the firm of Town and Davis in New York, the first fully developed architectural firm in the United States.[27] Ithiel Town, its founder, was a man of wide cultural attainments and seems to have been the administrative head of the firm. He was also an engineer who won world renown for his famous lattice truss, an ingenious device which was used as the main structural element in many of the covered bridges of New England. Alexander Jackson Davis, who joined the firm in 1829, was just the opposite of his partner. A true artist with numerous talents and an inexhaustible imagination, Davis approached architecture in a pictorial, not merely a structural, way. Sensing, as so many great artists have, the kinship between the visual arts and music, he always referred to himself as an "architectural composer," and tended to develop his buildings as much from a visual as from a purely geometric point of view. At the same time he appears as a confirmed rationalist, and his classical works in particular show remarkable qualities of structural invention.

Davis was enormously aided in his designing by his extraordinary fluency as a draftsman and water-colorist. He was thus able to develop his ideas with precision and warmth. Yet as the work of a true romantic, his designing has many facets, not all of them consistent with one another. Early in his career with the firm he designed some of the finest Greek buildings of the period. Later, his picturesque imagination seems sometimes to have prevailed over his sense of reason, and ultimately he became one of the most influential leaders in the romantic-eclectic movement of the first half of the nineteenth century.

And there were others, young men practicing in every center of population in America, to form the core of the new profession. Frequently

FIGURE 298. Henry Walters and A. J. Davis. Ohio State Capitol,
Columbus, 1838.

less harassed by the suspicions and other encumbrances which made
Latrobe's life so difficult, this new generation of architects won increasing
recognition for its professional competence. All of them worked in the
Greek style, but some, following the lead of Latrobe and Mills, performed in the rational style with emphasis on geometric form. In their
work, therefore, the more sophisticated aspects of the Neoclassical movement would be brought to wider reaches of the American scene. An excellent example is the State Capitol in Columbus, Ohio (Fig. 298). It
was designed by Henry Walters of Cincinnati in 1838. The history of
this building is too complex to recount here[28] but it is important to
record that Alexander Jackson Davis was called to Columbus to serve as
a consultant, and it seems probable that something of his own ideas are
reflected in the ultimate design.

The Ohio State Capitol is a long horizontal structure centered around
a colossal freestanding Greek Doric colonnade and has balancing wings
left and right. The columns of the colonnade are held back within the
plane of the wall so that there is no projecting portico. Both the rhythm
and the structural intentions of the columns, however, are carried into the
lateral wings by deep giant Doric piers. The entire façade, therefore, is
kept in a single plane, and it is unified at the top by a continuous, unbroken entablature which is common to both the columns and the piers.
Unlike its Greek prototype, the cornice is not the crowning element.
Instead, the entablature is topped by a low, completely unadorned parapet,

FIGURE 299. *Ithiel Town. Connecticut State Capitol,*
New Haven, 1827.

not unlike those used by Mills in his Monumental Church and in the
Fireproof Building. Set back from the plane of the entablature and
hovering above it, with no apparent structural relationship with the colonnade, is a depressed Doric pediment. The end façades of the building
are identical to the main façade except that they are shorter and do not
have a pediment. Centered above the entire design is a pure cylindrical
lantern, two stories high, with deep Doric pilasters and a perfectly plain
entablature.

The rational aspect of the building is seen at once in its pure geometric
character. The containment of the order within the plane of the wall,
and the combination of the cube and the cylinder, are familiar elements,
reminding us at once of Latrobe's Pump House in Philadelphia (Fig.
259), and less directly of Ledoux's Barrière de la Villette in Paris (Fig.
260). There is one feature of the design, however, which we do not find
in the earlier sources. This is the extension of both the rhythmic and
the functional purpose of the colonnade into the piers of the lateral wings.
In Greek architecture the column and the load-bearing wall are separate
things, each performing its own supporting role. In Roman architecture,
by contrast, the column was frequently engaged on the wall, as a purely
decorative device, and thus was robbed of its basic structural function. In
the Columbus Capitol the wall and the post-and-lintel systems are com-

bined. The deep piers, which seem to be merely part of the wall, are in fact performing as columns and are carrying the full weight of the entablature above. Because of this concentration of support the walls between the piers are drastically reduced in thickness and also contain the windows. What Walters and Davis have done, in other words, is to project the open post-and-lintel system of the Greek order around the entire building, as though it were a peripteral temple, and then to complete the enclosure they have simply added curtain walls between the posts. To be sure, their solution was locked within the rigid proportional system of the Greek order, and therefore enjoyed no freedom of extension. But it is a highly integrated and logical solution nevertheless and is one of the most rational developments of the period.

The origins of this are to be found in the work of Town and Davis and can be seen especially clearly in Town's design for the Connecticut State Capitol done eleven years earlier, in 1827, (Fig. 299). As seen in the original drawing, the building resembles a pure Greek Doric peripteral temple of the smaller type, such as the Theseum in Athens. But this resemblance is limited, for the only columns in the building are those which support the front and back pediments, six in each instance. The rest of the vertical supports, which extend along the two sides, are deep rectangular piers of the same proportions as the columns and spaced the same distance apart. Between these piers, and set well back so as to reveal the full supporting depth of the piers, are thin curtain walls and tall narrow windows which enclose a two-story interior. In this way the post-and-lintel structural system, on which the Greek temple was based, is maintained in its purest form; except for the change in shape from round to square, the rhythmic sequence of the supports has not been disturbed. At the same time, the full space behind the piers has been utilized for practical purposes. It is a highly ingenious scheme, comparable

FIGURE 300. *Alexander Jackson Davis.*
Project for a commercial exchange, c. 1860.

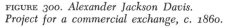

FIGURE 301. *Alexander Parris. Quincy Market,*
Boston, Mass., 1825.

in its simplicity to Mills's modular vaults, a scheme in which a coherent
structural system has been used to a practical end, yet which keeps alive
the fundamental geometry of the Doric temple.

Although cast in the visual form of an ancient architectural style, with
all its imposed limitations of proportion and decoration, the structural
idea developed by Town was exceptionally logical and seems to have
been the prelude to even more original applications by his partner A. J.
Davis.[29] Of these the most extraordinary is a later, unexecuted design for
a commercial exchange (Fig. 300). In a remarkable drawing in The
New-York Historical Society, which is dated about 1860, the architect
shows a simple Doric front of eight piers and an entablature. The building is without a pediment and is domed in the center. But between the
piers, for a height of four stories, and carried on pairs of tall and extremely
thin vertical supports, are windows which fill the entire space between the
piers. In this way Davis has transferred the support function from the
wall to the post, and thus, by utilizing the principle of the curtain wall
to the utmost, has made a clear visual separation between the weight
and density of the piers and the fragility and thinness of the glass and its
vertical supports. It is a priceless document of the artist's capacity to
combine the romantic and the rational in the same design.

Davis's primary means of achieving his contrast between support and
nonsupport is through scale. Between the heavy piers—whose proportions
were determined by their classical origin—Davis has placed secondary
supports which are as delicate and attenuated as the piers are thick and
dense. The bars which hold the glass are, in fact, so light that there can
be little doubt that the effect was made possible by the use of cast iron.

FIGURE 302. *Alexander Parris. Sears House, Boston, Mass., 1816.*

We know from his own testimony that Davis was among the first architects in America to use iron for structural and decorative purposes, and on the basis of other developments in iron during the same period, it seems certain that he achieved his remarkable effect of lightness and transparency by the use of the new material.[30] As a building, his exchange was designed to meet a contemporary need, and his proposed scheme was as visually inspired as it was rational. It was, to be sure, a masonry building, but in his concentration of support and his walls of glass, he anticipates by a quarter of a century the metal frame and curtain wall construction of the great commercial buildings erected in Chicago during the 1880's.

Davis was one of the most versatile and prolific architects of his time, and his work has qualities of excellence which set it conspicuously apart from that of his contemporaries. At a more plodding level, yet equally severe in its simplicity, is another important commercial building of the period, the Quincy Market in Boston, designed by Alexander Parris and built in 1825 (Fig. 301). The main building is a long extended horizontal block two stories high with a four-columned prostyle Doric temple at either end. In the center is a rectangular block, of squarish proportions, on top of which is a low dome of the Pantheon type. Windows are all cleanly cut without enframing surrounds, and are so large and closely spaced as to create the effect of pier rather than wall construction. Columns are unfluted, entablatures are plain, and nothing is permitted to penetrate

FIGURE 303. *Greek Revival house, 14 Louisburg Square, Boston, Mass., c. 1840.*

FIGURE 304. *Philip Hooker. Hyde Hall, near Cooperstown, N.Y., 1833.*

426 AMERICAN BUILDINGS AND THEIR ARCHITECTS

or project beyond the continuous flat plane of the mass. Constructed of Quincy granite, the building has less grace than Davis's design, but it is no less primitive in its geometry, and in the heart of red-bricked Federal Boston it must have been noticeably austere and heavy.

The Sears House on Beacon Hill (Fig. 302), also by Parris, is similar in effect. Here, in the sanctity of the most Bulfinchian part of Boston, and almost immediately adjacent to the master's third Harrison Gray Otis House, it presents an alien, protruding granite front. Built in 1816, only a decade after the Otis House, the sheer planes of its dressed ashlar masonry walls, and the bold projection of its semicircular bays (originally there was only one), taunt the flat gracious elegance of Bulfinch's finely scaled brick façade. Its highly rational geometry and crisply cut openings also set it apart from the other houses on Beacon Hill. The latter, even if built during the Greek Revival period, show no deviation whatsoever from the simple brick walls of the Bulfinch era. Indeed, they are Greek only because their doorways have Greek rather than Federal porticoes (Fig. 303).

Another example of domestic architecture from a different part of the eastern United States will serve to illustrate the permeation of the rational principles into the countryside as well as the city. Hyde Hall, near Cooperstown, New York, was designed by the Albany architect, Philip Hooker, and was built in 1833 (Fig. 304). Hooker, who died only three years after Hyde Hall was completed, spent most of his architectural career as a stanch disciple of the conservative Federal Style. In much of his work he combines its refined elegance with the local stone vernacular of eastern central New York State. Although the use of stone gives many of his buildings a large simplicity, he was not always able to reconcile its roughness of texture with the delicacy of Federal detail. Hyde Hall, however, as a late work, is clearly inspired by the rational doctrine and is one of the more accomplished provincial examples of the style.

The massing of Hyde Hall is conspicuously Neoclassical. The main block is a one-story horizontal rectangle, which is intersected in the center by a two-story block, topped by a pediment and fronted on the lower level by a severe Greek Doric portico. The basic geometrics could hardly be simpler or more clearly stated. The only significant projection from the straightforward planar theme is the portico, which has four unfluted Greek Doric columns and a plain entablature. This latter feature extends across the entire front of the building. The house is also without any ornamental embellishment. There are no curved moldings, and the windows are broadly proportioned and set low in the mass, with narrow horizontal recessed panels above. The building, however, is incoherent in scale. The second story of the central block has a diminutive pedimented temple front, with all of its elements much smaller in scale than the rest of the building. It appears as though it were a large building seen from the distance, and thus sits uncomfortably atop the bolder forms of the main block below. Although this is a contradiction which we would not find in Mills, the stark almost primitive character of the house gives it a strong Millsian flavor and one wonders whether Hooker was influenced by the work of the younger man.

FIGURE 305. *Larkin House,*
Portsmouth, N.H., 1815.

FIGURE 306. *Benjamin Latrobe. Burd House,*
Philadelphia, Pa., 1801–2.

Both the Sears House and Hyde Hall are stone buildings, and the exterior detailing in both has a Greek rather than a Federal flavor. Their identification with the rational phase of the Neoclassical movement is therefore complete. Equally interesting are those buildings of the period which were still Federal in detail, but which showed other qualities clearly inspired by rationalist principles. That the Sears House could have been built on Beacon Hill at all is symptomatic of a growing vitality in American architecture which could not be suppressed, a vitality which even enlivened the work of Bulfinch himself. The Lancaster Meetinghouse (Fig. 198), for example, leaves us with no doubt about the master's responsiveness to what the younger men were doing. More than that, what was true of Bulfinch was almost universally true throughout New England. In the midst of passive conformity were occasional flashes of rebellion, each adding in its own way to the changing character of the region. It is a delight to find one of the rarest of these in the very heart of one of the stanchest Federal strongholds in America, Portsmouth, New Hampshire. The Larkin House (Fig. 305), built there in 1815, would be a remarkable building under any circumstances, but amidst the doctrinaire three-story Federal fronts of Portsmouth it is like a sleek clipper ship in the company of blunt-nosed whalers. Not to look outlandish among its companions on the surrounding streets, the house has certain characteristics which are perfectly conventional. It is four-square, three stories high, and is crowned by a simple classical cornice. There are tall end chimneys, and on top of the whole is a widow's walk. But here the similarities cease. The four outer walls are pure unbroken planes of a superb red-orange brick, tightly and precisely laid up in Flemish bond. The central door, and the first- and second-floor windows of the façade, are all recessed beneath brick relieving arches. These are laid with stretchers, exactly in the plane of the wall. Except for the slight contrast in texture which results from the different patterns of the brickwork, there is no interruption of the taut flat surface.

The openings set within the wall arches are themselves round-headed and are framed in pure flat bands of white which project imperceptibly from the plane of the wall; crossing these surrounds at the spring of the arches are short horizontal white bands which join the inner and outer arches. The effect is not unlike a Palladian window set in a wall arch, the Adamesque device which was so popular during the Federal period. In fact, the first-floor windows are precisely that, with a large round-headed central window flanked by narrow square-headed side lights. In the door and second-floor windows, however, there are no side lights. Instead, these areas are filled in with brick rather than glass. The third-floor windows are small rectangles topped by flared white lintel stones. Over the main door is a circular fanlight of the simplest possible design. But nowhere in the building, except for the cornice, is there the slightest hint of authentic classical detail. All the elements which surround and support the windows and doors are stripped to the bone, without moldings of any kind, and are held exactly in the plane of the recessed wall.

We recognize here certain elements which we have already associated with the Federal Style. The flat brick wall with crisply cut openings, the refined scale, the recessed Palladian motifs within a recessed wall arch, all these recall Charles Bulfinch and in turn Robert Adam. Yet there is something unusually clean and unorthodox about this house. It is, in fact, so stripped of projecting elements and so distilled in detail that we are drawn irresistibly to an identification with rational rather than the traditional phase of the Neoclassical movement. The austerity and pure geometry of the building are very similar to what we have already encountered in Bulfinch's great essay in rationalism, the Lancaster church. Indeed, the Larkin House has been attributed to Bulfinch by local legend. One would like to believe this, for it is a building of the most delicately poised tensions, and is worthy of the great New Englander in every respect. But whoever designed it, its ties with rational Neoclassicism seem clear. A comparison with Latrobe's Burd House in Philadelphia (Fig. 306), built in the years 1801–2, leaves little doubt that the New England architect (or was he from Philadelphia?) knew the Burd House and borrowed freely from its highly original idiom.[31] Yet if anything, the Portsmouth house, with its fine harmony of parts and its more consistent scale, is even more coherent than Latrobe's design. It is a building of rare beauty which is made all the more provocative by its anonymity. As in the case of so many American buildings, it originated at that marvelous level of the unknown where the name of an individual can be set aside in favor of the building itself.

Another fruitful comparison, which will demonstrate the depth to which the rational ideals permeated American architecture, can be made between Bulfinch's Lancaster Meetinghouse and two other churches of the period, the Stone Temple in Quincy, Massachusetts, and the Congregational Church in Wellfleet on Cape Cod. The First Church of Quincy was designed by Alexander Parris, and was built in 1828 (Fig. 307). Because it is constructed of local granite it is known as the "Stone Temple." Now a Unitarian church, although originally Congregational, it is historically important because it was the church of the Adams family; in fact, the stone from which it was built was a gift from old John Adams, and both he and John Quincy Adams are buried in the crypt. It is therefore sometimes called the "Church of the Presidents."

Architecturally, the Stone Temple is both conservative and radically new. In its general massing it is conspicuously based on the Lancaster Meetinghouse, which was under construction when Parris was working for Bulfinch. Accordingly, Parris knew it well. That it should influence him is perfectly logical. At the same time, there are important differences between the two. The Quincy church is stonemasonry rather than brick, so that the walls are much heavier in scale; so too is the bold Greek Doric portico with its cylindrical unfluted columns and its unadorned entablature. The use of stone and the Greek portico, together with the recessed paneling in the clock tower, are familiar devices of the rational style, devices which Bulfinch avoided in his Lancaster church in favor of flat pilasters and large simple planes of finely scaled brick. Yet the Quincy church, with all its sturdy rationalism, is actually more derivative than the earlier design. In detail it is quite honestly—if naïvely—Greek,

FIGURE 307. *Alexander Parris. Stone Temple,*
Quincy, Mass., 1828.

and except for the fact that it is a Wren-Gibbs form of church, it is completely free of any of the traditional conventions of the Federal Style. In the directness of its adaptation it belongs unequivocally to the new movement.

The Greek Revival: Folk Manifestations

The Stone Temple is typical of a number of churches, built during the second quarter of the nineteenth century, in which both the formal aspects of the Greek style and the geometric largeness of the rational doctrine were combined with the traditional church form. It could hardly have been otherwise in Congregational New England. The fact that the Quincy church was stone, however, made it almost unique in its setting, as did its heavy scale and the severe character of the masonry. These qualities were the special mark of the new generation of architects, and were totally alien, both in scale and texture, to the wood architecture of America. It is all the more rewarding therefore to find the anonymous American builder, who was so utterly committed to wood, seeking ways to change the familiar material into forms which he admired but never really quite understood. In countless wood buildings of the period, the bold massing of Neoclassicism is there but not the coherence, the primitive geometry but not the substance; for the broadest expanses of surface, even when laid up with matched boards, cannot convey the weight and density of the load-bearing wall. The sheathed wood frame is membrane construction, a taut skin drawn over a stiffening and supporting armature. It is precisely because of this that Bulfinch's wood dome on the Massachusetts State House (Fig. 183) sits so uneasily on the brick wall below; it is also precisely because of this that the peripheral architecture of the Neoclassical period has qualities which separate it sharply from the high style rational buildings.

The First Congregational Church in Wellfleet, Massachusetts (Fig. 308), is extraordinary for its broad simple geometry. Cylinder, upon octagon, upon triangle, upon cube, these are the main ingredients.[32] Each geometric unit is sharply defined and distinct from its neighbor. All planes are expansive and uninterrupted. These are all familiar aspects of the rational style and in this building are executed with a provincial awkwardness which adds a brusque vitality to the strong primitivism implicit in its simple planes. Strange unorthodoxies transmute the classical elements. The depressed pediment and deep entablature of the portico betray the building's Greek origins, but the Doric pilasters seem to be over-tall in proportions, with recessed panels down their centers. This is a fairly common form of the Doric order in provincial Greek Revival wood architecture. Yet when examined closely each pilaster turns out to be not one but two extremely thin pilasters, so closely spaced as to appear as one. It is as though the builder, with his true loyalties still in the Federal Style, could not bring himself to make a pilaster in the proportions of the Greek Doric order. By putting two together he could create the effect without sacrificing principle. Similarly, although the pitch of the pediment over the portico is low in the Greek manner, the roof pitch is not. Here the traditional steep angle prevails, and the pediment is forced into unhappy isolation in a setting still resistant to change.

As a design, the Wellfleet Church is in no way remarkable. Indeed, it is a clumsy composite of unrelated and misunderstood elements, some drawn indirectly from the architectural ferment of the time, others persisting from a powerful tradition. It is provincial in the extreme. At the same time, it is a superb example of the ultimate permeation of the more creative aspects of Neoclassicism into the extreme periphery of American architecture. It belongs in the folk category of a building tradition which began in Europe as a philosophical and technical outburst of the Age of Reason, and finally spent its forces in rural America as a universally accepted symbol of democracy. Yet the significance of the Wellfleet Church derives not so much from the fact that it seems inspired by rational Neoclassicism as from the fact that it pretends to be "Greek." In our discussion so far we have had several occasions to refer to Greece, and we have also been making careful distinctions between rational Neoclassicism and what we have called "Greek Revival." Yet we have never fully

FIGURE 308. *First Congregational Church,*
Wellfleet, Mass., 1850. Spire, 1879.

demonstrated the Greek Revival, and to complete our story we must do so now.

The Greek Revival was the first pervasive and self-conscious nationalistic movement in American architecture. Although its initial impetus came at the professional level, where it was used for government buildings all over the land (Figs. 298, 299), the total national character came at the folk level, where it achieved the same fulfillment of aspiration toward architectural independence as Jefferson's idealistic adaptation of Roman architecture did more than a quarter of a century earlier.

Greek forms in the architecture of Latrobe and Mills and, to a lesser degree, in that of such innovative younger men as A. J. Davis were discreetly applied. In many instances they were so drastically modified and so tightly woven into a larger architectural purpose that they no longer appeared as Greek. In the work of some of the other younger men, however, such as Strickland and Walter, the Greek orders and the Greek ornamental system were used with deliberate authenticity. In the more extreme instances the closer the imitation of the Greek the more the work was revered, and in this drive for archaeological correctness we have one of the major ingredients of the Greek Revival.

Throughout the Neoclassical era, admiration for Greek architecture was almost universal, and came about primarily as a consequence of the ever-increasing body of specific knowledge about Greek buildings themselves. This knowledge was made available to American architects through books. Some of these were archaeological works, all of them published abroad, which provided specific and detailed data about actual Greek buildings. Others were builders' handbooks, some published abroad and some in this country, which carried the basic information about the Greek orders and Greek ornamental detail. The professional architects drew heavily on the more important archaeological publications. Ithiel Town, for example, brought together one of the largest architectural libraries in the country, as well as a large collection of engravings. He kept them in his home in New Haven and made them available to all his colleagues in the architectural profession. The local carpenters, however, relied on the builders' handbooks, books identical in intent and character to those used in the eighteenth century and differing only in that they presented Greek rather than Renaissance details. The most important ones published in the United States were by Asher Benjamin of Greenfield, Massachusetts, and Minard Lafever of New York. Benjamin's earliest publication, which appeared in

FIGURE 309. *William Strickland. Philadelphia Exchange, Philadelphia, Pa., 1832–34.*

1797, shows details in the Federal Style, but in the sixth edition of his *American Builder's Companion,* published in 1827, some Greek details were included. In his later works Greek orders and Greek ornament prevail. Lafever's first work was published in 1829. Subsequent editions by both men appeared as late as the 1850's. Since it was derived primarily from such sources, provincial Greek Revival architecture in America had a persistent bookishness. Certain house types, certain door motifs, certain ornamental details, would appear repeatedly over a wide range of the American scene, in a manner reminiscent of some of the stereotypes which left their mark on the architecture of the colonial years.

The first thing then that distinguishes the architecture of the Greek Revival from that of the rational Neoclassical movement was a much stricter adherence to the proportions and character of the Greek orders and the Greek ornamental system. William Strickland's Philadelphia Exchange, built between 1832 and 1834, is an interesting case in point (Fig. 309). Strickland was a contemporary of Robert Mills, and a fellow assistant in the office of Latrobe. Like Mills he was an engineer of commanding ability, and he shared Mills's enthusiasm for the Greek style. But his interest in it was less idealistic and more artistic. He was a more elegant designer than Mills, with a far greater sensitivity to the refinements of the Greek style. Where Mills saw its bold planes, Strickland saw its swelling curves and decorative richness, especially as found in the Ionic and Corinthian orders. Where Mills was moved by its rational geometry, Strickland was touched by its grace. Although the Philadelphia Exchange is conceived as a basic combination of cylinder and block, the walls of the primary cylinder are screened behind a circular Corinthian colonnade of the most delicate proportions and refined detail. Above the whole is a tall cylindrical lantern, based in shape and character on the Choragic Monument of Lysicrates in Athens. Like its prototype, it displays an elegant Corinthian order. Strickland, to be sure, has taken some liberties with the design of his Corinthian capitals, but in proportion and scale, and even in the details of the ornament, the Exchange is far more authentically classical in its outward grace than anything designed by Robert Mills.[33]

The same is true of Strickland even when he worked in the Doric style. His Second Bank of the United States in Philadelphia (Fig. 310) was the first public building in America to be based on the Parthenon (Fig. 1). It was designed in 1818, and was taken from the restored façade of the ancient building as illustrated in Stuart and Revett's *Antiquities of Athens.* Although for practical reasons Strickland does not extend the colonnade completely around the building, the proportions and details of the order itself, including the entablature, are closer to the Greek than anything built in this country up to that time, and the intention to create the image of the Doric temple front, isolated and standing by itself, is clear beyond question. The building may thus be regarded as the first truly Greek Revival building in America, as direct in its evocation of the Parthenon as Jefferson's Virginia State Capitol in Richmond (Fig. 212) was of the Maison Carrée.

FIGURE 310. *William Strickland. Second Bank of the United States, Philadelphia, Pa., 1818.*

At this point we must return to an earlier templelike building, Latrobe's Bank of Pennsylvania (Fig. 256), and inquire why Strickland's Bank is Greek Revival, while Latrobe's earlier design was not. Latrobe's building, after all, carried on both of its porticoes the first Greek order in America, and it had something of the form of a classical temple. Yet for two reasons it cannot be called Greek Revival. First, Latrobe's Ionic order was not a direct quotation from a specific Greek building. Although it seems to have been based on a type illustrated in Stuart and Revett, existing illustrations of the building indicate a general rather than a detailed relationship. Moreover, the architect tells us himself that he designed the building without any reference to books.[34] In any case, it is clear that a direct relationship with a specific Greek building was not intended by Latrobe, whereas it was by Strickland. Indeed, he tells us so himself. "In the design and proportions of this edifice," he wrote, "we recognize the leading features of that celebrated work of antiquity, the Parthenon at Athens."[35]

The second reason why Latrobe's design is not Greek Revival is that the pure temple form, which Strickland goes to such great lengths to preserve, is transformed by him into something else; and in the Bank of Pennsylvania it is that "something else," that bold intrusion into the temple of a domed central block, which makes of it a wholly different kind of building. In Strickland's design, on the other hand, except for slight variations of the wall plane, the temple block remains inviolate.

It does not follow from this that the Greek Revival architects did not work freely within the Greek forms. They did, and the work of Strickland himself was filled with ingenious solutions to varied and complex problems. But the Greek style, as it spread into the American back country, through ever more peripheral stages of diluted professionalism, became increasingly an architecture of quotations, of specific details faithfully rendered as they appeared in the books; and the more professional the architect, the more authentic the rendition. In part this reflected the immense enthusiasm of the American architects for both the symbolic and the artistic relevance of the Greek style. But equally important, this enthusiasm was one that was shared by the American patron as well. In the published notice of the competition for the Second Bank of the United States, the directors left no doubt as to their intention: "The building will be faced with marble and a portico on each front, resting upon a basement or platform of such altitude as will combine convenience of ascent with both proportion and effect. In this edifice, the directors are desirous of exhibiting a chase (sic) imitation of Grecian Architecture, in its simplest and least expensive form."[36]

The important word in this statement is "imitation." Although the Greek Revivalists did not copy specific buildings outright, they did "imitate" salient characteristics of the Greek style, and it is essentially this which distinguishes their work from that of the rational Neoclassicists. To the extent that Mills in his Washington work introduced specific Greek details (as he did in his Ionic order of the Treasury Building) he was a Greek Revivalist; and to the extent that Ithiel Town modified the Greek Doric order by extending its structural principle into wider functional possibilities (as he did in his Connecticut State Capitol) he was a rationalist. Elements of both rationalism and romanticism were found in the work of all the leading professionals of the period. The fact remains, however, that the Greek Revival was motivated by pictorial and sentimental, rather than by architectonic and rational, values, and the farther one gets from the professional creative core, the more this is true.

The most convincing architectural evidence for this is the central importance of the temple form as the primary motif of the Greek Revival. At the idealistic level the temple lived for the Americans as a noble object, a building form which was expressive of those qualities, both real and imagined, which they admired in ancient Greece and which they longed to achieve for themselves. Sentimentally, it provided an important link with their own architectural tradition. The simple pitched-roof houses which dotted the American landscape were, when faced squarely, no more than the classical temple form with its long side turned to the street. The churches, too, were temples short side to the front, with the tower and spire added. Other building types also bore the same shape. It was a simple matter, therefore, to give new meaning to a building by adding a Greek portico to the short end, at the same time that in its basic shape it maintained a vital kinship with its own past. Finally, from the practical point of view, the temple form was the simplest of all building types to construct. Altogether, it could not have been better suited to an ambitious, expanding America.

And so the temple took its place in the American scene. Its appropriateness for government and public buildings was understood by architect and patron alike. The American people demanded it as a symbol of their cultural ambitions, the leading architects treated it with responsive awareness as an expressive dignified form. Working in stone, and taking full

FIGURE 311. *Thomas U. Walter. Girard College,*
Philadelphia, Pa., 1833–47.

advantage of its symmetrical coherence, they placed the temple form
whenever possible in sharp isolation, so that it stood apart from its environment as an object of large and simple beauty, poised, rhythmic,
and absolute. It is in this light that we must see Strickland's Second Bank
of the United States (Fig. 310) and Town's Connecticut State Capitol
(Fig. 299). By ingenious arrangements of interior space each of these
buildings functioned reasonably well for the purpose for which it was
designed, and Town's imaginative exploitation of the Greek's structural
system gave to his building an even more provocative quality. But visually,
both were Greek temples, with all the salient features rendered with refined attention to detail.

Even more grandiose in its aspirations was the design for Girard College in Philadelphia, a scheme developed by Thomas U. Walter, and built
between 1833 and 1847 (Fig. 311). Closely associated with Walter in his
scheme was Nicholas Biddle, one of the most remarkable men of his
age. Biddle had done graduate work in the classics at the College of
New Jersey (now Princeton) and in 1806 had visited Greece. He thus
became one of the few Americans of his time to see Greek architecture
with his own eyes and he viewed it with the highest admiration. As a
member of the board of Girard College, he was determined to see the
new buildings cast in the image of Greece, and it was he who suggested
to Walter the main Grecian lines of the design. The principal building,
now Founder's Hall (Fig. 312), is a large Corinthian peripteral temple
with refined, authoritative detail. It makes no difference that on the inside
it contains an ingeniously planned three-story complex of groin-vaulted
spaces, entirely of the latest (Millsian) fireproof construction. None of this
is revealed on the outside. The great colonnade encircles the building in
stately rhythm, setting off precisely the limits of its simple shape, and
screening all behind its formidable lines. What mattered to Biddle was
that the building should be a Greek temple.

Equally important is the sharp isolation of the building, indeed of each
unit, in the total complex of the design (Fig. 311). Founder's Hall
stands at the center on a slight prominence and is flanked by four dormi-

FIGURE 312. *Thomas U. Walter. Girard College, Founder's Hall, Philadelphia, Pa., 1833–47.*

tory units, all identical templelike buildings, two symmetrically placed on either side. Most important is the clarity with which each building is made to assert itself. Biddle had seen the great Greek temples at Paestum, on the coast of southern Italy, and thoroughly understood the Greek sense of the absolute as expressed in the individual perfection of the temple. Each unit had to stand alone. Girard College, therefore, contrasts dramatically with Thomas Jefferson's University of Virginia (Fig. 232). Where Jefferson worked in a typical Roman manner, with a complex synthesis of many diverse spatial units, Walter balanced five separate temples, each standing alone, all related in shape, and all balanced in symmetrical orientation and placement.

Walter used the pure temple form on other occasions and for wholly different purposes. One, because of its location, is of particular interest. In 1835, the Hibernian Society of Charleston, South Carolina, a social and charitable group, advertised for designs for a new hall, and Walter won the competition. His project was a pure prostyle Ionic temple with an order based largely on that of the Erechtheum in Athens (Fig. 313). As well as meeting rooms, the interior boasts an elaborate double staircase, but as in the case of Girard College, none of this asserts itself on the exterior of the building. Here the temple form is simple and complete,

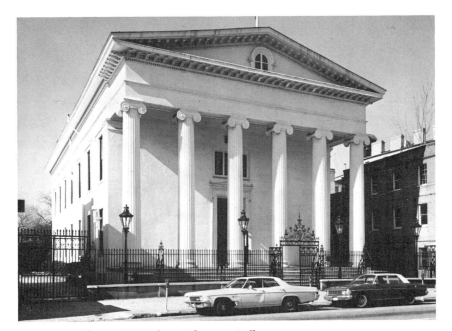

FIGURE 313. *Thomas U. Walter. Hibernian Hall,*
Charleston, S.C., 1835.

at the exclusion of all other considerations, and stands even today with
enough space around it to be comprehended as a coherent whole. The
lovely Ionic portico is finely proportioned in the best Greek manner, with
the only discordant note the modillioned cornice and the Italianate window in the pediment. Both were added in 1886 after an earthquake destroyed the original pediment.

Walter's Hibernian Hall is mentioned here because it characterizes a
fascinating and seldom recognized aspect of the city of Charleston itself.
Because of the commanding presence of St. Michael's Church, one of the
great masterpieces of the colonial years, Charleston is usually regarded
by most Americans as a Mecca of colonial architecture. Actually, however, large portions of the eighteenth-century city were destroyed in several disastrous fires, and except for a few significant clusters of important
colonial remains, the major architectural character of the city was determined in the nineteenth century, and a large part of it is Greek Revival.
Of the many churches built there during this era, seven are of the pure
Greek temple type, five Doric and two Corinthian. They include Baptist,
Methodist, Presbyterian, and Episcopal churches, and one synagogue. One
of these will suffice to illustrate them all. The Centenary Methodist Episcopal Church (originally built as a Baptist church) was designed and
constructed in 1842 by a local architect, E. B. White (Fig. 314). It is
a Greek prostyle temple in the order of the Parthenon, and can be identified as a church only by its tall six-light stained glass windows which
cut into the wall on either side. In its bookish adherence to the tenets
of the Doric order, in both profile and detail, it is an uninspired building,
and provides a revealing contrast with Robert Mills's Fireproof Building,
which is only six blocks away. To understand the difference between the

FIGURE 314. E. B. White. Centenary Methodist Episcopal Church, Charleston, S.C., 1842.

Greek Revival and rational Neoclassicism one need only compare these two buildings.

The other six Greek Revival churches in Charleston are identical in spirit if not in detail to the Centenary Methodist Episcopal Church, and as a group represent one of the most remarkable survivals of the period to be found anywhere. That they could all have been built in the same place at the same time is something which could have happened only in a cosmopolitan town like Charleston, where strong diversified religious groups were completely free of the entrenched conservativism of New England Congregationalism. The Stone Temple (Fig. 307) by comparison is evidence of this. But the Greek temple and Greek details made their way into New England churches, nevertheless, on a wide and pervasive front. In fact, some of the most refreshing works of the Greek Revival period are to be found in the permeation of the temple form into the wood architecture of rural New England.

This can be illustrated in a series of three churches, all built within a few years of one another. The first and most splendid is the Congregational Church in Madison, Connecticut (Fig. 315). It dates from 1838. Here the Doric front of the Parthenon (Fig. 1) has been rendered in wood with careful attention to proportion and detail. The entablature has a characteristic triglyph and metope frieze and the pediment is low pitched in the Greek fashion. In its direct evocation of the temple form the Madison church displays the same imitative qualities of the church in Charleston. But here the similarities cease. The use of wood rather than masonry gives the building a finer scale; edges are sharper, details flatter and thinner. Moreover, above and behind the pediment rise the characteristic

FIGURE 315. *Congregational Church,*
Madison, Conn., 1838.

tower and spire of the traditional New England church. To be sure, the
two stages of the spire are cylindrical, in the manner of the Choragic
Monument of Lysicrates, and carry Greek Ionic and Corinthian orders.
Furthermore, in the rectilinear character of the tower, with its flat Doric
pilasters and stripped-down entablature, and in the unbroken surfaces of
the walls, there is something of the geometric purity characteristic of
Neoclassicism in general. But the basic form of the Wren-Gibbs church
remains unchanged; and when one compares the earlier traditional Neoclassical church in Old Lyme (Fig. 174) with the Madison church, it
becomes apparent that the changes wrought in the latter were not changes
in concept, but changes in proportion and detail.

In Slatersville, Rhode Island, is another church of the Doric temple type
(Fig. 316). Built about 1840, it is more modest than its distant neighbor
in Madison, but it is a Greek Doric temple nevertheless and is typical

FIGURE 316. Church,
Slatersville, R.I., c. 1840.

of scores of smaller churches built in New England during the second
quarter of the nineteenth century. Also typical of the smaller Greek Revival churches is the treatment of the order. In the Rhode Island church
it is no longer an imitation of the Parthenon. In fact, there are numerous
interesting digressions from the classical norm. The Doric columns are
over-slender in proportion and are placed far apart, the entablature is
Ionic rather than Doric, and the raking line of the pediment is much too
steep in pitch. Again, the traditional tower intrudes upon the pure horizontal block to break the temple form. It is squarish in proportions and has
simplified Doric pilasters with recessed panels down their length. This
treatment of the pilasters is a virtual hallmark of the provincial Greek
Revival of the North. All these features give the Rhode Island church

FIGURE 317. *Chestnut Hill Baptist Church,*
Exeter, R.I., 1838.

a charming awkwardness, in contrast to the more coherent authoritative
grace of the one in Madison; it was obviously put together in patches and
pieces, from one or the other of the carpenters' handbooks, by a builder
too far removed from the main streams of archaeological authority to
show much concern for the authentic representation of the Greek style.

Still farther on the fringes of conformity is another Rhode Island church,
the little Chestnut Hill Baptist Church in Exeter (Fig. 317). It dates from
1838. Like its larger companions, it takes its fundamental character from
the Wren-Gibbs formula of a rectangular block and tower, but in the execution of the building everything has been reduced to its simplest possible
form. Indeed, one might ask in what way it is Greek. Except for the clumsy
Greek fret over the door, there is not a single feature which effectively re-

FIGURE 318. *Thomas U. Walter and Nicholas Biddle. Andalusia, Andalusia, Pa., 1836.*

sembles the ancient source. Yet, in its primitive unknowing way, it pleads to be Greek. Somehow, because of the pervasive force of the movement, the flat boards and rectangular moldings of the rural carpenter have been given shapes that dimly honor the ancient style. The four engaged piers with their recessed panels, even though they have no capitals, are acceptable mutations of the Doric column; the entablature has not a single Greek detail, yet is wide enough to hint at its remote ancestry; the triangle of the pediment is too steeply pitched, but it is a closed triangle nonetheless, which is the basic condition of the Greek pediment. The building's style seems to flow from an awareness on the part of the local carpenter rather than from knowledge. Its forms are those of an architectural illiterate groping toward a fashionable idiom with nothing to work with but plain boards, a saw, and a hammer. Yet it is strong and uninhibited, and in its awkward proportions and stark flat surfaces it is stanchly individual. Like the architecture of the New England hinterland during the colonial years, it debases the classical forms. It adheres to no bookish norms, makes no concessions to recognized authority. Within the limits of its primitive techniques it reflects innocently but boldly upon the Parthenon, probably the most subtle artistic achievement in the history of Western man; and it brought to those who built it, by whatever process of mutation, something of the immense power and wonder of that original moment, so remote in distance and time. This is the essence of all folk architecture, and the Exeter church is folk architecture at its best.

FIGURE *319. Ithiel Town and A. J. Davis. Russell House (now Honors College, Wesleyan University), Middletown, Conn., 1828–30.*

Precisely the same kind of metamorphosis may be traced in the domestic architecture of the period. Again, in the hands of the professional architect and the enlightened patron, an archaeological solution was the rule. In 1836, Nicholas Biddle commissioned Thomas U. Walter to build a Greek Doric portico around the main house of his estate, Andalusia, which was north of Philadelphia (Fig. 318). A peripteral temple form fronts and encloses the original house on three sides, asserting its own rhythm with compelling force, and in arrogant disregard for the older building it was designed to grace. One sees first the Greek temple, white and pristine, nothing else. Andalusia is, of course, a tour de force in archaeological revivalism, dictated we know by Biddle himself, and in all probability it was built by Walter against his own professional judgment. But the point is, Biddle wanted it and Walter had the knowledge to oblige him.

There were not many houses of the Greek Revival period, large or small, as brashly conceived as Andalusia, but there were hundreds that were cast from the same general mold, some authoritative, some bizarre, some pedestrian, but all of them moved by the same admiration for ancient Greece. The Russell House in Middletown, Connecticut, designed by Town and Davis, and built between 1828 and 1830, is one of the most imposing (Fig. 319). It is in the form of a prostyle Corinthian temple. Because of its order it is taller in proportion than Andalusia; it is also more coherent. Since the temple at Andalusia was simply wrapped around

FIGURE 320. *Ithiel Town and A. J. Davis. Russell House (now Honors College, Wesleyan University), Middletown, Conn., interior, 1828–30.*

an existing house, there is no tangible relationship between the rhythmic pattern of the windows and that of the colonnade; in the Russell House, however, they are part of a single design intention, and the windows fall in an alternating pattern between the columns. Furthermore, at the sides and back, the walls of the Russell House are brought out to the line of the columns so that throughout the design the dynamic presence of the inner spaces is integrated with the columnar rhythm. But the temple form is uncontested in both shape and orientation, and the short end of the building is glorified by the refined Corinthian order. Inside, too, the handling of detail is exquisitely elegant, with Greek fret and rinceau motifs dominating the design (Fig. 320). The knowledgeable but sensitive touch of the professional is on every hand.

In spite of its appealing simplicity the pure temple form was not the most common in American house design. Far more prevalent, probably because it offered greater variety in appearance and internal arrangements, was the temple with wings. It was an easy gracious form, severely classical in its symmetry, yet varied in profile, which produced some of the loveliest and most livable houses ever built in America. In fact, many of the most beautiful examples of the Greek Revival are to be found in houses of this type. Some, like the Elias Brown House in Old Mystic, Connecticut (Fig. 321), are extremely sophisticated in proportion and detail. Designed and built in 1835, it is a building of extraordinary ele-

FIGURE 321. *Elias Brown House,*
Old Mystic, Conn., 1835.

gance. This stems in part from the refined application of the Greek
Ionic order. Although the anonymous designer has taken some liberties
with the actual detailing of the capitals, the profiles and proportions
are impeccably correct, as is the delicate Ionic frieze. The side wings,
too, are sufficiently long to counter effectively the vertical mass of the
central temple unit, and the secondary colonnades on either side are appropriately scaled in relation to the principal portico. A conflicting element appears, however, on the top of the temple roof in the form of a
squarish cupola with Doric corner pilasters of the recessed panel type
already observed in the Slatersville church (Fig. 316). In the New England coastal communities these little towers occur frequently on houses
and may have been intended to take the place of the widow's walk found
in earlier examples. In the Brown House, however, it is difficult to relate
the cupola to the classic purity of the Ionic portico. Also curiously un-
Greek, but typical of the smaller houses of the period, is the location of
the door to the left of center. Here the internal planning requirements
obviously took precedence over the classical symmetry, and in a thoroughly practical way spare the house from being too smugly archaeological. But the off-center placement also adds an element of dynamic tension
to an otherwise stable design, a tension which is further animated by the
vivacious character of the door motif itself. The flanking pilasters are
Doric, but they support an Ionic entablature, and set *in antis* before
the recessed door are two Ionic columns, each coupled with the Doric
pilasters. This unorthodox combination is consistent with the asymmetry
and suggests a relaxed informality already implicit in the full-length win-

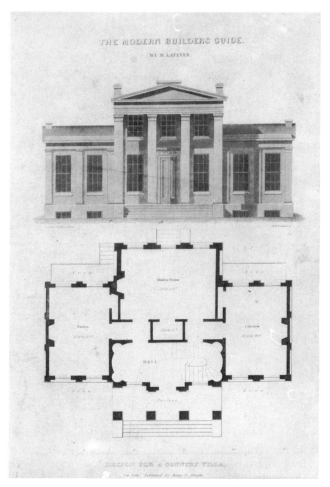

FIGURE 322. *Minard Lafever. Design for a country villa, 1833.*

dows and shaded wings. The house is practical as well as exquisitely and naturally beautiful.

Houses like the Brown House were popularized throughout the settled and expanding portions of the country by the books of Benjamin and Lafever (Fig. 322). A variety of provincial examples can still be found in many parts of the land, in Ohio, Indiana, Illinois and Michigan, as well as in the East and South, but among the finest is the Wilcox-Cutts House in Orwell, Vermont (Fig. 323). Far less sophisticated than the Brown House, it is set in superb isolation on the crest of an upland in the gently rolling Champlain Valley. Here it rules the Vermont farm land with a presumptuous dignity that is not altogether appropriate to the informality of its rural setting. Yet, at the time it was built, it was this very quality of dignity which gave substance to America's struggle for cultural independence. The attenuated Ionic columns loom high, their capitals crisply though flatly cut in wood, revealing in their linearity their origins in the sharp line engravings of a book source. The deep Ionic entablature encircles the house, all in the best Greek manner. The high shape of the pediment

FIGURE 323. *Wilcox-Cutts House,*
Orwell, Vt., 1843.

however, reflecting the steep pitch of the roof behind, concedes to the winter snows rather than to classical precedents. And there are other awkward moments such as the horizontal window in the pediment, and the short piece of wall which encloses the colonnade at the rear, and from which the side wings extend. The projection of the lower entablature of the wings into the space between two of the large columns is a particularly clumsy connection. These, of course, are the mark of a local carpenter, assembling the various components from the books at hand. They mix uneasily with the imposed formality of the classical system to give the house an untutored brusqueness which makes it seem more natural in its rural setting than its temple shape would imply.

On the inside, too, houses like the Wilcox-Cutts House are treated with bold simplicity. In the living room of the Joel Hayden House in Haydenville, Massachusetts (Fig. 324), all the elegant decorative graces, so conspicuous in the architect-designed Russell House (Fig. 320), have been stripped away in favor of broad flat casings and minimum moldings. A heavy Doric scale prevails throughout, and only the dog-eared door surrounds break the severe pattern of rectangles. Seen in the broader spectrum of middle-class American architecture, the Wilcox-Cutts and Hayden houses are but two of hundreds conceived in the same pattern.

FIGURE 324. *Joel Hayden House,*
Haydenville, Mass., living room, c. 1830.

Yet as one travels across the countryside it is a delight to discover that, thanks to the fierce independence of the rural carpenter, no two are alike. The Greek temple appeared in its simplest and most prolific form as the small pitched-roof house, identical in all basic respects to the small houses of earlier generations, except in its orientation. The Greek Revival houses were turned short end to the street, and in the more pretentious examples, such as one of several little anonymous houses in Eastham on Cape Cod (Fig. 325), attenuated Doric pilasters marked the front corners and gave visual support to a primitive entablature and pediment above. The door surrounds, too, were squared off by Doric pilasters and a flat entablature. Unlike the earlier houses, which were crowned at the eaves by a cornice alone, the Greek houses carried a full entablature all the way around. The pitch of the roof, however, and consequently the pitch of the pediment, was set at the traditional steep angle. To make possible a single front room on the first floor, the entrance door, just as in the Brown House, was pushed to the side. It did not bother the Yankee builder in the least that the sacred symmetry of the classical temple was thereby destroyed. It is, in fact, this very mutation in form, within the framework of a recognized style, this debasement of an ideal through the simple tools and hands of the local carpenter, that gives to the American Greek Revival its extraordinary diversity and strength.

At this, the folk level, the variations in the treatment of the temple form were as numerous as the regions, the towns, even the individual carpenters, who brought them into being. Yet, by no means all the houses of the Greek Revival were built as temples. Indeed the majority were not. The most common form was, in fact, the traditional colonial house type, with its door at the center of the long side, simply modified by the

FIGURE 325. *House,*
Eastham, Mass., c. 1850.

additions of Greek rather than colonial details. In some instances this
was done to houses actually built in the colonial era. In others, houses
in the traditional colonial form were built with Greek detail. A typical
example is the Westerman House in Orleans on Cape Cod (Fig. 326).
Built about 1840, it is a perfectly balanced rectangular block, long side
to the street. It has Greek Doric pilasters at the corners, a full entablature
encircling the house, and a squarish Doric surround enframing the central
door—this is all that makes it Greek, and it was houses like the Westerman House, which still abound throughout the eastern United States, which
marked the American Greek Revival in its most conservative form. It
was also houses like this which, together with the Wren-Gibbs type church,
maintained the strongest links with the past. In rural New England in
particular, they kept alive a powerful tradition down to the time of the
Civil War, and more than any other factor perpetuated the image of colonial architecture in nineteenth-century America. They have also been
responsible for the popular notion that colonial architecture was painted
white. For instead of displaying the earth tones of the colonial years,
the wood architecture of the Greek Revival was pristine white.[37] This was
the taste of the Neoclassical era, and it was so prevalent that many of

FIGURE 326. *Westerman House,
Orleans, Mass., c. 1840.*

the surviving colonial buildings were themselves repainted to bring them
into step with their newer neighbors. Thus was established a characteristic
of the New England village which survives to this day.

The Greek Revival in America, in spite of its diversity, was also homogeneous. It was homogeneous because of its universal acceptance of Greek
forms, it was homogeneous because of its whiteness, but it was also
homogeneous because it was motivated by the common aspirations of an
entire people. Thomas Jefferson's brief and highly personal Roman Revival was the product of an individual mind; the Greek Revival was the
product of a popular sentiment. The fact that it became expressive for
the whole of American society, from the erudite to the untutored, from
the capital to the village, from the city house to the farm, gave it a national
independence and set it apart from the architecture of Europe in a way
and to a degree that American builders had never before achieved. Indeed, at no time in the history of Western man had a single stylistic
form, however sentimentally conceived, been so spontaneously accepted
by a total society. It is in this sense that the Greek Revival must be
understood as America's first national style of architecture.

The Plantation Houses of the Deep South

There is one remarkable variation on this general observation, a kind
of rebellion within a rebellion, which we must consider to make our
story complete. This is the domestic architecture of the Deep South. The

great plantations of this region have long been classified by architectural historians as Greek Revival and there are persuasive arguments for doing so. This architecture was dominated almost entirely by the peripteral colonnade, it was an architecture which was almost without exception white, and it was all built during the Greek Revival period. Yet only in rare instances was the temple form used, and as often as not the order was Roman rather than Greek. There is no question, of course, that it was a part of the general Neoclassical movement, and the Greek style does appear. But there are so many aspects that set it apart from the developments we have just described in the North that it deserves to be treated as a unique product of a unique social and economic situation. For the plantation house spoke as eloquently for the cotton empire of the Deep South, as did the temple front for the coastal, rural, and early industrial towns of the North.

The cotton belt of the Deep South was that area which is now northern Louisiana, Mississippi, Alabama, and western Georgia. In the years when the young Benjamin Latrobe was making his way in the world of American architecture, this rich and fertile land was a wilderness. But with the invention of the cotton gin, settlement began, and by 1820 the first plantations had already been carved out of the area and their houses built. Forty years later, on the eve of the Civil War, virtually the entire region had been turned into productive fields of cotton: the plantation society of the cotton era was a firmly established fact. Out of this grew the legend of the Old South, the legend of a venerable aristocracy, seated in the stately porticoed plantation houses or riding in supreme command over their countless acres of cotton. With slaves to work the fields, the masters' life was one of leisure, sustained by a firm belief in a long-standing culture, and born easily amid the graces of a hospitable and genteel social behavior.

Modern historians now recognize this image of aristocracy for what it is, a legend. For those "aristocrats" who ruled over the life of the plantations, and who projected an image of cultured gentlemen in long-tailed coats and string ties, were in fact the very frontiersmen who a quarter of a century earlier had moved into the wilderness with gun in hand to conquer the virgin land; and, as described in contemporary literature, the society which they helped to shape was a typical frontier society, rough, ruthless, and speculative, far removed, indeed, from the chivalric aristocratic culture of the legend.[38] Nevertheless, enormous land holdings were acquired, and with these land holdings plus slave labor came financial success. Success brought cultural and social ambitions and the assumed postures of an aristocratic caste.

Into this promising and aggressive situation came the Classical Revival with all its potential for monumentality and dignified grace. Animated by ambitious dreams, modulated by an oppressive climate, and conditioned by the threads of an architectural tradition, the ancient styles were re-formed into a practical and gracious idiom, unique in its time and place. Never before in American history has so expressive a regional style taken shape so logically and quickly, or with more appropriateness

FIGURE 327. *Cahokia Court House,*
Cahokia, Ill., 1737.

to the conditions it was asked to meet. Although there was still much of the frontier beneath the frock coats and flowing dresses of plantation society, its aspirations were crystal clear and the Classical Revival provided the setting as no other style could. It was one of the fortuitous coincidences of history that the emergence of a plantation society and the development of the Classical Revival happened at the same time.

The basic character of the plantation house actually had nothing to do with the ancient world. Its roots were rather in the Mississippi Valley, where a primitive regional architecture had developed while the area was still part of the French empire. The French colonial possessions in the Mississippi Valley were enormous, ranging from the Gulf of Mexico to Canada to form the largest European colony on the North American continent. But in spite of its size very little building of any importance can be attributed to the French and virtually nothing has survived. In the area of domestic building, however, an important house type was developed which would later become the basis of the plantation house.

The type is seen in its simplest and oldest surviving form in the Cahokia Court House in Cahokia, Illinois (Fig. 327). Originally built in 1737 as a dwelling, it was sold in 1793 to be used as a county court house and jail. It is a simple single-story block with a double pitched roof and with stone chimneys on either end. The most unusual feature of the house is the roof. The lower planes are less deep than the upper, and continue out past the house in a sweeping overhang. This

FIGURE 328. *Homeplace Plantation,*
St. Charles Parish, La., c. 1801.

is· supported on simple wood posts, to form a covered area, or *galerie,*
which completely surrounds the house. Both the posts and the house
itself rest directly on the ground. It is essentially in this form that the
house spread down the Mississippi Valley and into the Louisiana bayou
country. But here the colonial builders were faced with a serious problem,
the constant danger of flooding. To overcome this, the entire house was
raised up on tall brick piers and foundations so that the *galerie* became,
in effect, an elevated porch.

The early plantation houses of the lower Mississippi Valley were in
this form, and one of the most characteristic surviving examples is
Homeplace Plantation in St. Charles Parish, Louisiana (Fig. 328). Built
about 1801, it is a simple two-story block completely surrounded by a
galerie. The walls and posts of the first floor are made of brick; those
of the upper floor of cypress timbers. A high hipped roof sweeps beyond
the house to enclose the *galerie* and is supported at the eave line by
slender wooden posts. The first-floor brick posts have the form of primitive
Doric columns, the wooden ones above are slender and turned. The
main floor, which is at the *galerie* level, is approached from the front
by a broad staircase and is surrounded by a balustrade. Full-length
windows open on to the *galerie* from the main living rooms.

The house type exampled by Homeplace Plantation developed slowly,
over a period of time acquiring features that were direct consequences
of climatic conditions: because of perpetual dampness the main living

FIGURE 329. *James Gallier. Belle Helene, Ascension Parish, La., c. 1850.*

area was elevated above the ground; to give protection from the sun and to provide comfortable space for outdoor living a covered porch was extended completely around the house; high-ceilinged rooms with full-length windows afforded air circulation while remaining shaded by the porch. Add to this the dignity and grandeur of the classical colonnade and the concept of the classic plantation house becomes complete. Indeed, it was exactly in this form that the majority of them were built. The colorful and gracious life of the plantation society of which they were the heart was brought to an end by the Civil War, and along with it many of the great houses themselves. But the shadowy ghosts of others remain, such as Belle Helene in Ascension Parish, Louisiana, built about mid-century (Fig. 329). Today this mournful house is screened behind a tangle of underbrush and dripping curtains of Spanish moss, rotting quietly and imperceptibly into oblivion. And on the leisurely ride up the old river road from New Orleans to Baton Rouge, one finds other touching reminders of both the strength and the weaknesses of the most tragic episode in American history.

Of the handful of plantation houses which still remain in anything like their original form, Oak Alley in St. James Parish, Louisiana, is the one that conveys most vividly the character of the society it was built to sustain (Fig. 330). Erected in 1836 for the planter J. T. Roman, and designed by an unknown architect, it is the epitome of the plantation house in every respect. Romantically situated at the end of a bowered vault of magnificent live oaks, the house itself, in spite of the pure clean rhythm of its classical colonnade, seems utterly caught up in the over-powering fecundity of the earth on which it stands. This is as it should be, for the plantation owed its very existence to the capacity of the land to produce, and to produce again and again in abundance. The house was possessed by the land, and isolated by the vastness of the surrounding plantation from neighbor and nation alike. That it should seem to be part of a perpetual process of growth was both symbolically and poetically just. At the same time, its self-contained classical symmetry rendered it sufficient unto itself, a serene cultural refuge in an environment of almost sinister opulence. It was this contradiction between growth and imposed order which gave the plantation house its vitality, and made the classical style so expressive of the social order which brought it into being.

The essential architectural feature of Oak Alley is its colonnade (Fig. 331). By using a colossal order the two floors of the earlier houses were unified behind the grand rhythm of the full-length columns, and the

FIGURE 330. *Oak Alley,*
St. James Parish, La., 1836.

FIGURE 331. Oak Alley,
St. James Parish, La., close view of house, 1836.

earlier spindly supports were transformed to ones of monumental classical
dignity. The style, however, is not Greek. Rather, the colonnade displays
a Roman order, and surrounds the building on all four sides without a
single pediment to give it the temple form. Moreover, the dormers show
round-headed windows with delicate Federal detail, and the main entrance has a graceful elliptical fanlight. Indeed, not one part of the
building is Greek.[39] There can be no doubt, of course, that the search
for classical identity which moved the Greek Revivalists of the North
also provided the incentive for the planters of the South. Oak Alley,
with its shaded porch and balcony and its stately colonnade, is an
extraordinary combination of the real and the unreal, of a practical
concern for the conditions of environment on the one hand, and a pretentious façade for a would-be aristocracy on the other. For a brief
moment in time the society of the South was brilliant, gracious, and
proud, and the classical colonnade had qualities of serenity and grandeur
which gave form to the dream.

Economically, socially, and spiritually the North and the South were
separate worlds. Wedded to the soil, the South was both created and
doomed by slavery. At the same time, in the North, the vital but ruthless

FIGURE 332. *Joel Hayden House,*
Haydenville, Mass., c. 1830.

FIGURE 333. *Hayden Gere and Co., Brass Works,*
Haydenville, Mass., c. 1840.

forces of industrialism were already at work fashioning a new culture which was as different from the plantation society of the South as the factory was from the cotton field. Before the Civil War the manufacturers of the North, like the planters of the South, saw their cultural destiny best fulfilled in the unshakeable authority of the classical past. The Joel Hayden House in Haydenville, Massachusetts (Fig. 332), built by a mill owner as a fashionable symbol of his authority, is a superb Greek Doric temple with flanking wings.[40] In its tight closed geometry, how different it is from Oak Alley. The plantation is more open, more diffused, more shadowed. It is isolated in its remote setting and engulfed by its surroundings. The positive self-assurance manifest in the little temple, on the other hand, derives not so much from its own prim perfection as from the factory which faces it across the street (Fig. 333). The two cannot be separated from one another, any more than Oak Alley can be divorced from the abundant verdure of the plantation it was built to glorify. The brutal reality of the Civil War would bring to a traumatic end both the Greek Revival in the North and the plantations of the South. For the factory not only provided the muscle which would defeat the South but also the dynamic forces which would create the future America.

When the factory emerged supreme after the Civil War the gentle classicism of the first half of the century would no longer gratify the aggressive taste of the new society and the new aesthetic. The architecture which came to take its place would be an architecture of movement, contrast, and dynamic largeness. Symmetry would give way to asymmetry, prim white to rough gray and brown, geometric simplicity to extravagant involvement. But beneath the flamboyant display would be a hard practical realism which would seek new directions for old materials and shape new forms in response to a new and exciting technology. And behind it all would be the shadow of men like Jefferson, Bulfinch, Latrobe, and Mills whose own celebration of practical truths had provided the substance upon which an expressive American architecture could be built.

CHAPTER I

1.1. From Philebus, as quoted by E. F. Carritt, *Philosophies of Beauty,* Oxford University Press, 1931, p. 31.

1.2. For a detailed and fascinating account of the building trades during the Georgian era, see John Summerson, *Georgian London,* New York, Scribner's, 1946, Chap. V.

1.3. Some of the most interesting timber construction in England during the Middle Ages is found in the great barns. For a discussion of this, see: Walter Horn, "The Great Tithe Barn of Cholsey, Berkshire," *Journal of the Society of Architectural Historians,* Vol. XXII, No. 1, March 1963, p. 13.

1.4. Although I have used numerous sources for my information about English architecture, I have relied primarily on Sir John Summerson's splendid work, *Architecture in Britain, 1530–1830,* Penguin Books, 4th rev. ed., 1963. This comprehensive and original volume is one of the Pelican History of Art series and is the finest general development of English architecture available.

I have not completely documented my debt to this work, but call attention to parts which were particularly useful to me and which might be of interest to the reader. See chapters IV and V of Summerson's work for a discussion of the prodigy house.

CHAPTER II

2.1. The fact that the only surviving houses of the seventeenth century are brick seems to suggest that brick was the more common material. But this was certainly not the case. Wooden houses must have far outnumbered brick houses, especially before 1650, and the fact that no wooden example remains intact indicates only that wood was more perishable in the Virginia climate. Available evidence suggests, however, that by the end of the century brick had become the principal material, especially for the more important buildings.

2.2. The Fairbanks House in Dedham, Mass., is also dated c. 1636, but in neither case is there sufficient hard evidence to determine whether it or the Adam Thoroughgood House is the earlier. New Englanders will claim the Fairbanks House, Virginians the Thoroughgood House.

2.3. The segmental arches and transom windows as restored in the Adam Thoroughgood House are complete conjecture but are based on other fragmentary evidence found in the area. See T. T. Waterman and J. A. Barrows, *Domestic Colonial Architecture of Tidewater Virginia,* New York, Scribner's, 1932, pp. 3–7.

2.4. There is no evidence for the brick brackets which now support the overhang at each corner. See *Idem.*

2.5. Henry Chandlee Forman, *The Architecture of the Old South: The Medieval Style, 1585–1850,* Cambridge, Harvard University Press, 1948, pp. 56–57. Plate 65 shows gables comparable to those at Bacon's Castle.

2.6. Forman, *The Architecture of the Old South,* pp. 60–61.

2.7. G. H. Cook, *The English Mediaeval Parish Church,* London, Phoenix House Ltd., 1954, p. 16.

2.8. Forman, *The Architecture of the Old South,* p. 80.

2.9. Another brick church was begun in 1639 at Jamestown, and also was Gothic. The tower, which dates from later in the century, is all that remains of the original structure, but the existing foundations make it certain that the body of the church was similar to St. Luke's. The third brick church was the Second Bruton Parish Church in Williamsburg, built in 1683. Excavations carried out during the restoration of Williamsburg indicate that it had a plan similar to St. Luke's, and a rough sketch made by a Swiss traveler in 1701 shows end gables which are Flemish and not unlike those at Bacon's Castle.

2.10. The present figural stained glass is nineteenth century. The original panes were clear glass, diamond-shaped, and set in lead.

2.11. James Grote Van Derpool, "The Restoration of St. Luke's, Smithfield, Virginia," *Journal of the Society of Architectural Historians,* Vol. XVII, No. 1, March 1958, pp. 12ff. Arguments for the early dating are found on pp. 17ff.

2.12. Cook, *The English Mediaeval Parish Church,* pl. 172.

2.13. Forman, *The Architecture of the Old South,* pp. 56–57; 85.

2.14. Cook, *The English Mediaeval Parish Church,* pls. 8, 10.

2.15. Summerson, *Architecture in Britain,* p. 106.

2.16. Forman, *The Architecture of the Old South,* p. 81.

2.17. For a thorough and fascinating account of the formation of a New England town see: Sumner Chilton Powell, *Puritan Village,* New York, Anchor Books, Doubleday & Company, Inc. For the actual methods of planning see: Anthony N. B. Garvan, *Architecture and Town Planning in Connecticut,* New Haven, Yale University Press, 1951, pp. 30ff. Garvan makes the interesting suggestion that the method of planning used in the colonization of Ireland during the first quarter of the seventeenth century may have set a direct precedent for the New England towns.

2.18. Land held in freehold was owned by the individual with rights to transfer title to lawful heirs, although in some instances the town maintained degrees of control over the transfer of title.

2.19. Garvan, *Architecture and Town Planning in Connecticut,* p. 54.

2.20. The word "summer" in summer beam derives from "sumpter," a pack horse which was capable of bearing great weight.

2.21. Besides the three houses discussed in this chapter several others should be noted. They are:
Massachusetts:
Fairbanks House, Dedham, c. 1636
Possibly the oldest surviving seventeenth-century house in New England.
Whipple House, Ipswich, 1639(?)
Turner House, Salem, c. 1668
The famous "House of the Seven Gables."
Ward House, Salem, 1684
Now part of the Essex Institute.
Scotch-Boardman House, Saugus, 1686
Maine:
McIntire Garrison House, York, c. 1640–45
Connecticut:
Whitman House, Farmington, c. 1660
See also: Hugh Morrison, *Early American Architecture from the First Colonial Settlements to the National Period,* New York, Oxford University Press, 1952, Chap. 3.

2.22. Successful efforts have been made by scholars to classify early New England dwellings according to structural, formal, and geographical types; but in spite of certain obvious relationships, a powerful individuality prevailed in the design of the New England houses, an individuality born in the peculiar nature of the New England community and nurtured by the varying and unpredictable exigencies of frontier life.

2.23. The date of the Capen House, which is carved on the chimney girt in the upper east chamber, has been given as July 8, 1683. However, a letter from Donald Millar to Bertram K. Little, which is in the files of the Society for the Preservation of New England Antiquities, makes it clear that this is a misinterpretation of the carving and that the date should read June 8, 1683.

2.24. The photographs are in the files of the Society for the Preservation of New England Antiquities at their headquarters in Boston.

2.25. The Parson Capen House was restored by George Francis Dow. In a letter to William Sumner Appleton, dated March 9, 1914, Mr. Dow states that the restored chimney is a reproduction of the one on the Hunt House in Salem. The Hunt House was destroyed in the late nineteenth century but full information about its chimney was available to Mr. Dow. The letter is in the files of the Society for the Preservation of New England Antiquities.

2.26. Evidence of this is seen in Photograph ∦1214, Series A, in the files of the Society for the Preservation of New England Antiquities. It is one of many made of the house during the restoration. I am indebted for this and other information about the Capen House to Mr. Abbott Cummings.

CHAPTER III

3.1. An important member of the group with which Jones traveled was Thomas Howard, Second Earl of Arundel, a brilliant young man whose wide cultural curiosity led him to become one of England's most important patrons of the arts. Since one of Arundel's objectives in going to Italy was to study Italian architecture, it is probable that it was Jones's knowledge of the subject, together with his experience in Italy, which prompted the young earl to include him in his suite.

3.2. Andrea Palladio (1508–80) was an Italian architect of the Renaissance. He studied classical art in Rome, and the architecture of ancient Rome was a central influence in his work. In regard to American architecture, Palladio's importance rests primarily in his theoretical writings. His *Four Books of Architecture* (*I quattro libri dell' architettura*, Venice, 1570) was translated into every modern European language and was a major factor in the spread of Renaissance ideas into northern and western Europe.

3.3. For a fuller discussion of Inigo Jones at the court of James I, see Summerson, *Architecture in Britain,* pp. 67ff.

3.4. In all probability it was Arundel's patronage which helped Jones attain this high post.

3.5. The tower of St. Luke's is one of several scattered examples of the appearance of classical elements in late seventeenth-century colonial architecture. See Fiske Kimball, *Domestic Architecture of the American Colonies and of the Early Republic,* New York, Scribner's, 1922, pp. 42ff.

3.6. For a fuller discussion of English middle-class society, see A. S. Turberville (ed.), *Johnson's England, An Account of the Life and Manners of His Age,* Oxford, Clarendon Press, 1933.

3.7. See Summerson, *Architecture in Britain,* pp. 154ff.

3.8. A superb example of this is found in Wren's additions to the Great Palace at Hampton Court.

3.9. Grinling Gibbons (1648–1721), the major wood carver for Sir Christopher Wren, was one of the virtuosos of his time. Although a sculptor responsible for several important works, such as the bronze statue of Charles II at Chelsea Hospital, he achieved real fame through the superb decorative woodwork that he produced for scores of houses and public buildings during the Wren era. Of all English art of the period his is probably the most Baroque.

3.10. For both the spires and the plans of the Wren London churches, see Eduard F. Sekler, *Wren and His Place in European Architecture,* New York, Macmillan, 1956.

3.11. Quoted in Morrison, *Early American Architecture*, p. 324.
3.12. The best and most authoritative account of Westover is given by Thomas T. Waterman in his splendid book, *The Mansions of Virginia, 1706–1776*, Chapel Hill, University of North Carolina Press, 1946.
3.13. William Byrd II actually came from a middle-class English background. His father, William Byrd I, was the son of a London goldsmith.
3.14. It is important to recognize that the architectural handbooks were not used in the colonies alone. They were written primarily for the English building trades, and the great body of small English houses derived from them in the same way that those in the colonies did.
3.15. Evelyn Byrd, the oldest daughter of William Byrd II, was one of the beauties of her time. While in London with her father she became engaged to the Earl of Peterborough, but her father objected because Peterborough was a Catholic. He brought her back to Westover, where she died a spinster. See Waterman and Barrows, *Domestic Colonial Architecture of Tidewater Virginia*, 1932.
3.16. See Waterman, *The Mansions of Virginia*, for some of the other houses built in Virginia during the first half of the eighteenth century.
3.17. See Nina Fletcher Little, *American Decorative Wall Painting, 1700–1850*, New York, Old Sturbridge Village with Studio Publications, 1952, p. 1.
3.18. There is no document to support this, and Wallace Nutting, who restored the Wentworth-Gardner House in the early twentieth century, left no records of his work; however, local opinion holds that when a later door was removed by Mr. Nutting the pattern of the old door was still visible. See John Mead Howells, *The Architectural Heritage of the Piscataqua*, New York, Architectural Book Publishing Co., 1965, figs. 81, 82.
3.19. Three areas particularly rich in gambrel roof houses are those around Newport, R.I., Portsmouth, N.H., and the Connecticut Valley (of which Deerfield is a part). Typical are: the Purcell (John Paul Jones) House, Portsmouth, N.H., the Hannah Robinson House, Narragansett, R.I., the Rowland Robinson House, Saunderstown, R.I., and the Rivera House, Newport, R.I. A more imposing use of the gambrel roof occurs at Connecticut Hall, Yale University, New Haven.
3.20. Nicholas Barbon (1640–98) was one of the notorious real estate speculators during the latter half of the seventeenth century in London. Using a high degree of standardization and mass-production methods, he built all over London, his enterprises including markets and professional buildings as well as squares of attached houses.
3.21. Strictly speaking, the Royall House was not a "town" house. It was built in the country, well up the Mystic River from the town of Boston, and even today is surrounded by attractive grounds. But its three-story form, with emphasis on the major façades rather than the ends, is exactly the town house type, and since none of the early eighteenth-century town houses of Boston itself survives, it will serve admirably as an example.
3.22. Little, *American Decorative Wall Painting*, pp. 6f.
3.23. The spire of Old North is not the original one. This was blown down during a hurricane in 1804, and in 1808 was replaced by one designed by Charles Bulfinch. Although Bulfinch followed the original spire carefully, he made the actual structure sixteen feet shorter. This second spire, in turn, went down in the hurricane of 1938. The one which replaced it is the present spire, and in the rebuilding it was returned to a height more closely approximating the original.
3.24. The wooden tower and spire on Independence Hall are not the original ones. By 1774, less than a quarter of a century after it was finished in 1753, the original woodwork was in such an advanced state of decay that it was necessary to take the tower and spire down. It was not until 1828 that they were replaced. The commission was given to the Philadelphia architect, William Strickland (see Chapter X), and in what

may have been one of the earliest historical restorations in the country, he rebuilt the tower along lines similar to the original. He seems to have taken for his inspiration Wren's tower on the Church of St. Magnus Martyr, London, England.

3.25. For a lively account of Newport in the eighteenth century, and of Richard Munday, see Antoinette Forrester Downing and Vincent Scully, Jr., *The Architectural Heritage of Newport, R.I., 1640–1915,* Cambridge, Harvard University Press, 1952.

CHAPTER IV

4.1. For a full account of the English Baroque, see Summerson, *Architecture in Britain,* Chaps. 16, 17.

4.2. For the development of the Palladian movement see Summerson, *Architecture in Britain,* Chap. 20.

4.3. For a fuller account of James Gibbs, see Summerson, *Architecture in Britain,* Chap. 21.

4.4. The plates in the English editions of Palladio have a more eighteenth-century pictorial quality than do the original Palladian engravings which inspired the English Palladians.

4.5. See Waterman, *The Mansions of Virginia,* Chap. 4.

4.6. Although Ariss's advertisement is the earliest document to suggest the presence of Gibbs's *A Book of Architecture* in the colonies, it is possible that Peter Harrison of Newport, whose work will be discussed later in this chapter, brought one over earlier. During 1748–49 he designed a summer house for the Redwood Estate in Newport, which he based on a design in Gibbs's book. See Carl Bridenbaugh, *Peter Harrison, First American Architect,* Chapel Hill, University of North Carolina Press, 1949, pp. 53–54.

4.7. Because of the radical differences in style between this group and other domestic architecture in Virginia, Waterman has attributed them to Thomas Jefferson. See Thomas T. Waterman, "Thomas Jefferson, His Early Works in Architecture," *Gazette des Beaux-Arts,* 6th Series, Vol. XXIV, 1943, pp. 89ff.

4.8. For a full account of the London town house, see John Summerson, *Georgian London,* New York, Scribner's, 1946, Chap. 5; also pp. 88–89.

4.9. A typical example is the Eagle House in Mitchum, Surrey, built in 1705 by a director of the South Sea Company.

4.10. During the years immediately preceding the Revolution Marblehead, Mass., was one of the most important ports on the Atlantic seaboard. At one time sixty merchants were active there and of these Jeremiah Lee was the most important. He maintained a far-ranging aggressive fleet of thirty ships, was an active citizen of great power and authority, and a patriot who participated in much of the pre-Revolutionary activity.

4.11. The Copley portraits of Mr. and Mrs. Jeremiah Lee are now in the Wadsworth Atheneum, Hartford, Conn. Full-size copies hang in the Jeremiah Lee Mansion.

4.12. For a fuller account of St. Martin's, see Summerson, *Architecture in Britain,* pp. 211ff.

4.13. Bridenbaugh has attributed the design of St. Michael's to Peter Harrison of Newport. The bases of this attribution are Harrison's personal and commercial connections with Charleston. There are no documents to sustain it, however, and there are several things about St. Michael's which are unlike Harrison's other work.

4.14. Joseph Brown was one of the more interesting gentleman-amateurs working in New England immediately before and after the Revolution. His Providence works include not only the First Baptist Meetinghouse, but also several houses, the most notable of which is the John Brown House on Power Street; College Edifice, one of the earliest buildings of Brown University; and a market house.

4.15. A French diarist writing in 1780 described the steeple of the First Baptist Meetinghouse as being painted in different colors. This was unquestionably the marbleizing technique which we have already seen in the Royall House in Medford, Mass. See Henry-Russell Hitchcock, Jr., *Rhode Island Architecture*, Providence, Rhode Island Museum Press, 1939, p. 23.

4.16. Bridenbaugh accords Harrison this honor as the title of his book, *Peter Harrison, First American Architect*, indicates.

4.17. See Bridenbaugh, *Peter Harrison*, p. 37.

4.18. See Bridenbaugh, *Peter Harrison*, pp. 168–70.

4.19. A water color drawing in the notebook of Pierre Eugène du Simitière shows the Redwood Library in its original form when it was a simple block with two little short wings. See Bridenbaugh, *Peter Harrison*, fig. 7.

4.20. See Bridenbaugh, *Peter Harrison*, pp. 48ff.

4.21. The portico of St. Michael's, Charleston, S.C. (1752–61), was actually built before the one on King's Chapel but it was not planned until after mid-century.

4.22. See Bridenbaugh, *Peter Harrison*, pp. 100f.

4.23. Bridenbaugh (*Peter Harrison*, p. 99) suggests a Dutch source for Harrison's arrangement and shows an illustration (fig. 31 in his book). With respect to the furniture arrangements there can be no doubt that some influence came from Holland, especially since Touro himself had been trained in Amsterdam. In regard to the architectural space itself, however, Touro Synagogue is much more akin to Newport's Trinity Church—which was already standing only a few blocks away—than it is to the Dutch model. It is remarkably similar, too, to the famous Drury Lane Theatre in London, which also had balconies supported on columns, and was similarly elegant in character.

4.24. For a complete account of William Buckland, see Rosamond Randall Beirne and John Henry Scarff, *William Buckland, 1734–1774, Architect of Virginia and Maryland*, Baltimore, Maryland Historical Society, 1958.

4.25. Buckland's library of architectural books was not as extensive as that of Peter Harrison. For a list of those which he owned, see the inventory of his estate in Beirne and Scarff, *William Buckland*, pp. 149–50.

4.26. Illustrated in Beirne and Scarff, *William Buckland*, p. 129.

CHAPTER V

5.1. The architecture of the French, especially in the lower Mississippi Valley, will be discussed in Chapter X.

5.2. The best summary of Dutch colonial architecture is found in Morrison, *Early American Architecture*, Chap. 4.

5.3. The name "New Mexico" was first used by the Spanish in the sixteenth century to define the country north of the settled Mexican provinces; later it became applied to the American Territory of New Mexico, which was officially recognized by Congress in 1850. When used in this chapter the term refers to the area now included within the present state of New Mexico.

5.4. For a more detailed discussion of adobe, see George Kubler, *The Religious Architecture of New Mexico in the Colonial Period and Since the American Occupation*, Colorado Springs, Taylor Museum, 1940, pp. 25–26. In addition, Kubler's book presents the best and most authoritative account of the New Mexico churches.

5.5. For a thorough discussion of this subject, see E. Boyd, *Saints and Saint Makers of New Mexico*, Santa Fe, Laboratory of Anthropology, 1946.

5.6. The Trasparente, by Narcisco Tome, is an elaborate altarpiece built over and around the Blessed Sacrament in Toledo Cathedral. Completed in

1732, it is a fantastic tour de force in illusionism, combining architecture, painting, and sculpture. Part of the effect of a heavenly vision is made possible by lighting from behind.

5.7. The most readable and informative work on the missions of the South-west is: Trent Elwood Sanford, *The Architecture of the Southwest, Indian, Spanish, American,* New York, Norton, 1950. See also Morrison, *Early American Architecture,* Chap. 6.

5.8. See George Kubler and Martin Soria, *Art and Architecture in Spain and Portugal and Their American Dominions, 1500–1800,* Baltimore, Penguin Books, 1959, pp. 2ff.

5.9. There are many eighteenth-century churches in Mexico which also have but one tower although two were obviously essential to the design. The reason for this was in part economic: churches of the period were taxed according to the degree of completion.

5.10. For a more detailed account of San Xavier, see Sanford, *Architecture of the Southwest,* Chap. 21.

5.11. Bernard L. Fontana, *Biography of a Desert Church: The Story of Mission San Xavier del Bac,* Tucson, The Westerners, 1961 (rev. ed. 1963), p. 9.

CHAPTER VI

6.1. Two attitudes toward borrowing from the past are determinable in nine-teenth-century America. The first, known as Revivalism, focused upon a single style. Thus we can identify a Greek Revival and a Gothic Revival. The second point of view is Eclecticism. In this instance, ingredients from several styles in the past may be incorporated in a single design, or an architect may work in one style at one time and in a wholly different style at another.

6.2. The best summary of the developments which led up to the Neoclassical movement is found in Summerson, *Architecture in Britain,* Chap. 25.

6.3. One of the most influential architectural books of the period was Robert Wood's *The Ruins of Palmyra,* published in 1753. Four years later he brought out a second and equally impressive work, *The Ruins of Balbec.* Robert Adam's first contribution was his monumental folio, *The Ruins of the Palace of the Emperor Diocletian at Spalatro in Dalmatia,* published in 1764.

6.4. A second edition of Laugier's *Essai* appeared in 1755. A detailed discus-sion of Laugier and his influence on eighteenth-century architecture may be found in two important works: Emil Kaufmann, *Architecture in the Age of Reason,* Cambridge, Harvard University Press, 1955; and Wolfgang Herrmann, *Laugier, and Eighteenth Century French Theory,* London, A. Zwemmer Ltd., 1962.

6.5. Stuart and Revett's impressive volumes were actually preceded by J. D. Leroy's *Les Ruines des plus beaux monuments de la Grèce,* published in 1758. The French work, however, was more pictorial and archaeological than Stuart and Revett's and therefore much less practical as a source for architects.

6.6. Two important works by Winckelmann had previously appeared: *Gedanken über die Nachahmung der griechischen Werke* (1756), which recommended imitation of Greek work; and *Anmerkungen über die Baukunst der Alten* (1762), which included a description of the archaic Greek temples at Paestum.

6.7. Other influential works by Piranesi were his famous *Carceri (Invenzioni capric. di Carceri all' acquaforte,* Rome, 1745) and his *Antichità romane de' tempi della Repubblica e de' primi imperatori,* Rome, 1748.

6.8. Laugier's influence is to be seen especially in the work of the radical French Neoclassicists Etienne-Louis Baulée, Claude-Nicolas Ledoux, and Jean-Jacques Lequeu. In England the writings of Laugier were regarded by

Sir John Soane as a basic text, which, it seems, he had his students read. The direct influence of these radical Europeans upon American architecture will be discussed later as it is relevant to our story.

6.9. Vitruvius (born c. 83–73 B.C.) was an ancient Roman architect and writer. Dating from about 30 B.C., his ten books on architecture are unique in that they are the only works on this subject that survive from ancient times. Vitruvius established firm proportional systems for the orders, and his methods formed the basis for the theoretical codifications of such Renaissance writers as Palladio.

6.10. The most radical of these were several projects proposed by Ledoux in his folio *L'Architecture*, published in 1804. Although none was ever built, they display a distillation of architectural form to its purest geometric components and are altogether indicative of the rational attitudes of the period. See Kaufmann, *Architecture in the Age of Reason,* and Herrmann, *Laugier.*

6.11. Because of the romantic tendencies which motivated the Neoclassical movement, it is frequently referred to by critics as "Romantic Classicism." See Henry-Russell Hitchcock, *Architecture, Nineteenth and Twentieth Centuries,* Baltimore, Md., Pelican History of Art Series, 1958, pp. xxi f; also p. 431, n. 1. In spite of its romantic character Neoclassicism was nevertheless based on the classical architecture of Greece and Rome, and to avoid confusion with the Romantic Eclecticism of the nineteenth century, which was inspired by the architecture of the Middle Ages and other romantic sources, I prefer the more traditional term, Neoclassicism. In this way, the rational work of men like Latrobe and Mills (Chapter IX) can be distinguished from works of the more irrational Greek Revival itself (Chapter X), at the same time that their common origins in the architecture of the classical world can be stressed. The romantic styles of the nineteenth century will be the subject of the second volume of this work.

6.12. See Chapter VIII.

6.13. See Chapter IX.

6.14. The only known vaulted building earlier than Latrobe's Bank of Pennsylvania was the old Philadelphia Jail, built shortly before the Revolution. See Talbot Hamlin, *Benjamin Henry Latrobe,* New York, Oxford University Press, 1955, p. 153, n. 5.

6.15. See Chapter X.

6.16. See Talbot Hamlin, *Greek Revival Architecture in America,* London, Oxford University Press, 1944, p. 48. Hamlin refers here to a fascinating book written by Frances Milton Trollope, *Domestic Manners of the Americans,* first published in London in 1832.

6.17. The Greek Revival as a national style in the United States is treated fully by Hamlin in his *Greek Revival Architecture.*

6.18. The best summary account of the work of Robert Adam is in Summerson, *Architecture in Britain,* pp. 264ff. For more detail, see James Lees-Milne, *The Age of Adam,* London, B. T. Batsford Ltd., 1947; and John Fleming, *Robert Adam and His Circle,* London, John Murray, 1962.

6.19. For a complete discussion of the Adam principles, see Lees-Milne, *The Age of Adam,* Chap. V.

6.20. The development in planning of varied and contrasting shapes goes back in French domestic architecture to the late seventeenth century. With the shift in social life from the pomp of Versailles, with its endless and tedious array of identical rooms, to the intimacy of the Parisian hotels, wholly new attitudes toward planning became possible. The irregular and difficult sites of many of the town houses, plus the increasing stress on functionalism, led French architects inevitably toward ingenious and convenient plan solutions. By the early eighteenth century, in the work of such masters as J. H. Mansart and Pierre Bullet, the concept of freely arranged contrasting rooms was firmly established. (See Anthony Blunt, *Art and Architec-*

ture in France, Baltimore, Pelican History of Art Series, 1954.) By the late eighteenth century these ideas were codified by J. F. Blondel in the six volumes of his *Cours d' architecture.* Blondel gives extensive consideration not only to questions of material and structure, but also to every practical aspect of planning, including the convenient relationships of the various internal parts of a building. Robert Adam stopped in Paris on his way to Italy and there can be no doubt that he was influenced by both French planning and French decorative systems. See Summerson, *Architecture in Britain,* p. 252.

6.21. See note 9 above.

6.22. Adam himself describes the Gallery at Syon House as being "in a style to afford great variety and amusement." (Summerson, *Architecture in Britain,* p. 267). The ornament in this room is prolific, covering almost the entire walls and ceiling, and shows the characteristic attenuated proportions, compartmentation, and delicate scale. The colors against which the ornament is drawn, however, are contrasting high value tints. There are also numerous small elements in stronger colors and an extensive use of gold. Altogether, the color effect is more complex and vivacious than the sober neutral tints and white of the American work.

6.23. For a detailed account of McIntire's work, see Fiske Kimball, *Mr. Samuel McIntire, Carver, the Architect of Salem,* Portland, Me., Southworth-Anthoensen Press, 1940.

6.24. The surviving examples are too numerous to list but the New England coastal communities of Providence and Newport, R.I., Salem, Marblehead, and Newburyport, Mass., Portsmouth, N.H., and Portland, Me., are particularly rich in well preserved examples. The early nineteenth-century town houses of Boston will be given special treatment in Chapter VII.

6.25. West College was built in 1790 and may have been the work of the Greenfield architect Asher Benjamin. It is a simple rectangular brick block, three stories high and laid in Flemish bond. As originally designed it served as dormitory, classroom, and chapel space for the College. It has undergone many changes in its long history and in 1951 it was completely gutted by fire. The current interior, therefore, is a modern reinforced concrete structure but the original walls still remain. The shape and arrangement of the window openings show the typical proportions and graded spacing of the Federal Style.

6.26. At a town meeting held in Boston in 1803 the town requested the General Court of Massachusetts to require by law that all buildings in Boston over ten feet high be built of stone or brick and covered with slate, tile, or other noncombustible material. Walter Muir Whitehill, *Boston, a Topographical History,* Cambridge, Harvard University Press, 1959, p. 50.

6.27. For discussion of the Charleston "single house," see Beatrice St. Julien Ravenel, *Architects of Charleston,* Charleston, S.C., Carolina Art Association, 1945, pp. 2f.

6.28. Next to Charles Bulfinch, Asher Benjamin was one of the most important architects in Boston during the Federal era. He is best known for his architectural handbooks, the first published in America, which were important in disseminating both the Federal and the Greek Revival style into the American hinterland. Ithiel Town was to become a partner in the firm of Town and Davis, the first architectural firm in the United States. His role in the development of the Greek and Gothic Revivals will be discussed later.

CHAPTER VII

7.1. For an account of the early town of Boston, see Whitehill, *Boston, a Topographical History.*

7.2. Quotation from Elias Boudinot, in Harold and James Kirker, *Bulfinch's Boston, 1787–1817,* New York, Oxford University Press, 1964, p. 204.

7.3. Among the Bulfinch papers in the Massachusetts Historical Society is a list, in Bulfinch's handwriting, of what he describes as the "Public Buildings Erected After the Designs and Under the Direction of Charles Bulfinch." Exclusive of his large housing projects and his work in Washington, this list includes thirty-six buildings. of a government, public, or commercial nature. (No domestic work is included.) Obviously, in a study of this kind, we cannot consider all of the works by each architect, and of the few Bulfinch buildings that still survive we will focus upon only two, the new Massachusetts State House and the Lancaster Meetinghouse. We will also examine in detail his several housing projects and the three mansions which he designed for Harrison Gray Otis. His commercial buildings will come under consideration when we discuss industrial architecture in America in the second volume of this work.

7.4. There is sufficient evidence in the public press of Bulfinch's time to make it clear that he was not only considered an architect but was generally regarded as the best one in Boston. Typical is the report of the dedication of the Lancaster Meetinghouse, published in the *Columbian Centinel* for January 4, 1817, which identifies Bulfinch as the architect and praises him for the quality of the design.

7.5. Unless otherwise specified, all the quotations from Bulfinch himself are taken from two sources: Ellen Susan Bulfinch, *The Life and Letters of Charles Bulfinch, Architect,* Boston, Houghton Mifflin, 1896; and Charles A. Place, *Charles Bulfinch, Architect and Citizen,* Boston, Houghton Mifflin, 1925.

7.6. Bulfinch was plagued by financial difficulties throughout much of his life, and in 1811, even though he was Chairman of the Board of Selectmen, he was forced to spend a month in debtors prison. E. S. Bulfinch, *Life and Letters of Bulfinch,* p. 188.

7.7. There must have been many simple drawings of the kind shown by Hitchcock for the Challoner House in Newport, R.I., built in 1735. The plan by Benjamin Wyatt shows the layout of the rooms and the location of stairs and chimney. See Hitchcock, *Rhode Island Architecture,* Fig. 5.

7.8. See Chapter VIII.

7.9. The most conspicuous example of this is his Lancaster Meetinghouse. See p. 270ff.

7.10. See Chapter IV, pp. 142f.

7.11. Bulfinch was preceded in Europe by Thomas Jefferson, who arrived there in 1784 to take up his duties as Minister to France. When Bulfinch arrived, Jefferson helped the young Bostonian to lay out his itinerary, particularly as it related to his interest in architecture.

7.12. The building used as the State House in Boston between 1776 and 1797 had been built as the city's second "Town-House" in 1712–13. It still exists at the head of State Street, between Washington and Devonshire streets, and is now the home of the Bostonian Society. Although radically changed because of fire and reconstruction, it is one of the few surviving relics of the Wren-Baroque style in Boston.

7.13. Bulfinch was not only the designer of the Federal Street Theatre he was also one of the prime movers in its establishment. This was not easily accomplished. Owing to a stanch Puritan sentiment, Boston society viewed the Theatre as detrimental to public morals, and a law of 1750 prohibited public theatrical productions. Bulfinch saw many plays during his trip abroad, and while he and his wife were staying in New York in 1789 for the inauguration of Washington they went to the theatre there and in Philadelphia. Bulfinch brought to Boston therefore an enthusiasm for the theatre which was immensely influential in overcoming public prejudice. His Federal Street Theatre, therefore, was a triumph in more ways than one.

7.14. The book was John Crunden, *Convenient and Ornamental Architecture,* London, 1785. Plate 35 of this book seems to have been the major source for Bulfinch.

7.15. The old photograph of the Tontine Crescent used for Figure 180 shows outside shutters on the windows. Bulfinch's drawing for the Crescent does not. It seems certain from both visual and other evidence that outside shutters were not planned for the buildings of the Federal period. These were a product of the Romantic era later in the century, and the long stretch of the Tontine Crescent façade, therefore, must be read as a clean continuous wall without the interruption of the dark pattern of the shutters.

7.16. There is nothing to prove that Bulfinch ever went to Bath, but on the other hand it seems incredible that he did not. Bath was world-famous for its crescents and it is absolutely certain that Bulfinch knew about them whether he ever saw them or not. He later purchased a book which showed six views of the Bath crescents: W. Watts, *Select Views of Bath and Bristol,* published in London in 1794. It is among the books owned by Bulfinch which are now in the library of the Massachusetts Institute of Technology.

7.17. A tontine (from which Bulfinch's crescent received its name) is a financial arrangement in which the shares of each participant pass upon his death to the remaining shareholders until one member is left holding all the shares. Although this method of financing had been used successfully in New York, it was held in suspicion in Boston and was one of the reasons for Bulfinch's failure.

7.18. See Summerson, *Architecture in Britain,* pp. 256ff. Chambers was born in 1723 and died in 1796; Adam was born in 1728 and died in 1792.

7.19. The stone buildings listed by Bulfinch are: the Courthouse, Boston; the State Prison, Charlestown; University Hall, Cambridge; the New South Church, Boston; Massachusetts General Hospital, Boston; the Massachusetts and Mechanick's Banks, Boston; the New England and Marine Insurance Company offices, Boston; the Grammar School, Boston.

7.20. The Boston ordinance of 1803 was not unlike various ones introduced in London in the eighteenth century. In the rapidly growing cities of America the question of fireproof construction became a matter of increasing concern, but it was not until the nineteenth century that efforts were made to meet it squarely.

7.21. Segmental vaults were a favorite structural device of the great English Neoclassicist Sir John Soane. Segmental vaults of pure masonry construction were first introduced into America by Benjamin Latrobe. See Chapter VIII.

7.22. See Chapter VIII.

7.23. See Kirker, *Bulfinch's Boston,* for a full account of Bulfinch's activity as an architect. A complete analysis of his total production has yet to be written.

7.24. Large-scale uniform housing units, built for speculation under individual or group proprietorship, and embracing whole squares of land, were a significant architectural development of eighteenth-century England, especially in London and Bath. See Summerson, *Architecture in Britain,* Chap. 23.

7.25. Colonnade Row was a typical proprietory arrangement. The land for the project was purchased by David Greenough and James Freeman, who in turn commissioned Bulfinch to design the houses. See Kirker, *Bulfinch's Boston,* pp. 179f.

7.26. The Park Street group is gone entirely but a small fragment of the Colonnade is still to be seen at the end near Mason Street. See Kirker, *Bulfinch's Boston,* pp. 179f.

7.27. The three Harrison Gray Otis houses together form a superb document of the turn of the nineteenth century in Boston, not only reflecting the character and ambitions of one of the city's most prominent and influential citizens, but also revealing the remarkable growth of Bulfinch as an architect. All three still exist and appear on the exterior very much as they did when first built (exceptions will be noted in our discussion of the buildings). The first Harrison Gray Otis House was built in 1795–96 at 141 Cambridge Street. It is now the headquarters of the Society for the Preservation of New England Antiquities and is open to the public. The second house, which dates from 1800, is at 85 Mt. Vernon Street, in the heart of the Beacon Hill residential section, and is privately owned. The third house, dating from 1806, is at 45 Beacon Street, facing the Common, is now occupied by the American Meteorological Society, and may be visited by the public.

7.28. There are numerous documents indicating the close relationship between Bulfinch and Otis; one of the most interesting, now among the Harrison Gray Otis papers in the Society for the Preservation of New England Antiquities, is a sworn testimony given by Bulfinch at a hearing held in Boston on December 27, 1839. Bulfinch was asked if he had ever built with or for Harrison Gray Otis. He replied, "I was employed as an architect to build a house for him."

7.29. I am indebted to Mr. Abbott Cummings, Associate Director of the Society for the Preservation of New England Antiquities, for this information.

7.30. The use of delicate white figures against pale neutral tints, so characteristic of Federal Style ornament, is not only related to the decorative work in English houses of the Adam period, but bears a remarkable similarity to the pottery of the great Josiah Wedgwood. Here, too, white figures in delicate low relief are set in contrast against backgrounds of neutral blue, green, violet, or gray.

7.31. One consequence of the aggressive commercial policies of the New England merchants was the opening up of the China trade. It not only brought increased wealth to the city of Boston and to other New England coastal communities but added exciting new elements, including many decorative items of Chinese manufacture. It is not surprising therefore to find Chinese decorative motifs mixed with the traditional English forms.

7.32. The design concept of a heavy basement supporting lighter upper stories was popularized by the writings of Palladio and became a virtual hallmark of European Renaissance architecture, especially in England.

7.33. All classical designs are balanced around a central axis. See Fig. 98.

7.34. See Chapter VI, p. 233; also Ravenal, *Architects of Charleston.*

7.35. The Romantic movement in America will be the subject of the second volume of this series.

7.36. The fierce Yankee individualism expressed in the disagreement over the direction in which the church should face led to an animated debate which was not without its lighter side. One reason given for facing the church toward the south was that an important member of the congregation approached from that direction. At this suggestion an eccentric named "Old Beeswax" rose to his feet and replied "that the reason just given reminded him of an invention of his which would remove all difficulty, and meet the minds of every person in town, no matter from what point of the compass he might come. His machine, he continued, was an improved bed-wrench, and by placing that under the meeting house each man as he came up could take hold of the handle and bring the house round toward himself. There was a shout of laughter and the meeting adjourned." A. P. Marvin, *History of the Town of Lancaster, Massachusetts, From the First Settlement to the Present Time, 1643–1879*, published by the town, 1879.

7.37. See Kirker, *Bulfinch's Boston*, p. 77.

7.38. Besides the Church of the Holy Cross and the Lancaster Meetinghouse, the churches which Bulfinch lists as having been designed by him are: New North Church, Boston; New South Church, Boston; a Gothic church in Federal Street, Boston; meetinghouses in Pittsfield, Weymouth, and Taunton. In addition, the Congregational Church in Peterborough, N.H., has been attributed to Bulfinch.

7.39. See Place, *Charles Bulfinch*, p. 231.

7.40. A full account of the laying of the cornerstone, and of the dedication sometime later, is given by Marvin, *History of the Town of Lancaster*, pp. 416ff.

7.41. Not only does Bulfinch list the Lancaster Meetinghouse among the churches which he designed, but several contemporary accounts refer to him as the architect.

7.42. The pilasters project beyond the surface of the piers only to the thickness of one brick, thus all of the headers in the pilasters penetrate the fabric of the piers and are bonded with them.

7.43. In 1881 the Thayer Memorial Chapel was added to the north end of the church auditorium. At this time the windows, four on each side, which originally flanked the pulpit were closed and the two doors which open into the chapel were added instead. The arched window was also turned into a door which gave access to the pulpit, and it is probable that the tabernacle which surrounds the arched opening was added at this time. The wall and ceiling decorations were probably part of this same renovation.

7.44. Place finds it probable that the pulpit was carved by a local cabinetmaker, Jacob Fisher, who was also a member of the Building Committee: *Charles Bulfinch*, p. 231.

7.45. After the addition of the Thayer Memorial Chapel, the pulpit was entered from the door into the Chapel rather than through the small doors below.

7.46. The second phase of English Neoclassicism was marked by increasing rationalism, stimulated in part by the writings of Laugier and by the example of the French architects of the latter part of the century. It will be discussed in greater detail as it relates to the Rational Phase of American Neoclassicism in Chapter IX.

7.47. Benjamin Latrobe and his role in American architecture will be discussed in Chapter IX.

7.48. The shortage of skilled stonemasons in America became a serious problem with the erection of the monumental buildings in the new national capital in Washington. It was so serious in fact that the commissioners recommended to Jefferson that he take measures to import one hundred Germans, as many of them stonecutters and masons as possible.

7.49. Thomas Jefferson was born in 1743 and died in 1826; Charles Bulfinch was born in 1763 and died in 1844.

CHAPTER VIII

8.1. The quotations from Jefferson which appear in this chapter are thoroughly familiar and have been quoted and requoted in all the works which deal with his architecture. They are also readily available in the standard collections of Jefferson's writings. Except in a few special instances, therefore, the source will not be indicated. The major works which deal with Jefferson's architecture are:

Fiske Kimball, *Thomas Jefferson, Architect*, Cambridge, Riverside Press, 1916.

I. T. Frary, *Thomas Jefferson Architect and Builder*, Richmond, Garrett and Massie, 1939.

Karl Lehmann, *Thomas Jefferson, American Humanist*, New York, McMillan, 1947.

Frederick Doveton Nichols, *Thomas Jefferson's Architectural Drawings,* Boston, Massachusetts Historical Society; Charlottesville, Thomas Jefferson Memorial Foundation and University of Virginia Press, 1961.

8.2. See Kimball, *Jefferson, Architect,* p. 20, n. 5.

8.3. Over a period of forty-five years Jefferson brought together a library of between six thousand and seven thousand volumes which contained the most significant collection of architectural books in the country. He systematically catalogued this library himself and later sold it to the Library of Congress. See E. Millicent Sowerby (ed.), *The Catalogue of the Library of Thomas Jefferson,* Washington, D.C., Government Printing Office, 1952–53.

8.4. For the most recent dating of Jefferson's early drawings, see Nichols, *Jefferson's Drawings.* The earliest plan for Monticello is dated by Nichols in 1767. This would place it three years before the fire at Shadwell. Since this and several other early Monticello drawings escaped the fire, it seems probable that they were being kept at Monticello. The southeast pavilion was finished by that time for we know from Jefferson's own account that he moved into it only twenty days after the fire.

8.5. Nichols, *Jefferson's Drawings,* gives a complete list of the existing Jefferson drawings. He includes 531 items.

8.6. See especially Thomas T. Waterman, "Thomas Jefferson, His Early Works in Architecture," *Gazette des Beaux-Arts,* 6th Series, Vol. XXIV, 1943, pp. 89ff.

8.7. The building described by Jefferson is not the one which has been restored at Colonial Williamsburg. The original capitol familiar to Jefferson was destroyed by fire and replaced. It is the second one which formed the basis of the restoration.

8.8. For the best account of Jefferson's drawing technique, see Kimball, *Jefferson, Architect,* pp. 105ff.

8.9. For a full account of Jefferson's use of the Morris book, see Clay Lancaster, "Jefferson's Architectural Indebtedness to Robert Morris," *Journal of the Society of Architectural Historians,* Vol. X, No. 1, March 1951, pp. 3–10.

8.10. For a full and thoroughly documented account of Jefferson's involvement in the Virginia State Capitol, see Fiske Kimball, "Thomas Jefferson and the First Monument of the Classical Revival in America," *The Journal of the American Institute of Architects,* III, 1915.

8.11. Peter Harrison's Redwood Library in Newport (see Chapter III) has been cited as the first use of the classical temple form in American architecture. This is not the case. There is nothing in Harrison's work to indicate that he knew anything about Roman architecture. In fact, Harrison's colonnaded front in Newport was taken directly from the frontispiece of an English edition of Palladio. Moreover, the building, even in its original form, had short side wings with sloping roofs which tended to create a second pediment. Jefferson's adaptation of the Maison Carrée, on the other hand, represents a direct application of the pure classical temple form. This expresses a wholly different attitude toward the architecture of ancient Rome and it was therefore Jefferson, and not Harrison, who initiated the classical revival in America.

8.12. For a fuller development of the relationship between Jefferson and Palladio, see Lehmann, *Jefferson, Humanist,* Chap. 10.

8.13. The terms I will use to identify the rooms at Monticello will be those used by Jefferson himself. I am indebted for this information to Mr. James Bear.

8.14. Anna Ticknor, *Life, Letters, and, Journals of George Ticknor,* Boston, Houghton Mifflin, 1909, vol. I, p. 34. Ticknor's letter, written to his father on February 7, 1815, also contains several interesting observations about the architectural character of Monticello which show him to be an unusually perceptive man. He says that in the center of the lawn, "Mr. Jefferson has placed his house, which is of brick, two stories high in the wings, with a piazza in front of a receding centre. It is built, I suppose, in the French style . . . the drawing-room, [———] a large and rather elegant room, twenty or thirty feet high, [———] which, with the hall I have described, composed the whole centre of the house, from top to bottom. The floor of this room is tessellated. It is formed of alternate diamonds of cherry and beech, and kept polished as highly as if it were of fine mahogany."

8.15. The most fascinating and authoritative account of Jefferson's interest in the Roman villa is to be found in Lehmann, *Jefferson, Humanist,* Chap. 11.

8.16. The translation of Horace, from *Epodes* II, is the one given in Lehmann, *Jefferson, Humanist,* p. 181. Lehmann and also Chinard (Gilbert Chinard, *The Literary Bible of Thomas Jefferson,* Baltimore, Johns Hopkins Press, 1928) have noted the relationship between the Virginia plantation and these parts of the poem which Jefferson copied.

8.17. H. A. Washington (ed.), *The Works of Thomas Jefferson,* Vol. II, pp. 35–36.

8.18. The print was published by Bohn and shows the University in 1853. The addition which projects from the rear of the rotunda in the Bohn print was the work of Robert Mills and has nothing to do with Jefferson's original intentions. The Rotunda and Mills's addition were severely damaged by fire in 1895, and when the Rotunda was rebuilt a second portico, like the one facing the lawn, was added to the north side. This too was not Jefferson's original intention. He seems to have had only a projecting pavilion on the north side.

8.19. The letter was reproduced in the *New York Times,* April 26, 1931, Sec. 8, p. 20. The pertinent part is quoted below: "Large houses are always ugly, inconvenient, exposed to the accident of fire, and bad in cases of infection. A plain, small house for the school and lodging for each professor is best. These connected by covered ways out of which the rooms of the students should open would be best. These may be built only as they shall be wanted: in fact, a university should not be a house but a village."

8.20. There is one possible connection between the Jefferson and Ramée designs. The idea of using a monumental rotunda for the central motif was suggested to Jefferson by Latrobe in a letter dated several years *after* Ramée had introduced a similar idea in his design for Union College. In 1815, Latrobe and Ramée were rivals in the competition for the Baltimore Exchange. Latrobe, therefore, was very much aware of Ramée's skills as an architect and must certainly have known of his work at Union. On the basis of this connection it is possible to assume that Latrobe took the idea for a central rotunda from Ramée's design and then passed it on as his own to Jefferson. Moreover, among the Ramée drawings preserved in the library at Union is a small sketch showing a rotunda which is not unlike the sketch which Latrobe sent to Jefferson.

8.21. Samuel A. Roberson is currently working on this aspect of Jefferson's architecture. I am indebted to him for this information.

8.22. For more about the relationship between the University and the Roman villa, see Lehmann, *Jefferson, Humanist,* pp. 185ff.

8.23. Jefferson gives an even more detailed description of his intention in a letter to T. J. Tazewell, written in November 1825 (published in the *New York Times,* April 26, 1931, Sec. 8, p. 20):
"Among the branches of the arts and sciences taught in the university are comprehended the Fine Arts generally, of which Civil Architecture is a prominent branch. The introduction of chaste models of the orders of architecture, taken from the finest remains of antiquity, and of specimens of the choicest samples of each order was considered as a necessary foundation of instruction for the students in this art. The bases and

capitals necessary for exhibition, might, of course, and with propriety, have been placed in our museum, but besides that their massiveness would have too much crowded that, we thought that, to show their just effect, they could nowhere be exhibited so advantageously as in connection with their column and its superincumbent entablature. We therefore determined that each of the pavilions erected for the accommodation of the schools and their professors should present a distinct and different sample of the art and, these buildings being arranged around three sides of a square, the lecturer, in a circuit attended by his school, could explain to them successively these samples of the several orders, their varieties, peculiarities and accessory circumstances."

8.24. Quoted in Talbot Hamlin, *Benjamin Henry Latrobe,* New York, Oxford University Press, 1955, p. 294. The original letter is in the Latrobe papers in the Maryland Historical Society Manuscript Collection.

8.25. Although it was Latrobe who suggested to Jefferson the idea of a rotunda for the central building in the plan of the University, the choice of the Pantheon as the model was strictly Jefferson's. For a complete documented study of the rotunda, see William B. O'Neal, *Jefferson's Buildings at the University of Virginia, The Rotunda,* University of Virginia Press, 1960.

8.26. Jefferson never seems to have owned the Ledoux book (1804) from which our plate is taken. Because of his interest in contemporary Parisian town houses, however, he must surely have been familiar with the Hôtel Guimard.

8.27. See Chapter X.

8.28. The Virginia State Capitol building and the University of Virginia are the only public buildings designed and built by Jefferson. On the basis of surviving drawings, however, a number of houses in Virginia and elsewhere in the South have been attributed to him. Certainly Jefferson must have been ready to make drawings and suggestions for his friends, and there are a number of houses which show strong Jeffersonian characteristics. But there is little evidence to indicate that Jefferson was ever actually involved in the construction of any of them. His role seems to have been that of the gentleman-amateur, and the houses when finally built were as much a product of the owner and the builder as they were of Jefferson. There is only one house besides Monticello that was actually designed and built by Jefferson. This was his second home, Poplar Forest, in the vicinity of Lynchburg, which he built as a retreat on land inherited from his wife. All the others, when compared with Monticello, must be considered Jeffersonian rather than by Jefferson.

CHAPTER IX

9.1. Summerson, *Sir John Soane;* see Note 3 below.

9.2. Except where otherwise noted, my information on Latrobe has come from Talbot Hamlin, *Benjamin Henry Latrobe,* New York, Oxford University Press, 1955. This superb, readable book is the definitive study of Latrobe.

9.3. For my information on Sir John Soane I have used:
John Summerson, *Sir John Soane,* London, Art and Technics, 1952.
Dorothy Stroud, *The Architecture of Sir John Soane,* London, Studio Books, 1961.
Summerson's book is a short but searching analysis of Soane's style; Stroud's is a check list of the architect's works with an introduction by Henry-Russell Hitchcock.

9.4. Quoted in Herrmann, *Laugier,* p. 181.

9.5. I am indebted to Professor Paul Norton, Chairman of the Department of Art at the University of Massachusetts, for the photographs of Hammerwood and Ashdown. He had them made specifically for a study he is making of Latrobe in England, and was kind enough to let me use them even though he has not published them himself.

9.6. From a letter by Latrobe to Robert Mills, dated July 12, 1806; quoted in Hamlin, *Latrobe*, p. 126.

9.7. According to Hamlin (*Latrobe*, p. 153) the Bank of Pennsylvania was not the first masonry vaulted building in America. Apparently the old Philadelphia jail, built just before the Revolution, was also vaulted. The Bank of Pennsylvania, however, was certainly the first monumental building in which the vault was conceived as part of the internal spatial effect.

9.8. Letter from Latrobe to Samuel Fox, dated July 8, 1805. Portions quoted in Hamlin, *Latrobe*, p. 55.

9.9. Latrobe discussed the architect in America in the letter to Mills referred to in Note 6 above. It is quoted in Hamlin, *Latrobe*, p. 149. Since it sustains so beautifully our own evaluation of the matter it is worth quoting in part here: "The profession of architecture has been hitherto in the hands of two sets of men. The first,—of those who from traveling or from books have acquired some knowledge of the theory of art,—but know nothing of its practice—the second—of those who know nothing but the practice,—and whose early life being spent in labor, & in the habits of a laborious life,—have no opportunity of acquiring the theory."

9.10. Latrobe's activities in Washington will be discussed further in Chapter X.

9.11. For a more detailed account of the relationship between Bishop Carroll and Latrobe, see Walter Knight Sturges, "A Bishop and His Architect," *Liturgical Arts*, Vol. 17, No. 2, February 1949, pp. 53ff.

9.12. For an account of the evolution of the Baltimore Cathedral, see Fiske Kimball, "Latrobe's Designs for the Baltimore Cathedral," *Architectural Record*, Vol. XLII, December 1917, and Vol. XLIII, January 1918.

9.13. My plans are based on the ones shown by Sturges in his article in *Liturgical Arts* (see Note 11 above).

9.14. The most interesting surviving work by Maximilian Godefroy is the Unitarian Church at Franklin and Charles streets in Baltimore. It was built between 1817 and 1818. The interior is strongly reminiscent of Sir John Soane's interiors in the Bank of England. The New York City Hall by Joseph-François Mangin and John McComb was built in 1811. It is one of the most monumental of the early Neoclassical buildings in America and has many strong French overtones. Its magnificent central stairway is one of the finest of the period. The most notable surviving work by George Hadfield is the famous Arlington House in Arlington, Va., built by the stepgrandson of George Washington. It later became the home of Robert E. Lee. The massive Greek Doric portico which now fronts the building was added in 1820 when the house was remodeled under the direction of Hadfield. William Jay was active in Savannah, Ga., between 1817 and 1824, where he built a number of houses. The best preserved example is the Owens-Thomas House.

9.15. Except where otherwise noted I have relied for my general information about Robert Mills on two books:
H. M. Pierce Gallagher, *Robert Mills, Architect of the Washington Monument, 1781–1855*, New York, Columbia University Press, 1935.
Talbot Hamlin, *Greek Revival Architecture in America*, London, Oxford University Press, 1944.
Mrs. Gallagher's book is the only biography of Mills and brings under one cover much important documentary material. It is enthusiastically written but does very little with the architecture itself. Hamlin's book is the basic work on the Greek Revival. Although the organization is difficult (it would be impossible as a reference book if it were not for the superb index) it is the most important book yet published on the subject of Neoclassicism in America.

9.16. From "The Architectural Works of Robert Mills," an outline for a paper or book, which was prepared by Mills himself. It is quoted in full in Gallagher, *Robert Mills,* pp. 168ff.

9.17. From "The Architectural Works of Robert Mills," in Gallagher, *Robert Mills,* pp. 170ff.

9.18. From "The Progress of Architecture in Virginia," an essay by Mills in Gallagher, *Robert Mills,* pp. 155ff.

9.19. From "The Tuscan Order," an essay by Mills, in Gallagher, *Robert Mills,* pp. 155–56.

9.20. From "The Architectural Works of Robert Mills," in Gallagher, *Robert Mills,* pp. 169–70.

9.21. Mills seems to have attempted to set up practice in Charleston, S.C. as early as 1805, and to have designed some churches there prior to that date. There is clear evidence that he went there to supervise their construction (see Hamlin, *Benjamin Latrobe,* p. 214, footnote 1). So far these churches have not been identified. In any case, Mills was back in Latrobe's office by 1807 where he stayed at least until his Philadelphia commissions. The exterior of the Sansom Street Church by Robert Mills is illustrated in Talbot Hamlin, *Greek Revival Architecture in America,* New York, Oxford University Press, 1944, Plate X. The interior of the Sansom Street Church, and the exterior of the Octagon Unitarian Church are both illustrated in Gallagher, *Robert Mills,* p. 78.

9.22. I have been unable to locate reliable plans of the Monumental Church in Richmond. Figure 275, therefore, is not a plan, nor is it to scale. It is a schematic diagram which shows the relationship in the church between the shape of the balcony and the octagon in which it is contained. It also shows the location of the rim of the dome as it too relates to the octagon.

9.23. From "The Architectural Works of Robert Mills," in Gallagher, *Robert Mills,* p. 168.

9.24. The use of iron as a structural material will be discussed at greater length in Volume II of this series.

9.25. Helen G. McCormack, "The Fireproof Building: New Home of the South Carolina Historical Society," *The South Carolina Historical and Genealogical Magazine,* Vol. XLIV, No. 4, October 1943, p. 206, footnote 8.

9.26. Hamlin, *Greek Revival Architecture,* p. 49.

CHAPTER X

10.1. One of the most interesting Baroque city plans to survive from the seventeenth century is Sir Christopher Wren's unexecuted plan for the city of London which he submitted to the King after the Great Fire of 1666. It consisted of a series of round points connected by radiating avenues with a grid of narrower streets superimposed. It was along very similar lines that the city of Washington was laid out.

10.2. Jefferson wrote to L'Enfant on April 10, 1791, and sent him plans for "Frankfort on the Mayne, Carlsruhe, Amsterdam, Strasburg, Paris, Orleans, Bordeaux, Lyons, Montpelier, Marseilles, Turin and Milan."

10.3. There is some evidence to suggest that it may have been Washington himself who selected the sites for the Capitol and the President's House. The best and most recent account of the early planning of the capital city is found in *Historical Study ⅜3—Executive Office Building,* prepared by the General Services Administration and published by the Government Printing Office. The first chapter, "Washington and the Plan," deals with Washington's role in the planning. Donald J. Lehman is the author of this publication, although his name does not appear on it.

I am deeply indebted to Mr. Lehman for much of the historical data

NOTES 479

about the city of Washington and the Treasury Building which I have included in this chapter. At the time I was investigating the Treasury Building, he was Information Officer for the Public Buildings Service of the General Services Administration. Mr. Lehman was just completing a comprehensive monograph on the Treasury Building and I was privileged to read that part of his unpublished manuscript which dealt with the Mills portion of the building. He also made available to me significant photographic material, including Mills's plan, which is reproduced here as Figure 291.

10.4. For a complete account of the planning and building of Washington, see Glenn Brown, *History of the United States Capitol*, Washington, D.C., Government Printing Office, 1900, and I. T. Frary, *They Built the Capitol*, Richmond, Va., Garrett and Massie, 1940. Brown's book, which is the official government publication, is biased in favor of Dr. William Thornton. Frary's book is less so but draws heavily on Brown.

10.5. Quoted in Frary, *They Built the Capitol*, p. 29.

10.6. The dome proposed by Latrobe was a typical Neoclassical dome with a low profile. It was severely criticized as having insufficient height for the nation's Capitol. Confronted with this situation, Bulfinch prepared several schemes which showed domes of various heights. Officials selected the highest of these even though Bulfinch himself seems to have preferred one lower in profile.

10.7. For a full and lucid discussion of Latrobe's work on the national Capitol, see Hamlin, *Latrobe*, Chap. 13. Hamlin's account of the complicated relationship between Latrobe and Thornton is far more objective than that of either Brown or Frary.

10.8. The original Treasury Building, designed by George Hadfield and completed in 1799, suffered a minor fire in 1801, and was burned by the British in 1814. After being rebuilt, it was again destroyed by fire in 1833. It is this last fire which Mills was asked to report and which led to the ultimate construction of his Treasury Building. See Gallagher, *Robert Mills*, pp. 59–60.

10.9. The controversy between President Jackson and the House Committee on Public Buildings and Grounds concerned both the location and the character of the new building. Jackson wanted a building which would house all government departments and which would be built on a new site. The Committee preferred a building housing both the Treasury and the State Departments and located approximately on the site of the old (burned) Treasury Building. Jackson finally acquiesced and Mills was summoned to carry out the assignment.

10.10. The old Patent Office has recently been completely renovated and now serves as the National Portrait Gallery. Although the upper portion of the building was gutted by fire in 1877 and was refurbished in a high Victorian manner, the stair hall still has Mills's magnificent groined vaults.

10.11. The violent criticism which has been leveled at Mills because of the interruption of the vista from the Capitol to the President's House is hard to understand, especially since most of the President's House lay north of the site line down Pennsylvania Avenue even as originally built. The President's House was therefore partially obscured from the very beginning. Even if this were not the case, Mills's south wing for the Treasury Building would not have interrupted the view. It was instead the wing designed by Walter, which extended an estimated one hundred and twenty-five feet farther than the one proposed by Mills, that cut across the vista.

10.12. From Mills's description of the Treasury Building in his *Guide to the Capitol and Public Buildings;* quoted in Gallagher, *Robert Mills*, p. 60.

10.13. Although Mills always intended an E-shaped building, he never achieved this end. He was relieved of his government post in 1841, and the designs for the extension were prepared by Thomas U. Walter. Construction was actually carried out, however, by the Treasury Department's Construction

Branch, a subdivision established in 1853. Walter provided the Department with only two drawings, a floor plan and an elevation of the south façade. Work over the years was directed successively by Captain Alexander H. Bowman of the Engineering Corps of the United States Army, Ammi B. Young, Isaiah Rogers, and Alfred B. Mullett. Walter's drawings provided so little information that Bowman was forced to make measured drawings of the original Mills details. This is one reason why the entire building has such a consistent Millsian character.

10.14. One might be tempted to interpret the pilasters on the Treasury Building as an intentional thickening of the wall at the points of concentration of thrust in order to buttress the groin vaults within. The pilasters are, indeed, bonded to the wall by iron clamps set deeply in the masonry and there can be no doubt that they do aid in containing the thrust. But we know from his own testimony that Mills's calculations were made on the basis of the buttressing power of the walls alone as built with hydraulic cement. Mills also introduced massive diagonal braces of granite into the spandrels of the groins which tied the front walls with the internal cross walls, thus helping to contain the pressure. The pilasters he viewed as decorative adjuncts and not as integral to the structure. See House Report No. 737, 25th Congress, Second Session, p. 24.

10.15. Letter to Congress, dated February 1838; quoted in Lehman's unpublished monograph.

10.16. Mills's original columns were so badly disintegrated that in 1908 they were replaced by granite columns.

10.17. House Report No. 737, p. 24.

10.18. House Report No. 737, p. 26. The colonnade on Mills's Treasury Building was not the only one of its time. A. J. Davis designed a Corinthian colonnade for a row house known as LaGrange Terrace, built in 1836 in New York City. The Charleston Hotel in Charleston, S.C., designed by Charles Reichardt and built in 1839, also had a Corinthian colonnade.

10.19. House Report No. 737, p. 26.

10.20. It should be noted that the Patent Office has a freestanding Greek Doric portico, but it was designed by William P. Elliot and built by Mills. In the Post Office Building Mills used a Corinthian order, but it was engaged and not freestanding. In neither instance was it a continuous colonnade.

10.21. House Report No. 737.

10.22. House Report No. 737, p. 13; see also p. 33. The "centres" referred to by Walter are the wood formwork used to support vaults while they are being built. Vaults may be buttressed by the counterthrust of opposing vaults or opposing buttresses, or they may be buttressed by what is called loading, that is, the application of dead weight from above. It is this second type of buttressing which is the point of contention in Walter's report. The Boston architect Alexander Parris was in Washington at the same time as Walter, looking for government work. He, too, was asked to report on the Treasury Building. His report sustained Walter's observations with respect to the structure, although he was less emphatic in stating his point of view. Both he and Walter accepted the then current standards of vaulting, all of which points up the innovative character of Mills's technique.

10.23. Appendix to the Congressional Globe, 25th Congress, Second Session, pp. 336–41.

10.24. Appendix . . . Globe, p. 421.

10.25. Appendix . . . Globe, p. 420.

10.26. For further information about William Strickland, see Agnes Addison Gilchrist, *William Strickland, Architect and Engineer*, Philadelphia, University of Pennsylvania Press, 1950.

10.27. For further information about Town and Davis, see Roger Hale Newton,

Town and Davis Architects, New York, Columbia University Press, 1942.

10.28. For the full story of the Ohio State Capitol, see Thomas E. O'Donnell, "The Greek Revival Capitol at Columbus, Ohio," *Architectural Forum,* Vol. XLII, No. 1 (June 1925), pp. 5–8. It is summarized in Hamlin, *Greek Revival Architecture,* pp. 287–88. Hamlin's book is also the most definitive work on the Greek Revival in general and demonstrates better than any other the degree to which the Greek forms permeated the entire nation from the Eastern seaboard through the Western Reserve and the South to California.

10.29. One of the most interesting of these which still survives is the North Carolina Hospital for the Insane in Raleigh, N.C., built in 1850. Two extensive wings have strip windows throughout the three stories.

10.30. See Newton, *Town and Davis,* p. 183. The use of iron as a structural material in nineteenth-century America will be discussed in detail in Volume II of this series.

10.31. It may seem strange that we have not considered the domestic architecture of either Latrobe or Mills. Both men did a number of houses and some of them still survive. But the major contribution of both architects was made in their monumental public buildings, while the influence of their domestic architecture was negligible. We have therefore concentrated on the major works. An important Latrobe house which still survives is the Decatur House at 748 Jackson Place in Washington, D.C. It was designed in 1817 and has recently been carefully restored. It now serves as the head-quarters for the National Trust for Historic Preservation. An important surviving house by Robert Mills is the Wickham House at 1015 East Clay Street in Richmond, Va. It was built between 1811 and 1814 and is now the Valentine Museum.

10.32. The original spire on the Wellfleet Congregational Church was a tapering spire of the traditional Wren-Gibbs type. This was destroyed in 1879 and the present circular cupola was put on in its place. One wonders whether those responsible for the new cupola did not have a long look at the one on the Stone Temple in Quincy.

10.33. One of the most important surviving buildings by William Strickland is the Tennessee State Capitol, in Nashville, which was begun in 1845 and finished ten years later. It is in the form of a Greek temple with an Ionic portico on either end. At the center of each long side there is also an Ionic portico without a pediment. Rising above the center of the building is a rusticated tower, crowned by a circular lantern based upon the Choragic Monument of Lysicrates. The addition of the tower to the roof of the temple form was unfortunate. When it is seen from the distance, its vertical direction creates the illusion that the roof is actually giving way beneath the weight. As in the case of all Strickland's buildings the Greek detail is handled with exquisite grace and authenticity.

10.34. See Hamlin, *Benjamin Latrobe,* p. 156.

10.35. Quoted in Gilchrist, *William Strickland,* p. 55.

10.36. Quoted in Gilchrist, *William Strickland,* p. 53.

10.37. Even when the main body of a Greek revival house was made of brick, as frequently happened, it was painted white. There are a number of fascinating provincial exceptions to this in the back country of Maine, New Hampshire, and Vermont. Here the power of the traditional Federal Style still held sway, even though the buildings might have Greek temple fronts.

10.38. W. J. Cash (*The Mind of the South,* New York, Doubleday Anchor Books, 1941, pp. 26–27) quotes at length from a fascinating account of the life in Alabama and Mississippi in the 1830's, Joseph Glover Baldwin's *The Flush Times,* New York, 1853.

10.39. There were a number of ante-bellum southern mansions which did employ the Greek orders. A particularly rich cluster is to be found in Athens, Georgia; there are some others in Natchez, Mississippi. But almost without exception they are the peripteral colonnade type, without any hint of the temple form. The few instances in which the pediment does occur were eccentric to the region; at the same time they bear no relationship to the temple type of houses of the north. They were plantation houses in every respect.

10.40. The Joel Hayden House was purchased in 1958 by the late Professor Karl Lehmann and his wife Phyllis. The acquisition could hardly have been more appropriate. Professor Lehmann, one of the world's greatest classical archaeologists, was a member of the faculty at the Institute of Fine Arts, New York University, and his wife Phyllis Williams Lehmann is professor of art at Smith College. She, too, is a classical archaeologist. Their joint work at Samothrace is one of the most important archaeological undertakings of the twentieth century. That Karl and Phyllis Lehmann should have chosen to live in a Greek temple has given the lovely house a meaning more relevant to its origins than anything ever intended by the original builder.

Glossary of Terms

ABACUS. The top member of the Doric capital. A flat rectangular slab, square in plan, it rests between the echinus block of the capital and the lowest member of the entablature above.

ACROTERIUM. A pedestal for a statue or similar decorative feature at the apex, or at each of the lower corners, of a pediment.

APSE. A semicircular part of a building, forming a projection from the exterior wall, and the interior forming a large and deep niche.

ARCHITRAVE. The lowest member of a classical entablature. A molded lintel spanning between two columns. See also ORDER.

ARCHIVOLT. The group of moldings following the shape of an arched opening.

ASHLAR. Squared and dressed building stone.

AXIS. An imaginary line to which are referred the parts of an existing building or the relations of a number of buildings to one another.

BAROQUE. That style of architecture which flourished in Europe during the seventeenth and eighteenth centuries. Although based on the architecture of the Renaissance, it was more dynamic, with circles frequently giving way to ovals, flat walls to curved or undulating ones, and separated elements to interlocking forms. It was also a monumental and richly three-dimensional style with elaborate systems of ornamental and figural sculpture.

BARREL VAULT. A continuous arched roof or ceiling of semicircular or semielliptical form over an apartment, corridor, or similar space.

BAY. The space between two such recurring members as columns, piers, or wall panels.

BRACKET. A supporting member projecting from the face of a wall. In American architecture it is frequently used for ornamental as well as structural purposes.

CAPITAL. The moldings and carved enrichment which form a finish to the top of a column, pilaster, pier, or pedestal. See also ORDER.

CASEMENT. A window having hinged or pivoted sash opening either outward or inward.

CHAMFER. The surface formed by cutting off a square edge at an equal angle to each face.

CHIMNEY GIRT. A major wooden girder, used in early American frame construction, which passes across the breast of a central chimney. It is supported at its ends by the outer girders of the building and sometimes carries one end of the summer beam.

CLASSICAL RECTANGLE (sometimes called golden section). A rectangle which is so carefully proportioned that neither the long nor the short side seems to dominate. The façade of the Greek Doric temple is the epitome of this formal concept.

CLERESTORY. That part of a building which rises above the roof of another part, and which has windows in its walls.

COFFER. A recessed panel, usually square or octagonal, in a ceiling. Such panels are common in the inner surfaces of cupolas and vaults.

COLLAR BEAM. A horizontal tension member in a pitched roof connecting opposite rafters, generally halfway up or higher. Its function is to tie the angular members together and thus prevent them from spreading.

COLONNETTE. Any diminutive column.

COMPOSITE ORDER. A late Roman order which combines elements of both the Ionic and Corinthian orders.

CONSOLE. A projecting, scroll-shaped member usually used as a corbel or bracket for support.

CORBEL. To build outward, by projecting successive courses of masonry beyond those below.

CORBELED CORNICE. A cornice made up of several projections each of which extends farther outward than the one below.

CORNICE. The crowning member of a wall or entablature. See also ORDER.

COURSE. A row of building blocks, such as bricks or stones, extending the full length and thickness of a wall.

COVED CORNICE. A cornice with a concave curved profile; its size varies according to use.

CROCKET. In Gothic architecture a small ornament consisting of bunched curved foliage placed at intervals on the sloping edge of gables, spires, etc.

CROWSTEP. Any one of the progressions in a gable that ascends in steps rather than in a continuous slope.

CRUCK. Pairs of bent trees roughly shaped, then joined together at the top but set apart at the bottom. Used to support the roof of the earliest types of English house and barn.

CUPOLA. A small structure built on top of a building, usually for ornamental purposes.

DENTIL. A small ornamental block, forming one of a series set in a row. A dentil molding is formed by such a series.

DEPENDENCY. A building, wing, or room, subordinate to, or serving as an adjunct to, the main building.

DORMER WINDOW. A window in a sloping roof, with vertical sides and front.

ECHINUS. A heavy molding with a curved profile placed immediately below the abacus, or top member, of the Doric capital.

ENGLISH BOND. Brick work in the colonies was laid in two methods, both traditional to English architecture. In English bond, the bricks are set in alternating courses of *stretchers* (bricks laid the length of the wall with their long side showing) and *headers* (bricks laid across the wall with their short end showing); in Flemish bond the stretchers and headers alternate in the same row. This creates a more animated texture than English bond and was favored in the more elegant buildings.

ENTABLATURE. The top member of a classic order, being a richly molded continuous lintel supported on columns. It is divided horizontally into three main parts: the uppermost is the *cornice,* the middle one the *frieze,* and the lowest the *architrave.* Each has the moldings and decorative treatment that are characteristic of the particular order. See also ORDER.

FENESTRATION. The arrangement in a building of its windows, especially the more important and larger ones.

FILLET. A relatively small and narrow flat molding; a rectangular section projecting from the general surface.

FINIAL. An ornament placed upon the apex of an architectural feature, such as a gable, turret, or canopy.

FLEMISH BOND. See ENGLISH BOND.

FLEMISH GABLE. A gable the upper slopes of which ascend in steps rather than in a straight line. These steps may be rectilinear or curved, or a combination of both.

FOLIATED. In the form of leaves or leaflike shapes.

FRET. A continuous ornament on a flat ground consisting of a series of narrow straight bands, turning at regular intervals through a succession of right angles.

FRIEZE. Any long and narrow horizontal architectural member, especially one which has a chiefly decorative purpose. In Greek, Roman, and Neoclassical architecture it is that horizontal band which forms the central, and usually the most important, part of the entablature. See also ORDER.

GABLE. A triangular-shaped piece of wall closing the end of a double pitched roof.

GAMBREL ROOF. A roof which has a double pitch. The lower plane, which rises from the eaves, is rather steep; the upper plane, which spans from the lower to the ridgepole, has a flatter pitch.

GARLAND. A curved hanging festoon of leaves, flowers, or drapery. Frequently used in combination with the swag as an applied ornamental device. See also SWAG.

GAUGED BRICKS. Bricks which are cut or rubbed to a uniform size and shape.

GIANT PILASTER (sometimes called colossal pilaster or colossal order). A pilaster which runs through the full height of a building, extending two or more floors.

GOLDEN SECTION. See CLASSICAL RECTANGLE.

GROIN. The curved edge formed by the intersection of two barrel vaults of the same height and same configuration.

HAMMER BEAM. A short cantilevered beam securing the foot of the principal rafter to the brace, strut, or tie. It is usually horizontal and forms part of at least two of the triangles of construction, namely the one above, connected with the principal rafter, and the other below, connected with a wall piece.

HEADER. A brick laid with its end face to the weather. See ENGLISH BOND.

HIPPED ROOF. A roof which pitches inward from all four sides. The external angle formed where an end plane and side plane meet is called the hip.

HOOD. A rooflike canopy over an opening.

IMPOST. The top part of a pier or wall upon which rests the springer or lowest voussoir of an arch.

IN ANTIS. Columns in antis are placed in an opening in the same plane as the wall into which the opening is cut.

JOIST. Any horizontal beam intended primarily for the construction or support of a floor or ceiling.

KEYSTONE. The central wedge-shaped stone at the crown of an arch.

KING POST. In a truss, the vertical suspension member which connects the tie beam with the meeting point of opposing principal rafters. Properly, it is not a post but a tie.

LANCET WINDOW. A window generally tall in proportions and topped by a sharply pointed arch; characteristic of early English Gothic. Specifically, a lancet arch is a pointed arch whose centers are farther apart than the width or span of the arch.

LINTEL. The horizontal structural member which supports the wall over an opening, or spans between two adjacent piers or columns. See also ORDER.

MASONRY. Structure produced by building with stone, brick, or some other hard and durable but workable material laid up in units and bonded by mortar.

MASSING. The grouping or arrangement of the primary geometric components of a building.

METOPE. In a Doric entablature, that part of the frieze which falls between two triglyphs. In the Greek Doric order the metope characteristically contains sculpture.

MODILLION CORNICE. A cornice supported by a series of small ornamental brackets under the projecting top moldings. It is common to the Corinthian and Composite orders.

MORTISE AND TENON JOINT. A joint which is made by one member having its end cut in a projecting piece (tenon) which fits exactly into a groove or hole (mortise) in the other member. Once joined, the pieces are held together by a peg which passes through the tenon.

MULLION. An upright post or similar member dividing a window into two or more units, or lights, each of which may be further subdivided into panes.

OCULUS. A circular opening in a ceiling or wall; common in vaulted construction as the opening at the top of a dome.

ORDER. The most important elements of classical architecture are the orders, first developed as a structural-aesthetic system by the ancient Greeks. An order has two major components, a *column* with its *capital;* together, they form the *post,* or main vertical supporting member. The principal horizontal member is the *entablature,* or *lintel.* The entablature consists of three horizontal parts. The lowest one is the *architrave,* an unbroken horizontal element which rests directly on the capitals and forms the principal part of the lintel. Above this is a second horizontal area called the *frieze,* which is generally decorated with sculptural ornament. The top member is the *cornice;* made up of various combinations of moldings, it overhangs the rest of the entablature and becomes the crowning motif. On the gabled end of a building, the cornice is continued up along the edge of the roof (now called a *raking cornice*) to form an enclosed triangle, or *pediment.* In classical architecture, the roof planes were pitched at a moderate angle, making the pediment a low, wide equilateral triangle. The Greeks developed three different types of orders, the Doric, Ionic, and Corinthian, each distinguishable by its own decorative system and proportions (see Figs. 1, 4, and 5). All three were taken over and modified by the Romans, who added two orders of their own, the Tuscan, which is a simplified form of the Doric, and the Composite, which is made up of elements of both the Ionic and the Corinthian. The Romans often used the orders as a structural system in the same manner as the Greeks. Unlike the Greeks, however, they also applied them as decoration to the surfaces of walls that were supported by other means.

OVERHANG. The projection of part of a structure beyond the portion below.

PALLADIAN WINDOW (sometimes called Palladian motif). An arrangement in which a round-headed window is flanked by lower square-headed openings and separated from them by columns or pilasters.

PARAPET. A low wall, at the edge of a roof, balcony, etc., sometimes formed by the upward extension of the wall below.

PAVILION. A wing or central unit which projects from a larger architectural unit and is usually accented by special decorative treatment.

PEDIMENT. The low triangular gable formed by the roof slopes on top and the horizontal enclosing member, generally a cornice, beneath. See also ORDER.

PENDENTIVE. A vaulted section in the form of a spherical triangle which forms the structural transition from a square plan to the circular plan of a dome. A segmental pendentive, like a segmental dome, is one constructed on a segmental profile.

PERIPTERAL. Surrounded by a single range of columns.

PIER. A freestanding mass, generally rectilinear in shape, supporting one side of an arch or one end of a beam, lintel, or girder. A thickening of a wall in the form of a vertical strip to strengthen it or to carry a heavy load for which the wall would not be strong enough.

PILASTER. The projecting part of a square column which is attached to a wall; it is finished with the same cap and base as a freestanding column. Also a narrow vertical member in a similar position.

PORTICO. A porch consisting of a low-pitched roof supported on classical columns and finished in front with an entablature and pediment.

PORTLAND STONE. A light-colored Jurassic limestone from the Isle of Portland, on the coast of Dorset in southern England.

POST AND LINTEL. A structural system in which the main support is provided by vertical members, or posts, carrying horizontal members called lintels.

PROSTYLE. Having a columnar portico in front, but not on the sides and rear.

QUATREFOIL. A type of Gothic tracery having four lobes. It is generally formed by four circles or near circles, each tangential to the next around a center.

QUOIN. The bricks or stones laid in alternating directions, which bond and form the exterior corner angle of a wall.

RAKING CORNICE. A cornice which adorns the ends of the sloping planes of a roof and thus forms the upper sides of the pedimental triangle. See also ORDER.

RAKING PARAPET. One which is pitched upward at an angle.

REED AND ROSETTE. A reed motif is a pattern of small half-round moldings arranged in a compact vertical cluster. In this case they form small rectangles which alternate with the round flowers of the *rosette* motif to form a pattern not unlike that of the triglyph and metope scheme of the Greek Doric frieze.

REPOUSSOIRE. A French term meaning to push back. When applied to Baroque architecture, it relates to those pictorial devices which intensify the sense of depth. Thus, a shadowed figure in the foreground against a brilliantly illuminated background would create a repoussoire effect.

REREDOS. A screen or wall at the back of an altar, usually with architectural and figural decoration.

REVEAL. That portion of the inner surface of an opening which is visible from the face of the wall back to the frame or any other structure placed within the opening. Thus the windows of an ordinary brick building may have reveals of about four inches, which is the depth of each brick visible outside the window frames.

RIDGE LINE. The line of meeting of two opposite roof slopes, especially the horizontal edge which is seen against the sky.

RIDGEPOLE. The board or plank at the apex of a roof against which the upper ends of the rafters abut.

RINCEAU. An ornamental device consisting of a sinuous and branching scroll elaborated with leaves and other natural forms.

ROCOCO. A late phase of the Baroque style; marked by elegant reverse-curve ornament, light scale, and delicate color.

RUSTICATION. Masonry in which the joints are revealed by narrow recessed channels.

SEGMENTAL ARCH. An arch formed on a segment of a circle or an ellipse.

SEGMENTAL PEDIMENT. A pediment the top of which is a segment of a circle rather than two sides of a triangle.

SEGMENTAL VAULT. A vault built on the segment of a circle rather than on an entire half-circle. Because of the resulting low profile, it is a particularly elegant form of construction. Domes built on segmental curves are sometimes referred to as saucer domes.

SPANDREL. The quasi-triangular space formed by two adjoining arches and a line connecting their crowns. In skeletal construction, the space between the top of a window and the sill of the window in the story above; in this case sometimes referred to as a spandrel panel.

SQUINCH. Normally an arch, lintel, or corbeling, or a system of such members, built across the interior corner of two walls to form one side of an octagonal base. This octagonal base serves as the structural transition from a square interior space to an octagonal or round dome.

STRETCHER. A brick laid with its long face to the weather. See ENGLISH BOND.

STRINGCOURSE (sometimes called belt course). A narrow horizontal band of masonry which projects slightly from the wall. It is used primarily as a space divider.

STRUT. In a truss, a rigid member which acts as a brace or support. It differs from a post in that it is commonly set in a diagonal position and thus serves as a stiffener by triangulation.

SUMMER BEAM. In early New England house construction, a large horizontal beam which runs from the chimney girt at right angles to the main girder in the outer frame, at a point opposite to the chimney.

SUPERSTRUCTURE. A structure raised upon another structure, as a building upon a foundation, basement, or substructure.

SWAG. A suspended cluster of leaves, flowers, or drapery; frequently used in combination with the garland as an applied ornamental device. See also GARLAND.

TABERNACLE. A canopied niche or recess framed by engaged columns or pilasters and topped by a pediment.

TIE BEAM. The horizontal tension member which ties together the opposing angular members of a truss and thus prevents them from spreading.

TRACERY. Decoration made up of curvilinear lines or of narrow bands and fillets, or of more elaborately molded strips. In Gothic architecture, the curved interlocking stone bars used to support the leaded stained glass.

TRANSOM. A horizontal bar, as distinguished from a mullion; especially one crossing a door or window opening near the top.

TRIGLYPH. One of the vertical blocks in a Doric frieze, suggesting, in stone, the outer ends of the ceiling beams that were used in primitive wooden construction. It has three narrow vertical elements which form two triangular channels.

TRUSS. To strengthen by fitting with braces, struts, or ties. Also refers to a rigid framework made of such elements.

TYMPANUM. The triangular wall of a pediment between its enclosing moldings, frequently ornamented with sculpture. The similarly placed wall over a square-headed door or window which is set in an arch.

VAULT. An arched roof or ceiling constructed in brick or stone. An arch or a combination of arches used to cover a space.

VOLUTE. A spiral scroll; especially that which forms the distinctive feature of the Ionic capital.

VOUSSOIR. A wedge-shaped stone or brick used in the construction of an arch. Its taper toward the center is made to coincide with radii of the arch.

WEATHERING. The inclination given to any upper exposed surface so that it will shed water.

Index

Italicized figures refer to illustrations